Edward Augustus Freeman

Old English history for children

Edward Augustus Freeman

Old English history for children

ISBN/EAN: 9783337818715

Printed in Europe, USA, Canada, Australia, Japan

Cover: Foto ©ninafisch / pixelio.de

More available books at **www.hansebooks.com**

FOR

CHILDREN.

BY

EDWARD A. FREEMAN, M.A.,

Late Fellow of Trinity College, Oxford.

WITH MAPS.

London:

MACMILLAN AND CO.

1869.

LONDON :
R. CLAY, SONS, AND TAYLOR, PRINTERS,
BREAD STREET HILL.

PREFACE.

THIS little volume is an experiment, but it is an experiment which I may say has already succeeded. Its object is to show that clear, accurate, and scientific views of history, or indeed of any subject, may be easily given to children from the very first. In truth the more rigidly accurate and scientific a statement is, the more easy it is for a child to take it in. The difficulty does not lie with the child, who has simply to learn, but with the teacher who often has to unlearn. A child finds no difficulty in attaching a correct and definite meaning to a word from the first time of his using it; the difficulty lies wholly with the teacher, who has often been used to a confused and unscientific way of using words, which he finds it hard to leave off.

I have, I hope, shown that it is perfectly easy to teach children, from the very first, to distinguish true history alike from legend and from wilful invention, and also to understand the nature of historical authorities and to weigh one statement against another. Here again the difficulty is not at all with the child, but wholly with the teacher.

I have throughout striven to connect the history of England with the general history of civilized Europe, and I have especially tried to make the book serve as an incentive to a more accurate study of historical geography. For this purpose I hope that the maps with which the book is illustrated may be found really useful. No error should be more carefully guarded against from the beginning than that of bondage to the modern map. A child should learn from the very beginning that names like England, Scotland, France, do not necessarily mean, and have not always meant, exactly the same as they do now. Without perfect accuracy in these matters, no clear view of history can ever be gained. Here again the only difficulty lies with the teacher, who may have to unlearn; to the child it is just as easy to learn the right names from the beginning as the wrong ones.

I have throughout striven carefully to distinguish history from legend, but I have not thought it right wholly to throw aside the tales which have so often usurped the place of true history. These tales ought to be known, if only because they have usurped the place of true history. They ought also in many cases to be known, sometimes on account of their real beauty, sometimes as excellent studies for the comparative mythologist. I have therefore not wholly left them out, but I have told them as tales, in a shape which clearly distinguishes them from authentic history. And in telling them I have taken as my model the best of all examples of simple narrative, the best of all examples of English slightly antiquated but still perfectly intelligible, our received version of the Old Testament.

The present book was begun a good many years ago, and was written bit by bit for the use of my own children, as they wanted it, or as I found time to write it. It will, I suspect, be found that the latter part takes for granted a much greater degree of general knowledge than is supposed in the early parts. This is owing to the obvious cause that the children for whom it was written grew older while it was being written. As the same change will doubtless happen to other hearers or readers of the book, I cannot fancy that any difficulty will arise on this score.

The book, being written for particular children, living in a particular part of the country, had from the beginning a certain local character, and it gave special prominence to West-Saxon and especially to Somersetshire affairs. This was done on two grounds. It was utterly impossible to give a detailed history of all the fluctuating states which made up our elder England. I therefore chose for special notice that state which in the end swallowed up the rest and which grew into the Kingdom of England. But besides this, I thought that it gave further life and interest to the story for those for whom it was at first meant, if I made those parts of the history which concerned Wessex, and especially those which concerned Somersetshire and the Somersetshire Bishoprick, to stand out in a more marked way than others. And when revising the book for publication I saw no reason to leave out or to change these local allusions. I believe they add somewhat to the life and reality of the story, and I hope that they may be also useful in another way. I have certainly had some advantages for my purpose in living in what was so long a border district, a battle-field of the Briton and the Englishman. But every shire, almost every neighbourhood, has its own contributions to English History, its own places and events of special interest. Very few of these could be directly mentioned in a book of this kind, but I hope that the sort of use which I have made of the facts and events special to my own neighbourhood may lead others to deal in the same way with the places and events which more closely concern them. I trust that intelligent readers and teachers will often be able to supplement my references to matters belonging to Somersetshire with references of the same kind belonging to other parts of England.

With regard to the spelling of Old-English names, I must plead guilty to a certain amount of inconsistency. My own feeling is in favour of always using the genuine spelling of the old names rather than the common Latin and French corruptions. But I find that many people are in a manner frightened at the unusual form which is thus given to names still in common use. I have therefore, somewhat at the expense of consistency, left some of the more common names, such as Alfred, Edward, and Edith, in their modern spelling; while other names which are less familiar to modern readers, and which often have no one generally received modern shape, I have left in their ancient form. On the subject of Old-English names and on one or two points connected with the Old-English language I have added a few remarks at the end of this Preface.

I ought to mention that this little work was begun, and a great part of it written, before I had so much as planned the History of the Norman Conquest. In the parts of the history where the two works come on the same ground, the smaller was, I believe, everywhere written before the larger. The influence of the larger work on the smaller has been twofold. First, it has brought it sooner to an end, and has thereby hastened its publication. My first intention was to go on to the reign of Edward the First, but I found that it was hopeless to think of doing so, while the larger work was on my hands. I therefore send forth the present portion, which I may or may not go on with at some future time. The other way in which the great book has influenced the little one has been this. The fuller and more careful researches which were needed for the greater work have enabled me to correct and improve many things in the smaller. Further than this the two works have no connexion. The smaller is not an abridgement of the greater, neither is the greater an expansion of the smaller. They are two independent narratives written at different times and with quite different objects.

I have only to add that the young reader who carefully goes through this little book will, when he comes to the end of it, still have very much to learn even on its immediate subject; but I earnestly hope that he may have nothing to unlearn.

SOMERLEAZE, WELLS,
July 27*th*, 1869.

A FEW WORDS ON OLD-ENGLISH
WORDS AND NAMES.

THE English tongue which we speak now is essentially the same tongue as that which our forefathers brought with them into Britain in the fifth and sixth centuries. In the course of fourteen hundred, and even of eight hundred years, it has changed so much that the Old-English cannot be understood except by those who study it on purpose. But this is the same thing that happens to all languages more or less. There is no part of Europe where the people could at once understand a book written in their own language eight hundred years ago. But the change has been gradual; we did not leave off speaking one language and take to speaking another, as the people of Gaul and Spain left off speaking their own tongues and spoke such Latin as they could, or as many of the Welsh in Britain have learned to speak English. We have no more changed from one language to another than our cousins in Germany have, though undoubtedly English has changed more in a thousand years than the High-Dutch or German has. The chief points of change are two. First, we have lost nearly all our *inflexions*, that is the endings which mark genders, cases, and the like, while the High-Dutch has kept more of them, though it too has lost a great many. The other is that we have lost a great many old Teutonic words which are kept in High-Dutch, and have taken to Latin or French words instead. But we have always gone on speaking the same tongue, and the changes have been very gradual. And our tongue has always been called *English* as far back as we can go; so that it is better to call it English at all times, and, when needful, to distinguish the older form as *Old-English*, than to talk, as many people do, about "Saxon" or "Anglo-Saxon," which makes people fancy that one language has been changed for another.

I have just now compared our language with the High-Dutch or German; but it must always be remembered that High-Dutch is not the tongue nearest to our own. English is in truth a form of the *Low-Dutch*, the language which in different forms spreads from Flanders right away to the Baltic. The High and the Low-Dutch differ in this kind of way. Where High-Dutch uses a particular letter, Low-Dutch often uses another, according to a fixed rule which seldom or never alters, which at the beginning of words I may say never alters at all. Thus a word which begins with *z* in High-Dutch must begin with *t* in English, and a word which begins with *d* in High-Dutch must begin with *th* in English. For *th* our fathers had, like the Greeks, a particular letter called *Thorn*, which is written þ at the beginning of a word and ð at the middle or end. Some people still write yᵉ for *the*, where the *y* is nothing but a þ badly written.

Our Old-English names, most of which have gone out of
use, though we use a few still, always had a meaning, just
as the Greek and Hebrew names had. But the Old-English
names, like the Greek names too, fall into two classes. In
some of them, if you have any knowledge of the language
at all, you cannot help seeing the meaning at once. But
there are others whose meaning is by no means so clear.
and even a man who knows the language well may be only
able to guess at the meaning, or perhaps may have to give
it up altogether. For instance, such names as Neoptolemos,
Peisistratos, Laodikê, in Greek, or Æthelberht, Eadgar.
Ælfgifu, in Old-English, at once tell their own meaning to
any one who has learned the language. But it is quite
another thing with names like Iasôn, Pêleus, Tydeus, or
again with names like Offa, Penda, Dodda. I should not
like to say positively what these names mean, without thinking a good deal about it, and turning to see what learned
men have said. But you may be sure that all names had
a meaning at first, and you may be sure that the names
whose meaning is not plain, which are often the names of
Gods or heroes, are the older class of the two. These older
names, you will see, both in Greek and English, are generally shorter than the later ones, and they do not seem to
be compound words. But the later names in both tongues
are generally made up of two words, the meaning of which
is commonly pretty plain. The English names and those used
by the Teutonic people on the Continent are made out of
the same Teutonic roots, but it so happens that not many

of the particular names are common to England and to the Continent. For instance we have plenty of names beginning with _Wil_, as Wilfrith, and we have plenty of names ending in _helm_, as Ealdhelm; but I never heard of an English Wilhelm, and I doubt your finding a Wilfrith or an Ealdhelm abroad. And some names which are common abroad are found, but very rarely, in England, as Carl, Karl, Charles; Hloðhere, Lothar; Hereberht, Charibert, Herbert; Frithric, Friedrich, Frederick. Two things have helped to make the Old-English names seem more strange and uncouth than they need be. One is that most of them have gone out of use, so that the foreign names are now more familiar. The other is that, oddly enough, the proper names, more than any other class of words, are mainly formed out of roots which have gone out of use. For instance, in such a name as Æthelwulf, the _wulf_ is plain enough, but we have quite lost the word _æðel_, though it still lives in High-Dutch as _adel_ = noble. So in Sige_berht_, especially if I use the later spelling Sige_briht_, I need hardly tell you the meaning of the last syllable; but we have quite lost the word _sige_, which means _victory_, though that too lives in High-Dutch. And even in a name like Ælfgifu, though we still use both the words of which it is formed, you might not at once see that it means _elf-gift_. It would be too long a business to tell you the meanings of all the names, but it will help you if you remember a few of the words which we have lost but which are often used in forming names. I have told you of _æðel_ and _sige_, which are found together as a name, Æthel-

sige. Wig, war, *here*, army, *ead*, wealth or possession, *wine*, man, fellow, *frið*, peace, *gar*, spear, *burh*, pledge, *mund*, protection, *red* or *ræd*, counsel (rede), *ric*, kingdom or government, *flæd*, birth, will help you to the meanings of a good many. One thing you must always remember that in Old-English all names and words ending in *a* are masculine, never feminine, as they commonly are in Latin. Yet we are so much more used to Latin than to our own tongue that people will go and write women's names with an *a*, Elgiva, Editha, Etheldreda, and so on : and I dare say they are sometimes surprised to find that Ida and Ælla are names of men.

Perhaps you may ask how you ought to pronounce all these old names and other Old-English words. I cannot always tell you. I know how people wrote a thousand years back, but I never heard them talk. And we may be quite sure that they pronounced, as indeed they wrote, differently in different parts of the country, as people do still. We see this both in names and in other words. In many words and names where a soft sound is now used in the South of England, a hard one is used in the North. Thus *Carlton* and *Charlton*, *Skipton* and *Shipton* are the same name. We may be quite sure that *C* was at first hard before all vowels, and that *Sc* was sounded hard like *Sk*. But it is also plain that, at all events in the South of England, the hard sounds got softened into *Ch* and *Sh*, so that we now say *Church*, *Chester*, *Ship*, &c., though we still talk of *Kent* and *King*. Now it is not easy to say exactly when this change happened, so that I cannot tell you for certain whether a thousand years back we sounded such a word as *Æsc*, which we now call *Ash*, with the hard or the soft sound. But in any case we may be sure that there had been a time when it was sounded hard. Still I may tell you a few things which seem pretty plain. *E* before a vowel at the beginning of words, as *Eadweard*, *Eoforwic*, was clearly sounded like *y* or the High-Dutch *j*. Thus we still write *York*, and *Yedward* is found in Shakespeare, and *Earl* is in Scotland sounded *Yerl*, like the Danish *Jarl*. *G* at the beginning of words has in modern English often sunk into *y*, as we say *year* for *gear*, and as in some parts of England *gate* is called *yett*. So in names, you know that the old name *Eadgyth* has got softened into *Edith*. In Domesday it is written *Eddid* and *Eddied*, which looks as if the *g* was sounded like *y*. But in *Eadgar* the *g* keeps its place to this day; no one would call Edgar *Edar*. I think that, if you sound the two names several times, you will tell why the *g* got first softened and then lost in the one name, while it still abides in the other. *G* between two vowels or at the end of a word must have been sounded much as it is in High-Dutch. But it is plain that by the eleventh century it was sounded very faintly, for it is often left out. So in modern English it is always left out in the middle of a word, as *Thegn*, *Thane; regen*, *rain;* while at the end of a word it becomes *y*, as *dæg*, *day; weg*, *way*. *Hl* at the beginning of words was no doubt sounded like *ll* in Welsh; a sound which we have quite lost, but which is easily made by breathing, neither before nor after the *l*, but *as* you sound it. *Hw* is simply what we now write *wh;* for I hope that everybody who reads this book takes care to distinguish *whet, which,* and *whether* from *wet, witch,* and *weather.* Long *i* with an accent, as *win, wif, tim, rim,* was certainly sounded as it is now, like *ei* in High-Dutch. We now mark the long vowel by an *e* at the end, *wine, wife, time,* and we ought to write *rime,* only printers choose to spell it *rhyme,* because they fancy it is a Greek word. *Rim,* meaning number, should thus be written *rime* without the *h;* while *hrim,* meaning hoar-frost, should be written *rhime. Hr* and *cn* at the beginning of words should be sounded fully, as a Welshman can still sound the *hr* and as a High-Dutchman can still sound the *cn. H* at the middle or end of a syllable, as U*h*tred, Ælfhea*h*, was doubtless a guttural, like the Scotch, Welsh, or High-Dutch *ch.* We commonly write it *gh* in modern English, but we either drop the sound or else sound it like *f.* Long *a* with an accent answers in modern English to *o*, as *stán, stone, áð, oath;* but I cannot be sure that it was sounded so, at least not everywhere, as in the North they still say *stane* and *aith,* while in High-Dutch we have *stein* and *eid. E* at the end of a word, as God*wine,* must have been sounded, but sounded very slightly. You should not sound the last syllable like *wine,* which, as I have just said, is *win.*

In what I have now been saying, I do not at all pretend to say all that might be said, or even all that I might be able to say myself in a larger book. But I think I have said enough to make you think about the matter and to try

b

OLD-ENGLISH WORDS AND NAMES.

and find out more for yourselves. About proper names you may learn a great deal from the second volume of Miss Yonge's "History of Christian Names."

As I have had to bring in a few Welsh names, and as the Welsh sound many letters very differently from the English, I may as well tell you how they are to be sounded. *F* is sounded like *v*, but *ff* like *f*; *w* as a vowel is sounded like *oo*, and *aw* like *ow*; *u* is sounded like *i* in *it*, and *y* like *u* in *but*, except when it is in the last syllable of a word, when it is sounded like *i* in *it*. *Dd* is sounded like the English ð or *th*; so you will see that the name Gruffydd, though it looks so odd, is sounded as we commonly spell it in English, *Griffith*. Also, remember in Welsh words of three syllables to put the accent on the second always, as Morgánwg, Llywélyn, Carádoc, Merédydd. The last name is in English often wrongly sounded Méredith; Carádoc has got shortened into Craddock, which is not so bad a change.

CHRONOLOGICAL TABLE.

CÆSAR lands in Britain . . . . B.C. **55, 54**
Caius threatens to invade Britain . . . . A.D. **40**
Claudius in Britain **43**
Caradoc subdued by Ostorius **50**
Revolt of Boadicea **61**
Agricola builds his line of forts **81**
Hadrian makes his wall **121**
Lollius makes the wall of Antoninus **139**
Severus builds his wall . . . . **207—210**
Martyrdom of Saint Alban **304**
Constantine proclaimed Emperor **306**
Theodosius recovers Valentia **368**
The Roman legions leave Britain **410**
The ENGLISH CONQUEST begins.—Hengest begins the Kingdom
  of *Kent* **449**
Ælle and Cissa begin the Kingdom of *Sussex* **477**
Ælle and Cissa take Anderida **491**
Cerdic and Cynric begin the Kingdom of *Wessex* **495**
Arthur defeats the English at Badbury **520**
Ida begins the Kingdom of *Northumberland* **547**
Ceawlin King of the West-Saxons **556**
Ælla King of Deira **559**
Battle of Deorham **577**
Gregory the Great Pope **590**
Augustine converts Æthelberht **597**
Æthelfrith defeats the Scots at Dægsanstan **603**
Æthelfrith defeats the Welsh at Chester **607**
Paullinus converts Edwin **627**

b 2

A.D.

Edwin slain by Penda at Heathfield **633**
Oswald defeats Cædwalla at Heavenfield **635**
Cwichelm and Cynegils first Christian Kings of the West-Saxons. . **639**
Oswald slain by Penda at Maserfield **642**
Ithamar of Rochester the first English Bishop **644**
Cenwealh defeats the Welsh at Bradford **652**
Oswiu defeats and slays Penda **655**
Wulfhere King of the Mercians **657**
Cenwealh defeats the Welsh at Pen **658**
Ecgfrith King of the Northumbrians **670**
Bæda born **672**
Sexburh Queen of the West-Saxons **672**
Wilfrith converts the South-Saxons **681**
Ceadwalla King of the West-Saxons **685**
Ine King of the West-Saxons **688**
The Church of Wells founded **704**
Battle of Wanborough **714**
Taunton burned by Æthelburh **722**
Ine goes to Rome **726**
Æthelbald takes Somerton **733**
Cuthred King of the West-Saxons **740**
Rebellion of Æthelhun **750**
Cuthred defeats Æthelbald at Burford **752**
Sigeberht King of the West-Saxons **754**
Sigeberht deposed by his Wise Men and Cynewulf elected **755**
Death of Æthelbald—Offa King of the Mercians **755**
Eadberht of Northumberland takes Alcluyd **756**
Charles the Great King of the Franks **768**
Offa takes Bensington **777**
Cynewulf killed by Cyneheard **784**
Lichfield an Archbishoprick **786**
First landing of the Danes **787**
Æthelberht murdered by Offa **792**
Death of Offa—Cenwulf King of the Mercians **794**
Charles the Great crowned Emperor—Ecgberht King of the West-
    Saxons **800**
Ecgberht ravages Cornwall **813**
Cenwulf of Mercia ravages Gwynedd **816**

A. D.

Cenwulf ravages Dyfed **819**

Beornwulf conquers Powys **822**

Ecgberht defeats Beornwulf at Ellandun, and gains the lordship over
Kent, Sussex, and East-Anglia **823**

Northumberland submits to Ecgberht **827**

Wiglaf receives the crown of Mercia from Ecgberht—submission of
the Welsh **828**

The Danes defeat Ecgberht at Charmouth—Ecgberht defeats the
Danes and Welsh at Hengestesdun **835**

Æthelwulf succeeds Ecgberht **836**

The Danes reach London **839**

Battle at the mouth of the Parret **845**

Alfred born **849**

The Danes take Canterbury and London, but are defeated by Æthelwulf at Ockley **851**

Æthelwulf helps Burhred of Mercia against the Welsh **853**

Alfred sent to Rome **853**

The Danes winter in Sheppey **855**

Æthelwulf goes to Rome **855**

Æthelwulf marries Judith on his way home **856**

Æthelwulf dies ; Æthelbald succeeds **858**

Æthelbald dies ; Æthelberht succeeds **860**

Æthelberht dies ; Æthelred succeeds ; the Danes land in East-Anglia **866**

The Danes take York **867**

Æthelred and Alfred help Burhred against the Danes **868**

The Danes conquer East Anglia ; martyrdom of Saint Edmund . . **870**

The Danes enter Wessex ; Battles of Englefield, Reading, Ashdown,
Basing and Merton ; death of Æthelred and election of Alfred ;
Battle of Wilton ; peace between the Danes and West-Saxons **871**

The Danes invade Mercia ; Burhred goes to Rome **874**

Alfred defeats the Danes by sea **875**

The Danes under Healfdene settle in Deira **876**

The Danes under Guthorm enter Wessex **876**

The Danes leave Wessex and settle in part of Mercia **877**

Guthorm enters Wessex ; Alfred takes shelter at Athelney ; Battle
of Ethandun ; Peace of Wedmore ; Æthelred Alderman of
Western Mercia **878**

Guthorm settles in East-Anglia **880**

A.D.

Alfred defeats the Danes at sea **882**

Alfred drives the Danes from Rochester; the Welsh Princes submit
to him **885**

Alfred repairs London **886**

Charles the Fat deposed and the Empire divided **888**

Arnulf defeated the Danes at Löwen **891**

Hasting lands in Kent and is helped by the Danes in East-Anglia. . **893**

Alfred takes Appledore; the Danes defeated at Buttington. . . . **894**

Birth of Æthelstan **895**

The war with the Danes goes on **895-6**

Alfred improves his navy; the Danes leave Wessex **897**

Alfred dies; Edward the Elder chosen King; revolt of Æthelwald,
who takes refuge with the Danes **901**

Æthelwald and the Danes attack Wessex; death of Æthelwald . . **904**

Peace between Edward and Guthorm. **906**

The Danish wars begin again; Battle of Tettenhall; Edward and his
sister Æthelflæd begin to fortify various posts **910**

Battle of Wednesfield; Æthelflæd rules alone in Mercia **911**

Rolf settles in Gaul; beginning of the Duchy of Normandy . . . **913**

The Danes driven away from Somersetshire and Wales **915**

Death of Æthelflæd; Edward annexes Mercia to Wessex **918**

All Essex, East-Anglia, and Danish Mercia submits to Edward . . **921**

The Welsh Kings "seek Edward to lord" **922**

Rægnald takes York **923**

All the Northumbrians, Scots, and Strathclyde Welsh "chose Edward
to father and lord" **924**

Death of Edward; Æthelstan chosen King. **925**

The Welsh, Scots, and Northumbrians submit to Æthelstan; he drives
the Welsh from Exeter and fortifies the city **926**

Edwin the Ætheling drowned at sea **933**

Æthelstan ravages Scotland. **934**

Battle of Brunanburh. **937**

Æthelstan dies; Edmund chosen King **940**

Edmund recovers the Five Boroughs; Richard the Fearless Duke of
the Normans **941**

Division of England between Edmund and Anlaf **942**

Birth of Edgar **943**

Edmund recovers Northumberland **944**

A. D.

Edmund conquers Cumberland and grants it as a fief to Malcolm of
Scotland 945
Edmund murdered by Liofa; Eadred chosen King; the Northum-
brians and Scots acknowledge him 946
The Northumbrians again acknowledge Eadred 947
The Northumbrians rebel under Eric 948
The Northumbrians finally submit and the land becomes an Earldom 954
Eadred dies; Eadwig chosen King; Edgar reigns as Under-king in
Mercia 955
Dunstan banished 956
The Mercians revolt; Edgar recalls Dunstan 957
Oda divorces Eadwig and Ælfgifu 958
Eadwig dies; Edgar chosen King; Dunstan Archbishop 959
Edgar at York 961
Edgar subdues Idwal's revolt 963
Edgar marries Ælfthryth 964
Westmorland harried 966
Thanet harried; Æthelred born 969
Edgar crowned at Bath; his triumph at Chester 973
Edgar dies; disputed election; Edward chosen King; disputes about
the monks and the secular clergy 975
Various synods held 977
Edward murdered; Æthelred chosen King 979
The Danish invasion begun again 980
Swegen King of the Danes 985
Invasion of Olaf; Hugh Capet chosen King of the French . . . 987
Battle of Maldon; death of Brihtnoth; money first paid to the
Danes ; Æthelred's dispute with Richard the Fearless . . . 991
Elfric's treason; victory of the English at sea 992
The Danes ravage Lindsey; flight of the three Thanes 993
Invasion of Swegen and Olaf; the two Kings beaten off by the
Londoners 994
Olaf makes peace and goes home; Swegen continues the war . . 995
The Danes go on ravaging 997–999
Æthelred ravages Cumberland ; the Danes go to Normandy ;
Æthelred's fleet ravages the Côtentin 1000
The Danes return and are driven back from Exeter; battle at Pen-
how 1001

A.

Æthelred marries Emma ; tribute paid to the Danes ; massacre of
Saint Brice . . . . 10⟨

Swegen takes Exeter ; treason of Ælfric ; Swegen burns Salisbury
and Wilton . . . . 10(

Swegen burns Norwich and Thetford ; drawn battle between him
and Ulfcytel . . . . 10(

Famine . . . . 10(

Ælfhelm murdered by Eadric ; the Danes ravage the inland parts
of Wessex ; Malcolm besieges Durham, but is driven back
by Uhtred . . . . 10(

Tribute paid again . . . . 10(

The Fleet made ready 10C

The Fleet at Sandwich ; flight of Wulfnoth ; invasion of Thurkill . 10C

The Danes in East-Anglia ; Battle of Ringmere . . . . . . 10?

Tribute again offered ; the Danes take Canterbury and keep Archbishop Ælfheah in bonds . . . . 10)

Martyrdom of Ælfheah ; Thurkill joins the English ; Eadric ravages
Saint David's 101

Invasion of Swegen and Cnut ; Northumberland submits ; London
holds out ; final submission at Bath ; Swegen acknowledged
King 101

Æthelred takes refuge in Normandy ; death of Swegen ; Cnut
chosen King by the Danes, but Æthelred restored by the
English Witan ; Cnut mutilates his hostages and goes back
to Denmark . . . . 101.

Witenagemót at Oxford ; Sigeferth and Morkere murdered by
Eadric ; Edmund marries Sigeferth's widow and establishes
himself in the Five Boroughs ; Cnut comes back ; the
West-Saxons submit to Cnut while Edmund holds out in
the North . . . . 101!

Northumberland submits to Cnut ; murder of Uhtred ; death of
Æthelred ; Edmund elected King in London and Cnut at
Southampton ; Battles of Pen Selwood, Sherstone, Brentford, Otford and Assandun ; conference at Olney ; division
of the Kingdom ; death of Edmund . . . . 101(

Cnut finally elected and crowned ; the Æthelings and others put
to death or banished ; Cnut marries Emma ; Eadric put to
death . . . . 101⁊

A.D.

A great Danegeld laid on ; Edgar's law renewed at Oxford . . . **1018**
Godwine made Earl of the West-Saxons **1020**
The body of Saint Ælfheah translated to Canterbury **1023**
Cnut's Pilgrimage to Rome ; birth of William the Conqueror . . **1027**
Cnut puts forth a code of laws . . . . (?) **1028**
Scotland submits to Cnut **1031**
Death of Cnut; disputed election between Harold and Harthacnut ;
    the Kingdom divided **1035**
Pilgrimage and death of Robert of Normandy ; William succeeds ;
    murder of the Ætheling Alfred **1036**
Harold King over all England **1037**
Harthacnut chosen King ; he lays on a Danegeld ; he digs up the
    body of Harold **1040**
Worcester ravaged by order of Harthacnut ; Edward the son of
    Æthelred comes back to England **1041**
Death of Harthacnut ; Edward chosen King **1042**
Edward crowned ; Emma despoiled of her treasures **1043**
Stigand Bishop of the East-Angles; banishment of Gunhild and
    others **1044**
Edward marries Edith the daughter of Godwine ; threatened inva-
    sion of Magnus of Norway **1045**
Swegen the son of Godwine overcomes Gruffydd of South Wales ;
    he throws up his Earldom and goes to Denmark **1046**
War in the North ; help refused to Swegen of Denmark ; William
    of Normandy defeats the rebels at Val-ès-dunes **1047**
England in alliance with the Emperor Henry against Baldwin of
    Flanders ; the restoration of Swegen's Earldom refused ;
    Swegen murders his cousin Beorn ; Bishop Ealdred defeated
    by the Welsh ; Ulf made Bishop of Dorchester **1049**
The Norman influence increases ; Robert of Jumièges made Arch-
    bishop of Canterbury **1050**
Edward remits the Heregeld ; outrages of Eustace of Dover ; God-
    wine demands justice ; meetings at Gloucester and London ;
    Godwine and his family banished **1051**
William of Normandy visits Edward ; death of Emma ; return
    of Godwine ; Archbishop Robert and other Normans
    outlawed **1052**
Death of Earl Godwine ; Harold Earl of the West-Saxons . . . **1053**

A. D.

Siward invades Scotland and defeats Macbeth; Bishop Ealdred
goes on an embassy to the Emperor to bring back the
Ætheling Edward **1054**
Death of Siward; Tostig Earl of the Northumbrians; Ælfgar is
outlawed and joins Gruffydd of North Wales; they defeat
Ralph, and burn Hereford; Harold's first Welsh campaign;
he restores Hereford; peace with Gruffydd; Ælfgar restored
to his Earldom **1055**
Invasion of Gruffydd and Magnus; death of Bishop Leofgar . . **1056**
Return and death of the Ætheling Edward; deaths of Earls Leofric
and Ralph; Earldoms given to Gyrth and Leofwine . . . **1057**
Harold goes on a pilgrimage to Rome . . . . (?) **1058**
The minster at Waltham consecrated by Archbishop Cynesige; he
dies and is succeeded by Ealdred; Walter and Gisa Bishops
of Hereford and Wells **1060**
Tostig, Ealdred and Walter and Gisa all go to Rome **1061**
Saint Wulfstan Bishop of Worcester **1062**
Harold's march to Rhuddlan; his great Welsh campaign; Wales
submits and Gruffydd killed by his own people **1063**
Probable time of Harold's visit to Normandy and oath to William;
murder of Gospatric and other Northumbrian Thanes by
order of Tostig **1064**
Ravages of Caradoc at Portskewet; revolt of the Northumbrians;
banishment of Tostig; sickness of Edward; consecration
of Westminster **1065**

1066
Edward dies; Harold elected King . . . . *Jan.* 5
Edward buried; Harold crowned . . . . ,, 6
Harold wins over Northumberland with the help of Bishop Wulf-
stan . . . . *Jan.* 15—*April* 16
Harold's Easter Feast at Westminster . . . . *April* 16—23
The Comet . . . . ,, 24—30
Tostig ravages Wight and Lindesey and takes refuge in Scotland *May*
Great preparations of Harold . . . . *May* —*Sept.*
Harold's army disbanded . . . . *Sept.* 8
Invasion of Tostig and Harold Hardrada; they ravage the York-
shire coast and land at Riccall . . . . ,,

A.D.
1066

Battle of Fulford . . . . *Sept.* 20
York surrenders to Harold Hardrada ; Harold of England reaches
    Tadcaster . . . . ,, 24
Battle of Stamfordbridge . . . . ,, 25
William sets sail from Saint Valery . . . . ,, 27
William lands at Pevensey . . . . ,, 28
William marches to Hastings . . . . ,, 29
Harold marches to London and collects troops . . . . . *Oct.* 1 · 12
Harold marches from London and encamps on Senlac . . ,, 12, 13
Battle of Senlac . . . . ,, 14
Edgar chosen King ; Edwin and Morkere withdraw to their Earl-
    doms . . . . *Oct.* 15 —*Nov.* 1
William returns to Hastings . . . . ,, 15
William marches to Romney . . . . ,, 20
Dover submits . . . . ,, 21
Canterbury submits . . . . ,, 29
William's sickness ; submission of Winchester . . . . ,, 31 —*Dec.* 1
Skirmish near London ; burning of Southwark ; William marches
    to Wallingford ; submission at Berkhampstead . . . .,,
Coronation of William . . . . ,, 25

CONTENTS.

CHAPTER I.

WHO FIRST LIVED IN BRITAIN 1

PAGE

CHAPTER II.

HOW BRITAIN WAS CONQUERED BY THE ROMANS . . 9

CHAPTER III.

HOW BRITAIN WAS A ROMAN PROVINCE . . 16

CHAPTER IV.

HOW BRITAIN BECAME ENGLAND 22

CHAPTER V.

HOW THE ENGLISH KINGDOMS IN BRITAIN WERE FOUNDED 32

CHAPTER VI.

PAGE
HOW THE ENGLISH BECAME CHRISTIANS 42

CHAPTER VII.

HOW THE KINGS OF THE WEST-SAXONS BECAME LORDS OVER ALL
ENGLAND 63

CHAPTER VIII.

HOW THE DANES CAME INTO ENGLAND, AND HOW ENGLAND
BECAME ONE KINGDOM. 100

CHAPTER IX.

OF THE KINGS OF THE ENGLISH FROM THE TIME THAT ENGLAND
BECAME ONE KINGDOM TILL THE DANES CAME AGAIN . . 148

CHAPTER X.

HOW THE DANES CONQUERED AND REIGNED IN ENGLAND . . . 187

CHAPTER XI.

THE REIGN OF KING EDWARD THE CONFESSOR. (1042—1066) . . 253

CHAPTER XII.

PAGE

THE REIGN OF KING HAROLD THE SON OF GODWINE. JANUARY 6
—OCTOBER 14, 1066 298

CHAPTER XIII.

THE INTERREGNUM. OCTOBER 14—DECEMBER 25, 1066 340

LIST OF MAPS.

To face page

1. NORTH-WESTERN EUROPE IN THE FOURTH CENTURY . . 17

2. BRITAIN AT THE BEGINNING OF THE SEVENTH CENTURY 39

3. NORTH-WESTERN EUROPE AT THE END OF THE NINTH
   CENTURY 134

4. BRITAIN IN THE NINTH AND TENTH CENTURIES . . . 144

5. BRITAIN AT THE DEATH OF EDWARD THE CONFESSOR,
   1066, SHOWING THE EARLDOMS AND DEPENDENT
   KINGDOMS 280

OLD ENGLISH HISTORY
FOR CHILDREN.

CHAPTER I.

WHO FIRST LIVED IN BRITAIN.

THE country in which we live is called England, that is to say, the land of the English. But it was not always called England, because there were not always Englishmen living in it. The old name of the land was Britain. And we still call the whole island in which we live Great Britain, of which England is the southern part and Scotland the northern. We call it *Great* Britain, because there is another country also called Britain, namely, the north-western corner of Gaul; but this last we now generally call Brittany. The two names, however, are really the same, and both are called in Latin *Britannia.*

In the old days then, when the land was called only Britain, Englishmen had not yet begun to live in it. Our forefathers then lived in other lands, and had not yet come into the land where we now live; but there was an England even then, namely the land in which Englishmen then lived. If you look in a map of Denmark or of Northern Germany, you will see on the Baltic Sea a little land called *Angeln:* that is the same name as *England.* I do not mean that all our forefathers came out of that one little land of Angeln; but they all came from that part of the world, from the lands near the mouth of the Elbe, and that one little land has kept the English name to this day.

B

It is a long time, fourteen hundred years and more, since our forefathers began to come from their old land by the mouth of the Elbe and to live in the Isle of Britain. And when they came here, they did not come into a land where no men were dwelling, so that they could sit down and live in it without any trouble. They found a land in which men were already living, and they had to fight against the men whom they found in the land, and to take their land from them. The men whom our forefathers found in the Isle of Britain were not men of their own nation or their own speech. They were the men who had lived in the land for many ages, and they were called by the same name as the land itself, for they were called the Britons. But our forefathers called them by another name, for they spoke a tongue which our forefathers did not understand, and in Old-English those who spoke a tongue which could not be understood were called *Welsh*. So our forefathers called the men whom they found in the land the Welsh. And the children of those men, the children of the men who lived in the Isle of Britain before our forefathers came into it, we call the Welsh to this day.

Now I wish you to remember from the very beginning that we Englishmen came from another land into Britain, that we found the Welsh living in Britain before us, and that the land which before was called Britain came to be called England because Englishmen lived in it. I shall have to tell you all this again more at length, and in a way which may make you understand it better; but I want you to get what I have said well into your heads from the very first, and you will understand it better as you go along. And perhaps some of you may not very well understand what I mean by different nations and languages, so I will try to explain that a little more fully before I go on any further.

I think you must all know that all people in all parts of the world do not speak the same tongue or language, that is, they do not use the same words when they mean the same things. Thus a Frenchman, a German, and an Englishman will often call the same things by quite different names. Thus what we call a *horse* a Frenchman will call *cheval*, and a German will call it *Pferd* or *Ross*. But some languages are much more like one another

than others. Thus in English and German all the most common
words, all the words without which we could not get on at all,
are really the same. Thus *horse* and *Ross* are really the same
word, and many words in English and German are yet more
like one another. When you begin to learn German, you will
find that all the commonest words, *man, wife, child, house,
father, mother, bread, water, ox, sheep,* are either exactly the
same in German and in English, or else so much alike that
you can see that they were the same once. That is to say,
there was a time, a very long time ago, when English and
German were only one language, and when the forefathers of
the English that are now and the forefathers of the Germans
that are now were only one people or nation. We commonly
say that men are of the same people or nation when they live
in the same country and speak the same language.

Now the different nations of the world have not always lived
in the same countries in which they live now. Many of them
have moved about a great deal and have gone into new lands,
as Englishmen now often go and live in Canada and Australia.
Very often one nation has gone and conquered the country of
another nation ; that is, it has overcome them in battle, and
perhaps driven them quite out of the land ; or perhaps it has
only made them subject to the conquering nation or to its king ;
or perhaps only part of a nation has done this, while another
part has stayed in its old land. Thus it often happens that we
find people in quite different parts of the world speaking the
same languages. or languages nearly the same, while people who
live close together speak languages which are quite different.
This is nowhere plainer than in this Isle of Britain. As I
said, we came into this island from another land, and we found
other men living here, and the children of those men whom
we found here live in our island to this day. So you will find,
and, if you think a moment, you will see that it is not wonderful that it is so, that the other languages which are spoken
in Britain are quite different from English, while languages
which are very much more like English are spoken much
further off. This is because the people whom we found in
Britain were not our own near kinsfolk, while those of our
own near kinsfolk who stayed in their own land and did not

come into Britain went on speaking their own tongue, and still speak languages which it is easy to see were once the same as our own.

I do not think I need tell any of you that the whole island of Great Britain, as well as Ireland and the smaller islands about them, now forms only one Kingdom. Queen Victoria is Queen over all of them, and her Parliament makes laws for all of them, except for two or three small islands. We are all now friends and fellow-countrymen, whether we live in England, Scotland, Ireland, or Wales. But it was not so always. There are still several different languages spoken in the British Islands, because quite different nations once lived in them, and those nations often fought against and conquered one another. We ought to be very glad that it is not so now; but we must take care to remember that there have been quite distinct nations living in these islands, or we shall never really understand the history.

There are now three languages spoken in the British Islands, our own English tongue and two others. I need not say that English is the chief language of the whole country. Everybody speaks it in England, and most people can speak it in the other parts of the islands. But there are still some people in Great Britain who cannot speak English at all, and there are many to whom English is not their own mother-tongue. That is to say, they speak their own language and English as well, just as you speak English naturally, and yet may some time be able also to speak French and German.

The other two languages spoken in the British Islands are the Welsh, of which I have already said something, and the Irish. Wales, the land of the Welsh, lies to the west of England, and we often reckon it as part of England. This is because for England and Wales there is only one law, while the laws of Scotland and Ireland are often different from the laws of England. But in Wales there are still some people who cannot speak English at all, and in a large part of the country most people speak both Welsh and English. In a large part of Ireland nothing but English is spoken. But in other parts people speak Irish too, and some do not understand any English at all. In the southern part of Scotland everybody speaks English. They do not speak it in quite the same way as we do ; but it is really the same language, and an Englishman and a Scotchman soon get to understand one another. But in the northern part of Scotland, which is called the Highlands, there is still another language spoken, called Gaelic. But Gaelic and Irish are so much alike that it is perhaps best to say that there are only three languages spoken in Great Britain and Ireland, namely, English, Welsh, and Irish.

Now I just now said that the other languages which are spoken in Britain are much more unlike English than some other languages which are spoken much further off, especially in the lands which I told you were our old homes. You cannot make out a Welshman's or an Irishman's language at all, unless you learn it on purpose. But if you take a book in the language spoken by the common people in the north of Germany, I do not say that you will understand every word; but if you are at all quick, you will see that most of the words are the same as English. That is to say, their language is a kindred language with English, a language of the same group or class. For it is not hard to arrange the chief languages of the world in groups or classes. Thus not only German and English, but also Dutch, Danish, and Swedish, are all so much alike that we may be sure that the people who speak them were once all one people. These are called the Teutonic languages. Again, though a Welshman and an Irishman cannot understand one another, yet there is a great likeness between the Welsh and Irish languages, so that we may be sure that the Welsh and the Irish were once one people. Their languages are called the Celtic languages. The people speaking those languages were once spread over a great part of Europe ; but Celtic is not now spoken anywhere but in Ireland, Wales, the Isle of Man, the Highlands of Scotland, and that part of Gaul which is called Brittany. And there are many other groups of kindred languages of the same kind.

But we can go a little further back still. I told you that there was one set of languages called Teutonic and another called Celtic, and that there was doubtless a time when all the Teutonic nations were only one nation, and when all the Celtic nations were one other nation. But besides this, learned men, who know many languages, have found out that these Celtic and Teutonic languages, and many others too, Greek,

Latin, Slavonic (which is spoken in Russia, Poland, Servia, and
other eastern parts of Europe), and the old language of Lithuania and Eastern Prussia, were all once only one language.
And, what perhaps you might not have thought of, the old
languages of Persia and India were also once the same. The
people who speak all these languages were once all one people,
and all of them are our kinsfolk, though some are much nearer
kinsfolk than others. Thus the Welsh themselves are, after all,
our kinsfolk, though the Germans and Danes and Dutch are
kinsfolk who are much nearer. The time when all these different nations were only one people was of course a very long
time ago, long before any books were written, and before we
know any history for certain. But those who know the languages well can find out from the languages themselves that
they were once all one language. These languages which were
once one, are generally called the Aryan languages, from Arya
or Iran, the old name of Persia. The nations who speak
these languages now occupy nearly all Europe and a great
part of Asia. But even in Europe there are some people who
do not speak an Aryan language. There are two nations,
the Hungarians and the Turks, who are not Aryans, and who
have come into Europe in later times since the Aryan nations
came into it. And there are still some people left in Europe,
in corners and out-of-the-way places, whose language is not
Aryan, and whose forefathers were doubtless living in Europe
before the Aryan nations came into it. These are the Fins in
the very north of Europe, and the Basques in those wild
mountainous parts of Spain which nobody has ever been able
thoroughly to conquer. Now these people no doubt once
occupied a much larger part of Europe than they do now, and
it is not unlikely that some of them may once have lived in
the British Islands before the first Aryan people came into
them. But, if so, they must have been quite destroyed,
and not merely driven into corners, for there certainly are none
of them living in Britain now.

Now I will tell you a reason for thinking it very likely that
some people who were not Aryan once lived in Britain. It
does not seem that any of the Aryan people were ever mere
savages, such as travellers and voyagers have often found in

distant parts of the world. Yet, from things which have been
found in old graves and elsewhere, both in Britain and elsewhere, it seems most likely that people once lived in Britain
who must have been mere savages, without the use of metal, people who lived wholly by hunting and fishing. They had arrows
and spear-heads of flint, and axes and hammers of stone.
Think what trouble it must have been to do the commonest
things with such tools. After them came a time when men
had the use of bronze, and, last of all, the use of iron, as we have
now. You may have heard of buildings, if we may call them
buildings, made of great rough stones, which are called *cromlechs*. These have often been mistaken for altars, but they
really are graves. Huge uncut stones were piled up without
being joined by any mortar, and they were covered over with
earth and smaller stones, so as to make a tump or barrow.
These cromlechs, it seems most likely, are the graves of the
first dwellers in the land, who had no use of metal. Of these
very early times we can find out nothing, except from graves
and such like remains, as of course we have no books that were
written then. But there is every reason to think that the people
who made these great and strange works were the oldest people
who lived in these islands, and that the Celts, the Welsh and
Irish, came into the land and quite destroyed them. Then, ages
afterwards, our own forefathers came from North Germany, and
destroyed or drove out the Celts from a great part of the Isle of
Britain. but left them in other parts, where they still stay and
still speak their own tongues. I wish I could tell you more about
our own forefathers before they came into Britain. You will of
course understand that the little which we know of them is
part of the history of Germany and not part of the history of
Britain. What little I have to say about them I shall say in
another chapter ; but I will tell you this much now, that there
is no doubt that our fathers had always been a free people,
and had never had any other people ruling over them in their
own land. Now it was not so with the men whom they found
in Britain ; for before the English came into Britain, the
Welsh had been conquered by the Romans. Who the Romans
were, and how they conquered Britain, I shall tell you in the
next chapter.

This present chapter I am afraid you may have thoug
rather hard, as there are no pleasant stories in it, such as ye
will often hear in other parts of my history.   But, to unde
stand thoroughly what comes after, you ought to keep clear
in your mind the succession of the different nations one aft
another.   And I do not think that I have written anythir
which you cannot understand, if you think a little and look we
at a good map.   So now I will put the whole together for ye
in a few words.

In the British Isles there are still three languages spoke:
English, Welsh, and Irish.   All these are Aryan language
Of these, English is a Teutonic language, while Welsh an
Irish are Celtic languages.   Our forefathers came from tl
countries near the Elbe, and conquered, but did not whol
destroy, the Welsh or Britons who were already living in tl
island.   All this we know for certain; but it also seems likel
though it is not certain, that, before the Celts came int
Britain, there was a savage people in the island whom th
Celts quite destroyed, and about whom we can tell nothinį
except from things which have been found in their graves.

CHAPTER II.

HOW BRITAIN WAS CONQUERED BY THE ROMANS.

`HE first people then who lived in the Isle of Britain of whom we really know anything were the Celts, that is to say, the Irish and the Welsh ; and the first people of whom we know anything in that part of the island which is called England were the Welsh or Britons. But we know very little of the times when the Welsh lived in Britain as their own land, before the Romans conquered them. There are a great many strange stories told about their history, but nothing was written about these things till hundreds of years after the times when they are said to have happened. Therefore we cannot really believe anything that is told us about them. In those old times all the greatest nations of the world, those which were what is called *civilized*, lived round about the Mediterranean Sea. There dwelled the nations who lived under the best laws, who could build the best buildings, who had the greatest and wisest men among them, who first did things worth being remembered, and who first wrote those things down in books, in order that men might remember them. There lived the old Greeks who were so famous, and the Romans and other nations of Italy who were so famous somewhat later. Some of you will some day learn their languages, Greek and Latin. These are both Aryan languages, and you will find it very pleasant when you learn Greek to see how many of the commonest words are really the same in Greek and in English. But in all the Northern and Western parts of Europe, where the Teutonic and Celtic nations lived, the people were still very rude and ignorant, and they and the civilized nations near the Mediterranean Sea knew very little about one another. You may perhaps be surprised to hear that many of the great Greek writers, whose names you may have heard, and whose books you may one day read, had most likely never heard of the Isle of Britain, and that they certainly knew nothing at all of the English in their own older land. Though the Greeks were very good sailors in their own seas, yet their ships were not made to go such long voyages as our ships can go now, and they hardly ever went out of the Mediterranean and the other inland seas ˙which join it. They knew very little of the Ocean or outer sea, and for a long time they did not think that it was a sea at all, but they fancied that Ocean was a river running round the earth.

But there were another people called the Phœnicians, who, though they were in most things not nearly so great and wise a people as the Greeks, were much more likely than the Greeks to find out something about the Isle of Britain. They were not an Aryan people, and the language which they spoke was much the same as the Hebrew, the language spoken by the Jews. We first hear of the Phœnicians in Tyre and Sidon and the neighbouring cities, which are often spoken of in the Bible. If you look at a map, you will see these cities and the old land of the Phœnicians at the very east end of the Mediterranean Sea. The Phœnicians were very fond of trade, that is, of buying and selling, and so getting rich ; and they were the first people who made long voyages in order to buy and sell. They were also the first people who began to plant *Colonies* in different places. Perhaps you do not very well know what a colony is, though I think you must have sometimes heard of our own English colonies in America and Australia and other lands far away. At any rate you know how the bees swarm ; how, when the hive is too full, the young bees fly away and live somewhere else. The young bees then found a colony, and men do just the same. When a land is so full that all the people cannot find room enough to live in it, or when many people are discontented with their own country and would rather live somewhere else, or even when they think that they can buy and sell better by living somewhere else, men will often go to some other land, and find themselves a new country there. They go somewhere where nobody lives, or where the people who do live are easily conquered. So our fathers did in Britain ages ago, and so we do now in New Zealand and other lands far away. Men thus leave their old land and take to themselves a new land and dwell in it, and build them cities and live as a new people. Such a new city and country is called a colony of the old land from whence its people first came. Now both the Greeks and the Phœnicians were great planters of colonies ; indeed, nearly the whole of the Mediterranean Sea had Phœnician and Greek colonies scattered along its coasts. I say along its coasts, for both the Greeks and the Phœnicians were people who loved the sea, and seldom liked to live very far inland. Thus you will find both Greek and Phœnician cities far away from old Greece and old Phœnicia, cities which were colonies of the old cities in Greece and Phœnicia themselves. Just so now-a-days there are Englishmen in America and Australia, and not only in England itself.

Thus both the Greeks and the Phœnicians loved the sea, and both loved trade, and both planted colonies and built cities in far-off lands. But the Phœnicians were the bolder seamen of the two ; they began to sail far away and to settle in other lands sooner than the Greeks did, and they sailed to and settled in lands further off from their own land than the Greeks ever did. There never was any Greek colony beyond the Strait which joins the Mediterranean Sea and the Ocean, and there were very few Greek colonies in any part of Spain at all. But the Phœnicians had passed the Strait and had built the city of Gades or Cadiz, before the Greeks had planted any colonies even in Italy and Sicily. Cadiz is the oldest city in Europe which still remains great and flourishing, for it has been a great and flourishing city ever since it was built by Phœnician settlers nearly three thousand years ago. And besides Cadiz there were many other Phœnician cities both in Spain and on the north coast of Africa, the greatest of which was the famous city of Carthage. Thus you see how the Phœnicians, who were bolder sailors and were not afraid of the Ocean, were more likely to find out something about the Isle of Britain than the Greeks were. Some people have thought that Phœnician traders themselves sailed as far as Britain, and bought the tin which is found in Cornwall and the Scilly Islands, and even perhaps worked the mines themselves. If this really was so, we must of course suppose that these were Phœnicians from Cadiz and the other

cities in Spain and Africa, and not from the old cities of Tyre
and Sidon.   But there is no good reason to believe that the
Phœnicians ever settled in Britain, and for my own part I very
much doubt whether they ever came to Britain at all.   Still
there can be no doubt that the Phœnicians learned something
about Britain from the people who lived nearer to the island,
and who sold them the tin and the other things which came
thence.   We can hardly tell for certain how it was, for there are
very few Phœnician books or writings left, and none which tell
us anything about Britain.   But we cannot doubt that, through
these Phœnician traders, some little knowledge about Britain
found its way to the nations round about the Mediterranean
Sea.   They at least learned that there was such an island, and
that tin was to be found there.

The time when we first begin really to know anything about
Britain is between fifty and sixty years before the birth of our
Lord Jesus Christ.   You know, I suppose, that that is the way in
which Christian nations reckon time ; such a thing happened so
many years before, or so many years after, the birth of Christ.
At that time the greatest people in the world were the Romans.
These were originally the people of the city of Rome in Italy.
They were not so bold at sea as the Phœnicians, nor were
they so clever and learned a people as the Greeks.   They could
not build such fine temples, or carve such beautiful statues, or
make such eloquent speeches and poems as the Greeks could ;
but they were the best soldiers and the wisest law-makers that
the world ever saw.   At Rome, in the best days of Rome,
every man knew both how to command and how to obey.
The Romans chose their own rulers ; but when they had chosen
them, they submitted to all their lawful commands.   They made
their own laws ; but they did not think that, because they made
the laws, they might therefore break them.   Thus they were
able gradually to conquer, first all Italy, and then nearly all
the world that they knew of, that is, all the countries round
about the Mediterranean Sea.   The people of Italy itself they
gradually admitted to the same rights as themselves, so that at
the time of which I am speaking, every Italian was reckoned as
a Roman ; but the lands out of Italy they made into *Provinces*,
and the people of those lands were their subjects.   There was

no King at Rome, but the people of the Provinces had to obey the laws made by the Senate and People of Rome, and to be governed by the magistrates whom the Romans sent to rule over them. The Romans were very proud of their freedom in having no King or master of any kind, and for a long time they were worthy of their freedom, and used it well ; but after a while the nation became much corrupted, and their freedom became little more than confusion and quarrelling with one another. The truth is that the Romans were now far too great a people to be governed in the same way which had done so well for them when they were the people of only one city. And for the Provinces it would always have been better if the Romans had had a King or even a Tyrant,[1] because one master is always better than many.

At this time the Roman governor in Gaul was named Caius Julius Cæsar. He is one of the most famous men in the whole history of the world. In many things he was a very bad man, and he thought more of his own greatness than of the good of his country ; but there was much in him which made men love him, and as a soldier and a ruler hardly any man has ever been greater. Before his time the Roman Province of Gaul was only a small part of the country ; Cæsar gradually conquered all Gaul, and he next wished to conquer Britain also, as it was so near Gaul, with only a narrow arm of the sea between them. He twice came over to Britain with his army, but he only visited the southern part of the island, and he cannot be said to have conquered any part of it. Britain did not become a Roman Province, nor did Cæsar leave any Roman governor or Roman soldiers behind him. Still this coming over of Cæsar to Britain was a very important event. From that time Britain became much more known to the rest of the world than it had ever been before. Now that Cæsar had conquered all Gaul, parts of Britain could be seen from parts of the

---

[1] A *Tyrant* originally meant a man who gets to himself the power of a King in a country where there is not any King by law. Under the Roman Empire it meant an usurper or pretender in opposition to a lawful Emperor. In neither of these cases does the word prove anything as to the goodness or badness of the *Tyrant's* government. But the word is now more often used to mean a cruel or bad ruler of any kind.

Roman dominions. A great deal more trade went on between Britain and other countries than had ever gone on before. And men at Rome often thought and spoke of making Britain a Roman Province as well as Gaul; but it was not till a good many years after Cæsar's time that this was really done.

Some years after Cæsar was in Britain there was a civil war among the Romans. Perhaps you do not know what I mean by a *Civil* war. It is a war, not between two nations, but between men of the same nation, between fellow-countrymen or fellow-citizens, who in Latin are called *Cives.* Thus there was a war between Cæsar and his party and another great Roman called Pompeius and his party, and the end was that Cæsar became master of Rome and of all the Roman dominions, with all the power of a King, though he was not called King, but Dictator. But many of the Romans did not like having a master; for though Cæsar was not a harsh or bloody ruler, they could not bear that any one man should take to himself a power which the laws of Rome did not give him. So they plotted together, and one day they slew Cæsar in the Senate-House. Then there were other civil wars for several years, till at last Cæsar's grand-nephew, Caius Julius Cæsar Octavianus, made himself even more fully master of Rome than his uncle had been before him. But even he was afraid to call himself King; so he was called Imperator or Emperor, Prince, and Augustus. He was the first of the Roman Emperors, and is generally known in history as the Emperor Augustus Cæsar. But all the Emperors after him were also called Augustus and Cæsar, even though they were of no kin at all to the first Cæsar the Dictator.

It was in the reign of Augustus that our Lord Jesus Christ was born; we now, therefore, reckon the years after Christ instead of before, and we say that Augustus died *Anno Domini*—that is, in the year of our Lord—14. Augustus several times spoke of conquering Britain; but he never did it, and he never really tried to do it. His successor Tiberius said that the Empire was large enough already. It was the third Emperor Caius (who is sometimes called Caligula) who first professed to go and conquer the island of which men had heard so much; but Caius was a very foolish and bad prince, or rather, to speak the truth, he was downright mad. He did all sorts of silly things;

he gave himself out for a god, and appointed priests to worship him—one of the priests being himself, and another his favourite horse. He was so fond of this horse that he was going to make him Consul or chief magistrate of Rome, when happily the horse died. You may suppose that such a man was not likely to conquer Britain or to do any other great thing. All that he did was to take an army to the coast of Gaul, near where the town of Boulogne is now. There he set sail in a ship, but at once came back again. The story says that he gave out that he had conquered the Ocean, and ordered his soldiers to fill their helmets with shells and to take them home by way of plunder. This was in the year A.D. 40, ninety-five years after the great Cæsar had first come over to Britain.

It was the fourth Emperor Claudius in whose time any part of Britain was first really conquered. Claudius himself came over in the year A.D. 43, and after him his generals, Plautius and Ostorius, went on with the war. There were then many tribes in Britain under different chiefs, and sometimes some submitted while others still held out. The British chief who held out the longest and the most bravely was Caradoc, whom the Romans called Caractacus. He was King of the Silurians, who lived in South Wales and the neighbouring parts. Caradoc and his people resisted bravely for several years, but at last he was defeated in a great battle, and he and his family were taken prisoners and led to Rome. When Caradoc saw that great and splendid city, he wondered that men who had such wealth and grandeur at home should come and meddle with him in his poor cottage in Britain. He was taken before the Emperor, who received him kindly and gave him his liberty, and, according to some writers, allowed him still to reign in part of Britain as a prince subject to Rome. The Romans had very often before this put captive Kings and generals to death, so that Claudius' kind treatment of Caradoc was really much to his honour.

The whole of Britain was never conquered by the Romans, and it was not till after more than twenty years more of fighting that they got full possession of what was afterwards the Roman Province. But perhaps this chapter is already long enough; so, as the submission of Caradoc makes a good break in the story, I will keep the rest for another chapter.

CHAPTER III.

HOW BRITAIN WAS A ROMAN PROVINCE.

AFTER the time of Caradoc the war between the Romans and the Britons went on. Many parts of the island were still not conquered, and in those that were conquered, the ill-treatment of the Romans sometimes made the people revolt; that is, they took up arms to try and drive the Romans out of the country. In particular there was one Boadicea, the widow of a King of the Icenians, who lived in what is now Norfolk and Suffolk, who made a great revolt against the Romans in the year 61, in the reign of the wicked Emperor Nero. The Roman governor Suetonius was then at the other side of the island, fighting in Mona or Anglesey. Boadicea and her people were thus able to defeat the Romans for a while, and to destroy several of the towns where they lived. Among these was London, which was already a place of much trade; others were Verulam, near Saint Albans, and Camelodunum, now called Colchester. You will understand that the Romans lived chiefly in towns, while the Britons, like all wild people, kept to the open country. So to attack and destroy the towns was to do the Romans the greatest harm that they could. Boadicea was a brave woman; she stood with a spear in her hand and a gold collar round her neck, and with her long hair streaming down, telling her people to fight well and to avenge all that they had suffered at the hands of the Romans. But though they were successful for a while, they could not stand long against the Roman soldiers, who knew how to fight so much better than they. When Suetonius came back there was a great battle near London; the Britons were quite defeated, Boadicea killed herself, and so the war in that part of the island came to an end.

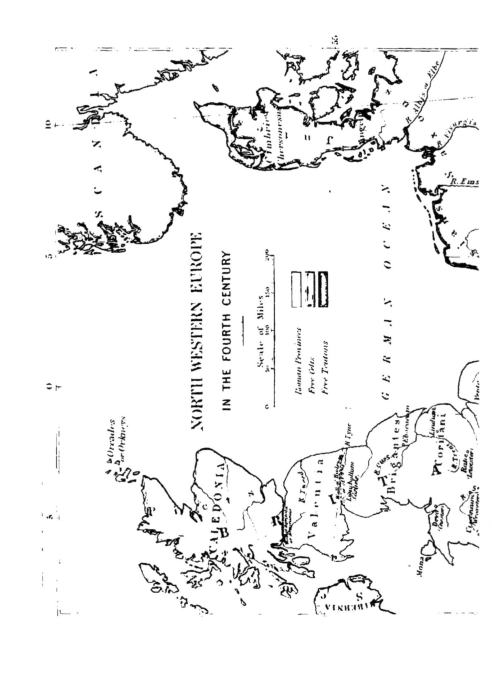

NORTH WESTERN EUROPE

IN THE FOURTH CENTURY

Scale of Miles

Roman Provinces
Free Celts
Free Teutons

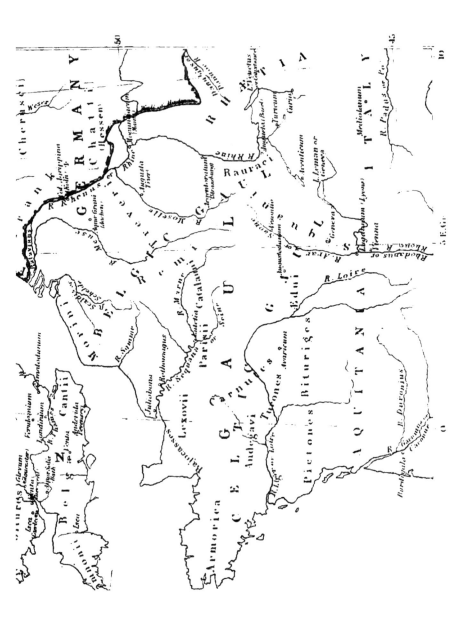

The man who at last really conquered Britain was Julius Agricola, who was the Roman commander here from 78 to 84. He was a good man as well as a brave soldier, and he did all he could to civilize the people as well as to conquer them.   He got further to the north than any Roman had done before him, and we may say that the Roman dominions now reached up to the line between the Firths of Forth and Clyde in Scotland.   If you look at your map, you will see that that is one of the points where the Isle of Britain is narrowest, much narrower than it is in any part of England, and narrower than most parts of Scotland.   Along this line Agricola built a chain of forts, that is, a number of small castles, to defend the Roman Province against the wild people in the north of Britain, who were never fully conquered. Agricola made several campaigns further into Caledonia, as Scotland was then called, and he sailed round the north of the island and found out the Orkneys, which before were hardly known.   But the part of Britain north of Agricola's forts was never really conquered ; there was always fighting along the border, and the barbarians sometimes got further south into the Province itself.

Thus all Britain, except the northern part of Scotland, was conquered by the Romans, and it remained a Roman Province for more than three hundred years.   The land was now ruled by Roman governors ; sometimes the Roman Emperors themselves came over into Britain, and sometimes Emperors were chosen by the soldiers in Britain.   The Britons soon found that it was better to submit quietly than to try to get rid of a yoke which they could not really cast off.   So we may say that the whole country became Roman.   Many Romans doubtless came to live in Britain, and many of the Britons tried to make themselves as much as they could like Romans.   They learned to speak Latin, and to dress and live in the same way that the Romans did.   Towns were built all over the country, and roads were made from one town to another ; for the Romans were among the best builders and the best road-makers that ever were in the world.   Many remains of Roman walls and other buildings are still found, sometimes in towns which are still inhabited, and sometimes in places which are now deserted.   Thus there are pieces of Roman work at Caerleon, Caerwent, Leicester, Lincoln, and many other towns, and also at places which are now forsaken, like Pevensey in Sussex and Burgh Castle in Suffolk. The Romans could not build such beautiful buildings either as the Greeks built before them or as Englishmen and Frenchmen have built since, but for building things which would last no people ever did better. A Roman wall is generally built of rows of small square stones, bonded together with courses of long thin bricks; the arches are round, sometimes made of the same sort of bricks, sometimes of larger stones; so it is easy to know them.

The Romans, and the Britons who had made themselves Romans, must have pretty well occupied the whole land, as we not only find remains of towns in all parts of the country, but also of villas or country seats. You know that now in England the noblemen and chief gentlemen do not live in towns. Most of them spend part of the year in London, but their homes are at their houses in the country. You know that the counties have their own magistrates and everything quite distinct from the towns, or, where it is not so, the people of the towns are under the magistrates of the county. But in the Roman times it was quite different. The towns were then almost everything. The men whom we should now call noblemen or rich gentlemen, though they had houses in the country where they spent part of their time, were citizens of some town, and filled offices there. A Roman town had a good deal of freedom in its own private affairs, but there was no freedom over the whole land. The Emperors did as they pleased throughout the Empire, and the governors whom they sent did much as they pleased in their several provinces. There were heavy taxes to pay, and much oppression in many ways. Still it always happens that a barbarous people gains something by being conquered by a more civilized people; Britain and the other provinces learned much from the Romans which they did not know before; commerce, agriculture, and all the arts improved; in short, they became civilized people instead of barbarians. Still, though the Britons to so great a degree became Romans, the old British or Welsh tongue could not have been forgotten. If it had been forgotten, Welsh could not be anywhere spoken now. I think that most likely things were

then much the same in all Britain as they are in Wales now.
In Wales, as you know, English is the language of the towns,
and in the large towns most people cannot speak Welsh at all.
And a Welsh gentleman can very seldom speak Welsh, unless
he has learned it, as he may have learned French or German.
But you know that the country people commonly speak
Welsh, and that some of them cannot speak any English. So
I fancy that, in these times that we are now talking about,
men spoke Latin in the towns, and also that those whom
we may call the gentry spoke Latin, but that the country
people still spoke Welsh. Welsh then must have gone on
being spoken, but most likely hardly anything was written in it.
There are a great many old stones still standing in Britain
with Latin writing upon them, but I do not think that there
are any with Welsh writing till long afterwards.

I told you that the time that Britain remained a Roman
Province was between three and four hundred years. That is
a long time in the history of any people, and you may expect
that in the course of so long a time many things must have
happened for me to tell you about. And you will find, as we
go on further in our history, that in the course of another
four hundred years very many things happened which I wish you
to remember. But in this particular four hundred years very
few things happened which I need tell you. And the reason
is because Britain was not free ; it was only a province of
Rome. I need not tell you the names of all the Roman
Emperors one after another, for that is rather part of the
history of Rome than of the history of Britain. And though
it sometimes happened that there was a separate Emperor
reigning in Britain, that does not show that Britain was really
independent of Rome. It only meant that the governor of
Britain had rebelled, and would have liked to be Emperor of
the whole Empire, if he could, but that he had been able as yet
only to get hold of a part. Many such rebellions happened
both in Britain and in other provinces. Sometimes the
governor who rebelled was conquered, and then he was said
to have been a Tyrant ; but sometimes he was able to overcome the reigning Emperor and reign in his stead, and then
he was called Imperator, Cæsar, and Augustus. But all the

C 2

time that the Romans were here, there was not any real struggle of the Britons themselves to get back their freedom, except so far as there was always fighting going on along the Northern border. In the year 120 the reigning Emperor Hadrian, who was very fond of travelling about through all parts of his dominions, came also to visit Britain. The next year he had a wall, by which is meant only a strong dyke or earthwork,[1] built from the Tyne to the Solway Firth, between the towns of Carlisle and Newcastle, to keep out the Barbarians. This, you will see, is a long way south of the line of Agricola; and to build the wall there was much the same as giving up all the country beyond it. But, not very long after, in 139, when Antoninus Pius was Emperor, another wall or strong dyke was made along the line of Agricola's forts. But the northern tribes often passed this boundary, and, between 207 and 210, the Emperor Severus came himself to Britain, and built a wall of stone along the line of Hadrian's wall. Severus died next year at York, which was then called Eboracum. Yet, long after, in 368, in the reign of Valentinian, the Roman governor Theodosius (father of the famous Emperor Theodosius) again conquered the country between the two walls. But, by that time, the power of the Romans was very much weakened, and they were not likely to keep their new province or anything else much longer.

You should remember the two walls, the wall of Hadrian or of Severus, and the wall of Antoninus, as they were some of the greatest of the Roman works in the island. Of the wall of Severus, parts are standing still, and it was very much more perfect till the last century, when a great deal was pulled down to mend the roads.

Now all the time which I have been talking about in this chapter was since the birth of our Lord Jesus Christ, and during all this time the Christian religion was making its way in the world. It is not really known who first preached the Gospel in Britain. But there is no doubt that there were Christians in Britain in very early times as well as in other parts of the Empire. And we may be sure that some of them

---

[1] The word *wall* does not always mean that it is of stone or brick, as we talk of a *sea-wall*, which is only a dyke.

were put to death for their religion here as well as in other places. The first martyr in Britain is said to have been Saint Alban, who was put to death at Verulam in 304, in the reign of Diocletian. A famous abbey was afterwards built there in his memory, and a town arose round it which still bears his name. Old Verulam, which stood a little way off, was forsaken, and the church and town of Saint Albans were built with its bricks.

The first Emperor who became a Christian was Constantine. He is said to have been born in Britain, and his mother Helen to have been a Briton. It is certain that it was in Britain that he was proclaimed Emperor in 306, on the death of his father Constantius. After his time, all the Emperors were Christians, except Julian, who became a heathen again. He is therefore often called Julian the Apostate, that is, one who falls away or forsakes his religion. But Julian was nevertheless in many things a good man and a good Emperor, very much better than many of those who called themselves Christians. When the Emperors became Christians, other people gradually followed their example, and the whole Empire was converted. Churches were built and Bishopricks founded. There are said to have been three Archbishopricks in Britain, at London, York, and Caerleon, those being then the three chief cities of the island. But very little is known for certain about the old British Church, and it does not really matter very much to us Englishmen. How our own forefathers became Christians I shall tell you another time.

If we reckon from the first coming over of Claudius, we may say that Britain was a Roman Province from 43 to 410; that is, 367 years. How the Roman power came to an end in the island I will tell you in my next chapter.

CHAPTER IV.

HOW BRITAIN BECAME ENGLAND.

AFTER Britain had been a Roman Province for about three hundred and fifty years, the Roman power began to get very much weaker. New nations began to be heard of, and they were often very troublesome to the Empire in different places. The Teutonic nations, that is, as I before told you, the race of men to which we ourselves belong, still for the most part remained free. The Romans could never conquer more than a small part of Germany; they could keep hardly any of the country either east of the Rhine or north of the Danube. They tried indeed very hard in the time of Augustus, and invaded Germany many times. But our kinsfolk always resisted them very bravely. There was especially one famous German chief, Irmin or Arminius, who destroyed a whole Roman army, and was called the deliverer of Germany.

Now I have told you about Caradoc and Boadicea, and it is right that you should know about them and care for them. But you should care for Arminius a great deal more, for though he did not live in our land, he was our own kinsman, our bone and our flesh. If he had not hindered the Romans from conquering Germany, we should not now be talking English; perhaps we should not be a nation at all. Happily the Romans never conquered Germany; and as for our other kinsfolk in Denmark, Sweden, and Norway, the Romans never even tried to conquer them—they hardly knew that there were such countries. So a large part of Europe was still quite free, though its people were still very wild and ignorant, what is called *uncivilized*. But we should always think with reverence of our own fathers and kinsfolk, and think what great nations have grown out of the people who were then looked down upon as *Barbarians.* For the Greeks, and after them the Romans, called all people who could not speak their tongue *Barbarians*, just as our forefathers called those who could not speak their tongue *Welsh.* There was a time when the Greeks called the Romans themselves *Barbarians*, and after that there was a time when the Romans called Gauls and Spaniards *Barbarians.* But, now that all people within the Roman Empire were reckoned to be Romans, *Barbarian* meant those nations who lived beyond the bounds of the Empire, and who did not speak either Greek or Latin. Most of the Barbarians whom we now hear of were Teutons, though, of course, in Ireland and Scotland the Barbarians were Celts. Now, towards the end of the fourth century after Christ, there was no longer any fear of the Romans conquering the Germans ; but, instead of that, the Teutonic nations began to press into the Roman Empire. Our kinsfolk were now something like what the Romans themselves had been ages before. They were strong and brave and hardy, and had many virtues which the Romans had lost. There was always more or less fighting going on along the borders of the Empire, and the Barbarians themselves often served in the Roman armies. Of course, as the Roman power grew weaker, and as good soldiers were less and less to be found within the Empire, the Roman armies became more and more filled with Barbarians who served as what are called *mercenaries.* By mercenaries I mean soldiers who are not fighting for their own country, but who are ready to serve any king or commonwealth that will take them into pay. But when any nation learns to trust chiefly to mercenaries, you may be sure that that nation will not long remain free. So it was with the great Roman Empire. The Teutons, by sometimes fighting against the Romans and sometimes serving with the Romans, gradually came to be better soldiers than the Romans themselves, and they at last learned to conquer those who had once conquered them. Various Teutonic chiefs with their followers pressed into the Empire, and though for some while they professed some sort of obedience to the Roman Emperors, they soon grew into independent kingdoms. Thus

the Franks pressed into Northern Gaul, and from them part of
Germany and part of Gaul came to be called *Francia* or the
land of the Franks; the name still remains in *Franken* or
Franconia, and also in *France*. The Burgundians settled in
the south-east part of Gaul, the part nearest to Italy, which was
for a long time after called the Kingdom of Burgundy. The
West-Goths, after wandering about the Empire for some time,
at last, under their King Alaric, took Rome in 410, but they did
not stay in Italy, and in the end they founded a great kingdom,
partly in Spain, partly in Aquitaine or Southern Gaul. The
Vandals first settled in Spain, and then crossed over into
Africa, and there founded a kingdom whose capital was the
famous city of Carthage. At last, in 476, an end was put for a
while to the succession of Roman Emperors in Italy. The Emperors still reigned in the East at Constantinople, but, first Odoacer, King of the Heruli, and then the great Theodoric, King
of the East-Goths, reigned in Italy. They professed to be subjects of the Empire, generals serving under the Emperor's authority, and they went on appointing a Roman Consul every year;
but they really were independent Kings. Thus Rome itself was
for a while cut off from the Roman Empire; I say for a while,
because in the sixth century both Italy and Africa were
recovered for a time by the Eastern Emperors. Thus the
Roman Empire went on in the East, where the Teutonic
nations did not settle, till its last fragments were destroyed by
the Turks, who took Constantinople in 1453. And during
all that time the people of the Eastern Empire, though they
spoke Greek and not Latin, still called themselves Romans,
and in many parts the Christian people who are now in bondage to the Turks call themselves Romans still.

Thus the Empire went on in the East, the people calling
themselves Romans, but being really not so much Romans as
Greeks. Meanwhile in the West the Teutonic nations settled.
Now in the Southern countries, in Italy, Spain, and Aquitaine,
the Goths and other Teutonic people gradually mixed with
the Romans. They became Christians—indeed most of them
were Christians before they settled within the Empire—and
they gradually learned to speak Latin. Of course the Latin
language became corrupted and mixed up with other tongues

and thus arose the languages of Southern Europe, Italian, Provençal,[1] Spanish, and French. These are called the *Romance* languages, because they are all derived from Latin, the language of Rome. But the French tongue came up much later than any of the others, because those of the Franks who settled in Northern Gaul, though they became Christians, did not mix so much with the Romans as the Goths and Burgundians did, but remained a purely German people for a very long time.

Now while the other Teutonic nations were conquering other parts of the Roman Empire, the greater part of Britain was also conquered by our own forefathers, the Angles and Saxons. But it was conquered in a very different way from the rest of the Empire. One difference, I think, must strike you at once, almost without my telling you. You know that we still speak, not a Romance, but a Teutonic tongue. A great many French and Latin words are mixed up with our real Old-English, but these words came in at a much later time ; they are mere strangers, many of which we could do just as well without. Some of you are learning French, and some day most likely you will learn German. You know that many words are the same in English and French, but those words are not the commonest words which we are speaking every moment. But when you come to learn German, you will find that those words which are the true life of a tongue, those without which we could not get on at all, are the same in German and in English, and are quite unlike French. You can make many sentences together about common things which shall not have one French or Latin word in them ; but you cannot make the shortest English sentence out of French or Latin words only, without using Teutonic words. So you see that, though English as we now speak it has many more foreign words in it than German, or Dutch, or Danish has, yet it still is a Teutonic tongue after all.

The reason of this is that our forefathers, when they settled in Britain, did not learn to speak Latin like the Goths

---

[1] That is the language of Southern Gaul, called from *Provincia* or *Provence*, that part of Gaul which first became a Roman *Province*, and which has kept the name ever since. The Provençal language is as different from French as Italian or Spanish is, and it must not be thought to be "bad French," as ignorant people often call it.

and Burgundians, but kept on speaking their own language. And they not only kept to their own language, but they also kept to their own religion. The Goths, Vandals, Burgundians, and Franks soon became Christians, but the English went on worshipping their old false gods, Woden and Thunder and the rest, for at least a hundred and fifty years after they settled in Britain. And if you look at a map you will easily see that in Italy, Spain, and Gaul, most places keep their old names. The towns and other places either have Latin names, or else they keep the old names of all that they had before the Romans came. But in England, nearly all the names are either English or Danish. That is, they are nearly all Teutonic of some kind ; the only names that are Latin or Welsh are the names of most of the rivers, of some of the hills, and of some of the oldest and greatest towns, like London, Gloucester, and Lincoln. In this Western part of England where we live, there are indeed a good many Welsh names ; but this is for a reason which I will tell you presently. But if you go into the Eastern and Midland counties, you will hardly find one Welsh name, except here and there the name of a river or a great town.

Now all this shows that the English conquest of Britain was quite another kind of thing from the Gothic conquest of Spain, or even from the Frankish conquest of Northern Gaul. The French are mainly Celts to this day, and to this day, as I said, they speak what we may call a kind of Latin. But we are not Welshmen but Englishmen, and we do not speak Latin but English. Now the reason of this is that our forefathers, the Angles and Saxons, were very much more savage and ignorant than the other Teutonic nations who settled within the Empire. Our old country at the mouth of the Elbe was a land which the Romans had hardly reached at all. Our fathers had not, therefore, like the Goths, become partly civilized by constant intercourse with the Romans, by either fighting against them or fighting for them. For the same reason our fathers were still heathens, for they had had no opportunity of hearing of the Christian religion from any of the Roman clergy. Therefore the Angles and Saxons made war in a much more savage way than the Goths did. The Goths, and most of the other Teutonic nations, thought it enough to conquer, but they did not destroy. As I told you, they often professed for a while to be subjects of the Roman Emperors. At any rate they neither killed all the Roman inhabitants, nor yet destroyed their towns. They made their own Kings rulers of the land, and they made themselves the chief men in it, and they seized on a large part of the land to maintain the King and his followers. But they generally left the Romans to live in their old way, and to be governed by their own laws. They generally admired the fine buildings which the Romans had made, and they preserved and imitated them as well as they could. And, as they were Christians, they respected the churches and clergy; and the clergy, who for a long time were mostly Romans, retained great power and large estates. Thus you see how the two nations gradually mixed together, and how it came to pass that in all the South of Europe the language and nearly everything else is still very much more Roman than Teutonic.

But the Romans in Britain and the Welsh, who, as we may say, had turned Romans, did not fare nearly so well at the hands of our own forefathers. The Angles and Saxons knew nothing and cared nothing about either the Christian religion or the arts and manners of Rome. They destroyed nearly everything which those Teutons who conquered the South of Europe took care to preserve. At first they seem to have destroyed all the towns which they took; but some of the great cities they seem not to have taken for a good while, till our fathers had become somewhat more civilized. And, instead of either mixing with the people, or else leaving them their own laws and part of their lands, they always either killed or made slaves of all the people that they could. Those who could get away no doubt escaped into Wales and Cornwall and the other parts of the island which the Angles and Saxons did not yet get into. Of the others you may suppose that those who fought against our forefathers were killed, and those who submitted were made slaves. The women of course would be made slaves, or they would sometimes be married to their masters. Thus there may doubtless be some little British and Roman blood in us, just as some few Welsh and Latin words crept into the English tongue from the very beginning. But we may be sure that we have not much of their blood in us, because we have so few of their words in our language. The few that there are are mainly the sort of words which the women, whether wives or slaves, would bring in, that is, names of things in household use, such as *basket*, which is one of the few Welsh words in English. Thus you see that our forefathers really became the people of the land in all that part of Britain which they conquered. For they had killed or driven out all the former people, save those whom they kept as mere slaves. Thus they kept their own language, their own manners, and their own religion. All this is very different from the conquests of the other Teutons in the South of Europe. There the Goths and the other nations did not really become the people of the land ; they either were rulers over the former people, or else they were altogether mixed up with them ; and everywhere they became Christians, and learned to speak such Latin as was spoken then.

Now you will perhaps say that our forefathers were cruel and wicked men thus to come into the land of another people, and to take the land to themselves and to kill or make slaves of the men to whom it belonged. And so doubtless it was. But you must remember that we were then both a heathen and a barbarous people, and that it is not fair to judge our fathers by the same rules as if they had been either Christians or civilized men. And I am afraid that men who called themselves both Christian and civilized have, even in quite late times, treated the people of distant countries quite as badly as ever our forefathers treated the Welsh. But anyhow it has turned out much better in the end that our forefathers did thus kill or drive out nearly all the people whom they found in the land. The English were thus able to grow up as a nation in England, and their laws, manners, and language grew up with them, and were not copied from those of other nations. We have indeed taken much from other nations in later times ; but then what we have taken we have always made our own, just as we have done with the foreign words which we have taken into our language. Had our forefathers done as the other Teutonic people did, though we might have known many things much earlier than we did, yet I cannot think that we should ever have been so great and free a people as we have been for many ages.

I have thus taken some pains to make you understand what sort of a conquest it was which our forefathers made in the Isle of Britain, and how unlike it was to the conquests which were made about the same time by our kinsfolk in other parts of the Roman Empire. I daresay this has been harder to understand than some other things which I have had to tell you; but it is well that you should know from the very beginning how it came to pass that we are Englishmen and speak English, while in the other countries of Western Europe they still speak languages which are so like Latin. And now you will ask me to tell you something about the men who were foremost in conquering Britain, and about the time when it happened. And very likely you may expect to hear some pleasant stories about it. I will tell you what I can, but I am sorry to say that it will be very little that I can tell you. For these are times of which we have hardly any history written at the time, so that we know very little of the deeds of this or that man; though we can make out a great deal from language and other things which are not written in books. When the first Teutons came into Britain it is not easy to say. Some people think that there were Teutonic people in the land even before Cæsar came, and that Queen Boadicea and her people were really of our own blood. But I do not myself believe this, and even if it were so, one can hardly fancy that, after being so long under the Roman power, the Teutons in Britain would be very different from the other people of the island. But towards the end of the fourth century, we first begin to hear something for certain about our own people. The Roman power in Britain was now getting weaker; the Romans had much ado to keep their province safe from the Picts and Scots in the north of the island, and the coasts now began to be ravaged by the fleets of the Saxons. Thus it is then, towards the end of the fourth century, that we first hear of our own forefathers trying to settle in Britain. It is very likely that the Angles and Saxons might have conquered Britain then, only in 367 there came into Britain a Roman governor named Theodosius (whom I have already spoken of), who was a wise and brave man, and who beat both the Scots and the Saxons, and won back the land for Rome as far as the wall of Agricola. This was, for the time, a great check to the Teutons who were trying to get into the island; but this *revival* or springing up again of the Roman power could not really last. In 400 the Romans had fallen back to the wall of Severus, which was then repaired. Ten years later everything in Italy was in confusion, and Rome itself was sacked by the Goths. Then the Emperor Honorius, the son of the Emperor Theodosius, and grandson of the Theodosius who had been in Britain, recalled the Roman legions from Britain, and left the people of the land to shift for themselves. It was now much more easy for the Angles and Saxons to come into Britain. They could now come, not merely to plunder and go away, but to settle and live in the land. Sometimes, it is said, the Britons were foolish enough to ask the Angles and Saxons to help them against the Picts and Scots who kept pouring in from the north. I need not tell you that, when our fathers were once asked to come into the land, they took care to stay there. However this may be, it is certain that, in the course of something more than a hundred years, in the fifth and sixth centuries, the Teutons from beyond the sea conquered much the greater part of Britain. At the end of the sixth century the Picts and Scots remained north of the Forth, and the Welsh in the west of the island, that is, not only in what is now Wales, but in all the land west of the Severn, and again in Cumberland and the neighbouring parts. and in Cornwall, Devonshire, and part of Somerset. But all the rest of the land was in the hands of our own forefathers.

We may be sure that a great many different Teutonic tribes had a share in this great movement across the seas. But they seem to have all been nearly akin to each other, and to have spoken much the same language. Three tribes especially are spoken of above all others, the Angles, the Saxons, and the Jutes; and of these it was that the land was mainly overspread. Of these three, the Saxons are those of whom we hear first; and this is most likely the reason why the Celtic people in Scotland, Wales, and Ireland call all Englishmen *Saxons* to this day. But the Angles took a greater part of the land than any of the others, so that it was they who, in the end, gave their name to the land and its people. As the Teutons in Britain began to grow together into one people, they were sometimes called the *Anglo-Saxons*—that is, the people made up of the Angles and Saxons—but more commonly they were called *Angles* or *English* alone. And when so much of Britain as the Teutons lived in came to have a common name, that name was ENGLALAND, or ENGLAND, that is, the land of the Angles, or ENGLISH. *Saxon* by itself always meant the people of those parts only where the Saxons settled, and the whole people was never called so except by the Celts.

Thus it was that our fathers came into the land where we now dwell ; and, like the men whom we read of in old times, they called the land after their own name. Of the different Kingdoms which they founded in Britain, the Kingdoms of the Angles, Saxons, and Jutes, I will tell you in my next chapter.

CHAPTER V.

HOW THE ENGLISH KINGDOMS IN BRITAIN WERE FOUNDED.

I HAVE told you that, among the Teutonic people who settled in Britain, the chief tribes were the Angles, the Saxons, and the Jutes. I have told you also that the Saxons were those who first began to trouble the British coasts before the Romans went away, which is most likely the reason why the Celts still call us all Saxons. But the Angles were those who took to themselves the greater part of the land, and who at last gave it their name, so that we have always called ourselves English and our land England. But, if our old traditions are at all true, the people who founded the first lasting Teutonic kingdom in Britain were neither the Angles nor the Saxons, but the Jutes. We cannot say much for certain about the English Conquest, because no account of it could well be written at the time, and the oldest accounts that we have were certainly not written till two or three hundred years after. But we can hardly think that the people in the different parts of England could have been quite wrong as to whence their forefathers came, and they may very well have remembered the names of the Kings and chief men who led them. So I do not at all mind telling you the story of the Conquest of Britain by our forefathers as it is told in the oldest books we have; for I see no reason to doubt that it is true in the main, though you should still remember that we cannot be so certain about it as about things which were written down at the time.

Our old Chronicle then, the oldest English history, the book which you should learn to reverence next after your Bibles and Homer, tells us that the first Teutonic kingdom in Britain began in the year 449. This was the Kingdom of Kent. It was

natural that Kent should be the first part of Britain to be
conquered, because it is the nearest to the mainland of Europe.
So the English Conquest began in Kent, just as the Roman
Conquest had done. And you should mark that Kent is one
of those parts of Britain which still keep their old British names ;
it is indeed the only part in the east of Britain which has done
so. Both the old kingdoms and the later shires in the east of
England have English names, all except Kent, which has never
changed. The land was still called Kent, and the English who
settled there called themselves Kentishmen. The Kingdom of
Kent was a kingdom of the Jutes. The Jutes were the tribe
who took to themselves a smaller part of Britain than any other,
only Kent and the Isle of Wight and part of what is now
Hampshire ; but their settlement is very important, for they were
the first Teutons who really fixed themselves in the land. The
names of their leaders when they came into Britain were Hengest
and Horsa. These names mean *horse* and *mare*, and some
people have thought that it is not likely that any men should
be called by such names, and they have said that all that the
story means is that the Jutes had a horse for the badge on their
standard. It is very true that the horse is the badge of Kent,
as you may see to this day on any sack of Kentish hops ; but I
do not see why men should not be called Hengest and Horsa
as much as Wolf, Lion, and Bear, or Bull and Lamb and Stag,
as many men have been called in all times. They may even
have taken the horse for their badge because of their own
names. However, this is one of the things of which we cannot
be certain ; but whether Hengest and Horsa were real men
or not, we need not doubt that the Jutes settled in Kent some
time in the fifth century, which is the chief thing to know.
The Welsh King whom they found in the land was called
Vortigern, and he is said to have asked them to come and
help him against the Picts. Later writers tell a story how
Vortigern fell in love with Hengest's daughter and married
her, and some go on to say that her name was Rowena.
But I find nothing about this in the old books, and no
Englishwoman was ever called by such a name as Rowena
at all. You will see that I say an Englishwoman, and I do so
because, though the Chronicle tells us that the people of Kent

were really Jutes, yet it calls them Angles or English from the very beginning. The English fought many battles with the Welsh in Kent, in one of which Horsa is said to have been killed. At last they founded two little kingdoms, East Kent and West Kent. Of these two East Kent was doubtless always the greater, and in it was the chief city, which was called in Old-English *Cant-wara-byrig*, that is, *Kentmensborough ;* we now call it, making the name a little shorter, *Canterbury*.

The next people who came were Saxons, who landed on the south coast under Ælle and his son Cissa in 477. They landed near the city which the Romans called Regnum, but which in English was called, from the name of Cissa, *Cis-sanceaster*,[1] the camp or city of Cissa, which we now cut short into *Chichester*. There was another Roman town in those parts called Anderida or in English *Andredes-ceaster*. It stood near where Pevensey now is, and the Roman walls are standing to this day. This town Ælle and Cissa took in 491. Our Chronicles tell us that they left not a Briton alive. And in the history of Henry of Huntingdon, who wrote in the twelfth century, there is a longer account of the siege, which seems to be made up from old ballads. You see it was easy for our fathers to land and settle in the open country, and to kill or drive away all the Welshmen, or here and there to make slaves of them ; but it was a good many years before they could take a town with Roman walls. So there was a great deal of fighting before the English could take Anderida. Thus was founded the Kingdom of the *South-Saxons*, which still keeps its name, and is called the county of *Sussex*.

Thus you see that Kent and Sussex were the first English kingdoms founded ; but neither Kent nor Sussex were among the greatest of the kingdoms which our fathers founded in Britain. The third English settlement came to much greater things than either of those two. This was also a settlement of Saxons, who, as they fixed themselves to the west of the Saxons who had first come, were called the *West-Saxons*, or the Kingdom of *Wessex*. The name of Wessex is not now in use as that of Sussex is, because Sussex has only had one shire, namely

---

[1] *Ceaster*, a tower or fortified place, from the Latin *castra*, one of the few Latin words which got into English from the very beginning.

Surrey, taken out of it, and the rest has kept its name, while the great Kingdom of Wessex took in at least seven shires. The West-Saxon Kingdom began, according to the Chronicle, in 495, in that part which is now called Hampshire. These Saxons came under two *Ealdormen* called Cerdic and Cynric his son. Perhaps you may be surprised at their title, as I dare say you have never heard the word *Alderman* used of any one but the magistrates of a town. But *Ealdorman* or *Alderman*, that is of course simply *Elderman*, used to be the highest title after *King*, just as in other countries you find rulers called by other names which at first simply meant *old men*, such as *Signore* or *Seigneur* (Senior), so in Latin *Senator* and in Greek γέρων. And so Cerdic and Cynric were Aldermen of the West-Saxons ; but they seem afterwards to have called themselves Kings, as the Chronicle says that the West-Saxon Kingdom began in 519. You must take care to remember Cerdic and his West-Saxons, because it was the Kingdom of Wessex to which all the other Kingdoms were joined one after another, till it became the Kingdom of all England, and from Cerdic were descended nearly all[1] the Kings that have reigned over all England. The Kings of the West-Saxons gradually conquered all the south-western part of Britain, and their Kingdom also stretched beyond the Thames over Oxfordshire and Buckinghamshire. But I will tell you more particularly what happened in our own western part of England. It is said that there was a Welsh prince called Arthur in Somersetshire, who fought bravely against the English and sometimes beat them. This is that King Arthur of whom you may have heard, and of whom many strange stories are told. Very likely there was such a man, but we can tell nothing about him for certain. Some of the Welsh Kings are spoken of in our Chronicle, but there is nothing about Arthur, and the Welsh writers who speak of him did not write till long after. It is said that he won a battle over the English at Badbury in Dorsetshire[2] in 520, and that he was buried at Glastonbury. This is not unlikely, as there can be no doubt that Glaston-

---

[1] All, except Cnut the Dane and his sons, Harold son of Godwine, and William the Conqueror. William's sons were descended from Cerdic in a roundabout way through their mother.

[2] *Mons Badonicus*, not Bath, as used to be thought.

bury was a great church in the Welsh times before the English came. And it is quite certain that the West-Saxon Kings did not conquer any part of Somersetshire till after the time when Arthur is said to have lived. The first of them who got so far west was Ceawlin, who began to reign in 556. He fought with the Welsh along both the Thames and the Severn, and even got as far north as what is now Shropshire. In 577 he won a great battle against the Welsh at Deorham in Gloucestershire, and took the three great Roman towns of Bath, Gloucester, and Cirencester. You see that Bristol, which is now a greater town than any of those three, is not spoken of, because it was not a Roman town, and most likely was not a town at all in Ceawlin's time. But the others were Roman towns, as you may know by their ending in *-ceaster*, for Bath too is called *Bathanceaster* in the Chronicle. The name, some of you will see, is a translation of the Latin name *Aquæ*.[1] Now it was that Ceawlin took the great stronghold on Worle-hill, and carried his frontier south as far as the Axe. So in those days Wookey[2] was in England, and Wells—or at least Glastonbury, for Wells was most likely not built—was in Wales. You have heard me say that there is *English Combe* near Bath, and you all know that there is *Wallcombe*, that is *Weala-cwm*, *Welshman's combe*, near Wells. These places show how the border ran. Thus it was that Somersetshire began to be English. The southern part of the county was not conquered till long after; but all between the Avon and the Axe has been English ever since 577, nearly thirteen hundred years ago. This part of Somersetshire always remained part of Wessex. But those who came after Ceawlin did not keep what he had conquered, and what the West-Saxon Kings before him had held either in Gloucestershire or in the other parts north of the Thames. Those parts afterwards belonged to the Anglian Kingdom of

[1] Other towns of the same name on the Continent keep the Latin name a little altered, as *Dax* (*De Aquis*) in Gascony, *Aix* in Provence, and *Aachen* in Germany, the city of the Great Charles, which Frenchmen call *Aix-la-Chapelle*.

[2] A village two miles from Wells, near the author's house, a ballad about which will be found in Percy's Reliques. On these local allusions see the remarks in the Preface.

Mercia. But you should remember that the Saxons under Ceawlin were the first Teutons who came into those parts. And this explains two things. First, it is another reason why the people of Wales call all Englishmen Saxons, because Ceawlin's Saxons were the first Teutons who came against them. Secondly, it explains why the speech of Gloucestershire and of several other shires within Mercia is much more like the Saxon speech of Somersetshire than it is like the Anglian speech of the shires further north. This is because, though those shires were afterwards part of an Anglian Kingdom, yet those who first conquered them were Saxons.

I have talked to you at greater length about the West-Saxons and Ceawlin for two reasons. First, because it was Ceawlin's Kingdom which gradually grew into the Kingdom of all England, and secondly because he did so much at places which you know, and because you have been born and lived in the part of England where he lived and fought. I must now go on with the other Kingdoms. But the Chronicle does not tell us so clearly about them as it does about Kent, Sussex, and Wessex, and we must put together our accounts how we can out of different writers who do not always tell the same story. The other Kingdoms are the one other Saxon King-dom, that of the *East-Saxons* or *Essex*, and the three Anglian Kingdoms of *Northumberland*, *Mercia*, and *East - Anglia*. These three, as you may see on the map, are altogether much larger than the Saxon and Jutish Kingdoms, so you see very well why the whole land was called *England* and not *Saxony*.[1] But some say that there were either Jutes or Saxons in the North of England, as soon or sooner than there were in the south. If so, there is another reason why the Scotch Celts, as well as the Welsh, call us Saxons. It is not unlikely that there may have been some small Saxon or Jutish settlements there very early, but the great King-dom of Northumberland was certainly founded by Ida the Angle in 547. It is more likely that there were some Teutonic settlements there before him, because the Chronicle does not say of him, as it does of Hengest, Cissa, and Cerdic, that he

---

[1] *Saxonia* does occur now and then, and it was really an older name than *Anglia*, but it soon went quite out of use.

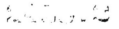

came into the land by sea, but only that he began the Kingdom. Most likely he began his Kingdom by joining several little districts, each of which had its own Alderman, into one. You must fully understand that in the old times *Northumberland* meant the whole land north of the Humber, reaching as far as the Firth of Forth. It thus takes in part of what is now Scotland, including the city of *Edinburgh*, that is *Eadwinesburh*, the town of the great Northumbrian King Eadwine or Edwin, of whom you will hear more presently. You must not forget that Lothian and all that part of Scotland was part of Northumberland, and that the people there are really English, and still speak a tongue which has changed less from the Old-English than the tongue of any other part of England. And the real Scots, the Gael in the Highlands, call the Lowland Scots *Saxons*, just as much as they do the people of England itself. This Northumbrian Kingdom was one of the greatest Kingdoms in England, but it was often divided into two, *Beornicia* and *Deira*, the latter of which answered pretty nearly to Yorkshire. The chief city was the old Roman town of *Eboracum*, which in Old-English is Eoforwic, and which we cut short into York. York was for a long time the greatest town in the North of England. There are now many others much larger, but York is still the second city in England in rank, and it gives its chief magistrate the title of *Lord Mayor*, as London does, while in other cities and towns the chief magistrate is merely the *Mayor*, without any *Lord*.

There is not very much to say about the Kingdoms of the *East-Saxons* and the *East-Angles*, which no doubt came up in the course of the sixth century. Their names speak for themselves. The East-Angles formed two divisions, the *North-folk* and the *South-folk*, whose names I think you will know as those of two counties. The East-Saxons had the old Roman town of Colchester, and one part of them, called the *Middle-Saxons*, though a very small people, had a greater city still, for London was in their land.

The great Anglian Kingdom of the *Mercians*, that is the *Marchmen*, the people on the *march* or frontier, seems to have been the youngest of all, and to have grown up gradually by

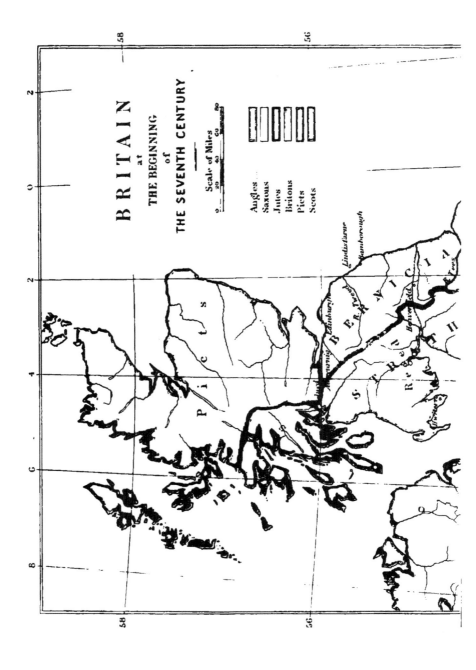

BRITAIN
at
THE BEGINNING
of
THE SEVENTH CENTURY

Scale of Miles

Angles
Saxons
Jutes
Britons
Picts
Scots

Picts

BERNICIA

Lindisfarne
Bamborough

STRETA

Edinburgh
Bamborough

joining together several smaller states, including all the land which the West-Saxons had held north of the Thames. Such little tribes or states were the *Lindesfaras* and the *Gainas* in Lincolnshire, the *Magesætas* in Herefordshire, the *Hwiccas* in Gloucester, Worcester, and part of Warwick, and several others. Most likely each of these little peoples had its own King or Alderman, who was independent if he could, but was generally more or less under the power of the Mercian King. When Mercia was fully joined under one King, it made one of the greatest states in England, and some of the Mercian Kings were very powerful Princes. It was chiefly an Anglian Kingdom, and the Kings were of an Anglian stock, but among the Hwiccas and in some of the other shires in southern and western Mercia, most of the people must really have been Saxons.

Thus it was that, during the fifth and sixth centuries, the Angles, Saxons, and Jutes settled in Britain, and made all the east part of the island English, from the English Channel northwards to the Firth of Forth. But in the more mountainous parts to the west, the Welsh still kept their ground. At the end of the sixth century, besides what is now Wales, all the land west of the Severn was Welsh, and so was all south of the Axe, not only Cornwall, but Devonshire and most part of Somerset. And to the north there was also a Welsh Kingdom, called the Kingdom of Strathclyde, which took in Galloway and the rest of the south-west part of Scotland, together with Cumberland, Westmorland, and Lancashire, all down to the river Dee and the city of Chester. So you see that a good deal of what we now call England was at the end of the sixth century still unconquered. And you must not think that all that was conquered was conquered at once ; the Roman towns especially often held out for a long time, and the Welsh were often able to hold their ground here and there while the English were settled around them. The English conquered one little piece and then another little piece, fighting a battle and taking a little more of the Welsh country after it. But generally the two nations did not mix, and there seem to have been hardly any Welshmen left in the English part of the country except those who were slaves.

I have thus told you about the founding of the seven old English Kingdoms, as we find it told in our oldest books. These Kingdoms are sometimes called the *Heptarchy*, from the Greek words ἑπτα, *seven*, and ἀρχή, *kingdom* or *government*. But I do not think this a good name. For ἑπταρχία in Greek would not mean seven Kingdoms close together, but rather a single government in the hands of seven persons. And the name Heptarchy also gives the idea of a more regular state of things than there really was, as if there had always been exactly seven Kingdoms, neither more nor fewer. But in truth, the different English peoples were always fighting with one another as well as with the Welsh, and sometimes one had the upper hand and sometimes the other, so that there were sometimes more than seven Kingdoms and sometimes fewer. And if we count small states with their King or Alderman tributary to a more powerful King, we might make up very many more than seven. Sometimes one King was so powerful as to get some sort of power over all the others; when this happened, he was called a *Bretwalda*. We have a list of Bretwaldas in the Chronicle, but we do not know exactly in what the power of a Bretwalda beyond his own Kingdom really consisted. It is plain however that it was a power which depended wholly upon the Bretwalda himself being a wise man and a great warrior, as it seems never to have stayed in the same kingdom or to have been handed on from father to son.

During all the time that I have been talking about, the English were still heathens. The Welsh do not seem to have ever tried to convert them, and, if they had tried, we cannot think that conquerors would have listened to people whom they thought fit for nothing but to kill or make slaves of. So our forefathers still worshipped Woden and Thunder and their other Gods, just as they had done before they came into Britain. They believed that their Kings were descended from Woden, and I suppose that no one who was not thought to be a descendant of Woden would ever have been chosen King in any part of England at this time. But though they always chose a descendant of Woden, they really chose their Kings, and the Crown did not always go in what we should call the right line. In such a state of things, when men are fierce and fond of fighting, a King's power depends very much upon what sort of a man he is himself. If he is a brave, open-handed warrior, he can do whatever he pleases; if he is a weak man who cannot fight well, he is very likely turned out of his Kingdom altogether. But our English Kings never ruled quite after their own will. They always had to consult the *Witan* or Wise Men of the Kingdom. And in every part there were smaller courts and assemblies for judging and settling matters, for we were a free people from the beginning. Yet high birth was held in great reverence, and men were divided into *Eorlas* and *Ceorlas*, that is, *Earls* and *Churls*,[1] according as they were noble or not. The churl was expected to live under some lord, and to follow him to battle when he was called on. The King had his own followers, who were called his *Thegnas* or *Thanes*, that is *servants*, but, as it was thought an honour to serve the King, *Thegn* became a title of honour. Still all men in the land were free, except those who were actually slaves. Men became slaves in two ways, either by being taken prisoners in battle, or by being made slaves by sentence of the law for certain crimes. In some parts of England there were very few slaves, in others there were very many. There were most of them in those shires which lay along the Welsh border, where of course many Welshmen were made prisoners and kept as bondsmen.

Such were our forefathers and the Kingdoms which they founded up to the end of the sixth century. In the last years of that century Christianity began to be preached to them; and, in the course of a hundred years after that time, all England became Christian. This is what I mean to tell you about in my next chapter.

---

[1] This word, like *villain, knave, boor, varlet*, meant at first simply a condition of life, and did not, as it now does, imply anything morally wrong in the man himself.

CHAPTER VI.

HOW THE ENGLISH BECAME CHRISTIANS.

THUS it was that Britain became England, and our fathers now dwelled in the land from the North Sea to the Severn, and from the Channel to the Firth of Forth. Now, as I before told you, the conquest of Britain by the English was not like the conquests made elsewhere by other Teutonic peoples; for elsewhere those who came into the land soon learned to speak Latin, and to believe in Christ, if they had not believed in Him before. But in Britain our forefathers still went on speaking their own tongue, and serving their own Gods. But about a hundred and fifty years after they began to settle in Britain, and a very little time after Ceawlin had won his great victories over the Welsh, the English first began to believe in the true faith. But they did not learn it from the Christians who still were in Britain, for they were all driven out or killed or made slaves, so that the Welsh were not likely to try to teach the English, nor were the English likely to listen to them if they had tried. Our fathers were first brought to the faith by the teaching of good men who were sent into Britain by Gregory, the Bishop of Rome, in the year 597. " In this year," says the Chronicle, " Gregorius the Pope sent into Britain Augustinus with very many monks, who *gospelled* God's word to the English folk." " Gospelled," you will see, is the same as " preached " or " taught;" they told them, that is, the *Gospel*, the *good spell* or *tale*, the *good news* of what God had done and would do for them.

Thus far the Chronicle ; but Bæda, a monk of Northumberland, who lived from 674 to 735, and who, for his learning and goodness, is commonly called Venerable Bede, tells us a great deal more. You see that Bæda did not live quite at the time, so that we still cannot be quite certain that we know everything exactly as it happened. Still the story as it is told by Bæda is so famous an one that you ought to know it, and there is no reason at all why it may not be true in the main.

Gregory, called the Great, was Pope,[1] that is, Bishop of Rome, the chief Bishop of the Western Church. As Rome was the first city in the world, and as the Roman Emperors were held to be lords of the world, the Church of Rome was naturally held to be the first of all Churches, and the Bishop of Rome to be the first of all Bishops. He was the Patriarch or chief Bishop of the West, as the Bishops of Constantinople or New Rome, of Alexandria, Antioch, and Jerusalem, were Patriarchs in different parts of the East. And as the Emperors had now quite left Italy and lived at Constantinople, the Pope, or Bishop of Rome, gradually became something more than merely a Bishop. He became the chief man in Rome and in Italy, and indeed in the whole West, and he had often to act for himself without consulting the Emperor. This happened especially when he had, as he often had, to deal with Kings and nations beyond the borders of the Empire. Thus the Bishops of Rome gradually gained very great power, much more than ever was gained by the Patriarchs of Constantinople, who had the Emperor near to control them. In after times, as you may have heard, the power of the Popes grew greater still, and it was often very badly used, and many abuses were brought into the Church, till at last our own Church and several other Churches found it needful to throw off their obedience to the Pope altogether. But there was nothing of this sort as yet in Gregory's days ; the Popes were still only the first Bishops of the Western Church, and they often did a great deal of good by acting as a sort of common father to all the nations, in days when there was so much war and confusion everywhere. Thus it was that the Bishop of Rome was the most natural person to undertake the conversion of the English, or of any other heathen nation in the West,

---

[1] The word *Pope*, *Papa*, παπᾶς, simply means *father*. In the East this name is given to every Priest, but in the West only to the Bishop of Rome.

and the more so as Britain had once been a Christian country and a province of the Roman Empire.

Now Bæda tells us that the reason which made Pope Gregory so anxious to make Christians of the English was as follows. Some time before he became Pope (which was in the year 590), perhaps about the year 574, he went one day through the market at Rome, where, among other things, there were still men, women, and children to be sold as slaves. He there saw some beautiful boys who had just been brought by a slave-merchant, boys with a fair skin and long fair hair, as English boys then would have. He asked from what part of the world they came, and whether they were Christians or heathens. He was told that they were heathen boys from the Isle of Britain. Gregory was sorry to think that forms which were so fair without should have no light within, and he asked again what was the name of their nation. "*Angles*," he was told.[1] "*Angles*," said Gregory; "they have the faces of *Angels*, and they ought to be made fellow-heirs of the Angels in heaven. But of what province or tribe of the Angles are they?" "Of *Deira*," said the merchant. "*De irâ!*" said Gregory: "then they must be delivered from the wrath"— in Latin *de irâ*—"of God. And what is the name of their King?" "*Ælla*." "*Ælla;*[2] then *Alleluia* shall be sung in that land." Gregory then went to the Pope, and asked him to send missionaries into Britain, of whom he himself would be one, to convert the English. The Pope was willing, but the people of Rome, among whom Gregory was a priest and was much beloved, would not let him go. So nothing came of the matter for some while. We do not know whether Gregory was able to do anything for the poor little English boys whom he saw in the market, but he certainly never forgot his plan for converting the English people. After a while he became Pope

[1] It must be remembered that in this dialogue, which of course was in Latin, Gregory's sayings take the form of a series of plays upon words, such as we call puns, all of which cannot (though some can) be preserved in English.

[2] Ælle or Ælla was King of Deira from 559 to 588. The conversation between Gregory and the slave-merchant therefore happened before 588. And it could not have happened before 574, when Benedict the First became Pope, for it was either of him or of his successor Pelagius that Gregory asked leave to go.

himself. Of course he now no longer thought of going into Britain himself, as he had enough to do at Rome. But he now had power to send others. He therefore presently sent a company of monks, with one called Augustine[1] at their head, who was the first Archbishop of Canterbury, and is called the Apostle of the English.

This was in 597. The most powerful King in Britain at that time was Æthelberht of Kent, who is reckoned as the third[2] Bretwalda, and is said to have been lord over all the Kings south of the Humber. This Æthelberht had done what was very seldom done by English Kings then or for a long time after: he had married a foreign wife. You know that now Kings and Princes almost always marry foreigners, because they think themselves too great to have anything to do with their own people. But it was not so in the old time. The Old-English Kings almost always married Englishwomen, the daughters either of other English Kings, or else of their own nobles; so our Kings then were true Englishmen. But King Æthelberht, for what reason we do not know, had married a foreign wife, the daughter of Chariberht,[3] one of the Kings of the Franks in Gaul. There were at this time several Frankish Kingdoms in Gaul, and this Chariberht reigned at Paris. Now the Franks, as you know, were Christians; so when the Frankish Queen came over to Kent, Æthelberht promised that she should be allowed to keep to her own religion without let or hindrance. So she brought with her a Frankish Bishop named Liudhard, and the Queen and her Bishop used to worship God in a little church near Canterbury called Saint Martin's, which had been

---

[1] You must take care and not confound Saint Augustine of Canterbury with the other Saint Augustine who, on account of the writings which he left, is reckoned as one of the "Fathers" of the Church. He was Bishop of Hippo in Africa in the fifth century, and is very famous for the books which he wrote. Our Saint Augustine does not seem to have left any writings behind him, except a few letters.

[2] Ælle of Sussex is reckoned the first, and Ceawlin of Wessex the second.

[3] This is the same name as *Herbert*. In Old-English it is *Herebarht*, from *here*, an old word for an army, and *berht* or *briht*, a word which we have hardly changed. But in writing the names of the old Frankish Kings, a *ch* is generally used for our *h*. Perhaps they sounded it harder than we did.

built in the Roman times.   So you see that both Æthelberht
and his people must have known something about the Christian
faith before Augustine came.   It does not however seem that
either the King or any of his people had at all thought of
turning Christians.   This seems strange when one reads how
easily they were converted afterwards.   For one would have
thought that Bishop Liudhard would have been more likely to
convert them than Augustine, for, being a Frank, he would
speak a tongue not very different from English, while Augustine
spoke Latin, and, if he ever knew English at all, he must have
learned it after he came into the island.   I cannot tell you for
certain why this was.   Perhaps they did not think that a man
who had merely come in the Queen's train was so well worth
listening to as one who had come on purpose all the way from
the great city of Rome, to which all the West still looked up as
the capital of the world.

So Augustine and his companions set out from Rome, and
passed through Gaul, and came into Britain, even as Cæsar had
done ages before.   But this time Rome had sent forth men not to
conquer lands, but to win souls.   They landed first in the Isle
of Thanet, which joins close to the east part of Kent, and
thence they sent a message to King Æthelberht saying why
they had come into his land.[1]   The King sent word back to
them to stay in the isle till he had fully made up his mind how to
treat them ; and he gave orders that they should be well taken
care of meanwhile.   After a little while he came himself into
the isle, and bade them come and tell him what they had to
say.   He met them in the open air, for he would not meet
them in a house, as he thought they might be wizards, and that
they might use some charm or spell, which he thought would

---

[1] They brought with them Frankish interpreters out of Gaul.   Perhaps
these men may have known English, or it may be that there was still so
little difference between Old-English and the Old-German which the
Franks spoke, that men of each tongue could understand the other.   But
in any case the Queen and her Bishop would understand them.   They
must also have understood Latin, or Augustine could not have made any
use of them.   Of course any priest, or any man of any education, in Gaul
at this time would speak both Latin and German.   It must be remembered that all intercourse between Augustine and the English, for some
time at least, must have been through these interpreters.

have less power out of doors. So they came, carrying an image of our Lord on the Cross wrought in silver, and singing litanies as they came. And when they came before the King, they preached the Gospel to him and those who were with him, telling them, no doubt, how there was one God, who had made all things, and how He had sent His Son Jesus Christ to die upon the cross for mankind, and how He would come again at the end of the world to judge the quick and the dead. So King Æthelberht hearkened to them, and he made answer like a good and wise man. " Your words and promises," said he, " sound very good unto me ; but they are new and strange, and I cannot believe them all at once, nor can I leave all that I and my fathers and the whole English folk have believed so long. But I see that ye have come from a far country to tell us that which ye yourselves hold for truth ; so ye may stay in the land, and I will give you a house to dwell in and food to eat ; and ye may preach to my folk, and if any man of them will believe as ye believe, I hinder him not." So he gave them a house to dwell in in the royal city of Canterbury, and he let them preach to the people. And, as they drew near to the city, they carried their silver image of the Lord Jesus, and sang litanies, saying, " We pray Thee, O Lord, let Thy anger and Thy wrath be turned away from this city and from Thy holy house, because we have sinned. Alleluia !"

Thus Augustine and his companions dwelt at Canterbury, and worshipped in the old church where the Queen worshipped, and preached to the men of the land. And many men hearkened to them and were baptized, and before long King Æthelberht himself believed and was baptized ; and before the year was out there were added to the Church more than ten thousand souls. When the King was baptized, he told them that they might build and repair[1] churches throughout the land. And now many more of the people were eager to do as their King had done ; but King Æthelberht did not, as many Kings have done since, force any man to do as he did and think as

---

[1] This shows that there must have been some of the old Roman churches still standing, though they were most likely in ruins. Or, if the word *restaurare* should be thought to mean to build again on the same place, it at any rate shows that men still knew where the old churches had stood.

he thought. Only he loved those men better who were his countrymen in the Kingdom of Heaven, as well as in his Kingdom on earth.

All this time Augustine was only a priest, but he knew that, according to the laws of the Church, he could not govern his new church rightly, nor make other priests, till he was himself made a Bishop. So he went back to Arles, in the south of Gaul, and was consecrated a Bishop by Ætherius, the Archbishop of that city. He then came back and, with the King's help, built, or rather repaired,[1] a church in Canterbury to be his cathedral or head church. He then consecrated it to the honour of our Lord Christ; and, though it has since been several times rebuilt, it still remains the head church of all England, and is still known as Christ Church in Canterbury. He also built another church with a house of monks belonging to it. which he called the Abbey of Saint Peter and Saint Paul, but which, after his death, was called the Abbey of Saint Augustine. What is left of it was some years back made into a College, where men are taught to go and preach the Gospel in other lands, as Augustine did in the land of Britain.

It would be too long if I told you all that Augustine did, and exactly how every part of England was converted by him and those who came after him. But there are one or two things which you must hear about. You will remember that the old Britons or Welsh, whom the English drove out, were, most of them at any rate, Christians, and so were the Irish or Scots,[2] both in Ireland and in what we now call Scotland. Now Augustine thought that it would be right to try and make friends with the Welsh Bishops, that they might join together in preaching to those of the English who were still heathens. So he went, with the help of King Æthelberht, to a place on the Severn in Gloucestershire, where he had a meeting with the Welsh Bishops under a great oak, which was therefore called Augustine's Oak, and from which the place is called Aust still.

---

[1] The words of Bæda show clearly that the Roman building was still standing, and as clearly that it was no longer used as a church.

[2] These words are used almost indiscriminately, because the Scots first came out of Ireland into Scotland. The word "Scotus" most commonly means an Irishman.

It is still one of the chief places for crossing the Severn, which was then the boundary of England and Wales. It was therefore a good place for meeting those who came out of Wales itself, and it was not so very far from the Welsh who were still in Cornwall, Devon, and Somerset, for you will remember that Ceawlin had not conquered further than the Axe, so that some of these Welsh Bishops may have come from those parts. But it was a long way for Augustine to go from his own home in Kent, but you will remember that Æthelberht was Bretwalda, with a certain power over the other Kings, so that no doubt any one who was protected by him could go safely even in those parts of the country which were not part of his own Kingdom. So Augustine went and talked with the British Bishops under the oak. But unhappily they did not agree, because, though the Welsh were Christians, they did not do in everything exactly as Augustine had been used to do at Rome. For instance, they did not keep Easter on the same day that the rest of the Western Churches did, and there were some other small matters about which they could not agree, though it does not seem that there was any difference between them about those things which all Christians ought to believe. No doubt there were faults on both sides, as neither side would yield to the other in anything. One cannot help thinking that Augustine must have forgotten some of the good advice which Pope Gregory had given him. For Gregory had told him in one of his letters that, in ordering his new Church, he was not bound to do in everything exactly as was done at Rome, but that it would be right to choose from among the customs of different Churches those which seemed most likely to suit the place and the people that he had to do with. The truth is that, though Augustine was a very good man, he was not nearly so wise and far-seeing as Gregory was, and he was too apt to think that everything must be wrong which was not exactly like what he had been used to at Rome. At any rate Augustine and the Welsh Bishops could not agree, and the Welshmen would not join him in preaching to the heathen English. Then it is said, but Bæda speaks as if he were not quite certain of it, that Augustine spoke thus to them : " If ye will not join me in preaching the way of life to the English, ye shall suffer the vengeance of

E

death at their hands." This was thought to be a prophecy, because, some years afterwards (in 607), when Augustine was dead, Æthelfrith, the heathen King of the Northumbrians, came and fought with the Welsh by Caerleon on the Dee,[1] and when he saw many monks[2] praying, he said, "If these men pray to their God that we may be beaten, it is all one as if they were fighting against us." So he smote the monks and slew them first of all, as many as twelve hundred, and then smote the rest of the Welshmen.

All the time of Augustine then, and for some years after, Northumberland was heathen. But after a time there arose a great King in Deira, called Eadwine or Edwin. He was Bretwalda, and he is said in the Chronicle to have been lord over all Britain save Kent alone. He was also, as you will soon hear, the first Christian King of Northumberland. But he was so famous a man that I must tell you his whole tale as Bæda tells it, only you must remember that as Bæda did not live quite at the time, it may not all of it be true.[3]

[1] *Civitas Legionum, Legeccaster, Caerlleon.* Bæda and the Chronicle give all these names, and they are in truth the same name in Latin, English, and Welsh. *Caer* in Welsh means a fortified place, just like *ceaster* in English, only it is put at the beginning of the word instead of the end. Thus *Caerlleon* and *Legeccaster* mean the same thing, the City of Legions. Just in the same way *Caergwent* is the same name as our Winchester, in Latin *Venta.* Both Winchester and Caerwent in Monmouthshire are *Venta* in Latin. So Caerleon-on-Usk, and Chester on the Dee, and Leicester in the middle of England, have all the same name, *Civitas Legionum, Legeccaster,* and *Caerlleon,* according to the language used. But the one which is meant here is neither the town which is now called Leicester, nor yet Caerleon, but Chester on the Dee.

[2] They were monks from Bangor, a monastery in Flintshire, not very far from Chester, which you must not confound with the Bishoprick of Bangor in Caernarvonshire.

[3] Stories like this of Eadwine, which contain a certain portion of marvellous, if not miraculous, incidents, cannot well be wholly left out, when they form an actual part of the history. The general truth of the history of Eadwine cannot be doubted ; on the other hand there are parts of it which can hardly have happened exactly as they are told. And we have no strictly contemporary writer to help us to check the story. The only fair way in such a case seems to be to tell the story as we find it, adding some such warning as I have given in the text. The case is of course quite different when we come to mere legends, not worked into the history, which can be either wholly left out or told as legends. It is different again

The Story of King Edwin.

Edwin, the son of Ælle, was born of the royal house of Deira, and his father Ælle was King of the land. But Ælle died when Edwin his son was but a little child, so Æthelfrith King of Bernicia came and took the kingdom of Ælle to himself and reigned over all Northumberland. Then they who loved the house of Ælle fled, and took with them the child Edwin, and they wandered to and fro through many lands, seeking shelter and help for the son of their master. So Edwin grew up in exile away from his own land, and he dwelt now among the Britons and now among the Mercians, till he came to the land of Rædwald, the King of the East Angles. Then he said to King Rædwald, "O King, I am Edwin of Deira, and Æthelfrith my foe hath seized my father's kingdom and seeketh my life. Let me, I pray thee, dwell in thy land, and deliver me not over into the hand of mine enemy." Then Rædwald had pity on him and said, "Thou mayest dwell in my land, and no man shall hurt thee or give thee over into the hand of Æthelfrith." But it was told Æthelfrith, saying, "Lo, Edwin dwelleth in peace in the land of the East Angles." Then Æthelfrith sent unto Rædwald, saying, "Slay me Edwin mine enemy, and I will give thee much gold and silver." But Rædwald would not hearken, and he said, "I will not slay him that hath sought shelter in my land, and dwelleth in peace in my house." Then sent Æthelfrith the second time. saying, "I will give thee greater gifts than I said aforetime, if thou wilt only slay Edwin mine enemy." But Rædwald would not hearken, and he answered the second time, "Be thy gifts unto thyself, for I will not slay Edwin." Then sent Æthelfrith the third time, saying, "Slay me Edwin, and I will give thee such gifts as thou hast not seen or heard of; but if thou wilt

when we have contemporary accounts with which we can compare a marvellous story. In the present case each man must settle for himself whether the marvellous part of the tale was a real miracle, or a dream. or a mere remarkable coincidence, or the misconception or invention of some one afterwards. In any case it is an essential part of the story, and cannot in fairness be separated from the rest.

not slay him or deliver him into my hand, then will I fight
against thee, and smite thee and thy people with a great
slaughter." Then Rædwald feared, for he knew that the
people of the Northumbrians were more than the people of the
East Angles, and he had heard how Æthelfrith was a mighty
man of valour. and how he had smitten the Welsh at Chester,
and how he had smitten the Scots at Dægsanstan,[1] and
Rædwald said in his heart, "If Æthelfrith cometh against me
to battle, I shall be even as one of them, and I shall not be
able to stand before the host of the Northumbrians." So
Rædwald spake to the messengers of Æthelfrith, saying, "Tarry
awhile in my house, and I will either slay Edwin or I will
deliver him into your hand."

Now Edwin had a friend who heard what Rædwald had said
unto the messengers of Æthelfrith. So he went to Edwin in
his chamber (for it was the first hour of the night), and he said,
"Come forth out of the house." So Edwin came forth out of
the house, and his friend said unto him, "Lo, Rædwald hath
promised to slay thee or to give thee into the hand of Æthelfrith. Follow me therefore, and I will in the same hour lead
thee out of this land, and hide thee where neither Rædwald
nor Æthelfrith may find thee." But Edwin said, "I thank
thee well for thy good-will, but I cannot follow thee. I have
sworn to Rædwald that I will dwell in his land, and I may not
go back from that I have spoken, while he hath done me no
harm nor hath wrought anything unfriendly against me. Nay
rather, if I must die, let me die by the hand of Rædwald, and
not by the hand of a meaner man. For whither shall I fly,
who have so long fled through all the kingdoms of Britain
seeking where I may dwell safely and may escape out of the
hand of them that seek my life?"

So his friend went his way, and Edwin sat alone on a stone
before the house. And his heart was very sorrowful, and he
knew not what to do or whither to turn him. Then there came
a man and stood before him, a man of strange countenance and
clad in strange raiment. such as Edwin had never before seen,
and Edwin feared as he saw him. Then said he, "Wherefore

---

[1] This was in 603. Ægdan King of Scots was utterly defeated.

dost thou, while other men sleep, sit thus alone and sad on a stone before the house?" And Edwin answered and said, " What is it to thee whether I abide this night within or without the house?" Then the strange man answered and said, "Think not that I know thee not who thou art, and why thou art sad and sleepest not, and why thou sittest thus alone before the house. For truly I know thee well who thou art, and wherefore thou art sad, and I know what evils they are that thou fearest lest they should come upon thee. But tell me, what reward wilt thou give unto him who shall free thee from all thy sorrows, and shall persuade Rædwald so that he shall neither do thee any harm nor deliver thee into the hands of them that seek thy life?" Then Edwin answered and said, "All that I have will I give as a reward to him that shall do this thing for me." Then the strange man answered and said, "And what wilt thou do if a man shall promise thee of a truth that thou shalt smite thine enemies and reign in their stead, and be a mightier King than were any of thy forefathers, yea or any of the Kings that have ever reigned over the people of the English?" And Edwin answered and said, "Yea verily, if a man shall do this thing unto me, I will give him such a reward as shall be fitting for his good deeds." Then the strange man spake unto him the third time, and said, "Yea, and when this thing hath come to pass, and when thou sittest on thy father's throne, and art mightier than all the Kings that have gone before thee, what wilt thou do, if he that promised thee all these things shall tell thee of a new life and a new law better than any that thou or thy fathers have known? Wilt thou then believe him, and obey him, and do such things as he shall speak unto thee for thy good?" And Edwin answered and said, "Yea verily, if such a man shall deliver me out of my sorrows, and set me on my father's throne, I will believe him and obey him in all things whatsoever he shall say unto me." Then the strange man laid his hand on Edwin's head and spake unto him, saying, "When this sign shall come unto thee, remember this night and remember thine own words, and delay not to do that which thou hast promised." Then the strange man vanished out of Edwin's sight, and he saw him no more, and he said in his heart, "This is not a man, but rather one of the great gods,[1] or one of the kind elves that hath spoken with me."

So Edwin sat alone before the house, and he rejoiced greatly in his heart at what the strange man had said unto him, and he greatly wondered who the man might be and whence he had come. Then came forth the friend who had before spoken to him, and he came with a joyful countenance, and said unto Edwin, "Rise up, and come into the house, and lay aside thy sorrows, and let thy limbs rest in sleep, for the King's heart is changed, and he will do thee no harm, but he will keep the promise that he hath sworn unto thee. For the King spake unto the Queen his wife, saying, 'I fear Æthelfrith, and his gifts that he promiseth are great, so I have said that I will give Edwin into his hand.' But the Queen said unto him, 'Sell not, O King, for gold thy friend that is in trouble, and do not for the sake of wealth lose thine honour, which is of more price than all jewels.'"

So Rædwald spared Edwin and gave him not over into the hand of Æthelfrith. And Rædwald gathered together an host, and fought against Æthelfrith by the river which is called Idle, by the northern border of the land of the Mercians. Now the host of Æthelfrith was greater than the host of Rædwald, yet was the victory with Rædwald, and he smote Æthelfrith that he died, and he smote his host with a great slaughter. Howbeit the son of Rædwald, whose name was Rægenhere, was slain there also.[2] So Edwin reigned over all Northumberland, and he was the mightiest of all the Kings of the Isle of Britain, and all the lords both of the English and also of the Welsh were his servants. And he went forth and warred with them that dwelt in the Isle Mona,[3] which is Man, and in the

---

[1] Bæda, clearly copying the words of more than one story in the Bible, says, "he understood that it was not a man but a spirit." But Edwin, as a heathen, would of course think that the wonderful person who had spoken to him was one of the gods whom he worshipped. It is easy to see that Bæda would not like to put heathen words into his mouth, but one may be sure that that was the way that the story ran when it was first told.

[2] One might almost have expected to be told that the death of Rægenhere was a judgement on Rædwald for having ever *thought* of giving up Edwin. The tale might be told in that way with great force, but I do not find it so in Bæda.   [2] Or Mevania.

other Mona which lieth by the land of the Welsh, and they became his servants. And because Edwin had conquered the isle, the name of the isle was no longer called Mona, but Anglesey, the Isle of the English.

So Edwin reigned, and he was a wise and just King and loved righteousness, and there was peace in the land wherever he reigned. And a woman with her sucking child might go through the land from one end thereof to the other, and no man would dare to harm her for fear of King Edwin. And he loved his people, and wherever there were springs of water by the wayside he put up stakes and hung brazen cups thereon, that men might drink, and no man durst steal those cups for love or for fear of King Edwin. And when King Edwin rode forth through the towns and villages of his Kingdom he had a banner borne before him, even as the Cæsars of Rome had, for that he was lord of the land of Britain, even as they were lords of the land of Rome.

Now it came to pass after these things, that Edwin sent messengers to Eadbald, King of the Kentishmen, saying, "Give me Æthelburh thy sister to wife." Now Æthelberht the great King was dead, and Eadbald his son reigned in Kent. And Eadbald answered, "I cannot give thee my sister to wife; for thou art an heathen man, and I may not give my sister, who believeth in the Lord Christ, to a man who knoweth not the law of our God." But Edwin sent again, saying, "Give me thy sister to wife, and I will not constrain her, but she shall worship what God she will, and she shall bring with her, if she will, servants of her God, whether they be men or women, and they shall serve your God after your law. Yea, and I will hearken to them, and I will learn what your faith and your law of which ye speak is. And if I find it to be better than mine own law and more worthy of God, I will even believe as ye believe." So King Eadbald let Æthelburh his sister go, and Edwin took her to wife. And she took with her a certain priest called Paullinus, who was hallowed as Bishop by Justus the Archbishop of Canterbury, that he might keep her in the right way, and might also preach unto the men of the land. But Edwin and the men of the land believed not, for that the god of this world had blinded their eyes.

Now in the next year Cwichelm the King of the West-Saxons sought to slay Edwin. And he sent one of his servants called Eomer, with a two-edged dagger dipped in poison, to smite Edwin and slay him. So Eomer came to King Edwin by the river of Derwent, and said unto him, "I am a messenger to thee, O King, from my lord King Cwichelm." But while Edwin hearkened, Eomer drew his dagger and struck at Edwin. But Lilla the King's Thane threw himself before his lord, so that the dagger smote him and went through his body and wounded Edwin. So Lilla died, and the men that were by him drew their swords and slew Eomer.

Now that day was the Feast of Easter, but Edwin and his people still served Woden and the other gods of their fathers. But in the same night Queen Æthelburh bare a daughter to Edwin, and Edwin gave great thanks to his gods. But Paullinus the Bishop gave thanks to the Lord Christ, and he said, " O King, I have prayed to my God whom I serve, and He hath granted thee this child, and hath given thee the Queen thy wife safe and sound." Then Edwin said, " I am going forth to battle against Cwichelm King of the West-Saxons, who hath sought to slay me by craft. If I return in peace, then will I believe in thy God and worship Him. Yea and the babe that the Queen my wife hath borne unto me, thou mayest baptize her as thou and her mother are baptized." So on Whitsunday Paullinus baptized the babe and eleven other of the King's household, and they called the babe's name Eanflæd. Now King Edwin's wound was healed, and he went forth to battle against the West-Saxons, and smote them with a great slaughter, and slew five of their Kings.[1] So Edwin came back in peace to his own land. And he no more served Woden and Thunder and the other gods of his fathers. Yet was he not at once baptized ; but he thought much of all that Paullinus had said unto him, and he often spake with him and pondered in his heart whether these things were so or no. And one day he sat by himself and thought thereon. Then came Paullinus to

---

[1] See the Chronicle A.D. 626. It must always be remembered that the *seven* Kingdoms were only the chief among many smaller ones. Here we have five Kings in Wessex besides Cwichelm the head King.

him and laid his hand on his head and said, "Knowest thou this sign?" And Edwin trembled and fell at his feet. Then Paullinus stretched forth his hand and lifted him up, and said unto him, "Be of good cheer, Edwin; the Lord whom I serve hath delivered thee out of the hand of the enemies whom thou didst fear, and He hath given thee the kingdom which thou didst desire. Defer not then to do the thing which thou didst promise." Then Edwin knew that it was he who spake to him by night as he sat at the gate of the house of Rædwald; and he believed.

Then King Edwin sent forth and gathered together his Aldermen and his Thanes and all his wise men, and they took counsel together. And men said one to another, "What is this new law whereof men speak? Shall we leave the gods of our fathers and serve the God of Paullinus, or shall we forbear?" And one spake on this manner and another spake on that manner. Then arose Coifi the High Priest of Woden and said, "Tell us, O King, what this new law is; for this one thing I know, that these gods whom we have so long worshipped profit a man not at all. For of a truth there is no man in thy land who hath served all our gods more truly than I have, yet there be many men who are richer and greater than I, and to whom thou, O King, showest more favour. Wherefore I trow that our gods have no might nor power, for if they had, they would have made me greater and richer than all other men. Wherefore let us hearken to what these men say, and learn what their law is; and if we find it to be better than our own, let us serve their God and worship Him."

Then another of the King's Thanes arose and said, "Truly the life of a man in this world, compared with that life whereof we wot not, is on this wise. It is as when thou, O King, art sitting at supper with thine Aldermen and thy Thanes in the time of winter, when the hearth is lighted in the midst and the hall is warm, but without the rains and the snow are falling and the winds are howling; then cometh a sparrow and flieth through the house; she cometh in by one door and goeth out by another. Whiles she is in the house she feeleth not the storm of winter, but yet, when a little moment of rest is passed, she flieth again into the storm, and passeth away from our eyes. So is it with the life of man; it is but for a moment; what goeth afore it and what cometh after it, wot we not at all. Wherefore if these strangers can tell us aught, that we may know whence man cometh and whither he goeth, let us hearken to them and follow their law."

So he spake, and the more part of the King's Thanes and wise men said that he had well spoken. Then arose Coifi the Priest the second time and spake, saying: "Let us even now hear Paullinus, and let him tell us what his new doctrine is." Then King Edwin commanded that so it should be; and Paullinus preached the Gospel unto them. Then spake Coifi yet again: "Truly I have long known that those things which we were wont to worship were naught; for the more I sought for truth in worshipping them the less I found it. But now say I openly that in that which this man preacheth I see plainly the truth which can give us the gift of health and happiness everlasting. Wherefore, O King, my counsel is that we do at once root up and burn down those temples and altars which we have hallowed, and yet have got no good thereby." Then King Edwin spake and said that he would henceforth worship the God of Paullinus and none other. And he said, "Who will be the first to throw down the altar and the temple of our false gods and the hedge which is round about them?" Then said Coifi, "I will. For who rather than I shall throw down that before which I have worshipped in my folly, now that God hath given me wisdom thereunto? Wherefore, O King, give me an horse and weapons withal, that I may ride to the temple of the false Gods and throw down the same." Now it was the law of the Angles that a priest might not wear weapons, nor might he ride except on a mare. So Coifi girded him with a sword, and took a spear in his hand, and he rode on the King's own horse to the place where was the temple of idols. Now it was at a place which is called Godmundingham, which lieth to the east of the royal city of Eoforwic (which men now for shortness call York), beyond the river of Derwent. And when men saw Coifi the Priest wearing weapons and riding on the King's horse, they said, "Of a truth Coifi the Priest is mad." But when he drew near to the temple he hurled his spear at it, and bade his fellows break down the temple and burn it with the hedge that was round about it.

Thus King Edwin believed, with all his Thanes and wise men and the more part of all the folk of Northumberland. And he built a church of wood in the city of York, and called it by the name of the Apostle Saint Peter, and therein he was baptized at the Feast of Easter;[1] and he bade that Paullinus should be Bishop of the city of York and should have that church for his see. Now after these things King Edwin reigned yet six years, and Paullinus dwelt at York and was Bishop there, and preached much, and baptized many of the men of the land all the days of Edwin. And King Edwin began to build him a church of stone in the city of York, but he lived not to finish the same, but Oswald his sister's son, who was afterwards King of the Northumbrians, finished it. For after six years Cædwalla the King of the Welshmen rebelled against King Edwin, and Penda the King of the Mercians helped him. So Cædwalla and Penda fought against King Edwin and smote him and slew him in the place which is called Heathfield, and many evil deeds did they throughout the whole land of Northumberland. For Penda was still an heathen man and worshipped the gods of his fathers, and he persecuted them that believed in Christ wherever he found them. In those days did Paullinus flee from York with Æthelburh the Queen and her young children and with the goodly things of the church of York, and they came and dwelt in Kent with King Eadbald the Queen's brother. And King Edwin's head was brought to York, and, when Oswald his sister's son reigned in Northumberland, it was buried in the porch of the minster of Saint Peter, which Edwin had begun to build, and which Oswald his sister's son finished.

I have told you the story of Edwin at length, because it is such a famous and beautiful tale, but for that very reason I must cut some other parts of what I have to say rather shorter. After the death of Edwin in 633, there was a time of great con-

[1] April 12th, 627.

fusion in Northumberland, during which many men fell back to their old gods, but after a while the kingdom came to Oswald, the son of Æthelfrith, and nephew of Edwin, who was not only a Christian but so good a man that he was reckoned as a saint and called Saint Oswald.   He fought a battle in 635 at a place called Heavenfield, near Hexham, where Cædwalla was killed, and the power of the Welsh was utterly broken.   After this we never again hear of the Welsh as really threatening any of the English Kingdoms; it was quite as much as they could do to keep the land west of the Severn.   Oswald now reigned as Bretwalda, like Edwin, but, like him, he could not stand against Penda of Mercia.   He died in battle against him in 642 at a place called Maserfield, and men counted him for a martyr. After his death Bernicia and Deira were again divided.   Oswine reigned in Deira and Oswiu in Bernicia.[1]   Oswine is described by Bæda as a very good King; however, war broke out between him and Oswiu, and I am sorry to say that Oswiu caused Oswine to be treacherously murdered.   We may hope however that Oswiu afterwards repented of this great sin, for he became one of the greatest and best Kings in England.   In 655 he won a great battle against Penda, who was killed, and for a while Oswiu held Mercia as well as Northumberland, and was called Bretwalda.   Under Oswald and Oswiu Christianity took firm root in Northumberland, partly through the help of Scottish missionaries.   This caused some disputings, for the Scots, like the Welsh, differed in some things from the Romans, and therefore from the English who had been converted by the Romans.   But in the end the English commonly thought it better to follow the Roman customs as to the time of keeping Easter and the other small matters about which the Scots thought differently from Augustine and Paullinus.   The Scottish Bishops however, of whom there were several both in Northumberland and in Mercia, seem to have been very good men, and perhaps they were better fitted to convert the English than the more learned and civilized men who came from Rome and other distant lands.

---

[1] Oswiu was brother of Oswald, son of Æthelfrith and sister's son to Edwin.   Oswine was a cousin of Edwin.   It should be remarked that most of the Northumbrian royal names begin with *Os*, as in Wessex they afterwards commonly begin with *Ead* and *Æthel*.

But before long Englishmen were found fit to be made Bishops, and they of course did better than either Scots or Romans. The first English Bishop was Ithamar of Rochester in 644.

Wessex was converted by a Bishop named Birinus, who was sent by Pope Honorius. The first Christian Kings of the West-Saxons were Cynegils and Cwichelm, Cwichelm being the King who had once tried to kill Edwin. They founded a Bishoprick at Dorchester in Oxfordshire in 639. After Cynegils' death his son Cenwealh fell back for a while into heathenism, but he was afterwards converted, and founded the Bishoprick of Winchester, which remained the Bishoprick of the West-Saxons, and Dorchester afterwards became a Bishoprick of the Mercians. You must remember that there was no Bishop of Wells as yet, and that as yet only a small part of Somersetshire was English. So much as was English must have been in the Diocese of Winchester.

Mercia became Christian after the death of Penda, under his sons Peada and Wulfhere. Wulfhere reigned from 657 to 675. The first Bishop in Mercia was Diuma, a Scot, but after him came Ceadda an Englishman, who is called Saint Chad and had his see at Lichfield. Mercia was, I think, the only King-dom which did not for a time fall back into heathenism. This we have seen happened in Northumberland and Wessex, and it was so also in Essex and East-Anglia, and even in Kent. For Eadbald the son of Æthelberht fell away and married his step-mother; so his mother the Frankish Queen must have died before her husband. But Eadbald afterwards came back to the faith, and it was then that, as I before told you, he gave his sister Æthelburh in marriage to Edwin, which brought about the conversion of Northumberland.

The last part of the main land of Britain to become Christian was Sussex. It was but a small state, and it seems to have been much more barbarous than other parts of England. The first Christian King was called Æthelwealh. He too had married a Christian wife, Eaba, from the little Kingdom of the Hwiccas, and he was himself baptized at the court of King Wulfhere in Mercia. But as yet few of their people were converted, till in 681 there came among them a Bishop named Wilfrith, who had been Bishop of York, but who had been driven out of Northumberland by the King Ecgfrith the son of Oswiu, who succeeded his father in 670. Wilfrith did much for the South-Saxons in the way of civilizing them as well as preaching to them. Amongst other things it is said that till he came they had no notion of catching any fish except eels, but he taught them to catch other fish as well. He founded the Bishoprick of the South-Saxons, the see of which was at first at Selsey, but was afterwards moved to Chichester.

Thus, in less than a hundred years from the coming of Augustine, all England became Christian. And the English Church was for a long time one of the most flourishing Churches in Christendom. Many churches and monasteries were built, and there were many good and learned men among Kings, Bishops, and others. And many Englishmen went out as missionaries to other lands, especially to our own old land of North Germany. Wilfrith, who preached to the South-Saxons, preached also to the Frisians, and there were many other English Bishops in other parts of Germany. The greatest of them was Winfrith. afterwards called Saint Boniface, who was the first Archbishop of Mainz, and who is called the Apostle of Germany. His see, Mainz. became the head church of Germany, as Canterbury is the head church of England.

In my two next chapters I shall tell you how the different English Kingdoms were all joined into one.

CHAPTER VII.

HOW THE KINGS OF THE WEST-SAXONS BECAME LORDS OVER ALL ENGLAND.

PART I.

I. HAVE told you how the Angles and Saxons founded many Kingdoms in Britain, and I have taught you the names of the chief Kingdoms among them, and I have told you that it often happened that one Kingdom got for a while a certain power over all or most of the others. But you know that now not only England, but Wales, Scotland, and Ireland too, make up altogether only one Kingdom. It is not so very long since Scotland and Ireland were fully united to England, and Wales kept its own Princes for many hundred years after the times that we have been talking about. What I have now to tell you is how England itself, that is the Kingdoms of the Angles, Saxons, and other Teutons who had come over into Britain, was made into one Kingdom. For in the tenth century, that is, about five hundred years after the English came into Britain, all England was for the first time thus thoroughly joined together, and since the eleventh century no man has ever thought for a moment of dividing it again. Only you must know that the northern part of Northumberland came into the hands of the Kings of Scots, so that some men of English blood and speech were cut off from the rest, and learned to call themselves Scots and forgot that they were really Englishmen. Thus it is that the land from the river Tweed to the Firth of Forth, though men have always spoken English there, has for many hundred years been counted to be part of Scotland. But all the rest of the Teutonic people in Britain were gradually joined together under the Kings of the West-Saxons. From the beginning of the ninth century, that power which I have told you that some one Kingdom often held over the rest became fixed in the hands of the Kings of the West-Saxons. From the beginning of the ninth century then, though there were still for some time other Kings in the land, yet the Kings of the West-Saxons were lords over them, and in the course of the tenth century there ceased to be any other Kings in the land at all. From that time, instead of being called Kings of the West-Saxons, they were called Kings of the English. And I have told you that nearly all the Kings who have since reigned in England have come of the blood of Cerdic the West-Saxon.

Now this did not happen all at once, so I must go back a little, and tell you some more about the West-Saxons and the other Kingdoms. But I shall tell you most about the West-Saxons, both because it was their Kingdom which in the end got the chief power, and because it is in the land of the West-Saxons that we ourselves dwell.

For a long time after Oswald and Oswiu of Northumberland no prince is mentioned in the Chronicle as bearing the title of Bretwalda. The next on the list, the eighth and last, is Ecgberht of Wessex, in whose time the West-Saxon Kings won a lasting power over all the others. We can therefore very well see why no Bretwalda is mentioned after him, as from the days of Ecgberht onwards the King of the West-Saxons for the time being had all the power, and more than the power, that the old Bretwaldas had had. But it is not so plain why no Bretwalda is mentioned between Oswiu and Ecgberht, as there were during that time several Kings both in Mercia and in Wessex who seem to have had as much power as any that were before them. One might almost have expected to find Penda himself on the list, and long after there reigned in Mercia a great King named Offa, of whom I shall speak again presently, who seems to have been quite as powerful as any one of the seven before Ecgberht. Perhaps Christian writers did not like to reckon such a fierce heathen as Penda in the same list as Edwin and Oswald, but one hardly sees why Offa is not reckoned. Still, however it may be, no Bretwalda is spoken of in the Chronicle between

Oswiu and Ecgberht.[1] It is certain that during this time, the first place among the English Kingdoms changed about very much. being sometimes in the hands of Mercia and sometimes in those of Wessex. Northumberland became of less consequence than it had been, and we do not hear much of the other four smaller Kingdoms. When we do, it is generally as being tributary either to Mercia or to Wessex. Kent, however, always kept up a certain degree of importance on account of its containing the head church of all England at Canterbury.

The last King of the West-Saxons whom I mentioned was Cenwealh, who founded the Bishoprick of Winchester. Like most of the West-Saxon Kings about this time, he had much fighting with the Mercians, and like all the other Kings both of Mercia and Wessex he had much fighting with the Welsh. In 644 Penda came against him, and drove him for a while out of his Kingdom, and it was perhaps now that Gloucestershire and some of the other West-Saxon lands north of the Thames and Avon became part of Mercia. But, if so, Cenwealh partly made up for this loss by a great gain in another quarter. You will remember that Ceawlin in 577 had conquered as far as the Axe. But the Welsh still kept a long narrow strip of country reaching from Frome up to Cricklade. Now I suppose it was in Cenwealh's time that this strip became English, for Cenwealh in 652 fought a battle against the Welsh at Bradford-on-Avon. In 658 he fought another battle at the hill called Pen or Peonna, and chased the Welsh as far as the river Parret. Now where is the hill called Pen? It is certainly one of our Pens in Somerset, but I do not profess to say whether it is, as many people say, Pen Selwood, or whether it is Pen Hill, a point of Mendip not very far from where I am now writing, or whether it is Pen or Ben Knoll, which is nearer still. *Pen* or *Ben* in Celtic means "head," and you

---

[1] Bæda gives the list of the seven Bretwaldas, though, as he writes in Latin, without using that name. (ii. 5.) The Chronicle adds Ecgberht. It may be that Bæda's list was copied by the Chronicler in the days of Ecgberht or one of his immediate descendants, and that, full of the glories of Ecgberht, he added his name to the seven in Bæda, but did not know or care enough about any King between them, especially of any King out of Wessex, to make him put down his name as well.

F

perhaps know that most of the mountains in Scotland are called *Bens, Ben Nevis, Ben Lomond,* and so forth ; and the Welsh name of the mountain which we call the Sugar-Loaf is *Pen-y-val.* These Pens are some of the cases in which Welsh names have lingered on through all changes, as they have often done in Somersetshire, and still more in Devonshire. It is said that the battle at Pen was a very hard one, and that the Welsh drove the English back for a while, but then the English rallied and beat the Welsh, and chased them as far as the river Parret. You must remember that these Welsh Kings, reigning over all Cornwall and Devonshire and most part of Somersetshire, were really very powerful princes, and that their dominions were larger than those of some of the English Kings. Thus it was a great matter to take from them all the country between the Axe and the Parret, which now, or soon after, became English. But it would seem that, now that the English were Christians, they did not so completely root out or enslave the old inhabitants as their heathen forefathers had done, so that many of the Welshmen still lived in the land as subjects of the West-Saxon Kings. So most likely many of the people in Devonshire and the greater part of Somersetshire are really descendants of the old Britons, who gradually learned to speak English, as we know they did in Cornwall. Amongst other places, Glastonbury now became English. The Abbey there had been founded in the British or Roman times : you will remember that, as long as the English were heathens, they destroyed all the churches and monasteries that they found in the land ; but now that the West-Saxons were Christians, they respected them, and we shall find the West-Saxon Kings giving great gifts to the church at Glastonbury. Thus it would seem that Glastonbury was the oldest of the great monasteries of England, having gone on being a famous church ever since the old British times. Of course I do not mean any of the buildings which are standing now, for they were built long after, chiefly towards the end of the twelfth century.

I need not tell you the names of all the West-Saxon Kings, but you should know that when Cenwealh died in 672, he was succeeded by his widow Sexburh. Now it was not usual in England or any other Teutonic country to be governed by women, and you will hardly find another case of a Queen *regnant*[1] in any of the Old-English Kingdoms. Sexburh is said to have been a brave and wise woman, but she reigned only one year. Some say she died then, others that she was driven out.

The next West-Saxon King whom I need tell you about is Ceadwalla, who began to reign in 685. He was of the royal house, but he seems to have come to the crown by some kind of rebellion against the reigning King Centwine. He had a brother called Mul, and, what seems strange, neither of them was baptized. Yet Ceadwalla was a believer in Christ, though his deeds were not of a very Christian kind. He reigned only two years, and spent that time in overrunning Kent, Sussex, and the Isle of Wight. But, though he was for the most part successful in these wars, yet in one of his inroads into Kent, his brother Mul was killed. Now what he did in Wight, as Bæda tells the story, is the best worth remembering. I told you that the Jutes settled in Wight and part of Hampshire as well as in Kent, and they made there a little Kingdom of their own, one of those which are not commonly reckoned among the seven. And perhaps I should not have said that the South-Saxons were the last of all to receive the Gospel, because the Jutes in Wight were still heathens in Ceadwalla's time, some years after Wilfrith had preached to the South-Saxons. But the South-Saxons were the last of the seven greater Kingdoms and the last people on the mainland of England to become Christians. The King of the Jutes in Wight at this time was named Arwald. I do not know whether Arwald had provoked Ceadwalla in any way, but the story reads almost as if Ceadwalla attacked the Jutes because they were heathens. He determined to conquer the island, to destroy the people, and put men of his own Kingdom to live there, and to dedicate a fourth of the land and of the prey to the Lord. This was indeed a strange way of spreading the Gospel, and very different from anything that the good Kings Æthelberht and Oswald had done. It seems that Bishop

---

[1] That is a Queen reigning in her own right, like a King, as Queen Victoria does. A Queen *consort* is one who is merely the wife of a King, like the late Queen Adelaide, the wife of King William the Fourth.

F 2

Wilfrith, whom I before mentioned to you as having converted the South-Saxons, heard of this, and came over and did what he could for both the souls and the bodies of the people.[1] Ceadwalla offered him the fourth that he had vowed to the Lord. So Wilfrith took a fourth of the land and with it a fourth of the people. Now there were in the whole island twelve hundred families, so that Wilfrith took three hundred. who, as far as we can make out, would otherwise have been killed with the rest. These people he put under Beorhtwine his sister's son, and left with him a priest named Hiddila, to preach to them and baptize them.

Meanwhile two boys, sons of the King of Wight, had fled from the island as Ceadwalla came near, and tried to hide themselves on the mainland. For as I just now said, there was a little piece of what is now Hampshire where the people were Jutes as well as in the island, and, though no doubt these Jutes were now subjects of Ceadwalla, the boys from the island may have thought that it would be easier to hide among people of their own race. But they were found out, and Ceadwalla ordered them to be put to death. Then a certain Abbot named Cyneberht, whose monastery was near to the place, went to Ceadwalla and asked that, if he would not spare their lives, he would at least let him, Cyneberht, try and make Christians of them before they died. So Ceadwalla, though he would not spare their lives, yet let Cyneberht teach them. So they believed and were baptized, and then Ceadwalla had them put to death.

Now we may suppose that Ceadwalla soon repented of all these cruel deeds; for, when he had reigned only two years, he gave up his Kingdom and left England altogether, and went to Rome. There he was baptized by the Pope Sergius at Easter in the year 689, and in his baptism his name was changed from Ceadwalla to Peter. In those days men who were baptized wore white

---

[1] The story as told in Bæda is not very clear, but this seems to be the meaning. We first read that Ceadwalla vowed to kill *all* the people ("omnes indigenas exterminare"), and then that Wilfrith received the three hundred families. One would think from this that, but for Wilfrith, they would have been killed also.

garments for a week after their baptism. But Ceadwalla or Peter fell sick while he still had his white garments on him, and he died at Rome and was buried there in the church of Saint Peter. So that he lived hardly longer after his baptism than the poor boys, the sons of King Arwald of Wight, had lived after theirs. Now after Ceadwalla there reigned in Wessex a great King whose name was Ine. He was not the son of Ceadwalla, but he was of the royal house of Cerdic, as also was Æthelburh his wife. He reigned as much as thirty-eight years, from 688 to 726. Like all the other Kings, he had much to do in the way of fighting, both against the Welsh and against the other English Kings, but he also found time for other things besides. He put together the laws of the West-Saxons so as to make what is called a *code*, being the oldest West-Saxon laws that we have, though there are Kentish laws which are older still, some even as old as the days of Æthelberht. He also divided the Kingdom of the West-Saxons into two Bishopricks. Hitherto all Wessex had been under the Bishops of Winchester; but now that the Kingdom was so much larger, Ine founded another Bishoprick at Sherborne in Dorsetshire. This is what is now called the Bishoprick of Salisbury, the See having been moved from Sherborne in later times. The first Bishop of Sherborne was named Ealdhelm; he had before been Abbot of Malmesbury in Wiltshire; he was a famous man in his time, and wrote many books, some of which still remain. There is a headland in Dorsetshire, the true name of which is Saint Ealdhelms Head, but it has got corrupted into Saint Alban's Head, because in later times the name of Saint Alban has been better known than that of Saint Ealdhelm. This new Diocese of Sherborne took in Wiltshire, Berkshire, Dorsetshire, and so much of Somersetshire as was now English; there was not a Bishop at Wells yet. But you will remember that, since the wars of Cenwealh, the English land reached to the Parret, so that both Wells and Glastonbury were in Ine's Kingdom. You should remember Ine, for it is said that it was he who, in 704, first founded Saint Andrew's church in Wells. That, you know, is now the cathedral church, but it was not a cathedral church then, because there was no Bishop. But there was a College or body of clergy belonging to it, making it what is called a collegiate church. And as Glastonbury was now in his dominions, Ine did much for the great monastery there. King Ine also fought much with the Welsh under their King Gerent. Gerent's name is mentioned in the Chronicle, which does not often tell us the names of any Welsh Kings, and we find that he was a notable man in the Welsh history. He seems to have had a good deal of power over the Welsh princes in Glamorgan and those parts ; and indeed, when Britain was cut up into so many small states, it was no small dominion to reign over Cornwall, Devonshire, and part of Somersetshire. But Gerent could not have long kept much, if any part of Somersetshire, for Ine went on with his conquests towards the west, and built the town of Taunton, which is beyond the Parret. Taunton was no doubt built as a fortress on the frontier, to guard the newly conquered land against the Welshmen in Devon.

King Ine had also much to do in fighting with the other English Kings. He fought against the men of Kent, and made them pay him much gold as the price of blood for his kinsman Mul. This price of blood paid to the kinsfolk of a slain man was called by the English and other Teutonic people the *wérgild.* He had wars also in Sussex and in East-Anglia, and in 714 he fought a great battle with Ceolred King of the Mercians, in which so many men were killed on both sides that they could not tell which side had won, so that it was what is called a drawn battle. This happened at *Wodnesbeorg* or Wanborough in Wiltshire, not far from Swindon, where as you go by on the railway you may see Wanborough church with both a tower and a spire on the top of the hill.

Towards the end of his reign, Ine seems to have been troubled by some rebellions among his own people, and also to have been less successful than before in his wars with the Welsh. One or two rebellions are mentioned, headed by Æthelings or men of the royal house, in one of which, while Ine was fighting in Sussex, the rebels seized the new town of Taunton. But Queen Æthelburh went against them and burned the town. This was in 722, and Ine reigned only four years longer. In 726, like Ceadwalla, he gave up his Kingdom

and went to Rome and died there. He must have been getting
old, and very likely he was troubled because the latter end of
his reign had been less glorious than the beginning. But his
wife Æthelburh is said to have persuaded him to leave the
world in a curious way which I will tell you, as it is a striking
story. But I only find it in William of Malmesbury,[1] who wrote
so long after as the twelfth century, so I do not feel so sure
that it is true, as if I read it in the Chronicle or in Bæda. So
here is the story.

Why King Ine forsook the World.

Now King Ine once made him a feast to his lords and great
men in one of his royal houses ; and the house was hung with
goodly curtains, and the table was spread with vessels of gold
and silver, and there were meats and drinks brought from all
parts of the world, and Ine and his lords ate and drank and
were merry. Now on the next day Ine set forth from that
house to go unto another that he had, and Æthelburh his Queen
went with him. So men took down the curtains and carried off
the goodly vessels,[2] and left the house bare and empty. Moreover Æthelburh the Queen spake unto the steward who had
the care of that house, saying. " When the King is gone, fill
the house with rubbish and with the dung of cattle, and lay in
the bed where the King slept a sow with her litter of pigs."
So the steward did as the Queen commanded. So when Ine
and the Queen had gone forth about a mile from the house,
the Queen said unto Ine, " Turn back, my lord, to the house
whence we have come, for it will be greatly for thy good so to
do." So Ine hearkened to the voice of his wife and turned

---

[1] It is not found even in all the copies of William of Malmesbury.

[2] In the days of Ine, and many centuries after, Kings and other great
men often went about from one house to another. There was not much
money in the land, so that a man could not, as he can now, take rent for his
lands and spend it where he would, but a man who had several estates
commonly went and stayed at one till he and his people had eaten up the
fruits of that estate, and then they went to another, carrying the most part
of their furniture with them on pack-horses. That the curtains and vessels
were taken away is not distinctly said, but it seems implied in the story,
and it is according to the custom of the time.

back unto the house. So he found all the curtains and the goodly vessels gone, and the house full of rubbish and made foul with the dung of cattle, and a sow and her pigs lying in the bed where Ine and Æthelburh his Queen had slept. So Æthelburh spake unto Ine her husband saying, " Seest thou, O King, how the pomp of this world passeth away? Where are now all the goodly things, the curtains, and the vessels, and the meats and drinks brought from all parts of the earth, wherewith thou and thy lords held your feast yesterday? How foul is now the house which but yesterday was goodly and fit for a King. How foul a beast lieth in the bed where a King and Queen slept only the last night. Are not all the things of this life a breath, yea smoke, and a wind that passeth away? Are they not a river that runneth by, and no man seeth the water any more? Woe then to them that cleave to the things of this life only. Seest thou not how our very flesh, which is nourished by these good things, shall pass away? And shall not we, who have more power and wealth than others, have worse punishment than others, if we cleave to the things of this life only? Have I not often bidden thee to think on these things? Thou growest old, and the time is short. Wilt thou not lay aside thy Kingdom and all the things of this life, and go as a pilgrim to the threshold of the Apostles in the great city of Rome, and there serve God the rest of the days that He shall give thee?" So King Ine hearkened to the voice of Æthelburh his wife, and he laid aside his Kingdom, and Æthelheard his kinsman, the brother of Æthelburh his wife, reigned in his stead. So Ine and Æthelburh went to Rome to the threshold of the Apostles, and Gregory[1] the Pope received them gladly. Now Ine lived no more as a King, yet would he not make a show in the eyes of men by shaving his head as monks do; but he dwelt at Rome as a common man for the rest of his days, and Æthelburh his wife dwelt with him.

Several things happened in other parts of England while these Kings reigned in Wessex, which it may be as well to

---

[1] That is Pope Gregory the Second. Gregory the Great, of whom you heard before, had been dead more than a hundred years.

mention. It was in Ine's time, in 690, that the first Englishman became Archbishop ; this was Beorhtwald or Brihtwold,
Archbishop of Canterbury ; for Wilfrith, though he was Bishop
of York, does not seem to have been called Archbishop. Up to
this time all the Archbishops of Canterbury had been Romans,
at least subjects of the Roman Empire; for the Archbishop
before Beorhtwald, Theodore by name, came from Tarsus in
Cilicia, the same town as Saint Paul, so that his native tongue
was Greek. This Theodore did much for the English Church
in many ways ; but by this time the English Church had, so to
speak, outgrown its childhood, so that it was time to put a man
born in the land at its head. And so after Theodore all the
Archbishops of Canterbury were Englishmen[1] for about three
hundred and fifty years, till the time of Edward the Confessor.

It was also during this time that the English missionaries
began to go into different parts of Germany to convert those
of their brethren who were still heathens. Such was Willibrord
who preached to the Frisians, and founded the Bishoprick of
Utrecht ; the Frisians are the people whose language comes
nearer to English than that of any other people on the Continent. ΄Such too was Boniface or Winfrith, of whom I spoke to
you before as being the first Archbishop of Mainz, and called
the Apostle of Germany. The English missionaries were much
helped in their good works by the Dukes and Kings of the
Franks, who were now the ruling people of Germany and Gaul,
and of whom you will hear more presently.

There were also many good men in different parts of
England who did much good in writing books and building
churches, and generally in making men more Christian and
civilized. Bishop Wilfrith was one of them, though he often got
into trouble, especially because he was too fond of the Pope.
For though all people in England acknowledged the Bishop
of Rome as the chief Bishop of the West, yet they did not
wish to have him altogether for lord over them, and Wilfrith
was often ready to set up the Pope's authority in a way to
which Englishmen in general could not agree. There was

---

[1] Oda in the tenth century was no doubt, strictly speaking, a Dane, but
we may count Englishmen and Danes as all one, as distinguished from
Romans and Frenchmen.

also one Benedict, called Biscop, Abbot of Wearmouth in
Northumberland, who did much to improve the art of building
in England, especially by first putting glass in the windows.
There was Caedmon, the first Christian poet in England,
whose verses remind one much of Milton's Paradise Lost.
There was our own Bishop Ealdhelm at Sherborne, and above
all there was Venerable Bæda, whom we have to thank for so
much of our knowledge of these times. He was born in 672
and died in 734, so that for all the time we have been lately
talking about he was what is called a contemporary writer.
He could know about Ine, and even a little about Caedwalla,
for himself; and about Cenwealh he could hear from people
who remembered him. But as he lived all his life in Northumberland, he does not tell us quite so much about our West-
Saxon Kings as we sometimes might wish. His greatest work
is called *Historia Ecclesiastica Gentis Anglorum*, that is,
Ecclesiastical History of the People of the English. I have
generally had it by me while I have been writing my story. All
his works were written in Latin, but King Alfred afterwards
translated some of them into English.

PART II.

After Ine was gone away the Kingdom of the West-Saxons
seems for a while not to have flourished so much as it had
lately done. You will remember that when Ine went to Rome,
his wife's brother Æthelheard reigned instead of him. Perhaps
this choice did not please all his people, for we read of an
Ætheling named Oswald,[1] a descendant of Ceawlin, who fought
against Æthelheard the very year that Ine went away. But two
years after, in 730, Oswald died. The Welsh too seem to have
recovered something of what they had lost, and there was also
war with the Mercians. There was now in Mercia a very

---

[1] It is unusual to find Oswald, a purely Northumbrian name, in Wessex.
Perhaps he was called in honour of Saint Oswald. Though some names
were common to the whole nation, others belong only to particular Kingdoms or families, and those which begin with *Os-* are much less common in
Wessex than in Northumberland.

powerful King named Æthelbald. In 733 he invaded Wessex, and got as far as Somerton. That, you know, is but a small town now, but it was then the capital of the *Sumorsætas*,[1] whence we have the name of *Somersetshire*. Æthelbald besieged and took Somerton, and brought all Wessex and all England south of the Humber into his power.[2]

In 740 Æthelheard died. Either he was very weak or very unlucky, for certainly things went on very ill in his time. His successor Cuthred did much better. He too had to struggle against both the Welsh and the Mercians, but he contrived never to have to fight against both at once. In some of his wars the Welsh helped him against the Mercians, and in others the Mercians helped him against the Welsh. Now he must have been a very clever man to have managed that. In 750 he was troubled by a rebellion at home, but he contrived to gain something even out of that. There was one Æthelhun "the proud Alderman," with whom he had a battle, in which Æthelhun was defeated and wounded. Now many Kings of those times would have taken some fearful vengeance on Æthelhun for this rebellion. Cuthred however seems to have forgiven him, and to have quite won his heart by his forgiveness. For, two years afterwards, Cuthred and his people could no longer bear the yoke of the Mercians, so Cuthred fought against Æthelbald in a great battle at Burford in Oxfordshire, not far from the borders of the two kingdoms. Now the West-Saxons won this battle, and the victory is said to have been greatly owing to the bravery of Æthelhun, who was the King's standard-bearer, and bore the royal ensign. The royal ensign of the West-Saxons was a golden dragon, and you will hear of the Dragon of Wessex in many battles that are to

---

[1] *Sætas* is the same as *settlers* (connected with *sit*, the Latin *sedere*, &c.), those who *settled* in any particular part of the country. The word is still preserved in the name Dorsetshire, as well as Somersetshire ; but in the case of the Wil*sætas* and Defn*sætas* (the people of Wiltshire and Devonshire) and the Mage*sætas*, who lived in Herefordshire, it is gone out of use. We get the same form in Els*ass* (*s* in the High-Dutch answering to *t* in English), the part of Germany which has been joined to France, and which Frenchmen call *Alsace*.

[2] Some however think that the Somerton which Æthelbald took was not our Somerton, but Somerton in Oxfordshire.

come. Æthelhun and the West-Saxons fought so well that King Æthelbald fled, and three years after, in 755, he was killed, perhaps in another battle.[1] From that time the Kingdom of Wessex grew and prospered, and was never again in bondage, yet we shall see that for a good while Mercia remained very powerful.

King Cuthred did not live to see the death of his enemy Æthelbald, as he died the year before him, in 754. He was succeeded by his kinsman Sigeberht; but Sigeberht reigned ill, so the Witan, the Wise Men, the Council or Parliament of the land, took his Kingdom from him and gave it to another kinsman named Cynewulf. I would have you mark this well, as showing that our forefathers were always a free people, and that from the beginning the Witan could choose their own King and could take his Kingdom from him if he reigned badly. You will find that our Parliaments continued to do this when it was needful, many hundred years after the time of Sigeberht. This was in 755, the year of Æthelbald's death. So Cynewulf was King of the West-Saxons, but Sigeberht was allowed to reign as Under-king of Hampshire. But after a while he killed one Cumbra, his Alderman, for giving him good counsel. So Cynewulf drove him quite away into the great wood of Andered in Sussex, where he was afterwards killed by a servant of Cumbra's. Cynewulf reigned a long time, and won many battles over the Welsh. But I must now tell you a little about some things which happened in other parts of Britain.

There is very little that I need tell you about the Kingdom of Northumberland in these times, but there is one thing which happened there which you should remember. There was a great King in that country called Eadberht, under whom Northumberland flourished greatly. Among other things,

---

[1] The Chronicle and Florence of Worcester mention that Æthelbald was killed in 755, but they do not say how. It is Henry of Huntingdon who says that he was killed in a battle with the West-Saxons. Henry did not write till long after, in the twelfth century; but he seems to have had books before him, or perhaps only songs, which we have not got now. But another late, though very good, writer, Simeon of Durham, says that he was killed by some of his own people.

Eadberht made an alliance with the King of the Picts in Scotland, whose name was Unust, and the two together made war on the Welsh in Strathclyde, and took their chief town of Alcluyd, near Dunbarton.[1] This was in 756. This is well worth marking, because it seems to have been now that the Kingdom of Strathclyde first became subject to Northumberland. Thus you see that now, three hundred years after the first coming of the English, the Welsh still held out against them in three parts, forming nearly the whole of the west side of the island. I mean in Strathclyde, in what is now Wales, which was then called North Wales; and in West Wales, that is in Cornwall, Devon, and Somerset. Eadberht got great fame by this conquest, so much so that Pippin, the great King of the Franks, made a friendship with him, and sent ambassadors with rich gifts. But after a while Eadberht, like so many other Kings about this time, gave up his Kingdom, and after him Northumberland did not prosper at all. There were great quarrrlings and confusions among different Kings and Aldermen, so that Northumberland soon became of no account at all, which made it the more easy for the Danes first to plunder and then to settle in that part of England, which I shall tell you more about presently.

I must now tell you something about Mercia, as some very notable Kings reigned there during the time that we have been talking about, and for some time things looked as if Mercia, and not Wessex, was going to be the head Kingdom of England. You have already heard of Æthelbald, and how for a time he held not only the smaller Kingdoms in subjection, but also Wessex itself. He tried to conquer Northumberland, but there Eadberht was too strong for him. But he calls himself in a Charter,[2] "King, not only of the Mercians, but of all the provinces which by a general name are called the South-English," that is, I suppose, all except Northumberland. And at the end he even goes so far as to call himself "Rex

---

[1] This is not in the Chronicle, but in Simeon of Durham, who is very good authority for Northumbrian matters.

[2] Its date is 736. The Latin words are "Rex non solum Mercensium sed et omnium provinciarum quæ generale [generali] nomine Sutangli dicuntur." See Kemble's Charters, i. 96.

Britanniæ" or " King of Britain." But you know that this greatness did not last, as I have told you how he was defeated by the West-Saxons at Burford in 752, and how he was killed three years afterwards. This King Æthelbald founded the great Abbey of Crowland in *Holland.* You know I do not mean Holland over the sea, but Holland in Lincolnshire. Both countries, I suppose, are so called because they are so low and flat, as if one should say *hollow land.*

A little while after Æthelbald there reigned a still more famous King in Mercia whose name was Offa. He founded St. Alban's Abbey; so the monks of that house had a great deal to tell about him, and some very strange things they told. I will tell you one story, but remember that it is a mere legend, which I do not wish you to believe.

The Tale of the Two Offas.

There was once a King who reigned over the Angles,[1] whose name was Wærmund. He had but one son, whose name was Offa ; he was a tall youth and fair, but he was dumb. Moreover he had been born blind, and saw nothing till he was of the age of seven years. Now when King Wærmund grew old and Offa his son was about thirty years old, men began to say, " Lo, Wærmund is old, and will soon die, and Offa his son is dumb ; how can a dumb man reign over the people of the Angles ?" Now there was one of the nobles of the Angles whose name was Rigan. And Rigan went to King Wærmund and said, " O King, thou art old, and thou hast no son save this Offa who is dumb, and a dumb man cannot reign over

---

[1] This story is told both by English and by Danish writers, and no doubt it is one of many old stories which are common to all the Teutonic nations. Or perhaps I should say that it is common to all the world, for you will easily see how like this story is to the tale of Croesus and his son in Herodotus. But while the Danish writers make Wærmund to have been a King of the Angles in their old country before they came into Britain, the English writers make him a King of the Angles in Britain. No doubt the story is one of those which the English brought with them, and for which they sometimes found a place in their new land ; I have therefore simply spoken of the " Angles," without saying where they lived.

the people of the Angles. Now behold me here, and choose me, that I may be unto thee as another son while thou livest, and that when thou diest I may be thine heir and reign in thy stead." But King Wærmund said to Rigan, "Thou shalt not be my son, neither will I give my Kingdom for thee to reign over." So Rigan gathered himself together an host to fight against King Wærmund. Then King Wærmund gathered together his Aldermen and his Thanes and all his wise men, and said unto them, "What shall we do, seeing Rigan cometh with an host to fight against us?" And they made a truce with Rigan, so that he and certain of his captains came and spake with the King and his wise men. And they sat for many days doubting what they should do, and one spake on this manner and another spake on that manner. For they would not that a dumb man should reign over them, and yet it pleased them not to cast aside the royal house which had so long reigned over the people of the Angles. Now on the last day Offa, the King's son, came and sat among the wise men. For though he was dumb, yet could he hear and understand the words that men spake. So when he heard men say that he was not fit to reign over the people of the Angles, it grieved him to the heart, and he wept. And when he was greatly moved, lo, the string of his tongue was loosed, and he spake among the wise men and said, "This now is wickedness, that any man should seek to drive me out of the seat of my fathers, so that a stranger should reign instead of me over the people of the Angles. Who is this Rigan that he should rise up against his lord the King and come with an host to fight against him? Now therefore, if he will stand up against me to battle, I will smite him and all that abide with him, but all that will abide with me and fight against him them will I greatly honour." So all men greatly wondered when they heard the dumb speak, and saw that he whom they despised had a strong heart within him. And the more part of them that had followed Rigan were afraid and went forth. But Rigan tarried yet awhile, and defied[1] the King and his son, and then went forth also. Then the wise men said to the King, "O King, thy son is of age

---

[1] *Diffiduciavit.* This is a technical term of feudal law, and implies renouncing of all allegiance.

and hath a stout heart; let him be girded with the belt[1] of a man of war, and let him lead us forth to battle against Rigan and them that are with him."

So Offa was girded with the belt of a man of war, and he went forth to fight against Rigan and his host. Now Rigan had two sons ; the name of the elder was Hildebrand, and the name of the younger was Swegen. And Hildebrand came forth to fight against Offa, but Offa smote him that he died. And when Swegen came to help his brother, Offa smote him also that he died. So when Rigan saw that both his sons were dead, he fled, and was drowned in crossing a certain river. So Offa returned to Wærmund his father with great joy. And Wærmund gave up his Kingdom to his son, and Offa reigned over the people of the Angles for many winters, and all the Kings that were round about honoured him.

Now after many years there was a man of the Angles who dwelt in Mercia, whose name was Thingferth, and he was of the seed royal of the Mercians, and he was an Alderman under his kinsman the King. Now Thingferth had but one son, whose name was Winfrith. And the child was lame, blind, and deaf ·from his birth ; so that his parents had great sorrow of heart. So they made a vow to God that, if He would of His mercy make the child whole, they would build a goodly monastery to His honour. Now after a while there arose in Mercia a King named Beornred, who was not of the seed royal. Wherefore he sought to slay all that were kinsfolk of the Kings that had reigned before him. And when Thingferth heard this, he fled, and his wife with him. But the lad Winfrith was left behind, for Beornred sought not to slay him ; for he counted that one who was deaf and blind and lame should never trouble his Kingdom. And when Winfrith was left alone, God had pity on him, and He opened his eyes and he saw. Then he stretched forth his limbs and walked. Lastly his ears were opened, and he essayed to speak and he spake plain. And he grew and waxed strong and became a mighty man of valour. Then men said, " Lo, this youth is like Offa in the old time, who spake not till Rigan came to fight against Wærmund his father." So

---

[1] The older ceremony, from which the later rites of making a knight seem to have been derived.

his name was no longer called Winfrith, but Offa. And all men that hated Beornred and loved the house of the old Kings, gathered themselves unto Offa, and he became their captain.

Now Beornred heard that Winfrith lived and had waxed mighty, and that men no longer called him Winfrith but Offa, and it grieved him sore, and he repented that he had spared Winfrith and had not slain him when he sought to slay the house of his father. So Beornred gathered him an host to fight against Offa and the men that were with him. And when Offa heard of it, he gathered together all his friends and all the men that followed him, even a great host, and went forth to the battle against Beornred. And the battle waxed very sore, but towards eventide Beornred was smitten that he died, and they that were with him fled, and were scattered every man to his own home. Then all men came to Offa and said, " Lo, thou hast vanquished Beornred the tyrant, and thou art of the house of our old Kings. Reign thou therefore over us, and we will serve thee and follow thee whithersoever thou leadest us." So they set the crown royal upon his head, and he reigned over all the people of the Angles that dwelt in Mercia. He sent for his parents back into the land, and when they died he buried them with great honour. So Offa was King, and he waxed mighty, and he smote the Welsh ofttimes, and he warred mightily with the other Kings of the Angles and Saxons that were in Britain. Moreover he made a league with Charles the King of the Franks, for that they two were the mightiest of all the Kings that dwelt in the western lands. Moreover he forgot not his father's vow, but he built a goodly minster and caused monks to serve God therein. And he called it by the name of Alban, who was the first martyr of Christ in the isle of Britain in the old time when the Romans dwelt therein. And he built the minster hard by the town of Verulam, where Alban had died. And men came to dwell round about the minster, so that there was a new town, and men called the name of that town no longer Verulam but Saint Albans.

And Offa reigned thirty-nine winters, and he died, and they buried him in a chapel by the river of Ouse, hard by the town of Bedford. But there was a great flood in the river which swept away the chapel and the tomb and the body of the great

King Offa, so that no man knoweth where he lieth to this day.

I must now tell you something of the real history of Offa. There is no doubt that, after the death of Æthelbald, the Kingdom of Mercia was held for a short time by one Beornred, who seems not to have been of the royal house. And there is no doubt that he was driven out by Offa the son of Thingferth, who was of the royal house, though not a son, or seemingly any very near kinsman, of the last King. Most likely it was only his name Offa and his driving out the usurper which made men think of the old stories about the hero Offa.[1] He seems to have been Alderman or Under-king of the Hwiccas (that is, you will remember, the people of Gloucester, Worcester, and part of Warwick[2]); but in 755, after he had driven out Beornred, he became King over all Mercia, and reigned thirty-nine years, till 794. Under him Mercia became the first power in Britain. He had a good deal of fighting with the other English states, both with the Kentish men and with the West-Saxons, and in 777 he defeated Cynewulf of Wessex, and took from him the town of Bensington on the Thames, just opposite Wallingford. I suppose it was now that Oxfordshire became Mercian instead of West-Saxon. But Offa is much more famous for his wars with the Welsh. Up to his time the Severn had been the boundary between the English and Welsh in this part of Britain. But Offa conquered a great deal of the Welsh country called Powys, which lies west of the Severn, and took the chief town, which was called Pen-y-wern, but which now became an English town by the name of Scrobbesbyrig or Shrewsbury. And to keep his new land safe, he made a great dyke from the mouth of the Wye to the mouth of the Dee, of which some remains are left still, and which is still called Offa's Dyke. This was doing very much

[1] In the pedigree in the Chronicle the real Offa comes in the twelfth generation from Offa the hero, and Offa the hero comes in the third place from Woden, from whom all the Kings of the Angles and Saxons professed to be descended.

[2] That is, the old Diocese of Worcester, before Henry the Eighth founded the sees of Gloucester and Bristol. The Bishop's Dioceses are generally the best guide to the boundaries of the old principalities.

the same as Hadrian and Severus had done long before, when they built the great Roman wall. But Offa's Dyke answered much better than the Roman wall, and it became the boundary of England and Wales, a boundary which has not changed very much from Offa's time till now.

And now I must tell you of a great change which Offa made in the Church, though it lasted only a little while. As Offa was the most powerful King in England, and especially as he had defeated the Kentishmen, he did not like the Church of Mercia to be subject to the Archbishop of Canterbury, but he wished to have an Archbishop of his own in his own Kingdom. So he held a Council in 786, and got leave from Pope Hadrian to make Lichfield an Archbishop's see, and for the Archbishop of Lichfield to be the head Bishop of all Mercia and East-Anglia. But this did not last long, for, as soon as Offa was dead, the next Archbishop of Canterbury persuaded the Pope —another Pope, named Leo—to take away the Archbishoprick of Lichfield, and to give back to Canterbury all that it had before. So there was one Archbishop of Lichfield, and only one. His name was Ealdwulf.

Thus you see King Offa was well known even out of our own island. I told you before that Eadberht of Northumberland had some dealings with Pippin King of the Franks, and now Offa had a great deal to do with Pippin's son, Charles the Great. This Charles is perhaps the most famous man in all history since the old times of the Greeks and Romans. He did many wonderful things both in peace and in war. He conquered the Saxons, I do not mean our Saxons in Britain, but the Old-Saxons in Germany, who till then were heathens and who often had wars with the Franks. So we may call him the first King of all Germany. And he was the first man of any Teutonic nation who was called Roman Emperor. You know that the Emperors had for a long time lived at Constantinople or New Rome, and they had for some while been gradually losing their power in Italy. Part of the country had been conquered by a Teutonic people called the Lombards, and in Rome itself the Popes were gradually getting to themselves the chief power. The Popes too, and the Romans generally, had a great deal of disputing with the Emperors on religious matters, because several of the Emperors wished to take away all images and pictures out of the churches, which the Popes did not wish to have done. There was a great deal of trouble about this matter during the whole of the eighth and ninth centuries, though we hear little about it in England. King Charles held a Council about it, and he and his Bishops agreed that it was lawful to have pictures and images, but that it was wrong to worship them. But the end of the matter was that the Emperors lost the greater part of their dominions in Italy; and though Rome still belonged to them in name, yet it was in name only. The Popes sent for the Kings of the Franks to help them both against the Emperors and against the Lombards. So both Pippin and Charles ruled at Rome, only they were called Patrician, and not King or Emperor. Charles indeed conquered the Lombards altogether, and joined their Kingdom to that of the Franks. So he ruled over all Germany and Gaul and part of Spain and Italy, and most of the nations to the east of Germany were more or less tributary to him. But he did many things besides fighting, for he made many laws, and greatly encouraged learning, and loved to have learned men about him, one of the chief of whom was called Ealhwine or Alcuin, an Englishman. Perhaps you will be surprised when I tell you that this great and wise King could not write. No doubt he could read, but he was not taught to write in his youth; he tried to learn when he was grown up, but he could not manage it. You know that writing was a more difficult business then than it is now, and few people in the West could write besides clergymen, and not all of them. But you must not fancy that because people could not write, it always follows that they could not read.

Now at last the people of Rome got tired of having anything to do with the Emperors at Constantinople. Just at the end of the eighth century the Emperor Constantine the Sixth was deposed by his own mother Eirênê, who put out his eyes and reigned herself. Then Pope Leo and the Romans said that a woman could not be Cæsar and Augustus, and they said that the Old Rome had as much right to choose an Emperor as the New. So they chose King Charles their

Patrician to be Emperor, and he was crowned at Rome by Pope Leo on Christmas Day in the year 800, by the name of Charles Augustus, Emperor of the Romans. And it was held for a thousand years after, down to the year 1806,[1] that the King of the Franks, or as he was afterwards called the King of Germany, had a right to be crowned by the Pope at Rome, and to be called Emperor of the Romans. But the Emperors at Constantinople still went on, and they too still called themselves Emperors of the Romans till the New Rome was taken by the Turks in 1453. Thus from 800 to 1453 there were two Emperors, one in the East and one in the West,[2] both calling themselves Roman Emperors, though the one was really a German and the other really a Greek.[3] Always remember that Charles the Great was a German, and spoke German, and lived mostly at *Aquægrani* or Aachen,[4] where he was buried. I tell you this because people often fancy that because he was King of the Franks, he must have been a Frenchman. But there was no such thing as yet as a French nation or language. Charles, Emperor of the Romans and King of the Franks and Lombards, spoke Latin and German; he understood Greek also, but he could not speak it.

King Charles, as I told you, was not crowned Emperor till the year 800, that is, not till after Offa was dead, so that, while Offa had anything to do with him, he was only King of the Franks and Lombards and Patrician of the Romans. But I thought it right to give you at once a little sketch of so famous

[1] In that year the Emperor Francis the Second, who was also King of Hungary and Archduke of Austria, resigned the Roman Empire and the Kingdom of Germany. Since then no Emperor has been chosen, but the Kings of Hungary have called themselves Emperors of Austria, as if our Queen should call herself Empress of Kent.

[2] There was not always actually an Emperor in the West, because some Kings of Germany were never crowned Emperors at all. But there was always either an Emperor or else a King who had a right to become Emperor, if he could get to Rome and be crowned.

[3] For a while, in the thirteenth century, there were Latin or French Emperors reigning at Constantinople, but the Greeks got the city back again; and while the French were at Constantinople, Greek Emperors still reigned at Nicæa and elsewhere.

[4] Called in French *Aix-la-chapelle*, but it is a pity to call German towns by French names.

a man, and one about whom people generally make so many mistakes, and we shall hear again of the Emperor Charles before we have done. Charles and Offa exchanged letters and gifts more than once, and gave each other's subjects various rights in each other's dominions. And in one of these letters Charles calls himself the most powerful of the Kings of the East, and Offa the most powerful of the Kings of the West. This sounds rather odd, as Offa was rather a King of the North, and one would have thought that the most powerful of the Kings of the East was the Emperor at Constantinople and that the most powerful of the Kings of the West was Charles himself. So Charles and Offa were for the most part very good friends, but they are said to have once had a quarrel in which neither Charles nor Offa seems to have acted very wisely. For when Charles asked Offa to give one of his daughters in marriage to his son Charles, Offa said he would do so only if Charles would give his own favourite daughter to Offa's son Ecgfrith. This made Charles angry, for he did not wish to part with his daughter, and perhaps he may after all have thought himself so much greater than Offa that he did not like to give his daughter to Offa's son. But Alcuin and other wise men reconciled the two Kings before any harm was done, but it does not seem that either of the marriages took place.

Offa is spoken of as being a man in many things not unlike Charles the Great himself. For besides all his fightings and conquests, he took care of other things, encouraging learning and making laws for his people. But I am sorry to say that he was guilty of one very great crime towards the end of his days. In the year 792 it had been settled that Æthelberht, King of the East Angles, should marry Offa's daughter Æthelthryth, but when he came to fetch away his bride, he was murdered in the King's court. Most writers say that this was done by Offa's own order,[1] or at any rate by that of his Queen Cynethryth. If so, Cynethryth acted very like Jezebel and Offa very like Ahab ; for even if he did not himself order Æthelberht's death, he at least took advantage of it to seize on

---

[1] The Chronicle says only that Offa had Æthelberht's head struck off, without any further account.

his Kingdom. As usual, he built churches and monasteries to atone for his wickedness, especially at Hereford, where Æthelberht was buried.[1] Some say that he went on a pilgrimage to Rome ; at any rate he gave much to churches at Rome and especially to the English school there.

Offa died in 794. In 785 he had his son Ecgfrith hallowed as King along with him ; but Ecgfrith reigned only a few months after his father was dead. After him reigned Cenwulf, whose reign was as prosperous as Offa's. He fought much against the Welsh and followed them as far as Snowdon. He had also wars with the Kentishmen and took their King Eadberht Pren prisoner, but afterwards let him go free. He died in 819, and, as far as I can see from the Chronicle, he was succeeded by his brother Ceolwulf ; but some tell a story here, which I may as well tell you.[2]

The Story of Saint Kenelm the little King.

When King Cenwulf died, he left only one son, whose name was Cenhelm, or, as we now write it, Kenelm. He was but a child of seven years, yet men set him on the throne of his father and called him King of the Mercians. Now King Cenwulf had left a daughter, whose name was Cwenthryth. And Cwenthryth envied her little brother, and she hoped that, if he were dead, the people of the Mercians would choose her to

[1] Æthelberht was looked on as a saint, and was held of great account both at Hereford and in his own kingdom. The cathedral church of Hereford was called Saint Æthelberht's minster, and his name is given to one of the great gateways leading to the cathedral at Norwich. That anything should be called after Æthelberht at Norwich shows that he was much thought of long after, for the church of Norwich was not founded till the eleventh century.

[2] The Chronicle has no mention of Cenhelm at all, and makes Ceolwulf succeed Cenwulf at once. But the story is found in Florence of Worcester, whom we generally believe next to the Chronicle. It is hard to see what should have made anybody invent such a tale, if nothing of the kind had ever happened. Yet it is a very unlikely story. For it was not the custom of the English then to choose either children or women to reign over them, so that, if Cenwulf left only a daughter and a young son, it is next to certain that his brother Ceolwulf would have been chosen King.

be Queen of the land. So Cwenthryth spake to Æsceberht, who had the care of the little King, and gave him gifts, and said, "Slay me my brother, that I may reign." So Æsceberht hearkened unto the voice of Cwenthryth, and he took his lord, even Cenhelm the little King, and led him into a wood and slew him, and hid his body in a thicket. Now the same hour men were praying at Rome in the church of Saint Peter. And lo, a white dove flew into the church with a letter, and lighted upon the high altar. And men took the letter from the dove and tried to read it, but they could not, because it was not written in the Latin tongue. And when many had tried to read the letter, at last one took it and read it, for he was an Englishman and he found that the letter was written in the English tongue. And the letter said how that Cenhelm the little King of the Mercians was slain and his body was hid in a thicket. So men told the Pope of this great wonder, and of what things were written in the letter which was brought by the white dove. So the Pope wrote letters to all the Kings of the English that were in Britain, and told them what an evil deed was done in their land. So men went forth to seek for the body of Cenhelm the little King. And as they went they saw a pillar of light shining over a thicket, and in the thicket they found the body of Cenhelm the little King. So they carried his body to Winchelcombe in the land of the Hwiccas, and buried it there in the minster. For they deemed that Cenhelm was an holy child, and they knew that he had been wickedly slain by the guile of his sister Cwenthryth. But over the place where they found his body, they built a chapel, and it is called Saint Kenelm's Chapel [1] unto this day.

Now, however this may be about the little King Cenhelm, it is certain that the next King of the Mercians was Ceolwulf the brother of Cenwulf. But two years afterwards he was driven out by one Beornwulf, and, after that, Mercia was of very little account. In the time of Offa and Cenwulf, it seemed as if Mercia was going to be the head Kingdom of all Britain. But so it was not to be. So I will now go a little way back,

[1] Near Hales Owen in Shropshire.

and tell you some more about the Kings of the West-Saxons. For we are now drawing near to the days of Ecgberht the great Bretwalda, who first made the Kings of the West-Saxons to be lords over all the land of the English.

PART III.

The last King of the West-Saxons whom I told you of was Cynewulf. He was killed in 784 by the Ætheling Cyneheard, a brother of the deposed King Sigeberht, and the Chronicle tells the story of his death at greater length than usual.[1] Cynewulf had ordered Cyneheard to go into banishment, but, instead of going, he gathered a band of men and plainly wished to make himself King. Now one day he heard that King Cynewulf was gone to visit a lady at Merton in Surrey, and had only a few men with him. So Cyneheard came with his men and beset the house where the King was. The King then went to the door, and fought for his life, and when he saw the Ætheling Cyneheard, he smote at him and wounded him, but the Ætheling's men pressed upon the King and slew him. But by this time there was a noise made, and the King's men came running to help him. And the Ætheling offered them great gifts, if they would follow him, but they hearkened not to him, but fought against him till they were all slain, save one, a Welsh hostage, and he was wounded. So Cyneheard the Ætheling seized the town of Merton and locked the gates. But in the morning came Osric the Alderman and Wigferth the King's Thane and many other of the King's men. And they tried to break the gate. Then came Cyneheard the Ætheling and spake boldly to them and said, " Let me be your King and reign over you, and I will give you broad lands and much gold. Ye see that Cynewulf is dead, and ye know that I am of the seed royal. Moreover there are with me many of your kinsfolk and near friends, who have sworn to follow me and to live and die with me." But Osric the Alderman and the men that were with him answered and said unto Cyneheard the Ætheling : " Of

---

[1] It is not however told in the right place, but long before, under the year 755, when Cynewulf began to reign.

a truth our kinsfolk are dear unto us, but no man is so dear unto us as our lord the King, whom thou hast slain." And they spake to their kinsfolk that were with Cyneheard, saying, " Come forth and leave Cyneheard the Ætheling, and not a hair of your heads shall be hurt." But their kinsfolk that were with Cyneheard answered and said, " We will not come forth, neither will we leave Cyneheard the Ætheling. And as for your promises, we will not hearken unto them, even as the men that were with Cynewulf yesterday would not hearken unto our promises." Now when Osric the Alderman and the men that were with him heard that saying, they pressed against the gate and brake it down, and fought against Cyneheard and the men that were with him. And they slew Cyneheard the Ætheling and all his company, even eighty-four men. Save only there was one whom they slew not, for that he was the godson of Osric the Alderman ; yet was he sore wounded. So they buried Cyneheard the Ætheling at Axminster, but King Cynewulf they buried in the royal city, even in Winchester. And the Wise Men chose Beorhtric that was of the seed of Cerdic to reign over them, and he reigned over the land of the West-Saxons sixteen winters.

Now this is a story which you may believe, because it is quite likely in itself, and because it is told in the Chronicle. It is a story worth thinking about, because it shows how much men in those days thought of faith to their own lord, whether he was the King or one in rebellion against the King. You see that both the King's men and the Ætheling's men were alike ready to die for their own chief.

King Beorhtric married Eadburh, a daughter of King Offa, of whom many stories are told, some of which I will tell you presently. But the chief thing which I read about in his reign in the Chronicle is that it was in his time that the Danes or Northmen first began to land and plunder in England, or at any rate in Wessex. You will hear a great deal more of these Northmen for a long time to come. The truth is that the time was now come when the English, in a great part of England, were to be dealt with in much the same way as their forefathers had dealt with the Welsh. That is to say, the country was gradually overrun by men from another land, and a great part of it was

settled by them. But the men who thus came in and partly conquered the English were not a people utterly strange to them,
as the English were to the Welsh. They were the people of
the North of Europe, whence they were called the Northmen,
people of our own race, speaking a Teutonic tongue like ourselves, and worshipping nearly the same Gods as the English
had worshipped before they became Christians. In truth, for
about two hundred years from this time, the Northmen played
much the same part as the Angles and Saxons had played three
hundred years earlier. They were always sailing about in their
ships, plundering by sea, plundering by land, and at last conquering and settling down in various parts of Europe, especially
Britain, Ireland, Gaul, and Russia. They also found out the
island of Iceland and the continent of Greenland. But this
was not till a good while after. We are now only at the very
beginning of the invasions of the Northmen, and at this time
they do not seem to have cared to settle anywhere, but only to
plunder and go away again. In their own country, in the
North, they gradually formed three Kingdoms, Denmark,
Sweden, and Norway. If you look at the map, you will see,
that we in Britain could not have much to do with the Swedes;
their conquests were made to the east, towards Russia. It
was naturally the Danes and Norwegians who came westward,
and those who came into England seem to have been mainly
Danes. So our writers often speak of the Northmen generally as
Danes, without taking much heed whether they all came from
Denmark or not. I suppose the Danes now must have been
much in the same state as the Angles and Saxons were when
they came into Britain. Perhaps they were somewhat stronger
and fiercer, but we can hardly tell, because we know so much
more of what the Danes did to our forefathers than we know
of what our forefathers had done to the Welsh. The Danes
were heathens, just as the English had been, and they seem to
have had a special hatred towards the Christian faith and towards all that belonged to it, and to have had a special delight
in destroying the churches and monasteries. And they did
many other cruel and horrible things at the time. But when
they had once settled in the land and had become Christians,
their language and manners differed so little from those of the

English that the Danes and the English soon became one
people. There is no doubt a great deal of Danish blood in all
the north and east of England, but the Danes and the English
did not remain as two separate nations in the way that the
English and Welsh did, so that the Danes may rather be said to
have become another tribe of Englishmen just like the Angles
and the Saxons. I think we may divide the Danish inroads into
three periods : First, When they merely landed to plunder and
then went away again. Secondly, When they came to conquer
some part of the land and to settle in it. Thirdly, When
Kings of all Denmark came to conquer the Kingdom of
England and to make themselves Kings of it. As yet we
have to do only with the first of these periods.

We first read of the landing of the Northmen in 787, the
year that Beorhtric married Eadburh. The crews of three
ships landed on the coast of Dorsetshire. When the reeve[1]
or magistrate who lived at Dorchester heard of it, he rode
down to the shore, and, as he did not know who the strangers
were, he ordered them to be taken to the King's town. Upon
this the Danes turned about and slew the reeve and all his
men. Soon after this we read a good deal of their inroads in
Northumberland. Most likely the invasions of the Northmen,
by helping to weaken the smaller Kingdoms, did a good deal
towards uniting all England under the West-Saxon Kings.

I must now first mention a very famous name, that of
Ecgberht, the great King of the West-Saxons, who was the
first to be lord of all England. We first hear of him in
Beorhtric's time, when we are told that Offa and Beorhtric
drove him out of the land for thirteen years,[2] which thirteen
years he spent in the land of the Franks where the great King
Charles reigned. When we are told that Offa helped to drive

---

[1] *Gerefa* or *reeve* means a King's officer of any sort, great or small.
Thus we have the *Scirgerefa*, the *Shire-reeve* or *Sheriff*, the *Port-reeve* or
Mayor of a town, and so on, down to the *Dykereeves*, who look after the
cleaning of the rhines in our moors. And in the English-speaking part of
Scotland a steward is called a *Grieve*. *Gerefa* is the same word as the
German *Graf;* but that title has risen in the world, while *Gerefa* has
fallen.

[2] The text of the Chronicle has *three* years, but it seems clear that this
must be a mis-writing for *thirteen.*

him out, it sounds as if Offa were afraid that he might stand in
the way of his daughter Eadburh's children, if she had any.
However this may be, when Beorhtric died in the year 800, the
same year that King Charles was crowned Emperor, the Wise
Men chose the Ætheling Ecgberht to be King of the West-
Saxons. And we read that the very same day there was a
fight at Kempsford in Gloucestershire between the Alderman
of the Hwiccas and the Alderman of the Wilsætas, and that
the Wilsætas had the victory. This was like the beginning of
the conquests of Ecgberht.

But before I tell you more of the reign of Ecgberht, I will
tell you the story of Queen Eadburh, as I find it in later
writers.[1]

The Story of Queen Eadburh.

Now Eadburh was the daughter of Offa the great King of the
Mercians, and she became the wife of Beorhtric the King of
the West-Saxons. But she was a proud woman and cruel, and
loved to have all power in her own hands. So when any man
withstood her or offended her, she told lies of him to the King,
that he might be put to death ; or if this might not be, she put
him to death herself by poison. Now there was a young
Alderman whom the King loved, whose name was Worr.[2] So
Queen Eadburh mixed her a cup of poison that Worr might
drink of the same and die. And he drank of the cup and
died. Moreover Beorhtric the King drank of the cup also, for
he wist not that there was death in the cup. And Beorhtric the
King died also. Then were all the people of the West-Saxons
very wroth against Eadburh the Queen, and they drove her out
of the land. Moreover they made a law that there should no

---

[1] The story is in William of Malmesbury, and also in Asser's Life of
King Alfred, the writer of which professes to have been told the story by
King Alfred himself. I shall speak more of Asser's book presently.
[2] The Chronicle mentions the deaths of Beorhtric and Worr in the
same year, as if they had something to do with one another. Asser and
William of Malmesbury speak of the young man whom Eadburh poisoned
without mentioning his name. Hence they have been generally thought
to be the same person.

more be a Queen in the land of the West-Saxons, because of the evil deeds that Eadburh the Queen had done. So the King's wife was no more called the Queen, but only the Lady, and she sat no more on a throne royal by the side of her husband, as the Queen of the West-Saxons had done of old time. And Eadburh, when she was driven out, crossed the sea and went into the land of the Franks to Charles Augustus the Emperor.[1]   And she found the Emperor standing with one of his sons, and she spake unto him and gave him gifts. Now Charles the Emperor was a merry man and loved to laugh and sport withal. So he said unto Eadburh, " Lo, Eadburh, here am I, and there is my son ; choose one of us twain that he may be thy husband." Then said Eadburh, " O Lord Cæsar, thou art old and thy son is young ; give me rather thy son, that he may be my husband." Then Charles the Emperor laughed again and said, " If thou hadst chosen me who am old, I would even have given thee my son who is young ; but since thou hast chosen my son, thou shalt have neither me nor my son." Moreover Charles the Emperor sent Eadburh to a monastery of virgins and bade her be their Abbess and rule over them. But she ruled over them ill and did wickedly in all things. So Charles the Emperor took her Abbey away from her that she might rule it no longer. And she went forth with only one slave to wander through the land. And she came to the city of Pavia, which is the royal city of the Lombards ; and there she begged her bread till she died. And in the days of King Alfred, who reigned over the West-Saxons and who was lord over all the Kings of the English, there were many men yet living who had seen Eadburh, the daughter of King Offa and wife of King Beorhtric, begging her bread.

And now I have come to the reign of Ecgberht, the great Bretwalda.   He was an Ætheling of the blood of Cerdic, and he is said to have been son of Ealhmund, and Ealhmund is

---

[1] As Beorhtric died and Charles became Emperor in the same year, Charles may have been only King when Eadburh came to him.   Asser indeed calls him " Francorum Rex."   But he may not have met him till the next year, when Charles was Emperor.

said to have been an Under-king of Kent. For the old line of the Kings of Kent had come to an end, and Kent was now sometimes under Wessex and sometimes under Mercia. I have told you how he spent thirteen years in banishment, and how, when Beorhtric died in 800, he was chosen King of the West-Saxons. He reigned till 836, and in that time he brought all the English Kingdoms, and the greater part of Britain, more or less under his power. The southern part of the island, all Kent, Sussex, and Essex, he joined on to his own Kingdom. and set his sons or other Æthelings to reign over them as his Under-kings. But Northumberland, Mercia, and East-Anglia were not brought so completely under his power as this. Their Kings submitted to Ecgberht and acknowledged him as their Over-lord, but they went on reigning in their own Kingdoms, and assembling their own Wise Men, just as they did before. They became what in after times was called his *vassals*, what in English was called being his *men*. They owed him a certain obedience as their lord, but they were not appointed by him or interfered with at all as long as they were faithful to him. But the other Kingdoms were rather what were afterwards called *apanages*, which he could keep in his own hands or grant out as he pleased. And besides the English Kings, Ecgberht brought the Welsh, both in Wales and in Cornwall, more completely under his power. But amidst all this greatness the Northmen often came, and sometimes they not only plundered, but defeated the English in battle. Now we cannot help thinking that in all that Ecgberht did he had before his eyes the model of the great Emperor at whose court he had lived so long. As Charles had joined Germany together, so Ecgberht did a great deal to join England together. As Charles had various nations besides his own Germans more or less under his power, so Ecgberht had the Welsh under his power. As Charles made his sons Kings under him over some of the lands which he conquered, so did Ecgberht. And lastly, both had to do with the terrible Northmen who were beginning to trouble the world. For though the Northmen did not do much damage in Germany and Gaul during Charles' own lifetime, yet they began their inroads, and did enough to show what they were likely to do in days to come. With the

Danes along their own border, along the river Eyder (which from Charles' time till 1866 separated Germany from Denmark), Charles had a great deal of fighting, and Northern pirates had begun to ravage the coasts of Gaul even while Charles was alive. So altogether the reign of Ecgberht was very like the reign of Charles on a small scale. Ecgberht made the West-Saxons the first people in Britain, much as Charles made the Franks the first people on the continent of Europe. Even Ecgberht being called Bretwalda was something like Charles being called Emperor; for the Bretwalda was much the same in Britain as the Emperor was in the rest of Western Europe. But I must now tell you some of the things which happened in Ecgberht's reign rather more in order.

Ecgberht's first wars were with the Welsh of Cornwall. He ravaged their country in 813, and it was perhaps then that Devonshire was conquered. Devonshire was certainly English ten years after, as in 823 we read that the men of Devonshire defeated the Welsh in a battle at Gafulford. Cornwall itself seems to have become tributary, but it certainly was not thoroughly conquered. For we shall often hear of the Welsh of Cornwall again, and I have told you that the Cornishmen kept their own Welsh language for many hundred years after this time, and the names of most of the places and people in Cornwall are Welsh to this day. Indeed even in Ecgberht's own time the Cornishmen revolted again with the help of the Danes, and ravaged the English country. But Ecgberht came and defeated them both in a great battle at a place called Hengest's-down (Hengestesdun). This was in the year before he died, in 835.

Thus far Ecgberht was only extending his own Kingdom of Wessex to the West, as Cenwealh and Ine had done before him. But he also did much more than they had ever done, for he gradually brought all the other English Kingdoms under his own power. His first wars were with the Mercians, with part of whom you will remember there was a battle the very day that he was chosen King. But we do not read much about Mercian wars till 823. In 821 one Beornwulf had turned out Ceolwulf, the last King of the Mercians that I told you of. I do not find how the war between him and Ecgberht

began ; but in 823 there was a great battle at a place called
Ællandun or Ælla's Down, and if that be, as some place it,
near Salisbury, it is clear that Beornwulf must have got a long
way into Ecgberht's dominions. It was a very hard battle, and
Hun the Alderman of the Sumorsætas was killed ; but at last
the West-Saxons won. There were songs made about it, of
which we find little scraps in some of our books. And one
chronicle written in rhyme a long time afterwards says :

> Ellandune, Ellandune, thy land is full red
> Of the blood of Bernewolf : there he took his dede (death).

Beornwulf however did not die at Ællandun, but was only defeated and fled. When Ecgberht had thus weakened Mercia,
he thought he might get back the lordship over the smaller
Kingdoms, which had once belonged to the West-Saxons, but
which the Mercians had lately held. So he sent his son
Æthelwulf with Ealhstan Bishop of Sherborne and Wulf-
heard the Alderman, and they drove out Baldred the King of
Kent, seemingly without any fighting. Then all the people of
Kent, Surrey, Sussex, and Essex submitted themselves willingly
to Ecgberht : for in most of those Kingdoms the line of the
old Kings had come to an end, and they did not care for the
new Kings who rose up of themselves, or whom the Kings of
the Mercians had put in. So they were quite willing to be
under Ecgberht, especially as his father had once been King of
Kent. And no doubt the people in Essex and Sussex, being
Saxons, liked the West-Saxons better than the Angles of Mercia,
and felt more akin to them. Thus you see Ecgberht was now
King of all the Saxons and Jutes, that is of all England south of
the Thames, and of Essex to the north of it. And if he had
Essex, he could hardly fail to have had also the great city of
London. Ecgberht, having got this large dominion, made his
son Æthelwulf King of Kent under him.

This was hardly done when the King of the East-Angles,
whose name we do not know, begged Ecgberht to come and
help him against the Mercians, who were greatly oppressing
him and his people. We can well believe that the East-
Angles had sorely hated the Mercians ever since their King
Æthelberht had been so treacherously killed by Offa. So

H

Ecgberht said he would help them. On this Beornwulf went against the East-Angles, swearing that he would destroy them utterly ; but the East-Angles stood up against him and fought a battle in which he was killed. The next King of the Mercians, Ludeca, came the next year, and was killed also, with five of his Aldermen. It does not seem clear whether the West-Saxons actually helped the East-Angles in this war, but one can hardly think that the East-Angles could have done so much all by themselves. At any rate, in 827, Ecgberht drove the next King of the Mercians, Wiglaf, out of his Kingdom and only let him come back as his man next year. Meanwhile Ecgberht had gone up towards Northumberland, but the Northumbrians met him at Dore in Derbyshire, just on the borders of Northumberland and Mercia, and submitted to him without any fighting. Northumberland was just now very weak ; for a long time various Kings had been rising and falling, whose names I need not give you, so the Northumbrians were not at all able to withstand Ecgberht.

Ecgberht was thus Lord over all the other English Kings, and the submission of Mercia seems to have led to the submission of the Welsh in what we now call Wales. Cenwulf of Mercia seems to have done a great deal to subdue them. The Welsh Chronicles tell us that in 816 he got as far as Snowdon, which the Welsh call Ereri, and in 819, the year of his death, he harried Dyfed or Pembrokeshire. And in 822 Beornwulf conquered Powys, the middle part of Wales on the borders of Mercia. So after the Mercians had submitted to Ecgberht, it is no wonder that we read that in 828, when he led his army into Wales, all the country submitted to him. Thus you see that Ecgberht had a greater power than any King that had ever been in Britain before him. For he was King of all the Saxons and Jutes, and Lord over all the Angles and at any rate over the most part of the Welsh. I say the most part, because I do not find anything said about the Strathclyde Welsh or about the Scots. They had, as you know, sometimes been more or less under the Kings of the Northumbrians ; but it is not likely that they had been so lately while Northumberland was in such disorder. But you must never forget that Northumberland then took in a great deal of what is now Scotland, namely all Lothian, with King Edwin's Castle, which is Edinburgh. So King Ecgberht was Lord from the Irish Sea to the German Ocean and from the English Channel to the Firth of Forth. So it is not wonderful if, in his charters, he not only called himself King of the West-Saxons or King of the West-Saxons and Kentishmen, but sometimes *Rex Anglorum* or King of the English.

But amidst all this glory there were the signs of great evils at hand. The Danes came several times. In 832 they ravaged Sheppey in Kent. The next year thirty-five ships came to Charmouth in Dorsetshire, where they fought King Ecgberht himself and defeated him. But in neither case do they seem to have made any attempt to stay in the land. And, as you know, in 835 Ecgberht beat the Welsh and the Danes together in the great battle at Hengestesdun.

The next year, 836, King Ecgberht died, and his son Æthelwulf, the King of Kent, was chosen King of the West-Saxons. And he gave his Kingdom of Kent, with Sussex, Surrey, and Essex, to Æthelstan his son.

CHAPTER VIII.

HOW THE DANES CAME INTO ENGLAND, AND HOW ENGLAND BECAME ONE KINGDOM.

I HAVE now told you the chief things which you need know about the history of our people down to the time when, under King Ecgberht, the West-Saxons became for ever the chief people of Britain, and their Kings became Lords over all the other princes of the island. I have told you how the English first came into Britain, how they won the land bit by bit from the Welsh, how they founded several Kingdoms, seven and more, how they became Christians, how sometimes one Kingdom and sometimes another had the chief power over the rest, and how at last that chief power became fixed in the hands of the Kings of the West-Saxons. A wise man might have been quite sure from the beginning that, sooner or later, all the different English Kingdoms would get joined together, but it was not at all clear which would be the one to get the upper hand over the rest. And till Ecgberht began to reign, perhaps nobody would have thought that Wessex was to be the head Kingdom. And it is worth while to stop and think what a great difference it has made to us that the chief power did come to Wessex rather than to any of the other Kingdoms. Let us suppose, for instance, that Northumberland had kept at the head, as it was in the days of King Edwin. We may be sure that, had it been so, two things at least would have been very different from what they are now. Our language, which is now much more Saxon than Anglian, would be much more Anglian than Saxon ; it would be more like what is now spoken in the Lowlands of Scotland. And we may be sure too that York would be the capital instead of London. Now if the

chief power had thus been placed in the north, most likely
Scotland would have been joined to England much sooner
than it was ; but on the other hand, through the chief power
being in the south, in the part nearest to the continent, England
has been able to take a much greater share in the general affairs
of Europe than it otherwise could have taken. You will find, as
you read more of history, that the importance of a country
depends very much on its position as well as on its size. Norway and Portugal, and Scotland while it was a separate Kingdom, were never of much account in Europe,[1] not only because
they were smaller than most other Kingdoms, but because they
were, so to speak, so far out of the way. Much smaller states,
and even single cities, if they were near the middle of Europe,
were thought much more of. I do not know whether you can
quite understand all that I have been just now saying, but I
think you can understand that it has made a great difference to
us that the chief power was fixed in the south of England and
not in the north. It is only quite lately, since so much of
trade and manufacture and mining has arisen in the north of
England, that the north has been of at all the same account as
the south. Perhaps now the north is of more account than the
south. But it is only quite lately that it has become so, and
the south of England was of much more account than the
north for many hundred years, and the reason doubtless was
because the chief power among the Old-English Kingdoms
came into the hands of Ecgberht of Wessex.

Another thing that I told you was how the Danes and other
Northmen were now beginning to come into England. A
great deal of what I shall have to tell you now will have to
be about the wars which the West-Saxon Kings had to wage
with these Danes, and about the way in which many of the
Danes at last settled in the land and became Englishmen.
And you must remember that the Danes, even while fighting
against the West-Saxon Kings, did in a manner help them to
become Kings of the whole land. This they did by weakening
and destroying the smaller Kingdoms. You will remember

---

[1] Whatever importance Scotland had came from the fact that the French
Kings were cunning enough to see that Scotland was an useful ally for
them against England.

that, under Ecgberht, Northumberland, Mercia, and East-Anglia still had Kings of their own, though their Kings were the *vassals*, or, as in Old-English it was called, the *men* of the King of the West-Saxons. But when we get to the end of the time of which I am now beginning to tell you, we shall find that the King of the West-Saxons has grown into the one King of the English. You will see that the question then was not whether the King of the West-Saxons or the King of the Mercians should have the upper hand in England, but whether the King of the English could defend his Kingdom, first against the King of the Danes and then against the Duke of the Normans.

I will now go on with the Kings of the West-Saxons who reigned after Ecgberht, though they were not Kings of any great account till we come to Alfred the Great, Ecgberht's grandson.

§ 1. THE REIGN OF KING ÆTHELWULF.

I have told you already that Ecgberht died in 836, and that his son Æthelwulf was chosen King of the West-Saxons, and that he gave the Kingdom of Kent and the other small states to his brother Æthelstan. Æthelwulf reigned twenty-two years, and died in 858. His reign was very much taken up with fighting with the Danes, who were always landing in different parts of the country. In 839 they got as far as London, and in 851 they seem to have taken or, as the Chronicle calls it, "broken," both Canterbury and London, and defeated Beorhtwulf King of the Mercians. And in 855 they wintered for the first time in the Isle of Sheppey. King Æthelwulf and his Aldermen had to fight many battles with them, in which sometimes the English had the better, and sometimes the Danes. I need tell you of only two of these battles. In 845 there was a battle at the mouth of the Parret, the river on which Bridgewater stands, when Eanwulf the Alderman of the Sumorsætas, Osric the Alderman of the Dorsætas, and Ealhstan the Bishop of Sherborne, with all the folk of their two shires, fought against the heathen men and smote them. Again in 851 there was another battle at Aclea or Ockley (that is Oak-lea) in Surrey, where King Æthelwulf himself and his son Æthelbald also fought against the Danes who had taken London, and smote them there. Bishop Ealhstan was a very famous Bishop in the time of Æthelwulf, and so was Swithhun Bishop of Winchester, who is said to have been Æthelwulf's tutor. This is Saint Swithhun about whom and whose day such strange stories are told. But of Swithhun we do not read anything except what seems to become the office of a Bishop, while you see that our Bishop Ealhstan fought in the battles just as much as a lay Alderman.

I must also tell you that in 853 Burhred the King of the Mercians with his Wise Men sent to their lord King Æthelwulf to ask for help against the North Welsh, who were troubling them at one end while the Danes were troubling them at another. So King Æthelwulf went forth with his army, and made the Welsh submit again to the King of the Mercians. Soon after this he gave King Burhred his daughter Æthelswyth to wife.

Now there are some parts of the reign of Æthelwulf which I feel some difficulty about. I always like to give you the authority for what I tell you, that you may know what you may believe quite certainly and what is doubtful. Now King Æthelwulf was the father of Alfred the Great, and the latter part of Æthelwulf's history is much mixed up with that of his son. I have told you that there is a book which professes to be the Life of Alfred written by Bishop Asser his great friend. Now if we could be sure that this was really written by Asser, this would be among our best authorities for these times. But it seems hardly possible that all of it could have been written by Asser, because it contains some things which there seems hardly any way of piecing on to the real history. Still it is most likely that it is Asser's book, only with some things put in afterwards by somebody else, as often happened. And I have one reason for thinking that most of it must be Asser's, which perhaps would not come into your heads. Asser was a Welshman ; now the writer of this book calls the English " Saxons," just as a Welshman would do both then and now, but as no Englishman in those days would have thought of doing.[1] Still,

---

[1] It might be said that a forger might imitate this custom to make his book look like a Welshman's book ; but this is very unlikely. And it

however this may be, we cannot put the same trust in the book called Asser as we do in the Chronicle, so that, in telling you my history, I shall always mark what is in the Chronicle and what is only in Asser.[1] I have been somewhat long about this matter, because most of the well-known stories about King Alfred, some of which I dare say you have heard already, come out of Asser. I shall therefore tell you them as tales, as I have done the other tales about which we cannot be quite certain.

In 853 King Æthelwulf sent his youngest son Alfred, who was then four years old, to Rome, where we read, what seems a very strange thing, that Pope Leo not only took him for his "bishop's son" or godchild, but hallowed him as a King. For it is hard to understand what a Pope could have to do with hallowing a King of the West-Saxons, or again how Æthelwulf could be certain that Alfred, his youngest son, ever would be King. However so it is said in one of the Chronicles. Two years afterwards Æthelwulf gave a tenth of his lands to the Church,[2] and then went to Rome himself. You may remember that both Ceadwalla and Ine had done this, but then they gave up the Kingdom and stayed at Rome for the rest of their days, but Æthelwulf only went on what is called a pilgrimage, to see the holy places and to pray at them, and after a year's time he came home again. On his way back he married Judith the daughter of Charles the Bald, King of the West-Franks. This Charles was grandson of Charles the Great, and was afterwards Emperor himself for a little while. Charles the Great was succeeded in the Empire by his son Lewis the Pious, during whose reign and after his death there was much quarrelling among his sons about dividing his dominions. At last they settled that the eldest son Lothar should be Emperor, and should have the great cities of Rome and Aachen, with a long narrow strip of

cannot be a forgery of quite late times, because a great deal of it is copied by Florence of Worcester, who lived at the beginning of the twelfth century.

[1] I shall quote the book as Asser, but without meaning to pledge myself to the genuineness of this or that part.

[2] Or perhaps charged his own lands with the payment of a tithe; but there is nothing at all to show that he laid any charge on the lands of other men.

country reaching from the Mediterranean Sea to the German Ocean. This land was called from Lothar, *Lotharingia*, and a small part of it is called *Lorraine* still. Lothar, as Emperor, was to have a certain supremacy over his brothers, Charles and Lewis, who were to reign to the west and east of him. This was the beginning of the modern Kingdoms of France and Germany, but the separation was not fully made till more than a hundred years after this time, and the Kingdom of the West-Franks under Charles the Bald was not nearly so large as France is now. Charles himself still spoke German, and so did the Kings of the West-Franks after him for a long while, but the French language seems to have been just beginning in his time ; for we have an oath which was taken by the soldiers of Charles and the soldiers of Lewis, each in their own tongue. The soldiers of Lewis of course swear in Old German, but the soldiers of Charles swear in what you would call a very strange language, something which one may say has left off being Latin, and which has not yet become French.

Now the Chronicle tells us only that Æthelwulf married King Charles's daughter and came safe home, and that his people received him gladly and that he died two years after. But the story in Asser tells us a great deal more, which is not in itself unlikely to be true, but which, if it is true, it is strange that the Chronicle should have quite left out.[1] We read there that Æthelbald, now the eldest son of Æthelwulf, conspired with Bishop Ealhstan and Alderman Eanwulf to keep his father out of the land, and that they made this conspiracy in Selwood, the great forest on the borders of the Sumorsætas and the Wilsætas, whence the town of Frome is called Frome Selwood. Most part of the great men of the land however were faithful to King Æthelwulf, but he, rather than have a civil war with his son, gave up to Æthelbald the Kingdom of the West-Saxons[2] and kept only the Kingdom of Kent and the other

---

[1] This part of Asser is copied by Florence of Worcester ; but Æthelwerd and Henry of Huntingdon follow the Chronicle.

[2] That Æthelbald was King for some time before his father's death seems clear, because the Chronicle says that he reigned five years, and it is plain that he could not have reigned five years *after* his father's death. But this does not prove that he rebelled against him. Æthelwulf may

lands which went with it.   It would seem that his eldest
son Æthelstan, the Under-king of Kent, was now dead, as we
hear no more about him.   King Æthelwulf, we are also told,
brought home his wife Judith, and set her by his side on a
royal throne, no man gainsaying him.   You will remember that
it is said that, after Eadburh had done such evil deeds, the
West-Saxons made a law that the King's wife should not be
Queen or sit on a royal throne.   If this story is true, it may
be that this law did not hold good in Kent, so that Judith
might be Queen there, though not in Wessex.

Before Æthelwulf died, he seems to have made a will
dividing his dominions, and, as we should say, settling the succession.   As this will was confirmed by the Wise Men, it was
much the same as an election made during the King's lifetime.
This was not often done in England, but it was very common
in Germany.   Æthelwulf then left the Kingdom of Wessex to
his sons Æthelbald, Æthelred, and Alfred in order, and Kent
to Æthelberht, who was not to have any right to the Kingdom
of Wessex.

King Æthelwulf died in 858 and was buried at Winchester.

§ 2. The Reign of King Æthelbald.
858—860.

Æthelbald succeeded his father, but he only reigned a little
while, and we read very little of him.   He married his father's
widow Judith,[1] as Eadbald of Kent had done long before with
his father's widow.   Such a marriage, I need not tell you, is
held unlawful among Christians, but it seems to have been an
old custom with some of the heathen Germans.   He died in
860 and was buried at Sherborne; he is said[2] to have been

very likely have joined him to himself in the Kingdom when he took his
journey to Rome.

[1] This is not in the Chronicle, but besides Asser, it is told us by two
good writers in Gaul, Prudentius of Troyes and Hincmar of Rheims.   This
shows us that some of the things in Asser which are not in the Chronicle
may be true, though we must be careful how we admit them.

[2] So says Henry of Huntingdon, whose account, as it often does, reads
like a scrap of an old ballad.

much lamented by his people. His widow[1] Judith then sold all that she had in England and went back to her father's court. She afterwards married a certain Baldwin, who became the first Count of Flanders. Baldwin was afterwards a very common name among the Counts of Flanders, so that the English sometimes called Flanders *Baldwinesland*. From this Baldwin and Judith was descended Matilda the wife of William the Conqueror, so that William's sons and all our Kings since them descended in the female line from Charles the Great, as we shall see that they also did from Ecgberht.

§ 3. The Reign of King Æthelberht.
860—866.

According to Æthelwulf's will, Æthelred ought now to have succeeded, but somehow or other, we are not told how, Æthelberht, King of Kent, came to the crown. Perhaps it was thought better that Wessex and Kent should be joined together. He too reigned only a little time, and he had much trouble with the Danes. We are now getting near the second period of the Danish invasion, when, instead of merely plundering, they began to try to settle in the land. In Æthelberht's time we read how they ravaged Thanet, and how another time they took Winchester the royal city, but the Aldermen of Hamptonshire[2] (which we now call Hampshire) and Berkshire came and smote them. King Æthelberht died in 866 and was buried at Sherborne.

§ 4. The Reign of King Æthelred the First.
866—871.

Æthelred now came to the crown. Nearly all that I have to tell you about his reign is taken up with fightings with the

---

[1] There seems no authority for saying that Bishop Swithhun made Æthelbald put her away. Hincmar calls her his widow (*relicta*).

[2] From Hampton, that is *South* Hampton, to distinguish it from *North* Hampton in Mercia. We now generally write the names in one word, *Northampton* and *Southampton*.

Danes. As you read or hear about them, you will do well to have your map always open before you, and to track the march of the armies and see what parts of England suffered most in these wars. Though the Danes were coming into England and trying to settle during the whole of Æthelred's reign, they did not come into Wessex just at first. So the only thing we hear of in Wessex during the first two years of Æthelred is the death of two men whom you have heard of several times, Bishop Ealhstan and Alderman Eanwulf. They both died in 867. Ealhstan, who had been Bishop fifty years, was buried in his own church at Sherborne; the Alderman of the Sumorsætas was buried at Glastonbury, as the greatest church of his shire.

Meanwhile the great Danish invasion had begun in the northern parts of England. There are many stories told in the old Northern Songs as to the cause of it. Some tell how Ragnar Lodbrog, a great hero of these Northern tales, was seized by Ælla King of the Northumbrians, and was thrown into a dungeon full of serpents, and how, while he was dying of the bites of the serpents, he sang a wonderful death-song, telling of all his old fights, and calling on his sons to come and avenge him. Others tell how Lodbrog, with only his hawk on his hand, was driven by a storm to the coast of East-Anglia; how Beorn, the huntsman of King Edmund, slew him; how King Edmund then put Beorn into a boat and let it drift on the sea; how the boat drifted to Denmark, and how Beorn made the sons of Lodbrog believe that it was King Edmund who had slain their father, and bade him come and avenge him. Others tell how the King of the Northumbrians took away the wife of one of his subjects from him, and how the husband went to Denmark, and bade the Danes come and avenge him.[1] Some of these stories may be true, and the tale of Ragnar Lodbrog is a very grand and famous story. Still they are only stories; what we really know is this. When the Danes began to come in Æthelred's time, Edmund was King

---

[1] This story is told in two ways. One makes the man a merchant of York, the other a Thane called Beorn; one calls the King Ælla, the other Osberht; one makes him bring in the sons of Ragnar Lodbrog, the other makes him bring in Guthorm or Guthrum, of whom we shall hear more before long.

in East-Anglia and Burhred in Mercia, while in Northumberland the King Osberht had just been deposed, and Ælla, who
was not of the kingly house, had been set up instead. The
Danes came first in 866 into East-Anglia, where they passed
the winter, the people having made peace with them. Next
year they crossed the Humber-mouth into Northumberland
and took York. The Northumbrians were too much divided
among themselves to do much at first; but after a while the
two Kings agreed and went with all their men against the
Danes. They got into the town, but both the Kings were
killed and many of their people, and the rest made peace with
the Danes. The Danes then set up one Ecgberht as King in
Northumberland, but he seems to have been a mere puppet in
their hands, and he was allowed to reign only in the country
north of the Tyne, the old Kingdom of Bernicia.[1] It would
almost seem as if they kept York and all the southern part of
Northumberland to themselves. Then in 868 the Danes got
into Mercia as far as Nottingham; so King Burhred sent to
his brothers-in-law, King Æthelred and the Ætheling Alfred,
to come and help him. So they went with their West-Saxons
as far as Nottingham, but there was no great fight, and the
Mercians too made peace with the Danes.

One hardly knows what this making peace with the Danes
means. Where it did not mean actual submission, it could at
most have meant merely giving them presents to go away for a
time. For, though the Northumbrians had made peace, we
find the Danes next year (869) at York, and in 870 they ride
through Mercia into East-Anglia. This invasion of East-Anglia
is a very important one in two ways. It was a real conquest;
the Danes took complete possession of the country, and made
it into a Danish Kingdom. The native East-Anglian Kings
came to an end, and the utmost that the West-Saxon Kings
could do for a long time was to try and get the same lordship
over the Danish Kings in East-Anglia which they had before
held over the native Kings. Thus we get the first distinct
Danish settlement in England.[2] This invasion should also be

---

[1] It is probably from this that the word Northumberland got its later
and narrower sense, meaning the country north of the Tyne.

[2] Yet it is certain that Danish names of places and the like are more

remembered, because of the famous story of the martyrdom of King Edmund, who is therefore known as Saint Edmund.[1] We are told that the Danish chiefs, Ingwar and Hubba, wintered at Thetford, and then King Edmund fought against them, but was beaten and taken prisoner. They then offered him his life and kingdom, if he would forsake Christianity and reign under them. When he refused, they tied him to a tree and shot at him with arrows, and at last cut off his head. So you may suppose that Saint Edmund has ever since been greatly reverenced, especially in his own Kingdom. In the churches of Norfolk and Suffolk you often see pictures of him pierced with arrows, especially on the rood-screens which divide the nave from the chancel. The Danes at the same time killed Hunberht the Bishop of the East-Angles, but he seems to have been almost forgotten in the fame of the King.

The Danes then ravaged the country, especially burning the churches and monasteries. They then went on into Mercia doing the same. They burned and broke down the great minster at Medeshamstead, which is now called Peterborough, and slew the Abbot and his monks. They did the like at Crowland, which is not far from Peterborough, many of the great abbeys in that country having been built on islands in the fen country, as Glastonbury is here. There is a very particular account of the destruction of Crowland, if we could only believe it, in the book which is called Abbot Ingulf's History of Crowland. Ingulf lived in the time of William the Conqueror, but it is quite certain that he did not write the book which is called by his name. Many things show that it must

common in some other parts of England, as in Yorkshire and Lincolnshire, than they are in East-Anglia. But perhaps this may be for the very reason that East-Anglia was the first complete Danish conquest. As it was conquered so easily, it is not unlikely that it was really less ravaged, and the English inhabitants less disturbed, than in some other parts. In other parts, even if the English were not driven out as the Welsh had been before them, yet at least the chief property in the land must have passed into the hands of Danes. I mean those parts where most of the places bear the names of Danish occupiers, Haconby, Kettilby, and such like. These names are very common in Lincolnshire, but are hardly found in East-Anglia.

[1] You must not confound this Saint Edmund the King with another Saint Edmund, who was Archbishop of Canterbury in the thirteenth century.

have been written several hundred years later. Still it is possible that whoever did write it may have worked in many stories from the old traditions and records of the Abbey; and though a great deal is certainly false, yet some things may be true. Anyhow you will like to hear how, while all the monks of Crowland were being killed, Thurgar, a boy of ten years old, had first seen Lentwine the sub-prior killed and thought he should die too; and how the younger *Jarl*[1] Sidroc pitied him, for he was so young and fair, and spared him, and took off his little monk's coat and put on him a Danish garment. So the young Thurgar hid himself and escaped, and lived to tell men all that he had seen when the Danes burned the minster at Crowland.

The next year, 871, the Danes for the first time entered Wessex. But as yet we hear of them only in the eastern part of the Kingdom, in Berkshire, Hampshire, and Surrey. The first place they came to was Reading, which of course was then a frontier town on the borders of Mercia. Nine great battles, besides smaller skirmishes, were fought this year, in some of which the English won and in others the Danes. First, Alderman Æthelwulf fought the Danes at Englefield in Berkshire, and beat them, killing one of their Earls. Four days after that there was another battle at Reading, where King Æthelred and Alfred the Ætheling and Alderman Æthelwulf all fought, but the Danes had the better of it and Æthelwulf was killed. Four days afterwards there was another more famous battle at Æscesdun or Ashdown, also in Berkshire. We are told that the heathen men were in two divisions; one was commanded by their two Kings Bagsecg and Halfdene, and the other by five Earls, Sidroc the Old, Sidroc the Young, Osbearn, Fræna, and Harold. And King Æthelred was set against the Kings and Alfred the Ætheling against the Earls. And the heathen men came on against them. But King Æthelred heard mass in his tent.[2] And men said, "Come forth, O King, to the fight, for the heathen men press hard upon us." And King Æthelred

---

[1] *Jarl* is the same as our *Earl*. This Danish title afterwards took the place of the English Alderman, but it was not till Cnut's time that it got into Southern England.

[2] This part of the story comes from Asser only.

said, " I will serve God first and man after, so I will not come forth till all the words of the mass be ended." So King Æthelred abode praying, and the heathen men fought against Alfred the Ætheling. And Alfred said, " I cannot abide till the King my brother comes forth; I must either flee, or fight alone with the heathen men." So Alfred the Ætheling and his men fought against the five Earls. Now the heathen men stood on the higher ground and the Christians on the lower. Yet did Alfred go forth trusting in God, and he made his men hold close together with their shields,[1] and they went forth like a wild boar against the hounds.[2] And they fought against the heathen men and smote them, and slew the five Earls, Sidroc the Old, Sidroc the Young, Osbearn, Fræna, and Harold. Then the mass was over,[3] and King Æthelred came forth and fought against the two Kings, and slew Bagsecg the King with his own hand. So the English had the victory, and smote the heathen men with a great slaughter and chased them even unto Reading. And after fourteen days there was yet another battle at Basing, and King Æthelred and Alfred the Ætheling fought again with the heathen men. But the heathen men prevailed against them and kept possession of the place of battle, yet took they no spoil.[4] Then came there other heathen men from beyond sea, and joined themselves to their fellows that were in the land of the West-Saxons.[5] And after two months there was again a battle at Merton, and King Æthelred and Alfred the Ætheling fought with the heathen men, and for a while they overcame them, but in the end the heathen men had the better and kept possession of the place of battle. In that fight was Heahmund Bishop of Sherborne slain. And at Easter-tide King Æthelred died, and

---

[1] Asser calls it a *testudo* or tortoise. This is the *shield-wall*, the famous tactic of the English and the Danes alike. We shall hear of it in all the great battles, down to the end.

[2] This is Asser's comparison.

[3] From Asser's account one would think that Æthelred's division had no share in the battle. But the Chronicle distinctly says that Æthelred fought against the two Kings, and Henry of Huntingdon adds that he himself killed Bagsecg, so this is the only way in which I can put the different stories together. I always take care never to *contradict* the Chronicle, even when I bring in details from other sources.

[4] Æthelweard.   [5] Asser.

they buried him in the minster at Wimborne in the land of the Dorsætas, and Alfred his brother reigned in his stead.

You see then that King Æthelred reigned but a few years, but that those years were very important and very fearful years. As he was a good man and fought bravely against the heathen, and most likely died of a wound in his last battle, men looked on him as a saint and a kind of martyr. You will find as you go on that many good and brave men were thus looked on as saints and martyrs, though they certainly were not actual martyrs in the way that Saint Edmund was. There is still a brass plate in Wimborne Minster which marks the burial-place of King Æthelred; but it is many hundred years later than his time, as late, I believe, as the time of Queen Elizabeth. This shows how long men remembered and reverenced him.

§ 5. THE REIGN OF KING ALFRED THE GREAT.
871—900.

We now come to our great King Alfred, the best and greatest of all our Kings. We know quite enough of his history to be able to say that he really deserves to be so called, though I must warn you that, just because he left so great a name behind him, people have been fond of attributing to him things which really belonged to others. Thus you may sometimes see nearly all our laws and customs attributed to Alfred, as if he had invented them all for himself. You will sometimes hear that Alfred founded Trial by Jury, divided England into Counties, and did all kinds of other things. Now the real truth is that the roots and beginnings of most of these things are very much older than the time of Alfred, while the particular forms in which we have them now are very much later. But people have a way of fancying that everything must have been invented by some particular man, and as Alfred was more famous than anybody else, they hit upon Alfred as the most likely person to give them to. But, putting aside fables, there is quite enough to show that there have been very few Kings, and very few men of any sort, so great and good as King Alfred. Perhaps the only equally good King we read of is Saint Lewis of France; and though he was quite as good, we

I

cannot set him down as being so great and wise as Alfred. Certainly no King ever gave himself up more thoroughly than Alfred did fully to do the duties of his office. His whole life seems to have been spent in doing all that he could for the good of his people in every way. And it is wonderful in how many ways his powers showed themselves. That he was a brave warrior is in itself no particular praise in an age when almost every man was the same. But it is a great thing for a prince so large a part of whose time was spent in fighting to be able to say that all his wars were waged for the deliverance of his country from the most cruel enemies. And we may admire too the wonderful way in which he kept his mind always straight and firm, never either giving way to bad luck or being puffed up by good luck. We read of nothing like pride or cruelty or injustice of any kind either towards his own people or towards his enemies. And if he was a brave warrior, he was many other things besides. He was a lawgiver; at least he collected and arranged the laws, and caused them to be most carefully administered. He was a scholar, and wrote and translated many books for the good of his people. He encouraged trade and enterprise of all kinds, and sent men to visit distant parts of the world, and bring home accounts of what they saw. And he was a thoroughly good man and a devout Christian in all relations of life. In short, one hardly knows any other character in all history so perfect; there is so much that is good in so many different ways; and though no doubt Alfred had his faults like other people, yet he clearly had none, at any rate in the greater part of his life, which took away at all seriously from his general goodness. One wonders that such a man was never canonized as a Saint; most certainly many people have received that name who did not deserve it nearly so well as he did.

Alfred, or, as his name should really be spelled, Ælfred,[1] was the youngest son of King Æthelwulf, and was born at Wantage in Berkshire in 849. His mother was Osburh, the first, or perhaps the second, wife of Æthelwulf. She was the daughter of Oslac the King's cup-bearer, who came of the royal house of

---

[1] That is, the *rede* or counsel of the *elves*. A great many Old-English names are called after the elves or fairies.

the Jutes in Wight. Now a story is told of Alfred and his mother which you may perhaps have heard already, and which is such a beautiful tale that I am really sorry to have to say that it cannot possibly be true. We are told that up to the age of twelve years Alfred was fond of hunting and other sports, but that he had not been taught any sort of learning, not so much as to read his own tongue. But he loved the Old-English songs ; and one day his mother had a beautiful book of songs with rich pictures and fine painted initial letters, such as you may often see in ancient books. And she said to her children, " I will give this beautiful book to the one of you who shall first be able to read it." And Alfred said, " Mother, will you really give me the book when I have learned to read it?" And Osburh said, " Yea, my son." So Alfred went and found a master, and soon learned to read. Then he came to his mother, and read the songs in the beautiful book and took the book for his own.

Now it is a great pity that so pretty a story cannot be true. And I must tell you why it cannot. Alfred was sent to Rome to the Pope when he was four years old ; and if the Pope took him as his " bishop-son " and anointed him to be King, one cannot help thinking that he would have him taught to read and to learn Latin. And it is quite certain that he could do both very well in after-life. Still this is not quite certain proof, as he might have learned afterwards. But this is quite certain. Alfred was not twelve years old till 861. By that time his brothers were not children playing round their mother, but grown men and Kings, and two of them, Æthelstan and Æthelbald, were dead. Moreover in 861 Alfred's father Æthelwulf was dead, and his mother must have been dead also, as Æthelwulf married Judith in 856, when Alfred was only seven years old. If then anything of the kind happened, it could not have been when Alfred was twelve years old, but before he was four. For in that year he went to Rome and could never have seen his mother again, even if she were alive when he went. And for a child of four years old not to be able to read is not so very wonderful a thing, even in our own time.[1]

---

[1] I have seen in different books two attempts to get out of this difficulty, but I do not think either of them will do.

First, some suggest that Osburh was not dead when Æthelwulf married

I have told you how, when Alfred was four years old, he was
sent to Rome by his father, and no doubt he came back with
Æthelwulf on his return.   We have seen also that he took a
leading part in the wars of his brothers against the Danes.   In
868, when he was in his twentieth year, while Æthelred was
King, Alfred married.   His wife's name was Ealhswith ; she
was the daughter of Æthelred called the Mickle or Big, Alderman of the Gainas in Lincolnshire, and her mother Eadburh
was of the royal house of the Mercians.   It is said that on the
very day of his marriage he was smitten with a strange disease,
which for twenty years never quite left him, and fits of which
might come on at any time.   If this be true, it makes all the
great things that he did even more wonderful.   In 871, on
Æthelred's death, he came to the Crown.   Æthelred had
some young children, but nobody thought of their succeed-
ing, so Alfred, the youngest son of Æthelwulf, became King
of the West-Saxons and Overlord of all England, as his
father had appointed so long before with the consent of his
Wise Men.

So Alfred was King, and he had at once to fight for his
Kingdom.   I have told you already of all the battles which were
fought in the year 871, before Æthelred died, and Alfred had
to fight yet another battle before the year was out.   This was
at Wilton near Salisbury, which I suppose was then the chief
town of the Wilsætas.   The modern city of Salisbury, or New
Sarum as it is still called, was not founded till long after, in
the thirteenth century, when the new cathedral was built ;

Judith, but that he had put her away, and that she might still have had her
children about her.   But of this there is no sort of proof ; and when we
read that a man, especially a good man like Æthelwulf, married a second
wife, we are bound to suppose that his first wife was dead, unless we have
some clear proof that she was alive.   And granting this, we still have the
difficulty that, when Alfred was twelve years old, his brothers were not, as
the story clearly implies, boys, but grown men and Kings, and that some
of them were dead.

Secondly, some suggest that the story really belongs not to Alfred's
mother Osburh, but to his step-mother Judith.   Now it is really ridiculous
to fancy that this young foreign girl would act as a careful mother to Æthelwulf's sons, some of whom must have been older than herself, and one of
whom she was unprincipled enough to marry.   Moreover in 861 Æthelbald
was already dead, and Judith had gone back into Gaul.

what is meant by Salisbury in these times is the old town, called Old Sarum, where the old cathedral[1] and the old castle were, but which has long been quite forsaken. It is a wonderful place indeed, with some of the greatest *fosses* or ditches that are to be seen anywhere. But the name Wilton seems to show that that town must have been the chief place of Wiltshire in those times. The battle of Wilton seems not to have been a very decisive one, as we read that the Danes were put to flight and yet that they kept possession of the field of battle. On the whole it is hard to see which side had the better in the mere fighting of this year, but you must remember that the Danes, being in a strange country, had nothing to lose but their lives, while the English not only suffered the loss of the men who were actually killed in the battles, but the mere marching about of the armies and the plundering and burning by the Danes must have been dreadful blows to them. But after the battle of Wilton the Danes seem to have been tired : we read that they made peace with the West-Saxons ; and there was peace, so far as Wessex was concerned, for a few years. But they were all the while fighting and plundering and settling in other parts of Britain, both in Northumberland and Mercia, and also among the Picts and the Strathclyde Welsh.

The Danes did not come again into Wessex till 876, but two very important things happened meanwhile in Mercia and Northumberland. In 874 Burhred, King of the Mercians, King Alfred's brother-in-law, ran away and left his Kingdom for fear of the Danes who had entered the country of Lindesey,[2] that is the northern part of Lincolnshire, and had got as far as Repton in Nottinghamshire. At Repton the minster is quite gone, but the monastery there was very famous in early times; there is some very ancient work in the parish church, which may very likely be as old as Alfred's days. Burhred, instead

---

[1] But you must remember that even Old Salisbury did not become a Bishop's see till the time of William the Conqueror. Wiltshire was first in the diocese of Winchester, then in that of Sherborne ; afterwards the Wilsætas had a Bishop of their own at Ramsbury.

[2] That is, the Isle of *Lindum*, the Roman city now called Lincoln. The name of Lincoln is from *Lindum* and *Colonia*, the town having been a Roman colony.

of fighting, like his brother-in-law Alfred, went out of the land, and went to Rome, like Ceadwalla and Ine, and died almost as soon as he got there. The Danes then gave the crown of Mercia to one of Burhred's Thanes named Ceolwulf; but of course he was a mere puppet in their hands; indeed he swore oaths to them, and had to do whatever they bade him. Thus the old Kingdom of Mercia came to an end. And this was one of the ways in which the coming of the Danes helped to make all England into one Kingdom. For of course, when the Danes were gone and there was some quiet again, it was easier, now that there was no King in Mercia, to join Mercia or part of it more completely on to Wessex, which I shall tell you about at the proper time. The other important thing is that, in the year 876, the year in which the Danes came again into Wessex, another party of them, under Healfdene, divided the lands of Northumberland among them, and began ploughing and tilling them. Thus you see, as I told you, the Danes were beginning to settle in the land, instead of merely coming to plunder and go away. Now, no doubt, it was that so many places in the North of England got Danish names. When we find villages in Yorkshire called Haxby and Thirkleby, we may be quite sure that they were once the estates of Danes called Hakon and Thurkill, and most likely these were the men to whom they were given by Healfdene in 876.

Though the West-Saxons had no fighting by land during these years, things were not quite quiet, for in 875 King Alfred had a fight at sea against some of the Danish pirates. This sea-fight is worth remembering, as being, I suppose, the first victory won by Englishmen at sea, where Englishmen have since won so many victories. King Alfred then fought against seven Danish ships, of which he took one and put the rest to flight. It is somewhat strange that we do not hear more than we do of warfare by sea in these times, especially when we remember how in earlier times the Angles and Saxons had roved about in their ships, very much as the Danes and other Northmen were doing now. It would seem that the English, after they settled in Britain, almost left off being a sea-faring people. We find Alfred and other Kings doing what they could to keep up a fleet and to encourage a naval spirit among their people. And in some degree they did so; still we do not find the English, for a long while after this time, doing nearly so much by sea as they did by land. This was a pity; for ships might then, as in later times, have been wooden walls. It is much better to meet an enemy at sea, and to keep him from landing in your country, than to let him land, even if you can beat him when he has landed.

But in 876 the Danes came again into Wessex; and we thus come to that part of Alfred's life which is at once the most terrible and the most honourable. It is the time when his fortune was lowest and when his spirit was highest. The army, under Guthorm or Guthrum, the Danish King of East-Anglia, came suddenly to Wareham in Dorsetshire. The Chronicle says that they "bestole"—that is, came secretly or escaped—from the West-Saxon army, which seems to have been waiting for them.[1] This time Alfred made peace with him, and they gave him some of their chief men for hostages, and they swore to go out of the land. This time they swore on the holy bracelet, which was the most solemn oath in use among the heathen Northmen, and on which they had never before sworn at any of the times when they had made peace with the English. But they did not keep their oath any better for taking it in this more solemn way. The part of the host which had horses "bestole away" to Exeter,[2] and it would seem that the rest stayed at Wareham. For we read that the next year (877) the army went from Wareham to Exeter, and a great fleet set out to go "west about," perhaps to go round the Land's End, or perhaps only to sail round the Isle of Purbeck to get to Exeter. For in those days, when ships were much smaller than

---

[1] Æthelweard says that they "joined with the western army, which they had never done before," as if some Danes had been staying all this time in Wessex, or perhaps more likely among the Welsh in Cornwall.

[2] Asser adds that they killed all the King's horsemen. He goes on to speak of the march to Exeter, adding that in the British tongue that city is called "Caerwisc." This is the sort of thing which a later forger would hardly think of, so this piece at least seems like a bit of the real Asser.

Exeter, Exanceaster, of course means the town on the "Exe, Usk, or Wise," "Isca Damnoniorum," as it is called in Latin, to distinguish it from "Isca Silurum," or Caerleon-on-Usk. The name of *Damnonii* is of course the same as that of the *Defenas* or *Defnsætas.*

they are now, they could get higher up the rivers, and then
Exeter was a great port. But now large ships cannot get so high
up the river Exe. So you may remember that Caerleon-on-Usk
was a great port in old times, but now ships only get up as far
as Newport. But there is this difference between the two *Isca*,
that Exeter still remains a large city, while Caerleon has quite
gone down in the world. However, wherever the fleet was
going, it did not get far. A great storm came on, and broke
many of the ships, so that they got no further than Swan-
wick or Swanage, in the Isle of Purbeck, not far from
Wareham. Perhaps it was this bad luck which made them
make peace again. For King Alfred rode after the Danish
horse as far as Exeter, but he did not overtake them till they
had got there, and were safe in the castle. Then they made
peace, swearing oaths, and giving as many hostages as the King
asked for. And this time the Chronicle says that they kept good
peace. That is to say, they went for the rest of the year out
of Wessex into Mercia. There, we read, they divided part of
the land and gave part to Ceolwulf. I suppose it was now
that they finally settled in Lincolnshire and the other parts of
Mercia where we hear most of the Danes afterwards, and where
Danish names are still common. In the parts of Mercia
which are near to Wessex we do not find Danish names.

And now we come to the terrible year 878, the greatest and
saddest and most glorious in all Alfred's life. In the very
beginning of the year, just after Twelfth-night, the Danish host
again came suddenly—"bestole" as the Chronicle says—to
Chippenham. Then "they rode through the West-Saxons' land,
and there sat down, and mickle of the folk over sea they drove,
and of the others the most deal they rode over; all but the King
Alfred; he with a little band hardly fared [went] after the
woods and on the moor-fastnesses." How can I tell you this
better than in the words of the Chronicle itself, only altering
some words into their modern shape, that you may the better
understand them? One hardly sees how it was that the country
could be all at once so utterly overrun, especially as there is
no mention made of any battle. There is indeed one account
which says that Alfred did not reign so well at the beginning
as he did afterwards, but that he did badly in many things and

oppressed his people, so that they would not fight for him ; but that he was rebuked by his cousin the hermit Saint Neot, and that after that he ruled well. But I do not at all believe this, because there is no good authority for it,[1] and it does not agree in the least with what went before and what goes after. It is more likely of the two, as some think, that the part of Alfred's dominions where the people were still of Welsh descent gave him some trouble, and that they did not join heartily with his own West-Saxons. But I do not see any very clear proof even of this, and anyhow it is quite certain that this time of utter distress lasted only a very little while, for in a few months Alfred was again at the head of an army and able to fight against the Danes. It must have been at this time that the story of the cakes, which I dare say you have heard, happened, if it ever happened at all. The tale is quite possible, but there is no proof of it being true. It is said that Alfred went and stayed in the hut of a neatherd or swineherd of his, who knew who he was, though his wife did not know him. One day the woman set some cakes to bake, and bade the King, who was sitting by the fire mending his bow and arrows, to tend them. Alfred thought more of his bow and arrows than he did of the cakes, and let them burn. Then the woman ran in and cried out,

" There, don't you see the cakes on fire ? Then wherefore turn them
     not ?
You're glad enough to eat them when they are piping hot ?"[2]

It is almost more strange when we are told by some that this swineherd or neatherd[3] afterwards became Bishop of Win-

---

[1] The story has got into some copies of Asser's *Life* from the book called Asser's *Annals*, which is undoubtedly a forgery. Most likely it comes from some life of Saint Neot, the author of which was anxious to exalt the saint, and did not mind how unfair he was to the King.

[2] The woman's speech is put into two Latin verses :—

> " Urere quos cernis panes gyrare moraris,
>   Quum nimium gaudes hos manducare calentes."

Most likely the whole story comes from a ballad.

[3] The story that Alfred took shelter in a herdsman's cottage is one story, and the story that Bishop Denewulf had been a swineherd is another story. But people have very naturally put the two stories together and have thought that Denewulf was the same man in whose hut the cake-story

chester.   They say that his name was Denewulf, and that the
King saw that, though he was in so lowly a rank, he was
naturally a very wise man.   So he had him taught, and at last
gave him the Bishoprick.   But it is hard to believe this, especially as Denewulf, Bishop of Winchester, became Bishop the
very next year.

We will go on with things that are more certain.   I do not
think that I can do better than tell you the story as it is in the
Chronicle, only changing those forms of words which you might
not understand.

"And that ilk [same][1] winter was Iwer's and Healfdene's
brother among the West-Saxons in Devonshire ; and him there
men slew and eight hundred men with him and forty men of his
host.   And there was the banner[2] taken which they the Raven
hight [call].   And after this Easter wrought King Alfred with
his little band a work [fortress] at Athelney,[3] and out of that
work was he striving with the [Danish] host, and (with him)
that deal [part] of the Sumorsætas that nighest was.   And on
the seventh week after Easter he rode to *Ecgbrihtesstan*,[4] by
the east of Selwood ; and there to meet him came the Sumorsætas all and the Wilsætas and of Hamptonshire the deal [part]
that on this side the sea was ;[5] and they were fain [glad] to see
him.   And he fared [went] one night from the wick [dwelling
or camp] to Æglea, and after that one night to Ethandun, and
there fought with all the host and put them to flight, and rode
after them to their work [fortress] and there sat fourteen nights.
And the army sold [gave] him hostages and mickle oaths, and
eke they promised him that their King should receive baptism.[6]

happened.   But no old writer distinctly says so, and indeed the two stories
come from different writers.

[1] That word is still used in Scotland.

[2] *Gu ð fana*, from *gu ð* (guth), which means *battle*, and *fana* (like the German or High-Dutch *fahne*), a *banner*.   It is the same word as *gonfanon*
or *gonfalon*, whence *gonfalonier*, the title of a magistrate at Florence long
after.

[3] *Æthelinga-ig*, the isle of the Æthelings or Princes.

[4] *Ecgberht's stone*, that is *Brixton* Deverell in Wiltshire.   You see how
the name has been cut short.

[5] That is, those who had not fled beyond sea for fear of the Danes.

[6] In Old-English *fullwiht* or *fulluht*, from *fullian*, to wash or make clean

And this they fulfilled. And three weeks after came the King Guthrum with thirty of the men that in the host were worthiest, at Aller, that is near Athelney. And him the King received at his baptism,[1] and his chrisom-loosing[2] was at Wedmore. And he was twelve nights with the King, and he honoured him and his feres [companions] with mickle fee [money]."

Thus you see how soon King Alfred's good luck came back to him again. And I do not doubt that you are the more pleased to hear the tale, because all this happened not very far from our own home. It was in the woods and marshes of Somersetshire that Alfred took shelter, and the Sumorsætas were among the first who came to his help after Easter. But we will take things a little in order. You see the first fighting was in Devonshire, where the Raven was taken. This was a famous banner of the Danes, said to have been worked by the daughters of Ragnar Lodbrog. It was thought to have wonderful powers, so that they could tell by the way in which the raven held his wings whether they would win or not in battle. Ethelweard tells us that the Danes besieged Odda the Alderman of Devonshire, and adds that, though their King was killed, still the Danes kept the battle-place. You see the time of utter distress lasted only from soon after Twelfth-night to Easter, and even during that time the taking of the Raven must have cheered the English a good deal. After Easter things begin to mend, when Alfred built his fort at Athelney and began to skirmish with the Danes, and seven weeks later came the great victory at Ethandun, which delivered Wessex. You must remember that, at this time, all the low country of Somersetshire, Sedgmoor and the other moors, as we call them now, was covered with water, or was at least quite marshy, so that any ground a little higher than the rest was really an island. You know how to this day very few people live quite

like a *fuller*. So *baptize* is from the Greek βάπτειν or βαπτίζειν, to dip, and in High-Dutch to baptize is *taufen*, which word you will see, if you change the letters rightly, is the same as our *dip*.

[1] That is, was his godfather.

[2] That is, he laid aside the chrisom or white garment (from Greek χρίω, to anoint, whence the name of *Christ*) which a newly baptized person wore for a certain time.

down on the moors, but the towns and villages, and even most
of the separate houses, are all built either on such islands, or
else on the slopes of the larger hills, as the villages between
Wells and Axbridge cling, as it were, to the side of Mendip.
Such islands were often chosen, as I think I told you before,
for building monasteries, and they were often useful in time
of war, when men could take shelter in such an island, where
it was hard for their enemies to get at them. Thus you will
find that, in later times, the Isle of Ely and other such places
served as a shelter to the English who were fighting against
the Normans,[1] and so it was when King Alfred made his
fort at Athelney. Then, when he thought he was strong
enough, he left the low ground and went up the hills, and
gathered his men together at Ecgbrihtesstan or Brixton,
which is in Wiltshire, near Warminster. Then he marched,
still north-east, to Ethandun, that is Edington, not far from
Trowbridge and Westbury, where he fought the great battle.
At Edington there is a very fine church, but that was not
built till many hundred years after Alfred's time, namely
in the reign of Edward the Third. Some say that the white
horse which is cut in the side of the chalk hills near there
was cut then, that men might remember the great battle of
Ethandun. But it has been altered in modern times to make
it look more like a real horse. There is another figure of
a white horse near Shrivenham, which has not been altered
at all, but is very old and rude, so that you might hardly
know that it was meant for a horse at all. Whether either
of them has really anything to do with King Alfred I do not
pretend to say. Perhaps the one near Shrivenham may be a
great deal older than Alfred's time, as it is very like the figures
of horses on some of the old British coins.

But all this time Alfred seems to have kept his head-quarters
at Athelney, for it was at Aller close to Athelney that
Guthorm came to be baptized. Thence they went to Wedmore,
because there the West-Saxon Kings had a palace. There the
Wise Men came together, and Alfred and Guthorm (or, to
give him the name by which he was baptized, Æthelstan)

---

[1] And later still, with the followers of Earl Simon of Montfort after his
death.

made a treaty. Guthorm-Æthelstan was to leave Wessex. but he was to keep East-Anglia, which he had already, and the north-eastern part of Mercia. The boundary ran along the Thames to the mouth of the Lea, then by Bedford and the river Ouse to the old Roman road called Watling-street. The south-western part of Mercia was to remain to Alfred. That is to say, speaking roughly, Alfred recovered that part of Mercia which had been originally West-Saxon and which was only conquered by the Angles in the seventh and eighth centuries. But you see that the Danes now got much the larger part of England. but Alfred contrived to keep London. All Northumberland and East-Anglia, most part of Essex, and the larger part of Mercia, thus fell to the Danes. The part of Mercia that Alfred kept he did not altogether join on to Wessex ; he did not keep it immediately in his own hands as he did Wessex ; West-Saxon Mercia, as we may call it. was still governed by its own Alderman, who held his own Assembly of Wise Men. But then the Alderman of the Mercians was now named by the King of the West-Saxons. One Æthelred, who had been Alderman of the Hwiccas, was now made Alderman of all the West-Saxon part of Mercia, and Alfred gave him in marriage his daughter Æthelflæd, who was called the Lady of the Mercians, and of whom you will hear again.

We shall find that Guthorm-Æthelstan did not always keep the treaty of Wedmore quite so well as he should have done. Still this treaty was very much better kept than any treaty with the Danes had ever been kept before. In 879 the army went away from Chippenham to Cirencester ; that is. they went out of Wessex into Mercia, though not as yet into their own part of Mercia. At Cirencester they "sat" for a year. seemingly by Alfred's leave, as we do not read of any fighting or of any mischief being done. Indeed some accounts say that only those of the Danes stayed who chose to become Christians, and that the rest went away into Gaul under a famous leader of theirs named Hasting. Anyhow, in 880 they went quite away into what was now their own land of East-Anglia, and divided it among themselves. Thus Alfred had quite cleared his own Kingdom from the Danes, though he was obliged to leave so much of the island in their hands. And even through all these misfortunes, the Kingdom of Wessex did in some sort become greater. For there was now no longer a King of the Mercians, but a great part of Mercia was governed by an Alderman, who was not only the man of the King of the West-Saxons, as the later Kings of the Mercians had been, but was appointed by him, and was in fact only a great magistrate acting under his orders. Remember that in 880, when Alfred had done so many great things, he was still only thirty-one years old.

I have now finished what I may call the second Danish War, and there was now peace for several years. Perhaps then this is the best place to bring in one or two stories about Alfred which are worth remembering in one way, whether they are true or false. For it at least shows how much people always remembered and thought of Alfred, that there should be so many more stories told of him than of almost any other of the old Kings. The only King of whom anything like so many stories are told is Edgar, and the stories which are told of Edgar are by no means so much to his credit as the stories which are told of Alfred.

One story is that Alfred, wishing to know what the Danes were about and how strong they were, set out one day from Athelney in the disguise of a minstrel or juggler, and went into the Danish camp, and stayed there several days, amusing the Danes with his playing, till he had seen all that he wanted, and then went back without any one finding him out. Now there is nothing actually impossible in this story, but we do not find it in any writer earlier than William of Malmesbury, who lived in the twelfth century. And it is the sort of story which one finds turning up in different forms in different ages and countries. For instance, exactly the same story is told of a Danish King Anlaf, of whom you will hear presently. So it is one of those things which you cannot at all believe for certain.

This is what you may call a soldier's story, while some of the others are rather what monks and clergymen would like to tell. Thus there is a tale which is told in a great many different ways, but of which the following is the oldest shape.

The Story of King Alfred and Saint Cuthberht.[1]

Now King Alfred was driven from his Kingdom by the Danes, and he lay hid for three years in the isle of Glastonbury.[2] And it came to pass on a day that all his folk were gone out to fish, save only Alfred himself and his wife and one servant whom he loved. And there came a pilgrim[3] to the King, and begged for food. And the King said to his servant. "What food have we in the house?" And his servant answered. "My Lord, we have but one loaf and a little wine." Then the King gave thanks to God, and said, "Give half of the loaf and half of the wine to this poor pilgrim." So the servant did as his lord commanded him, and gave to the pilgrim half of the loaf and half of the wine, and the pilgrim gave great thanks to the King. And when the servant returned, he found the loaf whole, and the wine as much as there had been aforetime. And he greatly wondered, and he wondered also how the pilgrim had come into the isle. for that no man could come there save by water, and the pilgrim had no boat. And the King greatly wondered also. And at the ninth hour came back the folk who had gone to fish. And they had three boats full of fish, and they said, "Lo, we have caught more fish this

[1] I have seen in many books so much of this story told as people nowadays think possible, namely the story of Alfred's charity to the poor man. Now it is quite possible that this may be true, and that the rest is an addition which has grown round about it. But we have no evidence that it is so, and we have no right to take a piece of a story by itself in this way. The writers who tell us one part tell us the rest, and, if we tell the story at all, we should tell the whole story. I therefore tell it simply as a legend, found only in writers who wrote long after the time. Some of it may be true, but it is not fair to pick out just so much as we think possible. and to tell that much as if it were certainly true.

[2] Here you will at once see two mistakes. Alfred was not hid for three years, and it was not at Glastonbury that he was hid. But the Life of Saint Cuthbert from which the story comes, was written in the north of England, and there they had no doubt heard of so famous a place as Glastonbury. but knew nothing of Athelney.

[3] The writer. by speaking of a pilgrim, clearly shows that he was thinking of Glastonbury rather than of Athelney, as there was no monastery at Athelney yet.

day than in all the three years that we have tarried in this island."
And the King was glad, and he and his folk were merry ; yet
he pondered much upon that which had come to pass. And
when night came, the King went to his bed with Ealhswith his
wife. And the Lady slept, but the King lay awake and thought
of all that had come to pass by day. And presently he saw a
great light, like the brightness of the sun, and he saw an old
man with black hair, clothed in priest's garments, and with a
mitre on his head, and holding in his right hand a book of the
Gospels adorned with gold and gems. And the old man blessed
the King, and the King said unto him, " Who art thou ? " And
he answered, " Alfred, my son, rejoice ; for I am he to whom
thou didst this day give thine alms, and I am called Cuthberht
the soldier of Christ. Now be strong and very courageous,
and be of joyful heart, and hearken diligently to the things
which I say unto thee ; for henceforth I will be thy shield and
thy friend, and I will watch over thee and over thy sons after
thee. And now I will tell thee what thou must do. Rise up
early in the morning, and blow thine horn thrice, that thine
enemies may hear it and fear, and by the ninth hour thou shalt
have around thee five hundred men harnessed for the battle.
And this shall be a sign unto thee that thou mayest believe.
And after seven days thou shalt have by God's gift and my help
all the folk of this land gathered unto thee upon the mount
that is called Assandun.[1] And thus shalt thou fight against
thine enemies, and doubt not that thou shalt overcome them.
Be thou therefore glad of heart, and be strong and very courageous, and fear not, for God hath given thine enemies into
thine hand. And He hath given thee also all this land and
the Kingdom of thy fathers, to thee and to thy sons and to thy
sons' sons after thee. Be thou faithful to me and to my folk,
because that unto thee is given all the land of Albion. Be
thou righteous, because thou art chosen to be the King of all
Britain. So may God be merciful unto thee, and I will be thy
friend, and none of thine enemies shall ever be able to overcome

---

[1] The writer evidently confounds *Ethandun* (Edington), the place of
Alfred's victory, with *Ascesdun* (Ashdown), where you will remember that
one of Æthelred's battles was fought, and perhaps with the real Assandun
where the great battle was long after in 1016.

thee." Then was King Alfred glad at heart and he was strong
and very courageous, for that he knew that he would overcome
his enemies by the help of God and Saint Cuthberht his patron.
So in the morning he arose, and sailed to the land, and blew
his horn three times, and when his friends heard it they rejoiced,
and when his enemies heard it they feared. And by the ninth
hour, according to the word of the Lord, there were gathered
unto him five hundred men of the bravest and dearest of his
friends. And he spake unto them and told them all that God
had said unto them by the mouth of his servant Cuthberht, and
he told them that, by the gift of God and by the help of Saint
Cuthberht, they would overcome their enemies and win back
their own land. And he bade them, as Saint Cuthberht had
taught him, to be pious towards God and righteous towards men.
And he bade his son Edward who was by him to be faithful to
God and Saint Cuthberht and so he should always have the
victory over his enemies. So they went forth to battle and
smote their enemies and overcame them, and King Alfred took
the Kingdom of all Britain,[1] and he ruled well and wisely over
the just and the unjust for the rest of his days.

Now is there any truth in all this story? I think there is
thus much, that Alfred, for some reason or other, thought he
was under the special protection of Saint Cuthbert. I have
two reasons for thinking so ; first, because it is rather remarkable that a Northumbrian writer should go out of his way to tell
so long a story about a West-Saxon King, unless he really had
something to do with his own Saint. And secondly, is not our
parish church in Wells called Saint Cuthbert's ? Now it is
not often that we find a church in the south called after a saint
who is hardly known except in the north. There must be some
special reason for it, and if, when Alfred was in Somersetshire,
any dream or anything else made him think that Saint Cuthbert
was helping him, we can understand why either he or other
men after him should call a church in that neighbourhood by
the name of a saint whom otherwise they were not likely to

---

[1] The writer seems to have had very little notion of the division of the
land between Alfred and Guthorm.

know much about.   But I will now go on to things which are
more certain.

For several years after 880 there was peace in the land, and for
a good many more years still there was much less fighting than
there had been before.   It was no doubt at this time that Alfred
was able to do all those things for the good of his people of which
we hear so much.   He had now more time than either before
or after for making his laws, writing his books, founding his
monasteries, and doing all that he did.   You may wonder how
he found time to do so much ; but it was by the only way by
which anybody can do anything, namely by never wasting his
time, and by having fixed times of the day for everything.
Alfred did not, like most other writers of that time, write in
Latin, so that hardly anybody but the clergy could read or
understand what he wrote.   He loved our own tongue, and
was especially fond of the Old-English songs, and all that he
wrote he wrote in English that all his people might understand.
His works were chiefly translations from Latin books ; what
we should have valued most of all, his note-book or hand-book,
containing his remarks on various matters, is lost.   He translated into English the History of Bæda, the History of Orosius,
some of the works of Pope Gregory the Great, and the Consolation of Philosophy by Boethius.   Perhaps you will ask why
he did not rather translate some of the great and famous
Greek and Latin writers of earlier times.   Now we may be
sure that King Alfred did not understand Greek at all ; very
few people in those days in the West of Europe knew any
Greek, except those who needed to use the language for dealing
with the men in the Eastern Empire who still spoke it.   Indeed
Alfred complains that, when he came to the Crown, very few
people, even among the clergy, understood even Latin at all
well.   And as for Latin books, no doubt Alfred thought that
the writings of Christians would be more edifying to his people
than those of the old heathens.   He chose the History of
Orosius, as a general history of the world, and that of Bæda, as
a particular history of England.   Boethius was a Roman Consul
in the beginning of the sixth century, who was put to death by
the great Theodoric, King of the East-Goths.   While he was in
prison he wrote the book which King Alfred translated   He

seems not really to have been a Christian, at least there is not a single Christian expression in his book. But people fancied that he was not only a Christian, but a saint and a martyr, most likely because Theodoric, who put him to death, was not an Orthodox Christian, but an Arian. Alfred, in translating his books, did not always care to translate them quite exactly, but he often altered and put in things of his own, if he thought he could thus make them more improving. So in translating Boethius, he altered a good deal, to make the wise heathen speak like a Christian. So in translating Orosius, where Orosius gives an account of the world, Alfred greatly enlarged the account of all the northern part of Europe, of which Alfred naturally knew much more than Orosius did. There was one Othhere, a Norwegian whale-fisher, whom Alfred employed to visit all the northern countries, and who brought him an account of all that he saw, which Alfred added to the account of Orosius. Besides writing himself, Alfred encouraged learned men, both Englishmen and men from other countries, to help him in writing and teaching his people. Such was Asser the Welshman. a priest from Saint David's, who wrote Alfred's Life ; such were Grimbald from Flanders and John the Old-Saxon, that is, a Saxon from Germany, as distinguished from one of Alfred's own West-Saxons in Britain.

Alfred was also very careful in the government of his Kingdom, especially in seeing that justice was properly administered. So men said of him in their songs, much as they had long before said of King Edwin in Northumberland, that he hung up golden bracelets by the road-side, and that no man dared to steal them. In his collection of laws, he chiefly put in order the laws of the older Kings, not adding many of his own, because he said that he did not know how those who came after him might like them. But it is curious that we have fewer accounts of meetings of the Wise Men under Alfred himself in Wessex than we have of the meetings of those of Mercia under Alderman Æthelred.

King Alfred was very attentive to religious matters, and gave great alms to the poor and gifts to churches. He also founded two monasteries ; one was at Shaftesbury in Dorsetshire, for nuns, of which he made his own daughter Æthelgifu Abbess.

The other was for monks at Athelney; you can easily see why he should· build it there. He also sent several embassies to Rome, where he got Pope Marinus to grant certain privileges to the English School at Rome; the Pope also sent him what was thought to be a piece of the wood of the True Cross, that on which our Lord Jesus Christ died. He also sent an embassy to Jerusalem, and had letters from Abel the Patriarch there. And what seems stranger than all, he sent an embassy all the way to India, with alms for the Christians there, called the Christians of Saint Thomas and Saint Bartholomew.

Lastly, there seems some reason to think that the Chronicle began to be put together in its present shape in Alfred's time, and that it was regularly gone on with afterwards, so that from the time of Alfred onwards we have a history which was regularly written down as things happened.

All these things happened mainly in the middle years of the reign of Alfred, when there was so much less fighting than there was before and after, and when some years seem to have been quite peaceable. Guthorm-Æthelstan and his Danes in East-Anglia were for some years true to the treaty of Wedmore, and the other Danes seem just now to have been busy in invading Gaul and other parts of the continent rather than England. Also King Alfred had now got a fleet, so that he often met them at sea and kept them from landing. This he did in 882, and we do not find that any Danes landed again in England till 885. In that year part of the army which had been plundering along the coasts of Flanders and Holland came over to England, landed in Kent, and besieged Rochester. But the citizens withstood them bravely, and Alfred gathered an army and drove the Danes to their ships. They seem then to have gone into Essex and to have plundered there with their ships, getting help from the Danes who were settled in East-Anglia or such of them as still were heathens.[1] Alfred's fleet however quite overcame them and took away their treasure, but his fleet was again attacked by the East-Anglian Danes and defeated. It would seem that in some part of this war Guthorm-Æthelstan was helped by Hrolf, otherwise called Rolf, Rou, and Rollo, the great Northern chief, who afterwards settled in Gaul and

---

[1] Æthelweard calls them *pagani*.

founded the Duchy of Normandy, and was the ancestor of all the Dukes of the Normans of whom you will hear so much afterwards. But Rolf did not settle in Gaul till some years after Alfred was dead.

It was about the same time, seemingly in the same year 885, that Alfred's authority was, according to Asser, greatly increased in another part of Britain. A little time before him there had been a very powerful prince in Wales called Rhodri Mawr or Roderick the Great, under whom Wales was much stronger and more united than it had often been before or than it ever was again. But in 877 Rhodri died, being killed by "the Saxons," according to the Welsh Chronicle. After him his dominions were divided among his sons, who had so many quarrels with one another, and with other Welsh princes and with the English on their borders, that several of the Welsh princes thought it best to put themselves under the King of the West-Saxons as their Overlord. Thus the Kings of Dyfed (Pembrokeshire), Morganwg (Glamorgan), Gwent (Monmouth), and Brecknock all became Alfred's vassals, and so did Anarawd the son of Rhodri himself, who is said to have agreed to be the King even as Alderman Æthelred and the Mercians were.

In 886 Alfred repaired London, which seems to have been much damaged in the Danish wars, and gave it over to Alderman Æthelred as part of his government.

From this time till the year 892 the Chronicle has nothing at all to tell us about things in England, except a few very small matters; it really tells us more of what was going on in other countries than in our own. For some very important things happened about this time, which I may as well tell you. The last thing that you heard about foreign parts was that the great Empire of Charles the Great was divided into three Kingdoms and sometimes more; the Emperor having a certain nominal supremacy over all. But about this time, in the year 885, the whole Empire, or nearly so, was joined together again under the Emperor Charles the Fat. He was son of Lewis, King of the East-Franks, whom I told you of before, and great-grandson of Charles the Great. You see how one Charles was great in mind and the other only great in body. I say the whole Empire or nearly so, because there was one Boso, who was not of the house of the Karlings, who was King in Burgundy,[1] between the Saône, the Rhone, and the Alps. But Charles was Emperor and King of Italy and King of the East and West Franks. But his people despised him, and in 888 he was deposed, and the Empire was again divided, and was never joined together again. Germany and France, as we may now perhaps begin to call them (though it is better to wait for another hundred years), and Italy were never all joined together again. The East-Franks chose Arnulf, who was of the house of the Karlings, and who was afterwards crowned Emperor. But the West-Franks chose Odo, Count of Paris, because he had been very valiant in resisting the Danes, and because his city, lying on the Seine, was very important in defending the country against them. In Italy two Kings, Berenger and Wido, disputed the crown. Thus counting Burgundy there were four Kingdoms. There now comes a hundred years of great confusion in the Western Kingdom. Count Odo was the forefather of all the Kings of France since 987; I say since 987, because it was not till then that the crown was fully fixed in his family. Between 888 and 987, there were some Kings of the House of Odo of Paris and some of the House of the Karlings, whose city was Laôn. In the Eastern Kingdom or Germany Arnulf's son Lewis was the last King of the male line of the Karlings. The crown then went into other families, though some of the Kings were descended from Charles the Great through females. One may say that after Charles the Fat there was no regular Emperor for nearly eighty years. Arnulf was crowned Emperor, and so were some of the Kings of Italy, but there was no Emperor acknowledged by every body till Otto the Great in 963. He joined the Kingdoms of Germany and Italy and was crowned Emperor at Rome. And from that time it was always held that the man who was chosen King of Germany had also a right to be crowned King of Italy at Milan and Emperor of the Romans at Rome.

I have gone on thus far about foreign matters, because you

---

[1] The name Burgundy has many meanings at different times. Besides this Kingdom of Burgundy, which was often divided into two, there was the Duchy of Burgundy, the Duke of which was a vassal of the King of the West-Franks.

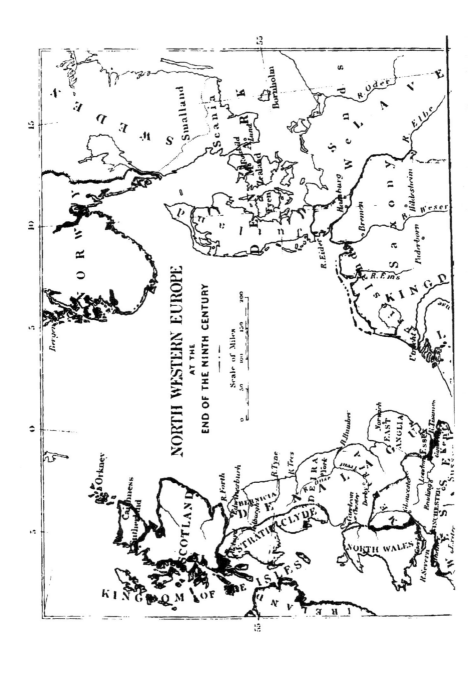

NORTH WESTERN EUROPE

AT THE

END OF THE NINTH CENTURY

Scale of Miles

0   50   100   150   200

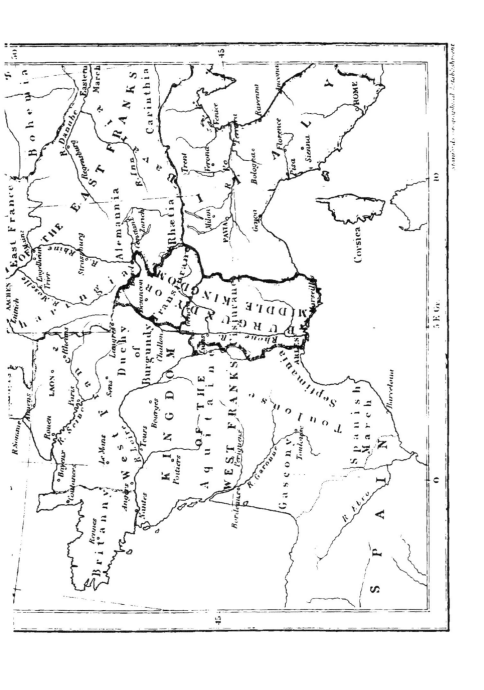

will find that we are getting to a time when England had much more to do with other countries than it had before, and several of the Kings of the East and West Franks will be spoken of in our English history as we go on. Also just at this time, as you have already seen, the same fleets of Danes were attacking both England and the opposite coasts, and, if they were driven away from one country, they generally crossed on to the other. Thus in 891 King Arnulf gained a great victory over the Northmen at Löwen in Brabant, which in French is called Louvain, after which they did very little mischief in Germany. But next year the same army came from " the east Kingdom " [*tham east rice*] to Boulogne[1] in Picardy, whence they came over to England. So the Danish wars began again in 893.

For five years now there was a great deal of fighting ; and we have very minute accounts, showing that the whole history must have been written down at the time. But I do not think that I need tell these wars at quite the same length as the wars in the early part of Alfred's reign, both because they are not nearly so famous and because they have not so much to do with our own part of England. Two large bodies of Danes, one of them under a famous chief called Hasting, landed in Kent in 893 and fixed themselves in fortresses which they built. And the Danes who had settled in Northumberland and East-Anglia helped them, though they had all sworn oaths to King Alfred, and those in East-Anglia had also given hostages. King Guthorm-Æthelstan had nothing to do with this, for he had died in the year 890. There was a great deal of fighting all over the south of England throughout 894, and the King had to go constantly backwards and forwards to keep up with the Danes. One time Alfred took a fort at Appledore in Kent, in which were the wife and two sons of Hasting. Now Hasting had not long before given oaths and hostages to Alfred, and the two boys had been baptized, the King being godfather to one of them and Alderman Æthelred to the other. But Hasting did not at all keep to his oath, but went on plundering all the same. Still, when the boys and their mother were taken, Alfred would not do them any harm, but gave them up again to

---

[1] *Bunan* in the Chronicle, from the Latin *Bononia*. The name is the same as that of *Bologna* in Italy.

Hasting. A little while after, while the King was fighting at Exeter with one party of them, another great host, many of them being from Northumberland and East-Anglia, went all the way up the Thames and then crossed to the Severn and went up the Severn. So Alderman Æthelred, and Æthelhelm Alderman of the Wilsætas, and another Alderman, Æthelnoth, who I suppose was Alderman of the Sumorsætas, went against them with all the men "from ilk borough[1] by east of Parret, both by east of Selwood and by west, both by north of Thames and west of Severn, and eke some deal [part] of the North-Welsh[2] kin." They followed the Danes up the Severn, as far as Buttington in what is now called Montgomeryshire, where they besieged them, and after a while fought a battle and defeated them. But a great many of them got away again into East-Anglia, and there left their wives, children, and spoil, and marched back as fast as they could to Chester. I mention this, because the Chronicle adds, what sounds very strange, that Chester was now a deserted place. This was still in 894. There was a great deal of fighting almost all over England, all the next three years. At last in 897 we read that Alfred made some improvements in his ships.

"Then had Alfred King timbered [built] long ships against the *æscs*[3]; they were full-nigh twice as long as the others ; some had sixty oars, some mo ; they were both swifter and steadier and eke higher than the others ; they were neither on the Frisian shape nor on the Danish, but as himself thought that they useful might be."

These new ships seem to have done good service, though one time they got aground, seemingly because they were so large, and the Danes were therefore able to sail out before them. The Chronicle says that the ships were not of the Frisian build, but King Alfred had many Frisians in his service. The Frisians, you should know, are the people along the north-coast, from

---

[1] *Burh, byrig, borough, burg,* that is any fortified place, great or small.

[2] "North-Welsh" here does not mean what we now call North-Welsh as opposed to South-Welsh, but rather the Welsh of what we call Wales generally, as opposed to those of Cornwall. They would doubtless be Alfred's new Welsh vassals, who were chiefly in what we now call South-Wales.

[3] The Danish long ships, from *æsc,* that is *ash.*

Holland up to Denmark. They are our nearest kinsmen on the continent, and speak a language nearer to English than any other ; in Alfred's time most likely the two languages were quite the same. These sea-fights along the south-coast were nearly the last things that we hear of in Alfred's reign. The crews of two Danish ships were brought to Winchester to Alfred and there hanged. One cannot blame him for this, as these Danes were mere pirates, not engaged in any lawful war, and many of them had been spared, and had made oaths to Alfred, and had broken them, over and over again.

This was in 897 ; the rest of King Alfred's reign seems to have been spent in peace. In 898 the Chronicle tells us only that Alderman Æthelhelm died, and also Heahstan or Ealhstan, Bishop of London. In 899 and 900 it tells us nothing at all. In 901 the great King died himself. He was then only fifty-two years old.

Alfred's wife, the Lady Ealhswith, lived a little while after her husband, till 903 or 905. They had five children, two sons, Edward, the next King, who had already begun to distinguish himself in the wars with the Danes, and Æthelweard. Of their three daughters you have heard of two, Æthelflæd, the Lady of the Mercians, the wife of the great Alderman Æthelred, and Æthelgifu, Abbess of Shaftesbury. The third was Ælfthryth, who married Baldwin the Second, Count of Flanders, the son of the first Baldwin and Judith. From this marriage descended Matilda, the wife of William the Conqueror, and thus it was that William's sons, though not William himself, were descended, in a kind of way, from Alfred, as they descended through Judith from Charles the Great.

King Alfred was buried at Winchester in the New Minster which he himself began to found and which was finished by his son Edward. It was then close to the Old Minster, that is the cathedral church. Afterwards it was moved out of the city and was called Hyde Abbey. But you cannot see King Alfred's grave there now, because everything has been destroyed, and the bones of the great King have been turned out, to make room for a prison.

§ 6. THE REIGN OF KING EDWARD THE ELDER.
901—925.

When King Alfred died, the Wise Men chose his son Eadweard or Edward to be King. It was not likely that they should choose anybody but the great King's own son, and one who had already shown himself valiant in his father's wars. But you may remember that Æthelred the eldest brother of Alfred left children, and his eldest son, according to the present law, would have been King instead of Alfred himself. But I have often told you that this was not the law in the old time, but that the Wise Men chose whom they would in the royal house. I tell you this again, because there was one Æthelwald an Ætheling, a son of Æthelred, who seems to have thought that he ought to be King. So he seized on two of the King's houses, Wimborne in Dorsetshire and Tweoxnam or Twynham, now called Christ Church, in Hampshire. But King Edward came against him with an army. Now the Ætheling had shut himself up in the town of Wimborne and said that he would live or die there. But when King Edward came near, he fled away, and that so fast that he could not be caught. This was a great pity, as he soon began to do a great deal of mischief. For he got away to the Danes in Northumberland and they made him their King.

King Edward, we are told, was as good a soldier but not so good a scholar as his father Alfred. We do not hear nearly so much as in Alfred's time of invasions of the Danes from abroad, but nearly all Edward's reign was taken up with fighting with the Danes who had settled in the north and east of England. They were always submitting and always rebelling. But in the end King Edward made himself lord over them and over the Scots and Welsh too. So King Edward was the first King of the West-Saxons who was Lord of all Britain. There was now no other English King, and the Kings and Princes of the Danes, Scots, and Welsh were all his vassals. So from his time our Kings no longer called themselves Kings of the West-Saxons or of the Saxons, but Kings of the Anglo-Saxons[1] or of

---

[1] Always remember that this does not mean *Saxons in England,* but *Angles and Saxons,* the nation made up by the union of the two.

the English, and sometimes Kings or Emperors[1] of all Britain.
But I do not find that King Edward speaks of himself in this
last way, as indeed he hardly could, as he was not Lord of all
Britain till quite the end of his reign. He commonly calls
himself *Rex Angol-Saxonum* or *Rex Anglorum.*

In the first two or three years of Edward's reign nothing
very great happened. There was a little fighting between the
Danes and the Kentishmen, the New Minster at Winchester
was hallowed, the Lady Ealhswith, the King's mother, died, and
such like. But in 904 Æthelwald began to give much trouble.
He came with a fleet to Essex, and the people submitted to
him, and the next year he persuaded the Danes in East-Anglia
to break the peace and invade Mercia. Indeed they got into
Wessex itself, for they came as far as Cricklade in Wiltshire and
thence they went on to Bredon in Worcestershire. Then they
went home. But King Edward went and harried all the Danish
land between the dyke and the Ouse, that is the western part
of East-Anglia, Cambridgeshire and thereabouts, and then
turned about to go home. But the Kentishmen would not
turn to come, though the King by his messengers bade them
seven times. So the Danes came and surrounded them, and I
suppose I must say defeated them, because the Danes kept the
battle-field. But the real victory was on the side of the English,
for many more of the Danes were slain than of themselves,
and among them Eoric the Danish King of East-Anglia, Æthelwald the Ætheling, and others of their chief men. But the
Kentishmen lost their two Aldermen[2] Sigulf (Sigewulf) and
Sighelm, and others of their chief men also.

The next year, 906, King Edward made peace with the
Danes both in East-Anglia and in Northumberland, and we are
told that the peace was made as King Edward thought good.
We have the terms of the treaty drawn up between Edward and

---

[1] Sometimes *Imperator*, very often *Basileus.* This was because the
Roman Emperors at Constantinople called themselves βασιλεύς, and
because our Kings wished to say that they were Emperors and not only
Kings, and that they owed no kind of service to the Emperors either of
East or West.

[2] Kent has two Bishops, Canterbury and Rochester, because in old
times there were two little kingdoms of East and West Kent. Most likely
each of them now had its own Alderman.

Guthorm, that is, no doubt, the son of Eoric and grandson of the old Guthorm-Æthelstan. Laws are put forth in the name of the two Kings, and both speak as Christians and command their people to give up all worship of idols. I do not know why the Chronicle should mention under this year the death of Alfred the town-reeve of Bath. I suppose he must have made himself remarkable in some way ; so, as it belongs to our own part of the world, I tell it you.

The war began again in 910, I hardly know how, for in that year we find King Edward attacking the Danes, though it is not till the next year that we read that the Danes broke the peace. So at least it stands in the Chronicle, but Florence makes them break a peace both years, which is certainly most likely. Anyhow in 910 King Edward won a battle over them at Tettenhall in Staffordshire, and in 911 he gained a still greater victory at Wodnesfield in the same shire. In 910[1] too we find the beginning of a system which goes on through all the rest of Edward's reign. In that year we read that Æthelflæd the Lady of the Mercians fortified Bramsbury, and from that time we find both the King and the Lady going on fortifying towns and castles almost every year. We find Æthelflæd mentioned and not Æthelred her husband ; most likely he was ill or getting old, for he died the next year, and Æthelflæd then ruled Mercia herself, only King Edward took London and Oxford into his own hands. For some years after the King and the Lady went on busily building in various places, chiefly along the line of frontier exposed to the Danes, as at Bridgenorth, Tamworth, Warwick, Hertford, Witham in Essex, and other places. No doubt all this was a great defence to the country. From this time we find the King and the Lady attacking the Danes instead of waiting to be attacked, and the only invasion of the Danes during these years is, not from the Danes settled in England, but from others who came from the south, no doubt out of Gaul.

I ought now to tell you how in 913 a very remarkable event took place in Gaul. A large body of the Danes or Northmen

---

[1] Or perhaps a little before, as in 907 we read that Chester was set up again : you may remember that in Alfred's time Chester was lying desolate.

settled there, something in the same way as Guthorm had done in East-Anglia. Charles the Simple who was of the house of the Great Charles, but who was very unlike him, was then King of the West-Franks, and reigned at Laôn, and Robert was Count of Paris and was called Duke of the French.[1] King Charles married Eadgifu, a daughter of our King Edward. Duke Robert was afterwards himself King for a little while. There was, as I said before, at this time a very famous leader of the Northmen called Rolf, who had done great damage both in England and in Gaul. He is said to have been called Rolf Ganger, that is the Goer or Walker, because he was too tall to ride, for when he sat on one of the small horses of the North, his feet touched the ground. After going about the world for many years, Rolf seemed inclined to settle somewhere, so King Charles and Duke Robert agreed with him that, if he would become a Christian and leave off ravaging the rest of the country, he should have a great province to hold in fief of the King, and should marry the King's daughter. So Rolf agreed to this, and was baptized by the name of Robert, after Duke Robert his godfather. But he still was better known as Rolf, just as we do not call Guthorm by his new name of Æthelstan. In Latin Rolf becomes *Rollo* and in French *Rou*. The story is told that when Rolf was to do homage for his Duchy he was ordered to kneel and kiss the King's feet. But Rolf said that he would not kiss the feet of any man, and told one of his soldiers to do it for him. The soldier did it in a kind of way, not by kneeling down, but by catching up the King's foot and lifting it to his mouth, so that the King and his throne were nearly upset. You may suppose that this was not the regular way of doing homage, and that King Charles and his nobles did not much like it, but

---

[1] It is not easy to say when, in talking of Gaul or West-France, one should leave off saying *Franks* and begin to say *French*. Perhaps the best way is to say *Franks* as long as one is talking of the old Karling Kings at Laôn, and *French* when one speaks of the new Dukes and Kings at Paris. For the Karlings were Germans and kept on speaking German to the last, while the Paris family were the ancestors of the later French Kings, and they seem to have spoken a Romance tongue all through this century. When the Paris Kings finally triumphed, we may look on the German power and the German tongue as having come to an end in Gaul, and modern France as beginning.

they were too much afraid of Rolf to say much about it, and they were obliged to let it reckon as good homage. So Rolf took possession of his Duchy, a territory on each side of the Seine, with the city of Rouen for his capital. He and his son William Longsword afterwards added greatly to it, till it took in six Bishops' sees besides Rouen the Archbishoprick. These are Bayeux, Evreux, Lisieux, Seez, Avranches, and Coutances,[1] besides Caen, which became a greater town than any except Rouen, though it never was a Bishop's see. This was a very fine and rich territory, and it made Rolf and his descendants great princes. He was called Duke or Count of the Northmen, and his land was the Land of the Northmen (*Terra Northmannorum*). Rolf seems to have ruled very well, and to have done all that he could to civilize his people and to undo the damage that he had done in past years. And his people gradually left off speaking Danish and learned to speak French, so that in the time of William, Rolf's son, nobody at Rouen talked Danish at all, but it was still spoken at Bayeux. So as Duke William wished his son Richard to speak both tongues, he sent him to Bayeux to learn Danish. And as the Danes learned to speak French, they softened their name from *Northmen* into *Normans*, and their land began to be called *Normandy* (Normannia). I tell you all this now because we shall hear so much more of the Normans and their Dukes, for Rolf and William and Richard were all forefathers of the great William, who, a hundred and fifty years after this time, became King of the English.

Now it would seem as if it had something to do with this settlement of Rolf in Gaul that not long after, in 915 or 918 (for the dates differ), a fleet of Danes came from the south, perhaps from Britanny. Very likely some of Rolf's people did not like settling on land, and so took to their old roving life again. Anyhow there came a fleet into the Severn under two Earls, Ohter and Hroald, and they did much damage on the coast of Wales. But the men of Gloucester and Hereford fought against them, and made them give hostages and promise to go away out of King Edward's dominions. And King Edward kept watch over the whole coast of Somersetshire,

---

[1] *Constantia*, from the Emperor Constantine or some of his family. It is the same name as the other *Constantia* in Swabia, now Constanz.

that they might not land anywhere. They tried to land both at
Watchet and at Porlock, but they were driven off at both places,
and most of them were killed, except those who could swim to
their ships. These few went and "sat" on one of the Holms,
the islands at the mouth of the Severn, either the Steep
Holm or the Flat ;[1] but they could get nothing to eat, so many
of them died, and the rest sailed away, first to Dyfed or Pembrokeshire and thence to Ireland.

This was in 915, and I think it is the last invasion from
foreign parts during the reign of Edward. We hear once or
twice of "vikings" helping the Danes in England, but not of
their coming wholly by themselves. For the wars with the
Danes in England still went on, and the King and the Lady
were still gaining upon them and building towns and castles.
Thus we find that the Lady took Derby in 917 and Leicester
in 918, and the same year she was treating for the surrender
of York, when she was taken ill and died at Tamworth and was
buried at Gloucester. Æthelflæd had ruled Mercia for seven
years after the death of her husband Æthelred. She was a
worthy daughter of Alfred and a worthy sister of Edward.
Besides her wars with the Danes, she had some fighting with
the Welsh, for in 916 she stormed the town of Brecknock, and
took the wife of the Welsh King prisoner. The Welsh chro- ·
nicles call Æthelflæd Queen, but she certainly had no such title.
She and Æthelred had no son, but they left a daughter named
Ælfwyn. If they had left a son, King Edward could hardly
have helped making him Alderman of the Mercians ; but it
was not usual for women to rule ; Æthelflæd herself was quite
an exception. So it is not at all wonderful when we read
that King Edward did not let his niece Ælfwyn rule in
Mercia, but took her away into Wessex in 919. And yet the
Chronicle tells it in a sort of complaining way, as if people
did not think it quite right. Very likely the Mercians still
liked to have an Alderman of their own, as the next thing
to having a King of their own. And it might have been
more generous if Edward had given his niece in marriage to

---

[1] Some copies of the Chronicle have "*Bradanreolice*," *Bread* or Flat
Holm, and some "*Steapanreolice*," which speaks for itself. But why
either of the Holms should be called *Reolic* I cannot say.

some valiant man, just as Alfred had given Æthelflæd herself to Æthelred, and had made him Alderman of the Mercians.[1] But in the long run it was a great gain to have Mercia and Wessex more closely joined together, as they were from this time. All this time, from 915 onwards, King Edward was building his towns and castles. In 915 a Danish chief called Thurcytel or Thurkill came to King Edward with many of his men, and "sought him to lord;" and five years after they went by sea to "Frankland," by King Edward's leave. Did they go to join Rolf in his new Duchy of Normandy? Meanwhile the King went on building at Bedford and Towcester and at Wigmore in Herefordshire. At last, in 921, the Danes seem to have made a great effort to resist him and to take all his towns and castles. So they attacked Bedford and Towcester and Wigmore and Maldon, but they were beaten and driven away everywhere. In the course of that year and the next Thurfrith, the Danish Earl of Northampton, submitted to Edward, and so did all the people in Essex and East-Anglia and the rest of Mercia, the English people who were under the Danes receiving him very gladly. But we do not find that King Edward at all oppressed the Danes, for, when he built Nottingham, he set both Englishmen and Danes to live in the town. That year, 922, all the Welsh Kings came to Edward and "sought him to lord." But some say that this was not till after a good deal of fighting, in which the Welsh, with some Danes and Irish to help them, had tried to get possession of Chester. The next year, 923, King Edward built Thelwall in Cheshire, and took Manchester "in Northumberland." But we read the same year that Rægnald (Reginald, Rainald) a Danish King took York, but he soon became King Edward's man. In 924 King Edward built another fort at Nottingham so as to secure both sides of the river Trent, with a bridge across it. Thus he had pretty well all Mercia in his hands. And now we read,

"And him chose then to father and to lord the King of Scots and all the folk of the Scots, and Rægnald and Eadulf's

[1] According to one story, which however is not in the Chronicle, Ælfwyn was sought in marriage by a son of the Danish King Guthred. If this be true, we can neither wonder at Edward nor blame him.

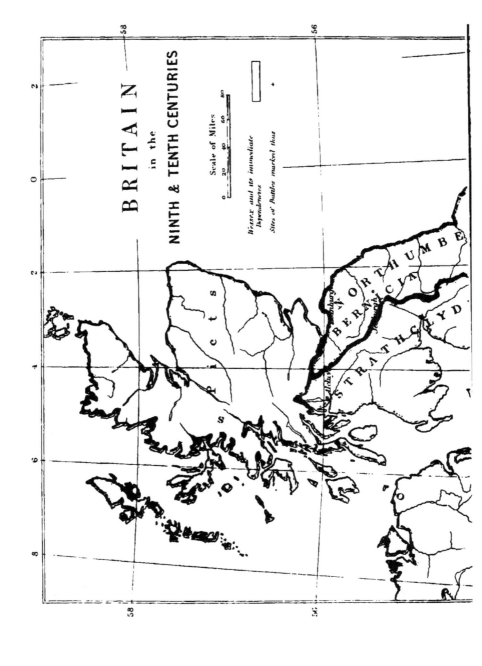

BRITAIN
in the
NINTH & TENTH CENTURIES

Scale of Miles

Desert and its immediate
Dependences

Sites of Battles marked thus

P i c t s

S

NORTHUMBE

BERNICIA

STRATHCLYD

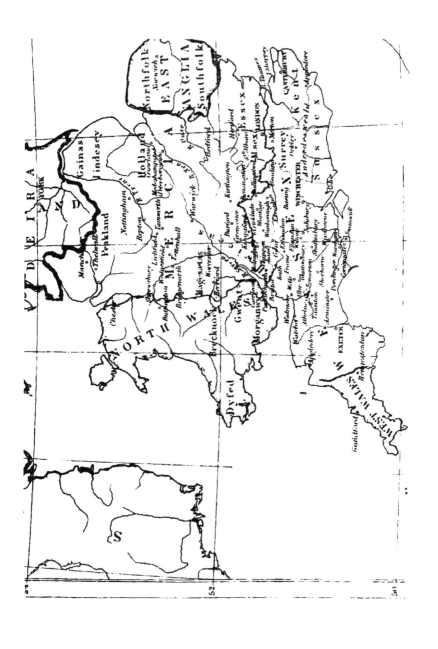

son, and all that in Northumberland dwell, whether English or Danish or Northmen or any others ; and eke the King of the Strathclyde Welsh and all the Strathclyde Welsh."

Thus did Edward, King of the English, become LORD OF ALL BRITAIN. Wessex, Kent, and Sussex he had inherited, Mercia, Essex, and East-Anglia he and his sister had won back from the Danes. Thus much was his own Kingdom. And all Northumberland, Wales, Scotland, and Strathclyde did homage to him as their Overlord. No one King in Britain had ever had so much power. None of the old Bretwaldas had so large a country in their own hands, none of them had extended their power so completely over the Welsh, and none of them, save those who reigned in Northumberland, had any power over the Scots at all. From this time the King of the English was the Overlord of the Welsh and the Scots, just as much as the Emperor and the King of the West-Franks were Overlords of any of the princes within their dominions who held their Duchies and Counties of them. You must well understand this, because otherwise you will get very wrong notions of some things in later times. When another King Edward, the first of the name after the Norman Conquest, made the Scots and Welsh do homage to him, he was not, as many people fancy, doing anything new or demanding anything unjust, but was simply defending the rights of his Crown which had been handed down to all the Kings of the English from the time of the first Edward, the son of Alfred.

The year after he had reached this height of power, the great King Edward died at Farndon in Mercia, that is in Northamptonshire, and was buried at Winchester. He left behind him a great many sons and daughters, most of whom became Kings and Queens. Three of his sons, Æthelstan, Eadmund, and Eadred, were all Kings of the English. Of his daughters five married foreign princes, either in their father's time or in their brother Æthelstan's ; another had to put up with a Danish King Sihtric in Northumberland ; and three became nuns. You know it was not usual in those days to marry out of the country, but King Æthelstan, through the marriages of his sisters, was brother-in-law

L

to most of the chief princes of Europe. For, as I think I told you, Eadgifu married Charles the Simple, King of the West-Franks ; and afterwards, when King Charles was deposed, she and her son Lewis took shelter with her father King Edward. Another Eadgifu married Lewis, King of Provence or Arles, that is the southern part of the Kingdom of Burgundy ; Eadhild married Hugh the Great, Duke of the French, son of King Robert, whom I mentioned before. And another sister made a greater marriage than all. For Henry, King of the East-Franks, sent to Æthelstan to ask for one of his sisters in marriage for his son Otto. So Æthelstan sent him two, Eadgyth or Edith and Ælfgifu, and bade him choose one for his son and give the other to one of his princes. So Ælfgifu was given to a prince near the Alps ; but Otto chose Edith for his wife. This was Otto the Great, who was afterwards Emperor, and who joined the Empire for ever to the Kingdom of the East-Franks, but this was not till after Edith was dead, so that she never was Empress. Of another sister, Eadburh, men told this tale.

The Story of Eadburh the Daughter of Edward.

Now when Eadburh, the daughter of King Edward and Eadgifu his Lady, was but three years old, it came into the King's heart to prove the child, whether she would dwell in the world or go out of the world to serve God. So he put on one side rings and bracelets and on the other a chalice and a book of the Gospels. And the child was brought in the arms of her nurse, and King Edward took her on his knees, and he said, " Now, my child, whether of these things wilt thou choose ? " And the child turned away from the rings and the bracelets, and took in her hand the chalice and the book of the Gospels. Then King Edward kissed his child and said, " Go whither God calleth thee ; follow the spouse whom thou hast chosen; and thy mother and I will be happy if we have a child holier than ourselves." So Eadburh became a nun in the city of Winchester, and served God with fastings and prayers all the days of her life.

Besides his three sons who reigned after him, King Edward had a son Edwin, of whom we shall hear again, and another son Æthelweard or Ælfweard, who is said to have been a great scholar and to have been in all things like his grandfather Alfred, but he died soon after his father. And some say that he had yet another son, named Gregory, who went away to Rome and became a monk, and thence went into the mountains of Swabia and became Abbot of Einsiedlen and got many gifts for his church from his brother-in-law the Emperor Otto. But I do not find anything like this in our English books, and I feel sure that no son of an English King in those days was called Gregory, though he may have changed his name to Gregory when he became a monk.

Also I must tell you that King Edward divided the Bishoprick of Sherborne into two, and gave the men of Somersetshire a Bishop of their own, and placed his see in the church of Saint Andrew in Wells which King Ine had founded. The first Bishop of Wells was Ealdhelm. Thus it was in the year 909 that Wells became a Bishop's see and Saint Andrew's a cathedral church.

I have now told you how the Danes came into England, and how England became one Kingdom. So I will end this long chapter here and begin another with the reign of the great Æthelstan, the son of Edward.

CHAPTER IX.

OF THE KINGS OF THE ENGLISH FROM THE TIME THAT ENGLAND BECAME ONE KINGDOM TILL THE DANES CAME AGAIN.

§ 1. The Reign of King Æthelstan.

925—940.

WHEN King Edward died, his eldest son Æthelstan was chosen King, and we find it specially' said that the Mercians chose him, so that the Mercians must still have had a meeting of their own Wise Men separate from the meeting of the West-Saxons. He was then hallowed as King at Kingston in Surrey, as were several of the Kings after him. You know that Westminster is now the place where our Kings are crowned, but this did not begin till the time of King Harold. King Æthelstan now gave one of his sisters, as I before told you, to Sihtric, the Danish King of Northumberland. But Sihtric died the next year, and then Æthelstan drove out his son Guthfrith or Godfrey, who had succeeded him, and took Northumberland into his own hands. Then the other princes of Britain, Howel King of the West-Welsh,[1] and Owen King of Gwent, and Constantine King of Scots, and Ealdred the son of Eadwulf of Bamborough, tried to fight against Æthelstan, but he overcame them in battle and made them do homage, and he

---

[1] The West-Welsh generally means the Welsh of Cornwall and Devonshire, but here it seems to mean the western part of Wales as opposed to Gwent or Monmouthshire. This Howel is a very famous King among the Welsh, on account of the Laws which he put together. He is called Howel the Good.

drove out Ealdred altogether. So Æthelstan was Lord of all Britain, as his father Edward had been before him. Thus much we learn from the Chronicle with a little help from Florence, who explains some matters a little more at large; but it is somewhat strange that, though Æthelstan was undoubtedly one of our greatest Kings, the account of his reign in the Chronicle is very short, and in some years there is nothing told us at all. To be sure we have the great song of the Battle of Brunanburh, which you may sing presently, but we have not much besides. On the other hand William of Malmesbury gives a very long account of Æthelstan and is full of stories about him. Æthelstan was a great benefactor to the Abbey of Malmesbury, and was buried there; so he was no doubt much thought of by the monks of Malmesbury, which is of course the reason why William writes of him at such length. But then we cannot trust William's stories as we can trust the history in the Chronicle. In one place indeed he professes to quote some writer who is now lost, but most of the tales are evidently made up out of songs or out of traditions of the Abbey of Malmesbury. I shall therefore take such parts of William's account as seem likely to be true history, and work them in with what I find in the Chronicle, and I will tell as stories such stories as seem worth telling in that way. Altogether there are perhaps as many stories about Æthelstan as there are about either Alfred or Edgar, but they do not generally seem to have been so famous in later times, or to be so well known now.

Æthelstan was thirty years old when he was chosen King. He was therefore born in 895, when his grandfather Alfred was still alive. He was a fair and graceful child, and his grandfather loved him, and is said to have made him a soldier while very young—for he was only six years old when Alfred died—and to have given him a purple cloak and a belt studded with gems and a sword[1] with a golden scabbard. After this,

---

[1] " Ensis Saxonicus." Does this mean the *sax*, the old, short, crooked sword, from which, according to some accounts, the Saxons took their name? The use of the word " Saxonicus" should be noted. As William can hardly be copying any Welsh writer, it would seem to imply something distinctly *Saxon* as opposed to *Anglian*.

he sent him to be brought up by his aunt Æthelflæd, the Lady of the Mercians, and by Alderman Æthelred her husband. So says William of Malmesbury, most likely out of some ballad. According to one story, Æthelstan's mother was a shepherd's daughter and was not the lawful wife of Edward, and on that account some people objected to his election. But Florence calls his mother Ecgwyn a noble lady (*mulier nobilissima*). And it is also rather strange that we find no mention of any wife or children of Æthelstan himself. To be sure Æthelstan had young brothers and sisters enough, so that there was no fear of the royal house coming to an end.

I just now told you that some people are said to have objected to Æthelstan's election. At their head was one Alfred, perhaps himself an Ætheling[1] who wished to be chosen King instead. Alfred was presently accused of conspiring to blind the new King at Winchester. I suppose that the evidence was not clear, and in such cases it was not unusual to allow a man to clear himself by swearing that he was innocent, and by bringing a fixed number of people to swear that they believed him. The oath was to be made before a Bishop, and, in this case, to make it the more solemn, Alfred was sent to Rome to swear before the Pope, John the Tenth. He there swore at the altar of Saint Peter's in the Pope's presence, but he at once fell down and was carried by his servants to the English school at Rome, where he died on the third day. Now this is a very strange story, and it is so like some other stories that one is tempted to set it down as one of those tales which go the round of the world, and which turn up in all manner of times and places. Yet William of Malmesbury does not tell it as if it came from any ballad or mere tradition, but he quotes a charter of King Æthelstan's own to the Abbey of Malmesbury, in which Æthelstan himself tells the story. For of course it was held that the death of Alfred was God's judgement upon him for a false oath, so that he was proved to be guilty of the treason with which he was charged. So the Wise Men gave Alfred's lands to King Æthelstan, and King Æthelstan gave them to the

---

[1] Perhaps he was a descendant of Æthelred, the elder brother of the great Alfred, like Æthelwald who opposed the election of Edward.

Abbey of Malmesbury. All this William of Malmesbury quotes from the charter, as if in Æthelstan's own words. So then, if the story be not true, and one can hardly think it is true, the charter must have been forged at some time between the days of Æthelstan and those of William of Malmesbury.

I will now go on with Æthelstan's wars, as far as they can be made out. I told you how, when Sihtric of Northumberland died, King Æthelstan took possession of his land and drove out his son Guthfrith or Godfrey. William of Malmesbury goes on to tell us a good deal more about this matter, which may very likely be true in the main, though it sounds very much as if it came out of a ballad. When King Æthelstan took possession of Northumberland, the sons of Sihtric, Anlaf[1] and Guthfrith, fled away, Anlaf to Ireland, and Guthfrith to Constantine King of Scots. So King Æthelstan sent to Constantine, bidding him to give up Guthfrith. Constantine was afraid of the English King, and agreed to give Guthfrith up, but he escaped again with one Thurfrith and sat down before York.[2] He there tried both with threats and prayers to make the citizens rebel against King Æthelstan, but they would not hearken. Soon after Guthfrith and Thurfrith were besieged in a strong place, and, lo, they escaped yet again. Thurfrith went out to sea and was shipwrecked and drowned and became food for the fishes.[3] But Guthfrith went to King Æthelstan and craved peace of him ; and the King received him kindly, and feasted him for four days. But after the four days, Guthfrith went back to his ships, for he was an old sea-robber and was used to live in the water like a fish. Meanwhile King Æthelstan plucked down the strong tower which the Danes had of old built at York, so that it might never be held against him, and the spoil that was in the tower he divided among his army, man by man. For King Æthelstan hated greediness and was alway bountiful to all men. Such is William of Malmesbury's story, who says

---

[1] This is how our Chronicles write the name, which is doubtless the same as Olaf.

[2] "Obsidens." The story therefore conceives him as having something of an army with him.

[3] This bit and the other bit directly after, comparing Guthfrith to a fish, must surely come from a ballad.

that Constantine, when he promised to give up Guthfrith, submitted himself and his Kingdom to Æthelstan, and that Æthelstan ordered Constantine's son to be baptized, and that he himself stood godfather to him. Now this reads as if William thought that the King of Scots was a heathen, whereas we know that the Scots had been Christians even longer than the English. I suppose all this is a confused account of what we read in the Chronicle and in Florence under the year 933 or 934,[1] how the King of Scots broke the peace—whether by receiving Guthfrith or in any other way I do not know—and how King Æthelstan went against him both with a fleet and a land army, and harried his land, till Constantine prayed for peace and gave the King large gifts and his son as a hostage.

William of Malmesbury also tells us a great deal about Æthelstan's wars with the Welsh in both parts of the island where they remained, that is to say, both in Wales and in Cornwall. He made all the princes of Wales do homage to him at Hereford ; he fixed the Wye as the boundary between England and Wales, and, what no English King had done before, he made the Welsh princes pay a tribute of gold, silver, oxen, hunting-dogs, and falcons. He then went against the other Welsh in Cornwall. Up to this time the city of Exeter, the greatest town in that part of Britain, had been inhabited by Englishmen and Welshmen, who had equal rights. But Æthelstan drove out the Welshmen from Exeter and fortified the city with towers and a wall of squared stones. Many towns and strong places at this time were fortified only with wood, or at most with quite rough stone, but William distinctly says that the walls of Exeter were built of squared stones. This shows that our forefathers were not such bad builders as some people have thought that they were. Æthelstan made the Tamar the boundary in this direction, so that the Welsh kept only what is still called Cornwall. This is said to have been in 926. Thus it took 349 years to make all Somersetshire and Devonshire English. I count from Ceawlin's coming in 577. And no doubt, from the Axe to the Tamar, and still more from the Parret to the Tamar, the people are still very largely of Welsh descent, though they

[1] In Simeon of Durham, who, for a northern matter, is perhaps better authority, it is 934.

have spoken English for many ages. In Cornwall itself, in the narrower sense in which we must now use the word, the old Welsh tongue went on being spoken for many hundred years after the time of Æthelstan.

I do not see any reason to doubt this account of William's, because it contradicts nothing of more authority and is quite credible in itself. And we know that Æthelstan was at Exeter, as some of his laws are dated there. When he had done so much for the city and for that whole country, he would very naturally have a meeting of the Wise Men there rather than anywhere else.

We now come to Æthelstan's great war and victory in the north in 937. He had then a great many enemies to struggle with at once. A Danish King Anlaf, who seems to be a different person from Anlaf the son of Sihtric, came back from Ireland with many ships, and he was joined by Constantine of Scotland and Owen of Cumberland, and by all the Danes, Scots, and Welshmen of the north. William of Malmesbury tells us that just before the great battle Anlaf came into the English camp in the garb of a gleeman and with a harp in his hand. And he sang and played before King Æthelstan and his lords, for they knew him not. And they were pleased with his song, and they gave him gold as men gave to a gleeman. And he took the gold, but he would not keep it, but buried it in the earth, for that it was a shame for a King to keep gold which had been given him for hire. And a soldier saw him hiding the gold, and knew him. And the soldier went to King Æthelstan and said, " My Lord O King, Anlaf thine enemy hath been in thy camp and hath seen thy power and where thou dwellest; for it was he that came and played before thee and thy lords in the garb of a gleeman." And King Æthelstan answered and said, " Wherefore then didst not thou give mine enemy into my hands when he was in thy power? Now art thou no true soldier, for that thou servest not thy lord the King faithfully." And the soldier answered and said, " My Lord O King, I was once a soldier of Anlaf's, and the same oath which I have taken to thee I then took to Anlaf. Now if I had broken mine oath to Anlaf and had given him into thine hand, then couldest thou not have trusted me that I should not do the like unto thee. But hearken now unto the voice of thy servant, and move thy tent from hence, and wait till the rest of thine host cometh, and then shalt thou fight against Anlaf and smite him." So King Æthelstan moved his tent to another place. And in the evening Werstan the Bishop of Sherborne came with his men to join the King's host. And Werstan pitched his tent where the King's tent had been pitched aforetime. And in the night came Anlaf with his host, and brake into the camp, and went straightway to the place where the King's tent had been, and slew Werstan the Bishop and all his folk. But when they found that the King was not there, they went on further, even to the place where the King's tent was now pitched. Now King Æthelstan slept, for he deemed not that Anlaf his enemy would come against him by night. But when he heard the noise and the tumult, he woke from his sleep, and bade his men arm themselves for the battle. And the King's sword dropped from his sheath, so that he found it not. Then prayed he to God and to Saint Ealdhelm, and he stretched forth his hand to the sheath, and found there a sword, and with that sword he fought against Anlaf his enemy; and that sword is kept in the King's treasurehouse to this day.

This is William's story. As usual, people are fond of telling so much of the tale as they think is possible, and leaving out all about the wonderful sword. But I do not think this is fair; so I tell it you, as I do the other tales, as a tale. You will at once see that part of it is the same as one of the stories about Alfred; no doubt it is one of those stories which, as I before said, get fixed sometimes to one man and sometimes to another.

It was in this campaign that the great battle of Brunanburh was fought. Brunanburh was somewhere in Northumberland, but no one knows exactly where. In telling of this great fight, it seems as if the Chronicler could not keep himself to plain prose, so he gives its history in verse, which I will give you with as little change as I can.

𝕿𝖍𝖊 𝕾𝖔𝖓𝖌 𝖔𝖋 𝖙𝖍𝖊 𝕱𝖎𝖌𝖍𝖙 𝖔𝖋 𝕭𝖗𝖚𝖓𝖆𝖓𝖇𝖚𝖗𝖍.

Now Æthelstan King,
Of Earls[1] the Lord,
To warriors[2] the ring-giver,
And his brother eke,
Eadmund Ætheling,   5
Eld-long[3] glory
Won in the fight
With the sword's edge
By Brunanburh.
The boardwall[4] they clave,   10
And hewed the war-linden,[5]
With hammer's leavings,[6]
Offspring of Eadward,
As to them kindly was
From their forefathers,   15
That they in fight oft
With every foeman
Their land should guard,
Their hoard and homes.
The foemen cringed,[7]   20
The Scottish people,

And the ship-floaters
Death-doomed[8] fell.
The field streamed
With warriors' sweat,[9]   25
Since the Sun up
At morning-tide,
The glorious star,
Glode over grounds,
God's candle[10] bright,   30
The everlasting Lord's,
Till the noble shape[11]
Sank to her settle.[12]
Here lay warriors many
By javelins pierced,   35
Northern men
Over shield shot,
So Scottish eke,
Weary war-sated.
And West-Saxons forth,   40
The life-long day,
In warlike bands,

---

[1] That is of *nobles*, or perhaps warriors in general. *Earl* did not, except among the Danes, become a special title answering to *Alderman* till Cnut's time.

[2] I hardly know how to translate the word *Beorn.* I am not clear that *Ber, Baron,* and the like, are not corruptions of it, but it would hardly do to talk of Barons so soon.

[3] Glory to last all his life, till his *eld* or old age.

[4] The wall of shields made of wood.

[5] Shields made of linden or lime wood.

[6] That is with the *sword*, what the hammer leaves after beating out the iron.

[7] In the literal sense, *fell* or *died ;* now we only use the word figuratively.

[8] *Fæge ;* the word *fey* is still sometimes used in Scotland for a man whose death is near, which is thought to be marked by some change in him, especially by his being unusually merry.

[9] That is *blood.*

[10] It is *candel* in the Old-English. This is one of the words which came into English very early and straight from Latin, no doubt as being an ecclesiastical word. Had it come through the French, we should say *chandle,* as we do call a man who makes candles a *chandler.* But we say *candle,* because it comes straight from *candela.*

[11] *Gesceaft,* the thing *shaped,* the creature, that is the sun.

[12] *Seat* or place—not a golden cup, as in the Greek story.

On the footsteps lay[1]
Of the loathed people.
Hewed they the flyers   45
Behind mightily
With swords mill-sharp.[2]
Nor did Mercians shrink from[3]
The hard handplay
With none of heroes,[4]   50
That with Anlaf
Over the ocean[5]
On the ships' bosom
The land sought.
Doomed to the fight,[6]   55
Five there lay
On the fightstead[7]
Kings young ;
So seven eke
Earls[8] of Anlaf,   60
Countless fighting men,[9]
Fleetmen and Scots.
There put to flight was
The Northmen's chieftain,
By need driven   65
To the ship's prow
With a little band.

Crowded[10] he his bark afloat,
The King out got him
On the fallow flood,   70
His life delivered.
So there eke the old one
In flight came
To his kith[11] northward,
Constantinus,   75
Hoary war-man.
Boast he might not
Of the swords' meeting ;
He was of kinsmen shorn,
Of friends bereaved,   80
On the folkstead[12]
Slain in the battle.
And his son left he,
On the slaughter-place,[13]
With wounds ground down,   85
Young in warfare.[14]
Vaunt him might not
The warrior with grey[15]
    hair,
Of the bills clashing,
That old deceiver.   90
Nor Anlaf the mo,

---

[1] That is *followed*.   [2] Sharp from the grindstone.
[3] Literally, *warned*.
[4] *Heleð*, the same word as the High-Dutch (or German) *held*.
[5] Why the sea is called "*ærgebland*" I do not know.
[6] There are so many words in the old tongue for *battle, warriors*, &c. that I cannot put a different word each time without using Latin words, which I avoid as much as I can. Here the word is *fight* (gefeaht), but in l. 57 the word is *campstede, camp* being of course the same as the High-Dutch *kampf*, and in l. 61 the word is *heriges*, cognate with the High-Dutch *heer*.
[7] See note 6.
[8] Here Earls means *Jarls*, the Danish title, like our *Alderman*.
[9] See note 6.
[10] That is *thrust, pushed, hastened*.
[11] That is land or home.
[12] The *stead* or place where *folk* meet, the trysting-place ; here the battle-field.
[13] *Wælstow*.
[14] *Guð* (Guth), yet another word for battle.
[15] "Beorn blanden feax :" *blond* here meaning *grey ; feax* is the same word that we find in the name Fair*fax*.

With their hosts' remnants;[1]
Laugh they might not
That in the war-work[2]
Better were they   95
On the fightstead[3]
In the banners' joining,
In the spears' meeting,
In the men's gathering,[4]
In the weapons' clashing,   100
Where on the deathfield
They then with Edward's
Offspring played.
Went forth the Northmen
In their nailed barks,   105
The darts', bloody leaving,[5]
On the roaring sea,
Over deep water,
Dublin to seek
And once more Ireland,   110
Ashamed in mood.
So too the brethren,
Both together,
King and Ætheling,
Their kith sought,   115
The West-Saxons' land,
In the war rejoicing.
Left they behind them

Corpses to feast on
With sallow coat,[6]   120
Both the swart raven
With horned nib,
And him of dusky coat
The erne[7] behind white ;
Carcases to eat ;   125
The greedy war-hawk,
And that grey deer,[8]
The wolf of the weald.
Never was slaughter more
In this island   130
Afore yet
Of folk o'erthrown
Before this
With the sword's edge,
As to us say books,   135
Men of old wisdom,
Sith from east hither
Angles and Saxons
Up became.
Over the broad sea   140
Britain they sought ;
The haughty war-smiths[9]
The Welsh overcame,
Earls[10] for glory eager,
A home they gat them.   145

---

[1] " Herelafum "—" leavings of the *here* " or army.   In High-Dutch *heer*.

[2] Another word for war, " *beadu*-weorca."

[3] " Campsted " as before.

[4] *Gumena gemôtes—Guma* means *man*.   We have the word in an odd corruption in " bridegroom," which should be " bridegoom," and has nothing to do with a *groom*.   The High-Dutch " Bräutigam " is nearer to the true form.   *Gemôt* is the word for a meeting, *Witenagemôt*, *Scirgemôt*, or any other.

[5] That is, those whom the darts left, who escaped from the darts.

[6] Seemingly the pale hue of the corpses, but the passage is very obscure.

[7] The real English name for the *eagle*, which word is of course from the French and Latin.

[8] "*Deor*," like θήρ and *thier*, means any beast: so Shakespere talks of " rats and mice and such small deer."

[9] A smith is one who makes or works anything ; so a soldier is a *war-smith* (wigsmið).

[10] *Earls:* see the note at the beginning ; the whole people are here clearly called *carls*.

I have given you this as a specimen of the songs in which our forefathers set forth the great deeds of their Kings and chiefs, and from which no doubt a good deal of our history, as it is called, was afterwards made up. There are several other such songs in the Chronicle, but this is the first, the longest, and the grandest. But I want you to mark the difference between this song and many others. There is in the song of Brunanburh nothing like a story or legend, nothing, if you strip it of its poetic language, except a few plain facts which the writer might have put into three or four lines of prose. " King Æthelstan and his brother the Ætheling Edmund fought a battle at Brunanburh against the Scots under Constantine and the Danes from Ireland under Anlaf, and gained a great victory. Five Danish Kings, seven Earls, and the son of the King of Scots were killed, while Constantine and Anlaf escaped. Then Æthelstan and Edmund went back in triumph to Wessex." This is really all, and you will see that the song tells us less about the battle as a political and military matter than is usual in the Chronicle. For instance, Did Constantine do homage again, and did he give more hostages, or anything of that kind? We are not told a word. Such a song is merely the history of the year in verse instead of in prose, and it is just as much to be believed as if it were in prose. But the kind of songs which William of Malmesbury speaks of, and which he often follows, are something quite different. They are *stories* and not *histories*, and we must judge of each as we can. We had one just before the battle, and I shall give you another presently.

The fight of Brunanburh was in 937. Of the two next years we read nothing, and in the year 940 King Æthelstan died at Gloucester, and was buried in the Abbey of Malmesbury, to which he had been so great a benefactor. A tomb is shown there which is said to be his, and very likely it is so, but it must have been made again some hundred years after his time, as was often done. Besides his gifts to Malmesbury, he built a church at Middleton, now called Milton, in Dorsetshire, and founded a college of priests in it, which was afterwards changed into an abbey of monks. Besides attending to war and religion, Æthelstan was, like so many of our old Kings, very careful in putting forth laws, and in having them rightly administered. I have already told you how some of his laws were put forth at Exeter, after he had driven the Welsh out of the city. Altogether Æthelstan was one of our greatest and best Kings. and though his grandfather Alfred was the best and greatest of all, yet we should not forget either him or his father Edward, especially as it was they who really founded the Kingdom of England. But what chiefly distinguishes Æthelstan from nearly all the rest of our old Kings is the great influence which he had in foreign parts, through having married his sisters to all the greatest princes in Europe. According to some writers his court was a sort of school for young Kings, who were sent to him to learn how to govern, but I do not see any ground for thinking this. For instance, there was one Hakon, King of the Norwegians, who is called "Æthelstan's foster," as having been brought up by Æthelstan, but it seems more likely that this means Guthorm in East-Anglia, who, you will remember, was baptized by the name of Æthelstan, and who has therefore got confounded with the great Æthelstan in one or two other stories. But one young King Æthelstan certainly did bring up. This was his nephew Lewis, the son of his sister Eadgifu, and of Charles the Simple, King of the West-Franks. There was much confusion in the Western Kingdom all this time, and much rivalry between the Kings of Laôn, who were descended from Charles the Great and spoke German, and the Counts of Paris, who were also called Dukes of the French, and two of whom, Odo and Robert, were Kings. Charles was deposed once or twice, and was at last murdered, and Eadgifu and her son were driven out of the country, and took refuge in England. But afterwards Hugh Duke of the French (who married King Æthelstan's sister Eadhild and who is called Hugh the Great) and William Duke of the Normans, and the other princes of the Western Kingdom, sent for Lewis to come back; so he was called *Ultramarinus* or Lewis from-beyond-Sea. King Æthelstan had much to do with sending him back, and it is plain that England was much thought of just now in other lands, and that the English fleet commanded the Channel.

I told you before that King Æthelstan had no children and, as far as we know, no wife, but that he had plenty of brothers and sisters. I also said that one of them was called Eadwine or Edwin. Now a tale is told about him, which, if it were true, would make Æthelstan guilty of a very great crime, but I am glad to say that I see no reason to believe it.

The Story of Edwin the Ætheling.

You have heard how Alfred the Ætheling conspired against King Æthelstan and sought to blind him in the city of Winchester, and how Alfred went to the great city of Rome and made oath before the Pope that he was innocent, and how the judgement of God showed that he was guilty. Then came evil men to King Æthelstan and spake falsely to him, saying, " Lo thy brother Edwin the Ætheling is one of them who had part with Alfred, and he also seeketh to take away thy life." And he who was the chief of them who told this false tale was the King's cup-bearer. Now when Edwin the Ætheling heard this, he sent messengers to his brother the King, saying, " Believe not these men, for I am guiltless of this thing." But the King hearkened not. So Edwin the Ætheling came himself to his brother the King, and he made oath before the King, as men make oath when they are charged with any grievous crime, and he sware that he had not done this thing, and that he had never sought to slay or to blind Æthelstan his brother. Howbeit King Æthelstan believed not Edwin his brother, but hearkened to the voice of his cup-bearer and of the other men who spake against him. And the King said, " I will not slay Edwin, for that he is my brother, and I fear to have my brother's blood on my head ; yet will I send him out of the land, and I will so send him out of the land that haply he may die as he goeth." So the King commanded, and they put Edwin the Ætheling, and one that was his armour-bearer, into a boat, and bade them sail away where they would. But the boat was old and leaky, and they had neither oars nor rudder to guide it. So the winds drave them into the midst of the sea, and no small tempest lay on them, and the heart of Edwin the Ætheling failed him. And he said, " It is better for me to die once than to live thus in fear of death." So he leaped into the sea and was drowned. But his armour-bearer took up his body, and he let the boat drift when the wind was for him, and he rowed as he might with his feet when the wind was against him, till he came to the haven of Witsand in Gaul which is over against Dover. And when King Æthelstan heard this, he was grieved, and his heart smote him, saying, "I have slain my brother." And he did penance in the church for seven years, as one that had slain his brother. And when the seven years were accomplished, he held a royal feast on a solemn day, and his cup-bearer served him as of old. And as the cup-bearer gave the King wine to drink, his foot slipped, and he bore himself up with the other foot, so that he fell not. And he said, "So brother helpeth brother." And King Æthelstan said, "Yea, brother helpeth brother, and I once had a brother who might have helped me, but thou didst beguile me that I slew him." And King Æthelstan wept and groaned for the death of Edwin his brother, and he bade the men that were with him seize the cup-bearer and smite off his head, for that he was the murderer of Edwin.

Such is the story in William of Malmesbury; now let us see how much truth there is likely to be in it. The Chronicle only tells us, in one copy, that in 933 Edwin the Ætheling was drowned in the sea; Florence says nothing about it; Henry of Huntingdon, who, I told you, lived long after, but who seems to have had writings before him which are now lost, speaks of Edwin's being drowned as a great misfortune and grief to Æthelstan, but does not in the least imply that he had any hand in his death. Simeon of Durham, on the other hand, says that Edwin was drowned by order of Æthelstan. Simeon, as I have told you, wrote long after, and he is not so good an authority for West-Saxon matters as he is for things in his own part of England. So I think you will see that the story rests on very slight grounds indeed. And the tale, as it stands in William of Malmesbury, is clearly made up of two or three of those stories which, as I say, go about the world. There are a great many stories about people being exposed in boats; you have already heard some of them in the history of Ragnar

M

Lodbrog and Ælla of Northumberland. The story about brother helping brother comes over again in the history of Earl Godwine, just as the story of the King going into the enemy's camp as a minstrel is told both of Alfred and of Anlaf. Then again the story seems clearly to be placed at the beginning of Æthelstan's reign, whereas Æthelstan had reigned eight years when Edwin was drowned in 933. And if Æthelstan did penance for seven years after 933, the story about the cup-bearer must have happened in the very last year of his reign, and his greatest victories must have been won while he was doing penance. Altogether the tale seems to me to be a mere legend, and I do not see how we can say anything more than that Edwin was drowned, but that we do not know how. I see no reason to charge any one with any blame because of it, any more than when another Ætheling, William, the son of Henry the First, was drowned at sea two hundred years after.

I have spoken of this at some length, because I think you should from the very beginning learn to distinguish between truth and falsehood, and to know how much more trustworthy one writer is than another.

§ 2. The Reign of King Edmund.

940—946.

There could not be much doubt who should be chosen King on the death of Æthelstan. As he had left no children, no one was likely to contend with Edmund his next brother, who had already won so much glory at Brunanburh. He was now eighteen, so that at the time of the battle he must have been only fifteen. So Edmund was chosen King by the Wise Men of Wessex and no doubt by the English of Mercia also. But the Danes both in Northumberland and in Mercia rebelled and broke their oaths, and sent for Anlaf from Ireland to be their King. So Edmund had just as much fighting to go through as his brother or his father. The next year he won back the Five Boroughs of Mercia, which the Danes held, and which seem to have formed a sort of Confederacy. These were

Leicester, Lincoln, Nottingham, Stamford, and Derby. This was thought so great a success that the Chronicle again throws it into the form of a song. But the next year Anlaf took Tamworth, and defeated the English, and took much spoil. And, according to other accounts,[1] the two Archbishops, Oda of Canterbury and Wulfstan of York, brought the two Kings to an agreement, something like that between Alfred and Guthorm, that Anlaf should reign on one side of Watling Street and Edmund on the other. Archbishop Wulfstan, strange to say, was on Anlaf's side, and was besieged with him in Leicester by Edmund. Anlaf died soon after,[2] and was succeeded in Northumberland by another Anlaf (namely the son of Sihtric, of whom we heard in the time of Æthelstan) and by Regnald the son of Guthfrith. They divided the land between them, and made friendship with Edmund and received baptism. But in 944 Edmund drove them out and gained possession of Northumberland. The Scots either kept quiet during these wars, or perhaps helped Edmund, for when in 945 Edmund conquered Cumberland, he gave it to Malcolm King of Scots, on condition of helping him by land and sea, and we hear of no more trouble with the Scots for some years.

Thus was Edmund, like his father and brother, Lord of all Britain. But he did not long enjoy his greatness. The next year, 946, he was keeping the feast of Saint Augustine of Canterbury at Pucklechurch in Gloucestershire, and there came into the hall one Liofa a robber, whom he had banished six years before. This man went and sat down by one of the chief Aldermen, near the King himself. The King bade his cupbearer to take him away ; but instead of going he tried to kill the cup-bearer. Then the King got up and went to help his cup-bearer, and seized Liofa by the hair and threw him on the ground, but Liofa had a dagger, and so he stabbed the King from below. Liofa was cut to pieces at once by the King's

---

[1] Simeon.

[2] It is very hard to get these events into their right order, because the Chronicle and Simeon give the dates quite differently, and because the two Anlafs get constantly confounded. In Northern affairs Simeon is perhaps the better authority.

men, but Edmund—Edmund the Magnificent[1] as he is called
—was killed.[2]

It was during the reign of King Edmund that a very
memorable man first comes into notice. I mean Dunstan,
Abbot of Glastonbury and afterwards Archbishop of Canterbury. It is a great pity that so many strange stories are
told of him, especially one very silly one indeed, because,
when his name is mentioned, people are apt to think of
those stories and not of his real actions. We shall soon hear
of him as the chief man of all England, but he was not so as
yet. He was born in the first year of Æthelstan, 925,[3] near
Glastonbury, where his father Heorstan was a great Thane.
His mother's name was Cynethrith. I do not think that I need
tell you all that is said about him, but I will give a little sketch
of his life up to this time. As a boy he was taught in the
school which belonged to the Abbey at Glastonbury. Afterwards
he was introduced to the court of King Æthelstan, where he did
not stay long, as it seems he found enemies there. As he grew
up, he greatly wished to marry a lady about the court, whose
name is not mentioned, but his kinsman Ælfheah, Bishop of
Winchester, with a good deal of difficulty persuaded him to
become a monk. He now gave himself up to the learning of
the time, and to various arts which were useful for the service
of the church, as music, painting, and metal-work. Both Æthelstan and Edmund seem to have taken a good deal of notice of
him from time to time, and at last in 943 King Edmund made
him Abbot of Glastonbury. As Abbot he did a great deal for
the monastery, rebuilding the great church and reforming the
discipline of the monks, according to the stricter rule of the
monasteries of Gaul. When King Edmund was murdered at
Pucklechurch, his body was brought to Glastonbury, and was
there buried by Abbot Dunstan.

[1] *Magnificus:* that is the doer of great deeds, in Greek μεγαλοπράγμων,
not magnificent in the way of mere pomp and show.

[2] I have tried, after Dr. Lappenberg's example, to put the story together
from the accounts of the Chronicle, Florence, and William of Malmesbury.
They do not contradict one another, but each gives some further details.

[3] The date is given in the Chronicle, yet it can hardly be right; as, if so,
Dunstan must have become Abbot of Glastonbury when he was only
eighteen.

§ 3. The Reign of King Eadred.

946—955.

King Edmund left two sons, Eadwig (whose name is often written Edwy[1]) and Edgar, but they were quite young children, so the Wise Men chose Eadred, brother of Edmund, to be King. He must have been a young man himself, as his elder brother Edmund was only twenty-four when he was killed. He is said to have been weak and sickly in health, but his reign was an active one, and things were wisely managed, for Abbot Dunstan was his chief minister.

King Eadred was hallowed at Kingston by Archbishop Oda, and at first the Northumbrians acknowledged him, as well as the Scots. The next year he went into Northumberland, and all the Wise Men of Northumberland, with Archbishop Wulfstan at their head, swore oaths to him. But in 948[2] they rebelled and chose for their King Eric the son of Harold Blaatand (Blue-tooth) King of Denmark. So King Eadred went and ravaged their whole country ; on which they submitted and drove out Eric. King Eadred made one Oswulf Earl[3] of the Northumbrians ; he seems to have been of the house of the old lords of Bamborough,[4] and the Earldom of at least part of the country remained in his family for more than a hundred years. Archbishop Wulfstan was deposed from his Bishoprick and put in prison at Jedburgh in Bernicia. This is worth noticing, because it shows that, even with Abbot Dunstan at the head of affairs, a churchman was as much subject to the law as anybody else. But after a little while Wulfstan was allowed to come out of prison, and though he was not

---

[1] I have seen it written *Edwin*, but this is quite wrong, as *Eadwine* and *Eadwig* are quite different names. See what I say about the meaning of names at the beginning of the book.

[2] Here again it is very difficult to get the dates into harmony. The Chronicle is nearer the time, but Simeon knew more about his own country.

[3] See pp. 144, 148.

[4] You see that in the Danish part of England the Danish title *Earl* was used, whilst in Wessex and the rest of the south, they still had *Aldermen.*

allowed to go back to York, where he had been so troublesome, he was given the Bishoprick of Dorchester. Dunstan
however caused the King to give largely to churches and
monsteries, and he is said to have had the royal treasure kept
at Glastonbury.

King Eadred died at Frome in 955, and was buried in the
Old Minster at Winchester. We do not read of any wife or
children of his.

§ 4. THE REIGN OF KING EADWIG.

955—959.

The Wise Men now chose Eadwig or Edwy, the eldest son of
King Edmund. He was still very young, but there was no one
else left in the royal family, and he seems to have been chosen
without difficulty and to have been acknowledged by the whole
country. It seems most likely that his younger brother Edgar
was made Under-king in Mercia from the beginning of Eadwig's
reign, but this is not quite certain, and at any rate he was only
Under-king with his brother as his superior lord. Eadwig's reign,
like those of his father and uncle, was very short, and, unlike
theirs, it was also very unlucky.

It is very hard to tell you about the reign of King Eadwig,
because the account in the Chronicle is very short, and because
all other accounts contradict one another so that one hardly
knows what to believe. The truth is that the history of this time
is greatly affected by what is called *party spirit*. That is to say,
people who are of any particular way of thinking in religion or
politics or anything else are too apt to tell everything so as to
make out their own side as good as possible and the other side
as bad as possible, whether it really was so or not. Now no party
ever was either all good or all bad ; in all such disputes there
are sure to be good and bad men on both sides, and moreover
nobody is so good as never to do wrong and nobody is so bad
as never to do right. So if any account makes out everything
done on one side to be all good, and everything done on the
other side to be all evil, you may be quite sure that that is not
a true account. Sometimes, in such cases, we have accounts

given by both sides, and then we must act as judges, and try and get at the truth by comparing and weighing one side against another. But this is often very hard to do. Now we have had nothing like this in our history as far as we have yet gone. Our accounts may have been influenced by *national* feelings—I mean that an Englishman and a Welshman would not always talk in the same way about a war between the Welsh and the English—but we have heard very little about *party* feelings, about religious or political differences between men of the same nation. We have had something like it when Augustine and the Welsh Bishops could not agree about the time of keeping Easter, and when there were disputes in Northumberland about the same matter some time after. And of course there is also something like it in the very change from heathenism to Christianity. Perhaps if we had a history of those times written by a heathen, Edwin might not seem so good nor Penda so bad as they do in our Christian accounts ; but at this we can only guess. But in this case of Eadwig we see that the story is distinctly coloured by party spirit. Eadwig was the enemy of Dunstan ; therefore the admirers of Dunstan have tried to make out Eadwig as bad as possible. On the other hand most modern writers have a prejudice against Dunstan, and try to make the best of Eadwig and the worst of Dunstan. If the Chronicle gave us a full account, we should know better what to believe. As it is, I will put the story together as well as I can by comparing different accounts.

The Chronicle does not tell us any harm of Eadwig, and Æthelweard[1] and Henry of Huntingdon give him a good character and lament his early death. On the other hand it is certain that he drove Dunstan out of the Kingdom. Now when we see how well things went on both under Eadred and afterwards under Edgar, when Dunstan was again in power, and how badly they went on under Eadwig, we shall think that to drive out Dunstan was a very foolish thing to do. Dunstan was a great and wise minister, but it was very natural for several

---

[1] Æthelweard was a man of the royal house who was an Alderman under King Æthelred. His history is but a poor one, but it is remarkable, because he is the only English historian of those times who was not a priest or a monk.

reasons that Eadwig should dislike him. Dunstan's great object was the reformation of the Church, according to his own notion of reformation. And there can be no doubt that he both aimed at and did a great deal of good, though his zeal in many things carried him too far. The monks at this time in many monasteries lived very irregular lives, not at all as monks should live, if there are to be monks at all. And there was no doubt much ignorance and vice among the *secular* clergy, that is, the clergy who were not monks, but who lived as the clergy do now, each man in his own house, being parsons of parishes and canons of cathedral and collegiate churches. These things Dunstan and Bishop Æthelwald of Winchester, and others who acted with them, set themselves heartily to reform. And so far as they tried to reform real ignorance or wickedness of any kind, so far they did right, though no doubt they would make themselves many enemies by so doing. But we cannot think that they were right when they went so far as to say that no clergyman, not even a parish priest, ought to marry, and when they tried to make those who were married leave their wives. This was not the law of the Church in the first ages, nor has it ever been the law of the Eastern Church, where old customs have always been kept up more strictly than anywhere else. But men in the West had long been thinking more and more that the clergy ought not to marry, partly because they thought that they would do their duties better if they had not wives and children to think about. And no doubt this is to some extent true, but on the whole experience shows that the law of the Eastern Church, which allowed the clergy to marry, was better than that of the West, which gradually came to forbid them. And when our own Church, and the Churches of Northern Europe generally, found it necessary to throw off all obedience to the Bishop of Rome, one of the chief points that was insisted on was that the clergy should be allowed to marry. And besides this, Dunstan and those who acted with him were very anxious to get all the cathedral and other great churches into the hands of monks instead of secular priests of any kind, whether married or not. This they did to a great extent in the days of Edgar, and other Kings and Bishops often did the same afterwards, so that several cathedral churches were served by monks instead of secular canons down to the time of Henry the Eighth. But in other churches the canons always remained; for instance, in our own church of Wells there never were any monks at any time, but it has always been a church of secular priests, as King Ine made it at first. At Glastonbury there always had been monks, and of course Dunstan did right to make them live according to their own profession. Altogether Dunstan was a great and good man, a zealous reformer of the Church and a wise governor of the Kingdom. But it is clear that his zeal in these two points carried him too far.

Now it could not but happen that different men should think very differently about changes like these, which, whether good or bad in themselves, must have caused much hardship to a great many people. There would naturally be two parties in the land, one for Dunstan and one against him. Now King Eadred had been Dunstan's friend throughout, and so was King Edgar afterwards. But King Eadwig took the other side. He does not appear to have been at all an enemy of the Church or a robber of monasteries, as some have made him out, for he was a benefactor to the churches both of Glastonbury and of Abingdon. But he did not like Dunstan and he did not approve of his schemes. So far from turning out secular priests to put in monks, he seems to have sometimes put secular priests into churches where there had always been monks. William of Malmesbury bitterly complains that secular priests were put into his own church at Malmesbury, making it what he calls "a stable of clerks," as if secular priests were no better than beasts. It is no wonder then that we find the whole history both of Eadwig and of Edgar perverted by *party spirit*. Dunstan's friends make out all the ill they can against Eadwig, and Dunstan's enemies make out all the ill they can against Edgar. Hence both Eadwig and Edgar are charged with crimes which most likely neither of them ever committed.

As far as I can make out, it is most likely that Eadwig, before he was chosen King or directly after, married a lady called Ælfgifu, whose name in Latin is written Elgiva. She was so near of kin to him that, according to the laws of the Church at that time, he could not lawfully marry her. The law then was much stricter on such matters than it is now, but whether the law was good or bad, we cannot blame Dunstan or anybody else for trying to put in force the law as he finds it. But some of Dunstan's party seem to have been needlessly violent about it, and as they did not hold the marriage to be a lawful one, they took a pleasure in speaking as if Ælfgifu had not been Eadwig's wife at all, a way of speaking which has led to great confusion in the history. It is said that, on the day of Eadwig's hallowing as King, when, as usual, there was a great feast made to his Aldermen and his Bishops and all his Wise Men, Eadwig left the hall where they all were, and went away to another room to visit his wife and her mother. If we look at this impartially, we shall see that this was anyhow a great insult to the great men of the Kingdom, and that it would especially offend those who held that Ælfgifu was not the King's lawful wife. So Abbot Dunstan and Cynesige Bishop of Lichfield went to try to bring him back, which with some difficulty they did. We may well believe that there was a good deal of strong language on both sides, and that neither Eadwig nor Ælfgifu ever forgave Dunstan. It so happened that a party among the monks of Glastonbury were displeased at Dunstan's changes. This is no more than was sure to happen, whether his changes were good or bad. But of course the King and Ælfgifu would be glad of such an opportunity; so in one of the next two years, either in 956 or 957, Dunstan was driven out of the Kingdom and took refuge in Flanders.

Now, either by his banishment of Dunstan or by his way of governing in general, Eadwig gave great offence to his subjects. In 957 Mercia and all England north of the Thames revolted ; and they chose the Ætheling Edgar, who was already most likely their Under-king, to be King in his own right.   Edgar King of the Mercians, as he is now called, at once sent for Dunstan to come to him, and he presently gave him the Bishoprick of Worcester, and afterwards that of London. Dunstan held both these Bishopricks at once, a thing as clearly against the laws of the Church as any of the evils which he was trying to reform. The next year, 958, Archbishop Oda at last made Eadwig separate from Ælfgifu. This we know from the Chronicle, and it looks very much as if people in Wessex were getting discontented as well as in Mercia, and as if Eadwig made this sacrifice to win them back. I can hardly tell what happened next. I only know for certain that Archbishop Oda died the same year that he divorced Ælfgifu, and that Eadwig himself died the year after, 959. But there are all sorts of stories told by later writers, of which I can make out nothing, because they are so utterly contradictory and so confused as to their dates. Some woman or other, by whom they seem to mean Ælfgifu, was, according to one account, killed by the Mercians in their revolt; according to another, Archbishop Oda had her branded in the face with a hot iron and then banished to Ireland, and when she ventured to come back, Oda's men caught her at Gloucester, and cut the sinews of her legs, so that she died in this horrible way. Now it is clear that Ælfgifu could not be killed in the revolt of Mercia, because she was divorced afterwards, and the other dreadful tale rests on no good authority. Some say that Eadwig himself was killed, but I find nothing about that either in any early writer. I can only say that Eadwig, King of the West-Saxons, as he is now called, died in 959 and was buried in the New Minster at Winchester.

§ 5. The Reign of King Edgar.

959—975.

On the death of Eadwig, his brother Edgar, King of the Mercians, was chosen King by the whole people of the English,[1] and he reigned over West-Saxons, Mercians, and Northumbrians. But he was not hallowed as King for many years after; perhaps he had been hallowed already as King of the Mercians, and it was not thought needful to have it done over again. Edgar was only sixteen years old when he was chosen King.

---

[1] "Ab omni Anglorum populo electus," says Florence of Worcester. "Ægðer ge on West-seaxum, ge on Myrcum, ge on Norðhymbrum," says the Old-English of the Chronicles. You should know the letter þ or ð, the letter Thorn, like the Greek Theta. I wish we had it still.

It is almost as hard to write about Edgar as about his brother, because the accounts which we have of him are very contradictory. The earliest and best writers glorify him as the best and greatest of Kings; the Chronicler can hardly speak of him without bursting forth into poetry; Florence says he was as famous among the English as Alexander among the Macedonians or Charles among the Franks. On the other hand there is no King about whom there are more stories to his discredit. Here again we can see party spirit. There is no doubt that under Edgar England was wonderfully prosperous and wonderfully peaceful. He was also the great friend of the monks. This last was enough to make one side call him everything that was good and the other side call him everything that was bad. Most likely he was neither so good as the one picture nor so bad as the other. But I may say this much. The prosperity of his reign is certain, while the crimes attributed to him are very doubtful. They come from stories in William of Malmesbury, who allows that he got them out of ballads. Some of them are evidently just the same sort of stories as those of which we have had so many.

One thing at any rate is very plain, namely that there was no time in the tenth century, or for a long time after the tenth century, when there was so little fighting in the land as in the reign of Edgar. Never was there so much peace abroad or so much quiet at home. We hear of no invasions of Danes or of anybody else, and of very little disturbance in Britain itself. There was a little fighting with the Welsh, and a little with the Scots just at the beginning of Edgar's reign. But on the whole the King's power never was so fully established within his own Kingdom nor so completely acknowledged by the Kings and Princes who were his vassals. To preserve his Kingdom from foreign invaders, Edgar, like Alfred, kept up a great fleet, which was always sailing about the coasts, so that the Danes could never land. But there may very likely have now and then been some fighting by sea; for instance in 962 we read how a certain King Sigeferth killed himself and was buried at Wimborne. Now it is hard to see what any King Sigeferth could have been doing anywhere near Wimborne, unless he was a Danish prisoner. King Edgar often went about with

his fleet himself, and he also went through the different parts
of the Kingdom to see that justice was done everywhere, and
he was very severe to all wrongdoers. Very severe indeed he
was, for we find that in 969 he caused the Isle of Thanet to be
harried or ravaged, because of some disobedience, of what kind
we are not told.[1] Of the general goodness of his government
there seems no doubt, only some accuse him of being too fond
of encouraging foreigners in the country, Saxons—that is, of
course, Old-Saxons from Germany—Flemings, and even heathen
Danes, and they say that the people learned from them different
vices to which they were not used before. But this is only the
sort of way in which old-fashioned and prejudiced people always
talk of any intercourse with strangers. No doubt Edgar tried,
as a wise King would, to bring his people into greater intercourse with the rest of the world by commerce and otherwise.
He was on good terms with foreign Princes, and his friendship
with the great Emperor Otto is specially spoken of. You will
remember that Otto was a sort of uncle of Edgar's, having
married his aunt Eadgyth or Edith, the daughter of King
Edward. But she was now dead.

The civil and military events of Edgar's reign are not very
many. Edgar the Peaceful had very little to do with fighting.
His chief war was with the Welsh, because Idwal the son of
Roderick the Great, a Prince in North Wales, refused to pay
the tribute which had always been paid since the time of
Æthelstan. So in 963 King Edgar went against him and
harried his land. William of Malmesbury tells a strange story
that Edgar ordered Idwal to pay a tribute of 300 wolves' heads
yearly, but that it was paid only for three years, because in the
fourth year there were no more wolves to be found. I do not
know how this may be, but I know that there were wolves in
Britain long after, and surely North Wales is one of the parts of
Britain where they were likely to linger longest.

Edgar's doings in the North of England were more important. You will remember how much trouble Northumberland
had given to all the Kings before him since Alfred ; how for a

---

[1] The *fact* comes from the Chronicle, the *reason* from Henry of Huntingdon. Roger of Wendover, who wrote much later, says that the men of
the isle had ill-treated some merchants of York.

long time the Northumbrians had Kings of their own, and
how at last King Eadred had put down the separate Kings and
had made Oswulf Earl of the Northumbrians. King Edgar
seems to have thought that Northumberland was a country too
great and too distant for any one man to govern. I suppose
there must have been some sort of disturbances in the country.
In 961 King Edgar kept his Christmas at York, and in 966 we
read that Westmoreland was harried, which seems to imply
some revolt. And the same year he divided Northumberland between two Earls; that is to say, he restored the old
division between *Beornarice (Bernicia)* and *Deornarice (Deira)*.
He made one Oslac Earl of Deira or the southern part, with
York for his capital. To Oswulf the old Earl was left the country
beyond the Tees, that is the present county of Northumberland
and what was afterwards the Bishoprick[1] of Durham. This was
no doubt the beginning of the division of Northumberland into
several shires, and the reason why the name of Northumberland
has stuck to a part of the old Kingdom quite away from the
Humber. Besides this it is also said that King Edgar granted
Lothian to Kenneth, King of Scots, to be held as his vassal.
You will remember that Northumberland reached as far as the
Forth, and that Edwinesburh, which we call Edinburgh, was
King Edwin's border castle. You know also that this part of
Northumberland called Lothian has long been part of the
Kingdom of Scotland. It certainly was held by the Scots before
the Norman Conquest, and this seems as likely a time as any
for it to have been granted out. As King Edgar wished to
divide Northumberland, and as Kenneth was already his vassal
as King of Scots, there was really nothing wonderful in his
granting him further territory on the same terms. Of this it

---

[1] The *Bishoprick* or *County Palatine* is the county of which the Bishop of
Durham was formerly a temporal Prince, a rank which he kept down to
the reign of William the Fourth. But before that time his power had been
greatly lessened. You must not confound the *Bishoprick* with the *Diocese*
of Durham, which takes in also the county of Northumberland. Thus
in the county of Northumberland the Bishop was simply Bishop, in
the Bishoprick of Durham he was a temporal Prince as well. But there
was no Bishop of Durham yet; the church and city of Durham had not
yet been founded, and the Bishop's see was at Cunegaceaster or Chester-le-
Street.

came that Lothian was ever after held by the Scottish Kings. But the people of Lothian were English or Danish, and retained their language, and were much more civilized than the natural Scots. So the Kings of Scots gradually came to think more of their English territories, and learned to speak English, and at last to live mainly in Lothian, so that the Kingdom of Scotland was leavened, so to speak, by this English part of it. Of the three places most famous in Scottish history, Edinburgh is, as you know, in Lothian, Stirling is just on the border, and Dumfermline just on the other side of the Firth of Forth.

It is hard to say why it was that Edgar was not crowned till he had reigned thirteen years. In 973 he was at last hallowed as King "in the old borough Acemannesceaster,[1] which by another name men Bath call," or, as another copy of the Chronicle says, "at the Hot Baths." After his hallowing he sailed with his fleet all round Wales to Chester,[2] and there six, or as some say eight, of his vassal Kings came with their fleets and did homage to him, and swore to be faithful to him by land and by sea These eight are said to have been Kenneth King of Scots, Malcolm of Cumberland, Maccus of the Isles, and five Welsh princes, whose names are given as Dufnal, Siferth, Huwal (Howel), Jacob, and Juchil. These eight Kings rowed the Lord of all Britain in a boat, while Edgar himself steered, from the royal palace at Chester to the minster of Saint John, where they prayed, and went back in the same way. This was thought to be the proudest day that any King of the English had ever seen.

As King Edgar had so much more power than any of the Kings before him, it is not wonderful that we find in his charters that he is not called merely King of the English or King of the Anglo-Saxons, but " King of the English and all the nations round about," " Ruler and Lord of the whole isle of Albion," " *Basileus* of all Britain," and so forth. There is a story told by William of Malmesbury, which may perhaps

---

[1] The first syllable of this word is the Latin *Aqua*, from the old name *Aquæ Solis.* See p. 36.

[2] In the Chronicle *Leicester* (Legerceaster, Lægecaster, Leicastre). You will remember that Leicester, Chester, and Caerleon all have the same name, which sometimes leads to confusion. Here of course Chester is meant.

have happened after the great gathering of Kings at Chester. Edgar was, so it is said, but a small man in stature, yet he was strong and skilful in arms. Now one day Kenneth of Scotland said at a feast, when his heart was merry with wine, " How strange it is that all of us, so many Kings as we are, should serve this one man who is smaller than any of us." Now this saying was told to King Edgar, and he bade Kenneth come apart with him, for that he would confer with him about a certain great matter. So he took Kenneth apart into a certain wood, where they were all alone. Then King Edgar took out two swords, and gave one to Kenneth King of Scots and took the other himself, and said, " Thou sayest that I am but a small man, and unfit to reign over thee and so many other Kings. Now then take this sword, and lay on manfully, and let us see whether of us twain is the fitter man to rule over the other. For it is not good that a King should be swift with his tongue, as thou art, unless he be also swift and strong in battle." But Kenneth King of Scots would not draw the sword against his lord the King of all Britain, but he fell at his feet, and craved pardon for that which he had said, for that it was only in jest that he had spoken. Thus were Edgar King of all Britain and Kenneth King of Scots made friends again as they were aforetime.

In matters belonging to the Church King Edgar seems to have done whatever Dunstan wished. Archbishop Oda died a little time before King Eadwig, and in his place Ælfsine Bishop of Winchester was appointed. But Ælfsine set out to go to Rome to get his *pallium* from the Pope, and died of the cold in crossing the Alps. The pallium was the special badge which distinguished an Archbishop from other Bishops. It was worn round the neck, something in the shape of the letter Y. It was now beginning to be the custom for every Archbishop to go to Rome to fetch his pallium from the Pope, and without it it was held that he could not exercise the power of an Archbishop. Then Brihthelm Bishop of the Sumorsætas was chosen, but he was not thought to be fit for the place, so he stayed at Wells. And I suspect that it was a great gain for the church of Wells that he did stay ; for I cannot help thinking that the real objection to him was that he was not of the party of the monks. As I told you, the monks never got into the church of Wells, and I suspect that it was Brihthelm that kept them out. When Brihthelm died, care was taken to make a monk named Cyneheard Bishop of the Sumorsætas, but this was only a little time before Edgar died, so perhaps he had not time to make any change.

As Brihthelm was not thought fit to be Archbishop, Dunstan was chosen in 959, the first year of King Edgar, and the next year he went to Rome and got his pall from Pope John. This Pope John to whom Dunstan went was John the Twelfth, who was one of the worst of all the Popes, but he is famous for crowning the Emperor Otto. For the time Dunstan had things all his own way ; and he and Æthelwald Bishop of Winchester, Oswald Bishop of Worcester, and others of their party, turned the secular priests out of many of the chief churches of England, and put in monks. This was done in both the minsters at Winchester, at Worcester, in King Æthelstan's minster at Middleton, and elsewhere.[1] Edgar also showed favour to the monks everywhere; he was a great benefactor to Glastonbury and Malmesbury, and founded churches and monasteries in various places. Now as so much of our history was written by monks, we can well believe that much of their praise of Edgar is owing to the favour which he showed to their own order. But this cannot be all. The laws of Edgar, his strict government, the peace and prosperity of England under him, and his authority over all the other princes of Britain, speak for themselves, and we cannot doubt that Edgar was one of our greatest Kings. No doubt Dunstan helped him in many things besides the government of the Church ; but much of the glory was Edgar's own. In short, unless we except Eadwig—and perhaps we should not except Eadwig —we have a most wonderful succession of great and wise Kings reaching from Alfred, or rather from Æthelred, to

---

[1] But it is very strange that the secular priests seem not to have been turned out of Dunstan's own church of Canterbury, for we find that there are secular priests there as late as 990, when they were driven out by Archbishop Sigeric. It is however possible, as we shall see presently, that these secular priests were put in at the beginning of the reign of Edward the Martyr.

N

Edgar. We shall see how sadly things changed when Edgar was dead.

In the year 975 King Edgar died, and was buried at Glastonbury. He was now only thirty-two years old. It is remarkable how young most of the Kings during this century were when they died. Alfred seems to have been the oldest. and he was only fifty-two.

King Edgar married twice. His first wife was Æthelflæd. called the White and the Duck,[1] daughter of an Alderman named Ordmær. By her he had a son Edward. After her death he married, in 964, Ælfthryth, called in Latin Elfrida, the daughter of Ordgar, Alderman of the Defnsætas, and, Florence adds, widow of Æthelwald, " the glorious Alderman of the East-Angles." She had two sons, Edmund, who died young in 971, and Æthelred. King Edgar had also a daughter named Eadgyth or Edith, who became a nun, and was afterwards reckoned as a saint. Her mother's name was Wulfthryth, who, according to some accounts, was a nun also.

I told you that William of Malmesbury has several stories about Edgar, not much to his credit, but which William allows are taken out of ballads. I will tell you one very famous one, but which I do not in the least believe. It seems to me to be made up out of bits of the Old Testament, Herodotus,[2] and so forth, and it is hard to make it agree with chronology.

𝕿𝖍𝖊 𝕾𝖙𝖔𝖗𝖞 𝖔𝖋 𝕰𝖉𝖌𝖆𝖗 𝖆𝖓𝖉 𝕬𝖊𝖑𝖋𝖙𝖍𝖗𝖞𝖙𝖍.[3]

In the days of King Edgar, who was King of the English and Lord of all Britain, there lived a man named Ordgar, who

---

[1] *Ened.* This is the Old-English word, the same as the Greek νῆττα, the Latin *anat-is*, and the High-Dutch *ente*. *Duck* is a sort of pet name, from the bird's habit of *ducking* (High-Dutch *tauchen*).

[2] I do not mean that those who told the story had read Herodotus, but only that the same story turns up in both places.

[3] This story is found in William of Malmesbury and also in the French history of England by Geoffrey Gaimar, whence it is copied into the Chronicle called Bromton's Chronicle, which is full of strange tales. I have tried to put together from the two what seems to be the earliest form of

was Alderman of the Defnsætas, and he had a fair daughter whose name was Ælfthryth. And men spake of the beauty of Ælfthryth before the King, so that the King thought to take her to wife, for that Æthelflæd the Lady was dead. So the King spake unto Æthelwald his friend,[1] and said, "Go now into the land of the Defnsætas, to the house of Ordgar the Alderman, and see Ælfthryth his daughter, and bring me word whether she be as fair as men say she is or no." So Æthelwald went to the house of Ordgar, and saw Ælfthryth his daughter, and behold, she was the fairest of all women. And Æthelwald loved her, and he could not bear in his heart that she should be the King's wife rather than his. So he spake unto Ordgar her father, saying, "Give me thy daughter to wife." Now Æthelwald had not told Ordgar wherefore he had come to his house, and Ordgar saw Æthelwald that he was young and tall and brave and a friend of the King's; so he said to Æthelwald, "Yea, I will give thee my daughter." Then went Æthelwald back to King Edgar, and said, "Lo, I have been to the house of Ordgar, and I have seen Ælfthryth his daughter, and she is not so fair as men said that she was. Truly her face is comely, but her form is spare and deformed, and she is not worthy to be the wife of a King. But as for me, I am a poor man, and Ordgar the Alderman is rich, and he hath no son, and Ælfthryth his daughter will be his heir. Let me, I pray thee, take her to me to wife." So the King said to Æthelwald, "Let it be even as thou sayest." So Æthelwald went back to the house of Ordgar, and took Ælfthryth his daughter to wife. But from that day Æthelwald feared the King, lest haply he should know how he had deceived him, and should slay him for

the story. I suspect that Gaimar gives the earlier form, and that William altered some things which he saw to be clearly absurd. For instance, both stories speak of a son of Æthelwald, but Gaimar speaks of him as a son of Ælfthryth also, while William speaks of him as a son of some other woman, he cannot tell whom. One may be sure that the original story made him Ælfthryth's son, and that William, or those whom William copied, changed this, because it was clearly impossible.

[1] His secretary, according to both accounts; Bromton adds "Alderman of the East-Angles." Now that Æthelwald was Alderman of the East-Angles we know from Florence, but I think it is clear that the ballad knew nothing about his having any such rank.

the sake of Ælfthryth his wife. And after a time Ælfthryth bare a son to Æthelwald, and Æthelwald prayed the King to hold the babe at the font, that he might be his son according to the laws of the Church. So King Edgar held the babe at the font and was his godfather, and called him after his own name Edgar. Then was Æthelwald glad, and said in his heart, " Now is the King my brother by the law of the Church, and Ælfthryth my wife is the King's sister.¹ I fear not now lest the King should slay me that he may take her to wife."

But after a while men spake to the King, saying, " Know, O King, that Æthelwald thy friend hath deceived thee, and hath told thee lies, and hath by craft taken to himself Ælfthryth the daughter of Ordgar to be his wife. For of a truth Ælfthryth is the fairest of women, and no man is worthy of her save thou who art the Lord of all Britain." Then the King said, " Now will I go even into the land of the Defnsætas² and see whether these things be so." And the King gathered him a company, and went into the land of the Defnsætas as it were to hunt. And in his hunting he came near to the house of Æthelwald. And he sent to Æthelwald saying, " Lo, I am hunting near thy house ; I will therefore come and tarry with thee, and see Ælfthryth thy fair wife, and Edgar thy son who is my godson." And when Æthelwald heard that saying, he was afraid, and said in his heart, " Now hath the King heard that which I have done ; and he cometh hither, and when he seeth Ælfthryth and her beauty he will slay me." So Æthelwald went to Ælfthryth his wife, and said, " O my wife, thou knowest not as yet what I did that I might have thee to wife. When thou wast a maiden in the house of thy father, the King heard of thy beauty, and he sent me to see thee, whether thou wert as fair as men said that thou wast. But when I saw thee, I loved thee, and I could not bear that thou shouldest be any man's wife but mine own. So I spake lies to the King, and said that thou wast not fair enough to be the Lady of all Britain, and I spake

---

¹ By the old Church law no man or woman might marry the father or mother of a child to whom he or she had been godparent, or any one who had been godparent along with him.

² The ballad-maker clearly did not look on Æthelwald as Alderman of the East-Angles, as he makes him live in Devonshire.

unto thy father, and he gave thee to me to wife. And now pardon me this thing that I have done for love of thee. For now the King hath heard of thy beauty, and he cometh to tarry in my house, and when he seeth thee and thy beauty, he will know all that I have done, and he will slay me that he may have thee to wife. Now therefore disguise thyself, and, if thou canst, hide thy beauty from him, that he may not be pleased therewith, nor seek to slay me for thy sake." And when Ælfthryth heard that, she was wroth in her heart, and her love to her husband was turned to hatred, and she said, "Now hath Æthelwald deceived the King, and he hath deceived me and my father, that I might not be Lady of the English and of all the Isle of Britain. Now will I this day have my revenge upon him who hath dealt thus with me." So Ælfthryth arrayed herself in the best apparel that she had, and she put on all her jewels and all her bravery, and she went forth to welcome King Edgar to the house of her husband. And King Edgar saw her that she was the fairest of all women, and he knew how Æthelwald his friend had lied unto him. And he loved Ælfthryth, and he sought to slay Æthelwald that he might take her to wife. And King Edgar sent through the land, and bade the Wise Men to come together to a Council in the city of Salisbury.[1] And the Wise Men came together. And the King said, "Lo, the Danes vex us in the land of Northumberland; I will therefore send some brave and wise man to the city of York, that he may dwell there and guard the land. And who is braver and wiser than Æthelwald my friend? Let us therefore send him to the land of Northumberland to watch over the city and over all the land." And the Wise Men said that it was well spoken. So Æthelwald rode forth to go to York to guard the land against the Danes. And he took with him his son Edgar. But on the road he tarried to hunt with the King in the wood of Wherwell, and when they were alone, the King smote Æthelwald with a javelin that he died. And when Edgar the son of Æthelwald came up and saw the body of his father lying dead, then Edgar the King said to him, "How

---

[1] Remember that this does not mean the city of Salisbury that now is, but *Old Sarum*, of which I shall have to speak again.

doth such a hunting as this please thee ?"   And the lad answered, " Whatever pleaseth thee, O King, pleaseth me also."[1]

And when Edgar the King saw that Æthelwald her husband was dead, he took Ælfthryth the daughter of Ordgar to wife. And she bare him two sons, Edmund the Ætheling, who died young, and Æthelred, who was afterwards King of the English. And as for her other son Edgar, whom she bare to Æthelwald, the King loved him much and did all that he might to comfort him. And Edgar and Ælfthryth, because of their sin that they had sinned, built a minster by the wood of Wherwell, and placed nuns therein, who should serve God with fastings and prayers night and day.[2]

---

[1] This story is evidently the same as that of Kambysês and Prêxaspês in Herodotus ; only in the one story the King shoots the father, and in the other the son.

[2] Two distinct versions may be traced in the latter part of the tale. According to one story, Edgar has nothing to do with the death of Æthelwald, who is killed by unknown persons, robbers or the like. But after Æthelwald's death Edgar commits the sin of marrying his widow contrary to the law of the Church, for which he is reproved by Dunstan. According to the other account, Edgar kills Æthelwald with his own hand, and speaks to his son as I have said in the text. These both seem original stories, and there is no reason why the former may not be true. But a third version, namely that Æthelwald was killed by people sent by Edgar, seems a mixture of the two stories, and the author of it probably had the story of David and Uriah in his head. William of Malmesbury knows nothing about the meeting of the Wise Men at Salisbury, but it seems to fit in very well with the state of things at the time. He makes Edgar kill Æthelwald himself, and he tells the story of the boy, whom he makes to be Æthelwald's son by another woman. This last is not in Gaimar and Bromton. Most likely William and Gaimar both saw the absurdity of making a son of Ælfthryth's already able to talk and act, and each altered the tale in his own way. William gave him another mother ; Gaimar left out the latter part of the story altogether. But the King's great affection for the boy, of which no one speaks but William, exactly fits in with his being his stepson and godson, of which Gaimar and Bromton speak and William does not. And where did the murder happen ? Gaimar makes it on the road to York without giving the name of the place. William says it was at Wherwell, but one manuscript adds, "which is called Harewood." Bromton says "Wherwell," but he makes it, like Gaimar, some days' journey on the road between Salisbury and York. As far as I know, Wherwell is in Hampshire and Harewood in Yorkshire. There is certainly some confusion, but it looks as if the journey to York was part of the original story.

I have told you that I do not believe this story at all, and I have given you some of my reasons. I can only say that Ælfthryth was the daughter of Ordgar and widow of Æthelwald. I do not know how Æthelwald died; but if it is true that he was killed by robbers in a wood, we can at once see how the story began.

§ 6. THE REIGN OF KING EDWARD THE MARTYR.

975—978.

As soon as King Edgar was dead, and before another King was chosen, there was a great movement against the monks. Ælfhere, Alderman of the Mercians, and others of the chief men, began to turn the monks out of several churches and to bring the secular canons with their wives back again. But Æthelwine, Alderman of the East-Angles, whom men called " the Friend of God," gathered a meeting of the Wise Men of his own Earldom, and they determined to keep the monks, and they joined with Brihtnoth, Alderman of the East-Saxons, and they even got together an army to defend the monasteries. Meanwhile there was a great question who should be King. Both the sons of Edgar were very young : Æthelred was quite a child, about seven, Edward about thirteen. If there had been a brother of Edgar's living, no doubt he would have been chosen, but there was no brother, nor any one else, as far as one can see, very near of kin to the late King. So there was nothing to be done but to choose one of the boys. Some were for Edward and some for Æthelred. Of the two it was most natural to choose Edward, and King Edgar before he died had said that he wished it to be so. 1 forget whether I have told you that, though a King of the English could not leave his crown as he pleased, yet the wishes of the late King always counted for a good deal with the Wise Men. So when the Wise Men met to choose a King, the two Archbishops, Dunstan and Oswald, insisted that Edward should be chosen, and so he was chosen and hallowed. There was a comet seen that year, and men thought that it foretold that great evils were to come upon the land.

As far as I can make out, the young King Edward did not put such complete trust in Dunstan as his father Edgar had done. At least we still hear of disputes going on, and of Alderman Ælfhere turning out the monks. Also in the next year Oslac Earl of the Northumbrians, "the beloved, hoary-headed hero," as the Chronicle calls him, was driven into banishment. In the next year, 977, there were no less than three meetings of the Wise Men, at Kirtlington in Oxfordshire, and at Calne and Amesbury [Ambresbyrig] in Wiltshire, and all seem to have been called to settle these questions about monks and secular priests. In the meeting at Calne a strange accident took place, which people at the time called a miracle, and in which modern writers have suspected a trick, but which most likely was neither the one nor the other. The Wise Men were met in an upper room, and the floor gave way, and some were hurt and some killed ; only the beam on which Archbishop Dunstan stood remained firm, so that he was not hurt at all. After this, so at least William of Malmesbury says, people believed in him more than they had done before.

The next year, 979, the young King Edward was murdered or, as they said at the time, martyred. Now certainly he was not really a martyr, either for the Christian Faith or for right and truth in any shape ; but he was a good youth and was unjustly and cruelly killed, so people looked on him as a sort of saint, and called him Edward the Martyr. The Chronicle greatly laments his death, and says that a worse deed had never been done since the English came into Britain. It does not however say who killed him, but only that he was killed at eventide at Corfes Gate. This is a place in Dorsetshire, now called Corfe Castle. It is called the Gate because it stands in a gap between two great ranges of hills. Some fine ruins of the castle still remain, and a small part is most likely as old as the time of Edgar. Henry of Huntingdon says that Edward was killed by his own people. Florence says that he was killed by his own people by order of his step-mother Ælfthryth. William of Malmesbury, in another part of his book, says that Alderman Ælfhere killed him, but in recording his death he attributes the crime to Ælfthryth. If Ælfthryth did it, it was no doubt to secure the succession to her son

Æthelred ; if Ælfhere did it, which I do not at all believe, he may have had some hope of being chosen King himself, as he is said to have been a kinsman of King Edgar's. I can only say for certain that Edward was murdered at Corfe ; and as Florence says that Ælfthryth had a hand in his death, it is most likely that it was so. His body was buried at Wareham, which is very near Corfe, without any royal honours, but the next year, 980, Alderman Ælfhere translated it with great pomp to King Alfred's minster at Shaftesbury.

This is all I know, but I may as well add the story as William of Malmesbury gives it.

The Story of the Martyrdom of King Edward.

When Edward the son of Edgar was King of the English, he was always good and kind to his step-mother Ælfthryth and to her son Æthelred his brother. But Ælfthryth hated him, for that she had wished her son Æthelred to be King, but the Wise Men had chosen Edward his brother before him. So Ælfthryth ever sought how she might slay King Edward. Now one day King Edward was hunting in the land of the Dorsætas, hard by the Gate of Corfe, where Ælfthryth and Æthelred her son dwelt. And the King was weary and thirsty, so he turned away alone from his hunting, and said, " Now will I go and rest myself at Corfe with my step-mother Ælfthryth and Æthelred my brother." So King Edward rode to the gate of the house, and Ælfthryth his step-mother came out to meet him, and kissed him. And he said, " Give me to drink, for I am thirsty." And Ælfthryth commanded, and they brought him a cup, and he drank eagerly. But while he drank, Ælfthryth made a sign o her servant, and he stabbed the King with a dagger ; and when the King felt the wound, he set spurs to his horse and tried to join his comrades who were hunting. But he slipped from his horse, and his leg caught in the stirrup, so he was dragged along till he died, and the track of his blood showed whither he had gone. And Ælfthryth bade that he should be buried at Wareham, but not in holy ground nor with any royal pomp. But a light from heaven shone over his grave, and wonders were wrought there. And now Ælfthryth rejoiced greatly, but Æthelred her son wept when he heard that Edward his brother was slain, for that Edward had always been kind to him. Then was Ælfthryth wroth, and she beat her son Æthelred because he wept for his brother.[1] But after a while she heard of all the mighty works which were done at the grave of King Edward, how the sick were healed and the lame walked, and she said, " Lo, I will go even unto Wareham, and see whether these things be so or no." But when she mounted her horse to ride, the horse would not stir ; and her servants shouted and beat the horse, yet would he not stir. So Ælfthryth saw that it was a wonder, and she repented of her sin that she had sinned, and she became a nun in the house of Wherwell which she and Edgar her husband had builded, and there she served God with prayers and fastings and watchings and scourgings all the rest of her days. Moreover Ælfhere the Alderman repented that he had driven the servants of God out of so many minsters, and he took up the body of the holy King Edward, and carried it with all pomp to the minster at Shaftesbury.[2] And there all the holy virgins and godly widows lamented him, and many wonders were wrought by God at his tomb.

I shall now end this chapter. I have gone through all the Kings who reigned after the first Edward, the first King of the West-Saxons who became King of the English and Lord of all Britain down to the second Edward the son of Edgar. I stop here, because in the next reign, that of Æthelred, the Danish invasions begin again and go on till the Danes had conquered all England.

[1] A tale is added almost too ridiculous to put in the text. As Ælfthryth had not a rod at hand, she beat her son with wax candles, wherefore Æthelred ever hated wax candles, and would have none burned before him all the days of his life.

[2] In the Chronicle called that of Bromton all this is given at much greater length than by William of Malmesbury.

CHAPTER X.

HOW THE DANES CONQUERED AND REIGNED IN ENGLAND.

§ 1. The Reign of King Æthelred the Second.

978—1016.

We now come to a very different time from that of which we have been reading lately. Since the time of Alfred we have heard very little of actual invasions of the Danes. There has been constant fighting with the Danes who were already settled in England, up to the time when they were finally subdued under King Eadred. But the fighting was almost wholly with the Danes who were settled in England, or at most with those who came over from Ireland. We hear but little of any Danes actually coming from Denmark, and, when we do, it is only to help their brethren in Northumberland, not to conquer or plunder in other parts of the country. But now the Danish invasions begin again. They begin at first with mere plundering, such as we heard of long ago, as far back as King Beorhtric's time in Wessex. But the invasions gradually get quite another sort of character. We soon find Kings of all Denmark and of all Norway coming to England, not to plunder but to conquer, till at last a Danish King became King over all England. This is then what I before called the third stage of the Danish wars. The first was the stage of mere plundering ; the second was the stage of settlements like that of Guthorm-Æthelstan ; this last stage is that of deliberate attempts to conquer the whole kingdom.

The reason of this seems to be that some great changes had

been lately going on in the North of Europe. Scandinavia,
which had been before divided into a great many small principalities, had now settled down into three great kingdoms,
Denmark, Norway, and Sweden. With the Swedes, whose
country lay wholly on the Baltic, we in Britain had little or
nothing to do; but with the Danes and Norwegians, who had
one side of their land to the Ocean, we had a great deal to
do. The Danes were finally brought into one Kingdom by a
King named Gorm, who, from the long time that he lived and
reigned, was called Gorm the Old. If it really be true that he
reigned from 840 to 935, he must have been very old indeed.
But this is hardly possible, and the date of his death is much
more certain than the date of his coming to the crown. The
Danes have a great deal to say about this King Gorm and his
wife Thyra.[1]   They are said to have made the Dannewerk, the
great dyke which was meant to defend Denmark against the
Germans, and which was often spoken of in the late wars in
those parts.   Gorm's Kingdom took in the Danish Islands,
Jütland, Scania, which is now part of Sweden, and the Northern
part of Sleswick, that beyond the Dannewerk. In Charles the
Great's time the boundary between Denmark and Germany
had been the Eyder. But there were often wars between the
Danes and the Germans, especially as Gorm and most of his
people were still heathens and persecuted such Christians as
were in their country. So Henry, King of the East-Franks,
called Henry the Fowler, came against Gorm and made him
ask for peace and perhaps do homage. Then King Henry
moved the boundary northwards from the Eyder to the Dannewerk, and made the country between them into a *Mark* or
border land under a Margrave, and planted a Saxon colony
there. Now though this Mark of Sleswick did not last very
long, for the Danes in Cnut's time got the frontier of the Eyder
again and kept it till our own days, still this German settlement north of the Eyder was the beginning of events of which
the world has lately heard a great deal. Gorm the Old was
succeeded by his son Harold, called Bluetooth, who reigned

---

[1] The Danish writer Saxo Grammaticus makes her out to have been one
of the daughters of Edward the Elder (whom he calls Æthelred) and
sisters of Æthelstan; but this is very unlikely.

fifty years, from 935 to 985. We read a great deal of him in the history of Normandy, but not much in that of England; only, as we have seen, the rebellious Northumbrians in Eadred's time chose his son Eric for their King. According to some accounts, Harold sent an army with Eric, but we do not hear of his invading or plundering anywhere but in Northumberland; he had also wars with his neighbours to the south, and in 975 the Emperor Otto the Second, son of Otto the Great, ravaged the whole of Jütland, and obliged Harold to do homage and receive baptism. His son Svein, or in English Swegen, was also baptized, and was called Otto after the Emperor, who was his godfather.[1] Harold seems, in the last years of his reign, to have done what he could to settle Christianity in Denmark. But Swegen cast off Christianity and wished to bring back the worship of the old Gods. So he and those of the Danes who were heathens rebelled against the old King Harold, and he was beaten in battle and fled away and was either murdered or died of a wound. Swegen then became King and restored idolatry. There seems reason to believe that he had a hand in some of the first incursions into England of which we shall soon read. At any rate it is certain that, after he was King of the Danes, his great object was to conquer England. You will now understand that the three northern Kingdoms were much more united and powerful than they had been hitherto. For, though the Emperors had cut Denmark short to the south and had made some of the Danish Kings do homage, this did not greatly affect the power of the Danes to do damage in other places, and the Danes presently recovered what they had lost. And the other Kingdoms of Norway and Sweden were quite out of the reach of the Emperors. So it was no wonder that the incursions of the Northmen began again at this time on a greater scale than ever.

After King Edward was dead, there was really no one to choose as King except his young brother Æthelred; so Æthelred was chosen and was hallowed at Kingston. He reigned

---

[1] Adam of Bremen says that he was called " Sveinotto." I suppose that his former heathen name was Svein and that he was called Otto in baptism : but he is always called Svein, just as Guthorm and Rolf are always called by their old names, not Æthelstan and Robert.

thirty-eight years, and the whole of his reign was one time of wretchedness and confusion. It is said that Dunstan, at his coronation, foretold what a wretched time it would be. As long as Dunstan lived, things were a little better; but when he was gone, all the badness and weakness of Æthelred's character came out. He was perhaps the only thoroughly bad King among all the Kings of the English of the West-Saxon line; he seems to have been weak, cowardly, cruel, and bad altogether. He was always doing things at wrong times and leaving undone what he should have done, so that he is called Æthelred the *Unready*, that is the man without *rede* or counsel. No doubt he had to struggle with very hard times, but the times now were no harder than the times which Alfred had to struggle against. We know how much he could do.

Dunstan lived ten years after Æthelred became King. The invasions of the Danes had already begun; we hear of them in 980, 981 and 982, but not again till 988, the year of Dunstan's death. This interval seems to answer to the time when Swegen was at war with his father Harold. And no doubt, as long as Dunstan lived, some better care was taken of the country, though even then men must have missed King Edgar and his great fleet sailing round the land every year and keeping all enemies away. But, when Dunstan was dead, things grew from bad to worse; for in 991, by the advice of Sigeric, who was then Archbishop, and of the Aldermen Æthelweard[1] and Ælfric, men began the foolish way of giving money to the Danes to persuade them to go away. Of course, as soon as they had spent the money, they came back again. This Ælfric was Alderman of the Mercians; he was a sad traitor, and we shall often hear of him again.

The invasion of 988 was in our own part of the country, for the Danes harried Wecedport or Watchet, and Goda, a Devonshire thane, and other good men were killed, but the Danes were at last beaten and driven away. In the course of these

---

[1] This Æthelweard seems to be the man who wrote the Latin Chronicle which I have sometimes quoted. He was of royal descent, being sprung from Æthelred the brother of Alfred; but this kindred seems not to have been near enough to give him the title of Ætheling, or for him to be thought of when men were choosing a King.

years, from 978 to 991, we hear of a great many other misfortunes besides the coming of the Danes, such as a great murrain among cattle, a quarrel between the King and the Bishop of Rochester, in which Æthelred ravaged the Bishop's lands, and the burning of London in 982. As this is not said to have been done in any war or disturbance, it was most likely an accidental fire, like the more famous one in 1666. You must remember that in those days most of the houses were of wood, so that for a town to be burned was no very uncommon thing. In 991 there was a great invasion of the Danes or, as this time they seem more truly to have been, Norwegians, in the eastern part of England. There came two brothers called Justin and Guthmund, and with them there also seems to have come one whose name was Olaf. This is Olaf Tryggvesson, who was afterwards a very famous King of the Norwegians, and of whom we shall hear again. They harried or plundered Ipswich and then went into Essex, and sailed up the river Panta or Blackwater to Maldon. But then Brihtnoth the Alderman of the East-Saxons came against them, and there was a battle in which Brihtnoth, after fighting very bravely, was killed. You have heard of Brihtnoth before ; he was very bountiful to the monks, and helped to found the famous Abbey of Ely, which in Henry the First's time became a Bishoprick, and where is what I suppose I may call altogether the grandest church in all England. There Brihtnoth was buried, and there his wife Æthelflæd offered a piece of tapestry, on which she had worked the picture of all her husband's great actions. I wish we had it now, as well as the Tapestry at Bayeux which is so useful for our history seventy years later.

But I want you specially to remember Brihtnoth, because we still have the longest and grandest of our old songs, though it is not in the Chronicle, which describes the Battle of Maldon at length, though unluckily the beginning and the end of the song are both lost. I think that I cannot do better than give it you as I gave you the Song of Brunanburh, altering it from the Old-English as little as I can, but explaining such things as may need to be explained. I want you specially to take notice how nearly the whole song is about Brihtnoth's own personal following, his own Thanes and companions, who were bound to him by a special tie to fight for him and to avenge him.   So here I give you

The Song of the Fight of Maldon.

.   .   .   .
Bade he then youths each
Horse to forsake,
Far to hasten,
And forth to gang,
To strive with hands.   5

.   .   .   .
. That Offa's kinsman
First out found
That the Earl would not
Wretchedness thole ;[1]
He let there of his hands   10
Liefer[2] fly
Hawk for the wood,[3]
And to the fight stepped.
By that man might know
That the knight would not   15
Weak in the fight be,
When he to weapons took.
Eke to him would Eadric
His Elder serve,
His chief in fight ;   20
Gan then forth to bear
The spear in battle.
He gave God thanks
The while with hands
Hold he might   25

Board[4] and broadsword ;
Troth then he plighted
That well before his lord[5]
Fight he should.
Then there Brihtnoth gan   30
Warriors to trim.[6]
Rode he and rede gave,
And his men he taught
How they should stand
And their stead[7] hold,   35
And bade that their rounds[8]
Right they hold
Fast with hands,
And at nothing frightened be.
When he had the folk   40
Fairly ytrimmed,
He lighted there mid the men
That to him liefest were
Where he his hearth-bands[9]
Most faithful wist.   45
Then stood on the brink,
Sternly calling,
The wikings' herald ;
With words he spake ;
He then the threats bade   50
Of the sea-farers,
An errand to the Earl,

---

[1] Bear, endure.

[2] *Leof, dear.* We still sometimes say, " I would as *lief* do a thing." In l. 43 we have the word *liefest* again in the sense of *dearest.*

[3] This sounds as if Brihtnoth was hawking when he heard of the enemy's landing, and let his hawk fly, and at once made ready for battle.   But the whole of this part of the poem is mutilated and very obscure.

[4] The shield made of wood.

[5] *Frea*, the masculine of the High Dutch *Frau*, but we have lost both words.

[6] To arrange, or marshal.   "Warriors" is *Beornas*.   See the song of Brunanburh, l. 3.

[7] Their place or rank.   We talk of *steady* and *instead.*

[8] Their round shields.

[9] His household troops ; his companions bound to him by a special tie.

There as he over [1] stood.
"Me have sent to thee
The seamen swift ;[2]   55
They bade to thee say
That thou must rathly[3] send
Bracelets [4] for safety ;
And to you it better is
That ye the spear-rush   60
With gavel [5] buy off,
Than that we so hard
A battle deal.
Need we not each other slay ;
If ye speed [6] to this,   65
We will with the gold
A peace make fast.
If thou this aredest,
That here richest art,
That thou thy people   70
To loose [7] art willing ;
To sell [8] to seamen,
At their own doom [9]
Fee [10] with peace,
And take peace with us,   75

We will with the scot [11]
To our ships gang,
On the fleet to fare [12]
And with you peace hold."
Brihtnoth out spake,   80
His board [13] heaving ;
Shook he the weak ash [14]
With words spake he,
Ireful [15] and steadfast
He gave them answer.   85
"Hearest thou, sea-farer,
What this folk sayeth ?
They to you for gavel
Spears will sell,
The poisoned edge [16]   90
And the old sword,
The harness [17] that you
In fight shall help not.
Sea-men's bode,[18]
Bid back again,   95
Say to thy people
Mickle evil spell,
That here stand undaunted

---

[1] Opposite.   [2] *Snelle*, High-Dutch *schnell*.

[3] Swiftly ; we now use only the comparative *rather*.

[4] *Beagas*, as Æthelstan, and Brihtnoth some way on, are called *Beah-gifa*. It is odd that this Teutonic word which we have lost should survive in the French *bague*.

[5] *Gafol*, tribute.   [6] Agree.   [7] Save, redeem.   [8] Give, pay.

[9] That is, as much as the Danes should ask for.

[10] Money. You will remember that this year 991 was the time in which money was first paid to the Northmen.

[11] Treasure, payment, like High-Dutch *Schatz*. We still talk of "paying *scot* and lot," "going *scot*-free," &c.

[12] To go = High-Dutch *fahren*. We now use the word only metaphorically, excepting when we talk of "wayfarers" and "seafaring men." See p. 122.

[13] His shield.   [14] The slender shaft of ash wood.

[15] You must not think that *ire* is *derived* from the Latin *ira*, though of course it is *cognate* with it. Here the Old-English is "*Yrre* and anræd."

[16] This is the literal meaning, but we cannot think that our forefathers, we can hardly think that the Danes, really used poisoned weapons. I suppose it means only "sharp and deadly."

[17] The word for "weapons" is *heregeatu*. Thence the *heriot* paid in certain cases by a vassal to his lord, being originally a gift of weapons.

[18] Messenger, one bidden.

O

An Earl with his band,
That will defend　　　100
This our own land,[1]
Æthelred's home,
Mine elder's,[2]
His folk and ground ;[3]
Now shall fall　　　105
Heathens in battle.[4]
Too shameful me thinketh
That ye with our scot
To ships gang,
Unbefoughten.　　　110
Now ye thus far hither
On our earth
In have yeomen,
Ne shall ye so soft[5]
Treasures go and win.　　115
Us shall point and edge
Ere[6] judge between,
Grim war-play,

Ere we gavel sell."
Bade he then boards bear,　　120
And the men gang,
Till they on the water-brink[7]
All stood.
Ne might there for water
Band come to others ;[8]　　125
There came flowing
Flood after ebb ;
Locked them[9] the lake-streams ;[10]
Too long it them thought[11]
When[12] they together　　130
Spears could bear.
They there Panta's stream
With throngs[13] bestood,
East-Saxons' front-rank,[14]
And the ash-host ;[15]　　135
Nor might of them any
Other hurt,
But who through arrows flight

---

[1] The word is *ebel*, which means a man's very own land, which he holds of nobody else.

[2] "The home of Æthelred my Elder." You know what I have told you about the meaning of *Ealdor* and *Ealdorman*. See p. 35. In Latin of the time we might say, "*Æthelredus senior meus*."

[3] "Folc and foldan," but I cannot keep the alliteration in modern English, as *foldan* does not mean a *fold*, which in Old-English is *fald*.

[4] "The heathen shall fall in battle."　　[5] Easily.

[6] *Ær, ærest.* We use the words in a slightly different sense ; thus *ær* just below can quite be translated *ere.* In High-Dutch you know that *erst* is the common word for *first.*

[7] *Water* here is *ea*, thence *ealand*, which should in modern English be *eyland*, but which people spell, "*island*," as if it had something to do with *insula* and *isle.*

[8] That is the water hindered the band from getting at the enemy.

[9] *Locked* them, kept them from fighting.

[10] *Lagu-streamas. Lagu,* lake, does not at all mean stagnant water only. In many names like Hart*lake,* Stan*lake,* &c., it means running water.

[11] *Thought,* seemed, as we say *methinks.*　　[12] Till.

[13] "Mid prasse bestodon." Nobody seems to know what *prasse* means. Conybeare translated it *throngs,* and I know nothing better.

[14] *Ord,* point ; therefore the front rank.

[15] "Æsc-here," the host of the ship, that is the Northmen. One meaning of *æsc* or *ash* is *ship,* as being made of ashen wood. *Here* (High-Dutch *heer*) is the word always used of the Danish armies. The levy of the people of England is *fyrd.*

Their fall could work.[1]
The flood out went ; 140
The fleet-men stood ready,
Wikings many
For warfare eager.[2]
Bade then the heroes' guard[3]
To hold the bridge 145
A warman hard in war ;
He hight Wulfstan,
Quick with his kin,
That was Ceola's son,
Who the foremost man 150
With his franca[4] off-shot,
That there boldest
On the bridge stepped.
There stood with Wulfstan[5]
Warmen unfearing, 155
Ælfhere and Maccus,
Moody[6] twain ;
Who would not at the ford
Flight work,
And they fastly 160

'Gainst the fiend[7] warded,
The while that they might
Wield their weapons.
When they[8] that well knew,
And saw with gladness,[9] 165
That they[10] the bridge-wards
Bitter found,
Gan then to use guile
The loathly guests.[11]
Prayed they then that they 170
Up might gang,
Over the ford might fare,[12]
And their bands lead.
Then the Earl began,
For his overmood,[13] 175
To leave of land too much
To the loathly people.[14]
Began to call then
Over cold water
Brihthelm's bairn ;[15] 180
The warriors listened.
" Now to you is yielded,

---

[1] None could wound the enemy but those who could hit them and make them fall with arrows.

[2] *Georne*—High-Dutch *gern.* We have lost the noun and the adverb, but we keep the verb to *yearn.*

[3] " Heleþa hleo," "shelter or safeguard of heroes," meaning Brihtnoth. *Heleð* is the same as the High-Dutch *held.*

[4] *Franca,* a javelin. Some say that hence comes the name of the *Franks,* and that of the Saxons from the *seax* or short-sword.

[5] You will see how exactly Wulfstan is like Horatius, and Ælfhere and Maccus like Lartius and Herminius, in the " Lays of Ancient Rome."

[6] *Modig,* full of *mood* or spirit ; we use the word in a different sense, but in High-Dutch you have *muth* and *muthig* in the old sense.

[7] The *foe* = High-Dutch *feind.*

[8] *They,* that is the English. [9] *Georne :* see l. 143.

[10] *They,* that is the Danes. The Danes found the *bridge-wards*—Wulfstan, Ælfhere, and Maccus- *bitter* to them.

[11] *Guests,* strangers, enemies. So the Latin *hostis* at first meant only a stranger, and so Amompharetos in Herodotus calls the Persians ξεῖνοι.

[12] *Fare,* to go. See above, l. 78.

[13] His high spirit.

[14] *þeod.* We have quite lost the word, but it is found in many proper names, like Theodric, Theo(d)bald, &c., and we shall afterwards find *þeoden, lord,* coming from it.

[15] Brihthelm's son ; that is Brihtnoth.

Go straightway to us,
Men [1] to battle ;
God only wots   185
Who shall hold fast
The place of slaughter." [2]
Waded then the slaughter-wolves, [3]
For water they mourned [4] not,
The wikings' host ;   190
West over Panta,
Over sheer [5] water,
Shields they carried : [6]
The shipmen to land
Their lindens [7] bore.   195
There gainst the fierce ones
Ready was standing
Brihtnoth with warriors ; [8]
With the boards hight he [9]
Work the war-hedge, [10]   200
And made his host stand
Fast against foemen. [11]
Then was it fought nigh, [12]

Glory in battle,
Then was the tide [13] ycome   205
That the fey [14] men,
There should fall.
Then were shouts a-heaved ; [15]
Ravens wound round,
Ernes [16] for corses greedy ; [17]   210
On the earth was shouting.
Then let they from their hands
The file-hard spears, [18]
The sharply grounden
Javelins fly ;   215
Bows were busy,
Boards the point received, [19]
Bitter was the war-rush ;
Warriors fell ;
On either hand   220
Youths lay dead.
Wounded was Wulfmær,
Rest from fight [20] chose he,
Brihtnoth's kinsman, [21]

---

[1] *Guma*, a man. See the Song of Brunanburh, l. 99.

[2] The *wæl-stow*, the field of battle. The old chroniclers, in recording a battle, always say which side kept possession of the *wælstow*, as this was the sign of victory. So in old Greece, the defeated had to ask for their dead, which the victors were bound to give them.

[3] *Wæl-wulfas ;* of course the enemy.   [4] Recked, cared.

[5] Pure, clear.   [6] *Wegon ;* as if one could say *wayed*.

[7] Shields of linden wood.

[8] *Beornas*, as before.   [9] *He hight*, bade.

[10] That is, he had made his men form the *shield-wall*, a sort of fortress made by holding their shields close together. This is described at the beginning of the poem.

[11] *Feondum*, as before.   [12] Then the close combat began.

[13] *Tid*-time, as we say Christmas-*tide*, even-*tide* and the like, in High-Dutch *zeit*. The *tides* of the sea are so called because they keep to a certain known *tide*.

[14] *Fæge men ;* men doomed to death. See the Song of Brunanburh, l. 22.

[15] Lifted, upraised.

[16] Eagles. See the Song of Brunanburh, l. 124.

[17] *Georn*, as before.   [18] Sharpened hard with the file.

[19] That is, the javelins stuck in the boards or shields. *Onfeng* from *onfón*, to take, seize hold of. We have lost the verb, but we have the noun *fang*.

[20] *Beadu-ræs*, yet another word for war.

[21] *Mæg*, *may*, kinsman of any sort.

His sister's son,[1] 225
With bills was he
Sorely forhewn,[2]
There was to wikings
Back-reward given.[3]
Heard I that Eadward 230
One man slew
Mightily with his sword ;
From the blow warned[4] he not,
When at his feet fell
The fey warrior ;[5] 235
Thereof to him his lord[6]
Thanks said,
To him his bower-thane[7]
When he peace had.
So were meeting, 240
Stern of purpose,
The youths in battle.
Thought they gladly
Who there with spear-point
Foremost might be 245
From the fey men

Their life to win,[8]
Warriors with weapons.
Slaughter fell on earth ;
Stood they stedfast ; 250
Brihtnoth arrayed them :
Bade he that each youth
Should think on battle,
Who with the Danes would
For their doom[9] fight. 255
Raged[10] then the war-hard man,[11]
Weapons up-hove he,
His board to shield him,
And towards the warrior stepped ;[12]
Went then stedfast 260
The Earl against the Churl,[13]
Either for the other
Evil was thinking.
Sent them the seaman
A southern dart,[14] 265
Therewith wounded was
The lord of warriors ;[15]
He shoved[16] them with his shield,

---

[1] Among all the Teutonic nations, a sister's son was held to be almost as near to a man as his own children.

[2] *Forheawen ;* that is cut down, mangled.

[3] *Wiðerlean ;* I have translated it literally, but one misses the fine old English word.

[4] That is, *shrunk* or swerved.

[5] *Cempa :* we have lost the word, but it lives in High-Dutch in *Kampf* and other kindred words.

[6] *þeoden* from *þeod* or people, like *Cyning* from *cyn.* See l. 177.

[7] Steward or chamberlain. Edward must have held this place in Briht-noth's house.

[8] That is, to struggle with the enemy, and *win* or take away their lives.

[9] The *doom* of the Danes : that is, the victory of the English.

[10] *Wôd,* a verb, like the adjective *wood,* angry, sometimes mad ; the word is, I believe, still used in Scotland.

[11] That is, the Danish chief.

[12] That is, stepped close to Brihtnoth.

[13] The *Earl* is Brihtnoth ; the English poet calls the Danish leader a *churl.* On the words see p. 41.

[14] This is said to mean a Southern, that is an English dart, hurled back again ; but this sounds very harsh.

[15] That is, Brihtnoth.

[16] *Shoved.* This is an instance of the way in which words, so to speak, go down in the world. We should not talk now of *shoving* in battle, but of pushing or thrusting.

That the shaft burst,
And the spear snapped   270
That it sprang again.
Wrathful was the war-man ;
He with his dart stung[1]
The proud wiking,
That to him the wound gave. 275
Skilled was the leader,[2]
He let his franca[3] wade[4]
Through the youth's halse ;[5]
His hand he guided
That he from the robber[6]   280
His life he took away.
Then he another
Swiftly shot,
That the corslet burst ;
He was in breast wounded   285
Through the ring-fold ;
In his heart stood
The poisoned point.
Then was the Earl blithe,
Laughed the moody[7] man.   290
Said to his Maker thanks
For the day's work
That his Lord gave him ;
Hurled then some fellow[8]

A dart from his hands,   295
From his hand it flew,
That all-through it pierced
Through the noble one,
The Thane of Æthelred.
By his half[9] stood   300
A youth unwaxen,[10]
A knight[11] in the war,
He full quickly
Drew from the warrior[12]
The bloody dart,   305
Wulfstan's bairn [was he],
Wulfmær the young.
Let he the hard spear
Fare[13] once yet again ;[14]
The point through-waded,   310
That he on earth lay
Who his chieftain[15] ere[16]
Sadly had reached.
Then came a wily
Fighting-man to the Earl ;   315
He would the warrior's
Bracelets[17] fetch away,
His robe[18] and rings,
And jewelled sword.
Then Brihtnoth drew   320

---

[1] We now use this word only of insects with *stings*, but it used to mean to pierce in any way. In the Chronicle we read that Liofa *stung* Edmund.

[2] The *fyrd-rinc*, the man of the *fyrd* or army : that is, Brihtnoth.

[3] See l. 151.   [4] *Go*, in a wider sense, like *sting*.

[5] *Neck ;* the word is used in Scotland still.

[6] *Sceaða*, one who does scathe or damage.

[7] See l. 157.

[8] That is, one of the enemy. The poet speaks contemptuously, as when he spoke of a *churl*.

[9] By his *half :* that is, by his *side.* We still speak of doing a thing on a man's *behalf.*

[10] Not yet *waxed* or fully grown up.

[11] *Cniht* first meant a boy or youth ; then a page or follower, and so on to his later use, changing its meaning, much like *Thegn* and other words.

[12] The *Beorn ;* see above. That is, Brihtnoth.

[13] See l. 78.

[14] That is, he threw back the spear which had struck Brihtnoth.

[15] See above, l. 236.   [16] See l. 117.   [17] *Beagas,* see l. 58.

[18] *Reif ;* this seems to be one of the words which got into French from Teutonic, and which have come round to us again through French.

His bill[1] out of sheath,
Broad and brown-edged,[2]
And on the corslet smote ;[3]
Rathly him then let[4]
Of the shipmen some one,   325
That he the Earl's
Arm did mar.
Fell then from his hands
His sword of fallow[5] hilt,
Nor might he hold   330
The hard falchion,
Or his weapon wield.
Yet a word quoth
The hoary war-man ;
The daring youths   335
Bade he gang forth,
His good companions.[6]
Might he not on feet long
Fast now stand up ;
He to heaven looked ;   340
"Thank Thee, Nations' Wielder,
For all the good things[7]
That I in the world have bode ;[8]

Now I own, mild Maker,
That I most have need   345
That Thou to my ghost
Good should grant,
That my soul to Thee
Now may make its way,
To Thy kingdom,   350
Lord of Angels,
With peace[9] to journey.
I am praying to Thee
That it hell-fiends[10]
Hurt may never."   355
Thereon hewed him
The heathen soldiers ;[11]
And both the warriors
That near him by-stood ;
Ælfnoth and Wulfmær both   360
Lay there on the ground
By their lord ;[12]
Their lives they sold.[13]
Then bowed[14] they from the fight
That there to be would not ;[15]   365
There were Odda's bairns

---

[1] *Bill* is commonly an axe ; here it must be a sword.

[2] *Brown* sword is a common epithet in old ballads.

[3] Literally *slew*, like *schlagen* in High-Dutch, but we can hardly use the word so.

[4] *Hindered*, as several times in the Prayer Book.

[5] *Fallow*, that is yellow or golden.

[6] *Geféran*. This is a word which seems to have fallen very low indeed, into *gaffer*. But *fere* was a good word much later.

[7] "*Wynna ;*" we have lost the substantive, but we keep the word *winsome*.

[8] *Bode, abode :* that is, experienced or enjoyed.

[9] *Frið*, like the High-Dutch *friede*.

[10] *Hel-sceaðas ;* that is, fiends or dæmons. See above, l. 2So.

[11] *Scealcas :* servants, soldiers ; in High-Dutch *Schalk*. So in the proper name *Gottschalk*, in Low-Dutch *Godescalc*, and in *Marescalc*, one who looks after mares or horses, the same as *Maréchal* or *Marshal*, the word having come back to us through French.

[12] *Frea;* see l. 2S.

[13] We still sometimes talk of men " *selling* their lives dearly."

[14] That is, *turned*, ran away.

[15] *Noldon*, "would not," as if we could say *nould*. In Old-English there are a great many negative words found in this way with an *n* at the beginning, as we still say *one* and *none*, *ever* and *never*, *yea* and *nay*.

Erst [1] in flight ;
Godric from battle [went],
And the good man forsook
That to him ofttimes   370
Horses had given. [2]
He leapt on the horse [3]
That his lord had owned, [4]
On the housings
That it not right was, [5]   375
And his brothers with him
Both hurried off,
Godrinc and Godrig ;
For battle they recked not,
But went from the fight,   380
And the wood sought they ;
They fled to the fastness
And their life guarded.
And of men mo [6] [fled]
Than it any reason was,   385
If they the earnings [7]
All had minded
That he to their good
To them had done ;
As Offa on a day   390

Ere to them said
On the speech-stead, [8]
Where he a meeting had, [9]
That there moodily [10]
Many men spoke,   395
That yet in battle
Would not endure.
There was fallen
The folks' Elder,
Æthelred's Earl ;   400
All then saw
Of his hearth-companions [11]
That their lord lay [dead].
Then there went forth
The proud Thanes,   405
The undaunted men
Hastened gladly ; [12]
They would then all
One of two things,
Either life forsake,   410
Or the loved one [13] wreak. [14]
So them emboldened
The bairn of Ælfric,
Warrior of winters young

---

[1] First, foremost. See l. 117.

[2] Literally, " mares had sold ;" *mare* originally meaning a horse of any kind.

[3] *Eoh*, a word which we have quite lost, cognate with the Latin *equus* and the Greek ἵππος.

[4] You will remember that Brihtnoth did not fight on horseback, but rode to the field and then got down to fight. Godric got on the horse which was kept ready for the Earl.

[5] Because he had no right to ride the Earl's horse.

[6] *More ;* it is still sometimes used in verse.

[7] *Earnings*, that is, rewards.

[8] The place of speaking.

[9] " Þa he *Gemôt hæfde.*" I told you (see p. 131), how the separate *Gemôts* or meetings of the different kingdoms still went on.

[10] *Boldly.* See l. 157.

[11] His own followers, the youths who attended him and fought near him. The word is "heorð [hearth]-*geneatas,*" a word that we have lost, but which is found in High-Dutch as " Eid*genossen,*" " Bundes*genossen,*" &c.

[12] *Georne.* See above, l. 143.

[13] That is, Brihtnoth.

[14] That is, to *avenge.* We cannot now talk of *wreaking* in this way, but we talk of *wreaking vengeance* on any one.

With words spake. 415
Ælfwine thus quoth he.
" The bold speeches mind
That times have we oft
At the mead ¹ spoken,
When we on benches 420
Our boasts upheaved,
Heroes in hall.
Round us is hard fight,
Now may we ken
Him that bold is. 425
I will my high-birth ²
To all make known,
That I was in Mercians
Of mickle kin ; ³
Was nine old father ⁴ 430
Ealdhelm hight,
A wise Alderman,
Rich in world's wealth. ⁵
Neither on that folk ⁶
Shall the Thanes twit me ⁷ 435
That I from this host
Away would go
To seek my home.
Now mine Elder lieth
Hewn down in battle ; 440
To me is that harm most ;
He was both my kinsman

And my lord."
Then he forth went
On feud ⁸ minded. 445
That he with spear-point
One man reached
Of the folk of the fleetmen,
That he on earth lay
Smitten down with his weapon. 450
Again he his fellows ⁹ cheered ;
Friends and companions,
That they forth should go.
Offa then spake.
His ash-wood he shook, 455
" How thou, Ælfwine, hast
All our Thanes
In need-time cheered.
Now our lord lieth,
The Earl on the earth, 460
That of us each one
Others should embolden,
Warmen to the war,
That while we weapons may
Have and hold, 465
The hard falchion,
Spear and good sword.
Us Godric hath,
Base bairn of Odda,
All betrayed. 470

---

¹ At the drinking of *mead*, that is at the feast, as a wedding feast is called a *bride-ale*, now cut short into *bridal*.

² *Æðelo*, nobility. The same word that we find in so many names and words, as *Æthel*stan, *Æthel*ing and *Æthelinga*-ig or Athelney. In High-Dutch they can still say *adel*.

³ As we should say, " of a great family."

⁴ That is, *grandfather*.

⁵ *Worold-sælig*, happy or blessed in the world. In High-Dutch *selig* still means blessed, but in English it has sunk into *silly*.

⁶ Does this mean among the East-Angles as distinguished from his own Mercians ?

⁷ Another word that has gone down in the world. I remember an account of Saint John Baptist *snubbing* Herod.

⁸ *Fæht*, like the High-Dutch *fæde*. We can still talk of having a *feud* with any one. Here it means that he was minded to deal wrathfully with the enemy.

⁹ The word is " winas" from "wine," a word which we have quite lost, but which we find in so many proper names. *Godwine*, "a good fellow ;" *Leofwine*, " a dear fellow," &c.

Weened there too many men,
As he on mare[1] rode
Proudly through the fight,
That it was our lord.[2]
Therefore was'here in field   475
The folk all scattered,
The shield-wall[3] broken.
Perish this his deed
That he so many men
To flight hath driven."   480
Leofsuna spake out,
And his linden heaved,
His board[4] to guard him ;
He to the warrior quoth,
" I this promise   485
That I hence nill[5]
Fly a footstep,
But will further go,
To wreak in the fight
My lord and comrade.   490
Nor by Stourmere[6]
Any stedfast hero[7]
With words need twit me,
That I lordless
Homeward should go,   495
And wend from the fight ;
But me shall weapons meet
Point and iron."
Full of ire he waded,

Fought he [sted]fastly,   500
On flight he thought not.
Dunnere then quoth,
His dart he made quake,
The valiant churl,
Over all he cleped ;[8]   505
He bade that warriors each
Brihtnoth should wreak ;
" Nought may he fear
Who to wreak thinketh
His lord among the folk,   510
Nor for his life mourn."[9]
Then they forth went,
For life they recked not.
Began then the house-men[10]
Hardly to fight,   515
Fiercely spears bearing,
And to God they prayed[11]
That they might wreak
Their lord and comrade,
And on their foes[12]   520
A fall might work.
Then there a hostage gan
Gladly to help ;
He was in Northumberland
Of a hard[13] kin,   .   525
Ecglaf's bairn,
Æseferth was his name.
Nought then feared he

---

[1] See above, l. 371.
[2] They thought that Brihtnoth himself was flying when they saw Godric on Brihtnoth's horse.
[3] See in the Song of Brunanburh, l. 10, 11, and above, l. 200.
[4] See this too in the Song of Brunanburh, l. 10, and above, l. 120.
[5] On the negative words, see above, l. 365. This particular word we keep in the phrase, " will he, *nill* he."
[6] A lake or fen in Essex, near which Leofsuna seems to have lived.
[7] See the Song of Brunanburh, 50.
[8] *Called:* we still sometimes use the participle *yclept.*
[9] That is, think, care, reck. See l. 189.
[10] " *Hired-men,*" the men of the *hired* or court of the Aldermen; his own personal companions and followers. Do not think it means men *hired* with money.
[11] *Bædon;* as in High-Dutch *bitten,* and as we talk of a *bedesman* and of telling *beads.*
[12] Strictly *fiends.* See above, l. 161.
[13] Stout, valiant.

In the war-play,
And he poured forth 530
Arrows enough ;
One while he on board[1] shot,
One while a warrior teased,[2]
Ever and anon[3] he sold[4]
Some wounds, 535
The while he weapons
Still might wield.
Then yet in rank[5] stood
Eadward the Long.
Ready and yearnful ;[6] 540
Bold words spake he
That he would not flee
A footstep of land,
Overback to bow,
While his better lay. 545
He broke the board-wall,
And with the warriors fought,
Till he his gift giver[7]
On the seamen
Worthily wreaked, 550
Ere he in slaughter lay.
So did Ætheric,
Noble comrade,
Eager forth to go,[8]

Fought he earnestly, 555
Sibriht's brother,
And so many other
Clave the keeled board.[9]
Keen they were,
Burst they the boards, 560
And the hauberk sang
A grisly lay.[10]
There in the fight slew
Offa the seamen,
Till he on earth fell, 565
And Gadda's kinsman
The ground sought ;
Rath was in battle
Offa down hewn,
Yet had he furthered[11] 570
That he his lord had pledged,
As he ere agreed
With his ring-giver[12]
That they should both
To the borough ride 575
Hale[13] to home,
Or in the host cringe[14]
On the slaughter-place,
Of their wounds die.
He lay thanelike[15] 580

---

[1] See above, l. 483.

[2] That is, *troubled, annoyed, wounded ;* here is another word which has sadly come down in the world.

[3] " Æfre embe stunde." " Ever from time to time." " *Stunde* " in High-Dutch has got the special sense of *hour*.

[4] *Gave*, as above. See p. 122.

[5] *Ord*, the word often used for *point* or *edge ;* here the *edge* of the army.

[6] *Yearning*, eager. See above, l. 143.

[7] He who had given him gifts or treasures, his *hláford* Brihtnoth.

[8] " Fús and *forðgeorn* " = *forth glad*, eager to go forth.

[9] The shield from its curved shape, like the keel of a ship.

[10] "Gryre leo'e." That is, made a fearful noise. " Leo'e" is the same as the High-Dutch *Lied*. This word again has come back to us in a new shape, through the French *lai*.

[11] Carried out as far as he could.

[12] " Beah-gifa." See at the beginning of the Song of Brunanburh, and above, l. 58.

[13] That is, unhurt in the battle.

[14] Fall, die. See in the Song of Brunanburh, l. 20.

[15] *þegenlice ;* like a Thane, like a good and faithful follower, falling back on the first meaning of *þegen.*

His lord hard by.
Then were boards broken,
Seamen waded on,
In the fight wrathful.
The spear oft waded through 585
The fey man's life-house.[1]
Forth then went Wistan
Thurstan's son,
With the warmen fought he,
He was in the throng, 590
Banesman [2] of three of them,
Ere him Wigeline's bairn
In slaughter low laid.
There was stern meeting;[3]
Stood they fast 595
Fighters in battle;
Fighting they cringed,
With their wounds weary;
Slaughter fell on earth.
Oswold and Ealdwold 600
All the while,
Both brethren,
The warriors trimmed;[4]
Their fellow-kinsmen
With words they bade, 605
That they there at need
Them should bear up,
And unweakly [5]
Their weapons use.
Brihtwold then spoke, 610
His board heaving,
He was an old comrade;[6]

His ash [7] he made quake;
He full boldly
The warriors learned;[8] 615
"Mind shall the harder be,
Heart shall the keener be,
Mood shall the more be,
As our main [9] lessens.[10]
Here lies our Elder, 620
All down hewn,
A good man in the dust;
Ever may he groan
Who now from this war-play
Of wending thinketh. 625
I am old of life;
Hence stir will I not,
And I by the half [11]
Of my lord,
By such a loved man 630
To lie am thinking."
So Æthelgar's bairn
Then all cheered on,
Godric to battle :
Oft he the dart let go, 635
The death spear wound he [12]
On the wikings.
So he on the folk
The foremost went,
He hewed and slew them 640
Till he in fight cringed.
This was not the Godric
Who from the fight fled.[13]

---

[1] That is, his body.

[2] *Bána*, a *bane*, a destructive person; we now use the word only of things. That is, he killed three of the enemy.

[3] *Gemót.* See the Song of Brunanburh, l. 99.

[4] See above, l. 41.   [5] That is, strongly.

[6] *Geneat.* See above.   [7] See above, l. 82.

[8] *Læran*, like the High-Dutch *lehren.* In the Psalms we say, "*learn* me thy statutes."

[9] *Mægen*, strength; as we say with his might and *main.*

[10] "*Lytlað*," grows *little;* but we have lost the verb.

[11] See above, l. 300.

[12] Made go in a winding course.

[13] *Forbah :* literally bowed before the fight; that is, was afraid and ran away.

So the brave and good Alderman Brihtnoth died. It is a great pity that there were so few men like him. You see how he refused to pay money to the invaders, but it was in this very year, after Brihtnoth was dead, that Archbishop Sigeric and the two Aldermen advised paying money. They paid ten thousand pounds, a very large sum in those days, to Justin, Guthmund, and Olaf. In after times men had to pay much larger sums still.

Still, after all this, the English in 992 showed some spirit to resist. The King and his Wise Men ordered a fleet to be got together at London, and so it was. But Alderman Ælfric, who was one of the commanders, sent word to the Danes and afterwards joined them himself. However, the English put both him and the Danes to flight, and took Ælfric's ship, but he himself escaped. It was no doubt out of vengeance for this treason of Ælfric's that King Æthelred next year caused the eyes of Ælfric's son Ælfgar to be put out. And a base and cruel deed it was, as there is nothing to show that Ælfgar had any hand in his father's crime. The same year, 993, the Danes harried a great part of Northumberland and also Lindesey,[1] that is, the northern part of Lincolnshire. The people resisted them bravely, but their three leaders,[2] Fræna, Frithegist, and Godwine, being themselves of Danish descent, took to flight, and so betrayed them to the enemy.

It is not quite certain whether Swegen himself, Swegen with the Forked Beard as he was called, had any hand in these earlier invasions, but the Chronicle distinctly tells us that Swegen and "Anlaf" came in 994. This Anlaf was Olaf Tryggvesson, of whom you heard at Maldon, and who was now King of the Norwegians or Northmen. So we now have two Kings of all Denmark and of all Norway coming against England. They first attacked London, where the citizens bravely beat them off, and then they ravaged the south coast of England. But again King Æthelred could think of nothing better than to give them

---

[1] *Lindesey*, or *Lindesige*, the isle of *Lindum*. Do not forget that Lincoln is *Lindi Colonia*.

[2] *Heretogas*, leaders in war, the same word as the High-German *Herzog*. The *Heretoga* in war is the same as the Alderman in peace, but it does not follow that all these three had the rank of Alderman.

more money. So they stayed through the winter at Southampton,
and seemingly did no more damage, at least not till they wanted
more money. But King Æthelred sent Ælfheah Bishop of
Winchester[1] and Alderman Æthelweard to King Olaf, and they
brought him to Andover, where the King was. Olaf was now
a Christian. Some say that the year before, when he was
twenty-five years old, he had been on one of his voyages to
the Orkneys, where Sigurd the Earl of the country persuaded
him to be baptized. The Orkneys were then inhabited by Norwegian settlers, and had an Earl of their own. Others say that
he was converted by an Abbot in the Scilly Islands. So Olaf
and Æthelred made a treaty; and Æthelred had Olaf confirmed by Bishop Ælfheah and adopted him as his son. Olaf
then promised that he would never invade England again, and
he kept his promise very faithfully. He became a zealous·
Christian, and the introduction of Christianity into Norway is
in a great measure owing to him. But he did not set about it in
the same good and wise way as our own Kings Æthelberht and
Edwin, who won over their people by persuasion and their own
example. For King Olaf Tryggvesson compelled his people to
become Christians whether they would or not, and cruelly persecuted those who stuck to the old Gods. At last he died in a
sea-fight against Swegen of Denmark.

From this time we have no more to do with invasions from
Norway till Harold Hardrada came against our King Harold
seventy years after. But we have a great deal more to do with
Swegen Forkbeard and his Danes. It is very hard to put the
English and Danish stories together. According to some accounts, Swegen had once been driven out of his Kingdom by
Eric, King of the Swedes. He then wandered about, seeking
a refuge first in Norway and then in England. But Hakon the
King of the Norwegians would not take him in, neither would
our King Æthelred. So he went to the King of Scots, and
stayed with him till he was able to get back to his own Kingdom. So Swegen remembered the wrong, as he called it, that

---

[1] This Ælfheah was afterwards Archbishop of Canterbury, and was
martyred in a way that I shall tell you of. He is generally called Saint
Alphege, but that makes nonsense of his name, which is *Ælf-heah*, *Elf-
high* ; you know how many names come from the *elves.*

Æthelred had done him, and he invaded England to avenge it. I do not know how this may have been, but that both Swegen and Olaf came into England in 994 is quite certain. Olaf, as we have seen, went home and kept his promise honourably, but Swegen's fleet and army stayed, and in 997 they began to plunder again, sailing up the Bristol Channel, plundering again at Watchet and other places on both sides. They then doubled the Land's End, and burned the minster at Tavistock, which had been built by Alderman Ordgar, the father of the Lady Ælfthryth. The next year, 998, they ravaged Dorsetshire and Wight and got provisions from Hampshire and Sussex, and defeated the English whenever they came against them. The next year, 999, they besieged Rochester and defeated the Kentishmen who came to help the town, and then, getting themselves horses, they ravaged all Kent. Then at last King Æthelred thought it was time to do something, and he and the Wise Men ordered that a fleet and army should be got ready. But when they came together, they only made matters worse ; for the soldiers and their leaders oppressed the people and did nothing against the enemy. We may suppose that things would have been very different if King Edgar had been in the fleet, or if Alfred or Edward or Æthelstan or Edmund had been there to lead the people to battle.

The next year was the year 1000. It really seems like madness when we read that Æthelred, who could not or would not defend Wessex against the Danes, must needs go and ravage Cumberland. Our own earliest accounts give no reason at all for this. Henry of Huntingdon indeed makes it an expedition against the Danes, who he says were settled in Cumberland,[1] and he says that the Danes were defeated. But I cannot help thinking that, if it had been an expedition against Danes, the Chronicle would have made it more clear. And there is another account which, though it is found only in a much later Scottish writer named John Fordun, seems very likely in itself. King Æthelred called on Malcolm, the Under-king of Cumberland, to give him money towards paying the Danes.[2] Mal-

---

[1] "Maxima mansio Dacorum." The Danes are, oddly enough, often called *Daci*.

[2] That is, he wanted him to pay the tax called *Danegeld*, or money

colm answered that he had never promised to pay money for anything, but only to follow the King of the English in war ; and he added that it was disgraceful to pay money to the enemy. So Malcolm said that if the King would go out to battle against the Danes, he would go too, according to his duty, but that he would not pay any money.   Alfred or Edgar would have been delighted with such a vassal, but this foolish and wicked Æthel-red was angry with him, and took the trouble to go all the way to Cumberland to punish Malcolm by harrying his country, while the Danes were still in the English Channel.   He ordered his fleet to sail round North Wales and meet him in Cumberland. But the fleet got no further than the Isle of Man, which was harried, we are not told why; perhaps the King of Man had made the same answer as Malcolm.

And now we come to a matter which, if it really happened. as seems most likely, shows Æthelred to have been even more utterly senseless than he seems in this Cumbrian expedition. You know how very little England had hitherto had to do with the countries on the Continent, and how the little that England has had to do with them had been almost wholly of a friendly kind.   We have now and then seen a marriage or a treaty, but there has not been a single war between England and the Emperors or the Kings of the West-Franks or any other foreign princes.   There has been plenty of fighting, but it has always been either with the other nations in Britain or else with the Danes who invaded the land.   You will indeed think that this was a strange time, when the Danes were harrying the country everywhere, for Æthelred to rush into a war on the Continent. Yet it really seems to have been so.   We have indeed no distinct account in our own writers, but the Norman writers tell of it ; and though their account is most likely exaggerated, it seems on the whole more likely that our writers have passed it by or slurred it over than that the Normans should have altogether invented it.   So I tell the tale as a thing which is very likely, without being quite certain about it.   This same year then, the year 1000, Æthelred sent his fleet to invade Normandy, or, as the Chronicle calls it, *Ricardesrice*, just as Flanders is called *Bald-*

for paying the Danes, an impost which began now and lasted long after there were any Danes to pay.

winesland. The Duke of the Normans now was Richard the Second, called Richard the Good. He was the son of Richard the Fearless, who was the son of William of the Long Sword, who was the son of Rolf Ganger. Richard the Fearless reigned from 941 to 996, and Richard the Good reigned from 996 to 1026 ; so it is not wonderful if it seemed as if the Duke of the Normans must always be a Richard. The land was hardly yet called Normandy ; so our people seem to have called it Richard's *rice*[1] or dominion. The Normans had now become quite French in their ways, and they spoke the French tongue. You see I do not mind saying *French* now, because the old German Kings of the West-Franks, the Karlings who reigned at Laôn, had come to an end. In 987 Hugh, commonly called Hugh Capet, who was Lord of Paris and Duke of the French, was chosen King of the French, and his city of Paris became the royal city and has remained so ever since. Moreover the descendants of Hugh were Kings in France all the time from 987 to 1848, save only the years from 1792 to 1814, during part of which years there was a Republic and afterwards Napoleon Buonaparte was Tyrant. No royal house has ever lasted so long in the male line as the house of the Kings of Paris. These kings gradually got into their own hands nearly all the dominions of their own vassals, besides conquering and winning in one way and another a great part of Germany and Burgundy. So that now, whereas the real old frontier of France was the Rhone and the Saone, France now reaches in some places to the Alps and even to the Rhine. But for a long time these new Kings, though they called themselves Kings of the French, had very little power beyond their own Duchy of Paris. In Aquitaine for a long time nobody took any notice of them at all ; and though the Dukes of the Normans called themselves their vassals, they were really quite independent. Now these Paris Kings did not speak German like the descendants of Charles the Great, and the German tongue seems now to have quite died out in the Western Kingdom. And from this time the Eastern and Western Kingdoms had nothing to do with one another. So now that the two Kingdoms are quite

---

[1] The same word as the High-Dutch *Reich.* We keep it in the endings of words in the shape of *rick* and *ry*, as Bishop*rick*, Jew*ry*, &c.

separate, and as the West has got a new language and a new capital and a new line of Kings, I shall leave off talking about the Franks or West-Franks and talk of the *French*. But I shall perhaps sometimes talk of Gaul still, because the whole land was still called *Gallia*, and *Francia* generally means only the King's own dominions. The King of the French then at this time was Robert the son of Hugh, and the Duke of the Normans, as I said, was Richard the Good. The Normans, as I told you, had now all learned to speak French, unless perhaps a little Danish was still spoken at Bayeux. Still the Normans kept up a certain friendship for their former brethren in Denmark, and King Harold Bluetooth proved a very good friend to Duke Richard the Fearless more than once. The Normans had before this offended Æthelred by receiving Danish ships into their ports and letting them sell the plunder that they had taken in England. Æthelred and Duke Richard the Fearless had once before, in 991, quarrelled about this matter, and were very nearly coming to a war. But Pope John the Fifteenth, acting as a Pope should act but as the Popes did not very often act, stepped in and made peace between them. This time, in 1000, if our story be true, Æthelred sent his fleet against Normandy. According to the Norman account, he bade his people ravage the whole land, save only Saint Michael's Mount and the great monastery on it, which they were to spare. As for Duke Richard, they were to bring him to England with his hands tied behind his back. Foolish as Æthelred was, we need not believe that he was quite so foolish as all this. So the fleet went over and they began to harry the peninsula of Coutances—the great peninsula of Normandy, the only peninsula in Europe, except Jütland, which looks to the North. But Nigel or Neal, Viscount of Saint Saviour's, led the people of the country against the English, and drove them away, without Duke Richard having any need to help them. So King Æthelred's great expedition came to nothing. But from this time begins the connexion between England and Normandy, of which we shall soon hear so much; for Æthelred and Richard soon became friends, and in 1002 Æthelred married Emma the sister of Richard. He had been married before to an English wife, whose name is not quite certain, as she is not mentioned in the Chronicle, and later writers call her by different names and make her the daughter of different fathers. By her Æthelred had many sons and daughters. The eldest seems to have been Æthelstan, but the most famous was Edmund, who was afterwards King, and who was called Ironside, from his great strength and daring. I suppose that his mother was now dead, for Æthelred now married Emma, the first foreign Lady that we have seen since Judith the wife of Æthelwulf. Many of our Kings' daughters had married foreign princes, but none of our Kings from Æthelwulf to Æthelred had married any foreign prince's daughter. Emma was a clever and beautiful woman, and we shall hear a great deal of her for the next fifty years or so, but I cannot say that we shall hear much good. Perhaps you will be surprised to hear that the English did not like her name, and thought it so strange that she was called in England Ælfgifu. We now know the name of Emma very well, and we should think Ælfgifu a strange name. That is because we have dropped our good Old-English names, all but a few, and have taken to foreign names instead.

All this while the Danes were going about as usual. In the year 1001 they attacked Exeter, but were driven off by the citizens; they then ravaged all Devonshire, and defeated the Defnsætas and Sumorsætas in a battle at Penhow near Exeter, and went back to their ships with much spoil, and harried all Wight, Hampshire and Dorsetshire. The next year, the year of the King's marriage, he again gave them money to go away, but afterwards, later in the year, he caused all the Danes who stayed in England to be massacred. This was done on Saint Brice's day, 1002. It is said that no age or sex was spared, and that among those who were killed was Gunhild the sister of King Swegen, who was a Christian, and who was living in England. She was the wife of one Pallig, a Danish Earl, who had entered Æthelred's service and had then gone over to the Danes again. Æthelred, who put out the eyes of Ælfric's son, would be quite capable of putting her to death for her husband's treason. We are told that Gunhild's husband and her young son were both killed before her eyes, and that before she died she foretold the woes that would come because of this wicked deed. But there is no doubt much exaggeration in this

P 2

story, as it cannot be true that all the Danes in England were killed, when all the chief men of a large part of England were in one sense Danes. It can only mean the Danes who had stayed behind from Swegen's army. The reason given is that they had made a conspiracy to kill the King and his Wise Men, and to seize all the country for themselves. If this was so, it still could not be right to kill them all in this way without trial. And besides its being wicked, nothing could be more foolish. Such an act could do nothing except enrage Swegen and put him in some sort in the right. It is said that Æthelred was advised to do this by one Eadric, surnamed Streona, a man of low birth, who became his chief favourite, and to whom he gave his daughter Edith in marriage. Of this Eadric we shall hear a great deal for some years. All this, you will remember, was done just after the King's marriage ; a strange beginning for his young wife.

You may suppose that Swegen came again next year, more angry than ever because of the murder of his sister and of so many of his people. He again besieged Exeter, whose brave citizens had driven him off so gallantly two years before. But things were different now ; the commander was "the French churl[1] Huga, whom the Lady had set there to reeve." You see that the King's wife is still, according to the old West-Saxon law, spoken of only as the Lady and not as the Queen. Indeed she is always called so in the Chronicle,[2] save once or twice at a later time, so that I have been wrong if I have ever spoken of a West-Saxon King's wife as Queen. Exeter had been given to Emma as her marriage-gift, and she had used her power only to bestow a high office on one of her countrymen. Here we have the first Norman who ever held any command in England, and a bad beginning it was. Hugh was either careless or treacherous ; so Swegen took and plundered the city and broke down a great part of the fine stone wall that King Æthelstan had built. Then he went away into Wiltshire,

---

[1] It is *ceorl* in all the versions of the Chronicle, but Florence has "Nort-mannici *comitis*," as if he had read *eorl*.

[2] In the Chronicle for 888 Alfred's sister Æthelswith is called Queen, but she was wife of Burhred King of the Mercians, in whose Kingdom the West-Saxon law would not be in force.

and there the men of that shire and of Hampshire were gathered together, bravely to resist him. But here again there was a traitor in command; Æthelred had let Ælfric come back again, and had put him at the head of an army. Ælfric pretended to be sick and would do nothing; so the army dispersed, much against their will. So Swegen burned the towns of Wilton and Salisbury—that is, of course, Old Sarum—and went back to his ships.

In Devonshire and in Wiltshire the people were quite ready to fight, but they had no leaders. In the next part of England that Swegen attacked, the leader was all that could be wished, but the people were in fault. This was in East-Anglia in the next year, 1004. Here, you may remember, the people were largely Danes, descendants of those who had settled under Guthorm, so they were not so ready to fight against a Danish King as the Saxons in Wiltshire, and the mixed Saxons and Welsh in Devonshire and Somersetshire. Swegen went first against Norwich and harried and burned the town. The Alderman or Earl of the East-Angles at this time was named Ulfcytel, whose name shows that he was of Danish descent. Like Eadric, he had married one of the King's daughters, Wulfhild by name; but he was very different from Eadric. For he was a brave man and did his duty well. Yet even he at first consulted with the Wise Men of the East-Angles,[1] and they agreed, as the King has so often done, to buy peace of Swegen, before he did any more harm. But when Swegen broke his promise, and, instead of going away, left his ships and went up the country to Thetford, then Alderman Ulfcytel bade his men go and destroy the ships. But his men disobeyed him. However he got together such troops as he could, and fell upon Swegen as he had just harried and burned Thetford, and was going back to his ships. The Danes said that their battle with Ulfcytel was the hardest "handplay" they had ever had in England. Many men were killed on both sides, and it seems to have been what is called a drawn battle, where the victory is not very clearly on either side. However, this brave resistance of Ulfcytel seems to have done some good, as we

---

[1] This shows that East-Anglia was still distinct enough to have its own Assembly under its own Alderman.

hear of no plundering the next year, but the fleet went back to Denmark and stayed there a little while. But that year, 1005, though there was no war to ravage the land, there was a dreadful famine. In 1006 Ælfheah, Bishop of Winchester, who, I told you, is commonly called Saint Alphege, became Archbishop of Canterbury; we shall hear of him again. And some cruel things were done through the influence of the King's wicked favourite Eadric, which must have withdrawn the minds of the people still more from Æthelred and his government. There was one Wulfgeat, who had been a chief favourite, who was driven from all his honours and his goods seized. This is said to have been because of his misconduct in office, but it looks very much as if it were done to please the new favourite Eadric. And there is no doubt that Eadric caused Ælfhelm, Earl of Deira, to be treacherously murdered at Shrewsbury. Eadric bade him to a feast, and on the third day took him out on a hunting party; but suddenly the town-hangman, whom Eadric had bribed and put in ambush, sprang out upon the Earl and killed him. And presently Ælfhelm's two sons had their eyes put out. One can hardly wonder that men would not fight well for such a King. However, the Danes came again in July this year (1006), and King Æthelred got together an army against them, but the Danes never would fight a pitched battle, but ravaged the whole of Wessex, getting much further inland than they had ever done before, namely to Reading and Wallingford, both which towns they burned. The furthest points from the sea that they had reached before were Salisbury in Wessex and Thetford in East-Anglia; but now you see they had got quite into the heart of England. So the King and his Wise Men promised to give them more money, which was paid next year (1007), and they went away and did not come again for two years. King Æthelred now made his favourite Eadric Alderman of the Mercians, which no doubt added to the discontent of the people.

This year (1006) there was also an invasion of the Scots. Malcolm King of Scots,[1] the son of Kenneth, came and be-

---

[1] This story comes from Simeon of Durham, who, as I have often said, is very good authority for Northumbrian matters, but he has put it in a wrong year, 979; it must have been in 1006.

sieged the new city of Durham. Waltheof, the Earl of Bernicia, was old and did nothing, but his son Uhtred, being a brave young man, got together a band both from Bernicia and Deira. He then fell on the Scots, killed most of them, and put their King to flight. He then took those among the heads of the slain Scots which had the finest hair, and caused four women to wash them, and then he set the heads on the walls of Durham, and gave each of the women a cow for her pains. For this service King Æthelred gave Uhtred not only his father's government, but also that of York or Deira, so that he was Earl of all Northumberland. You will remember that King Edgar had divided Northumberland between two Earls. Of this Earl Uhtred we shall hear a good deal again. He was a brave man, as you see, but he did some strange things. He put away his wife, who was the daughter of Ealdhun, the first Bishop of Durham, to marry the daughter of a rich man named Styr the son of Ulf (evidently a Dane), on condition that he should kill Styr's enemy Thurbrand. This he failed to do, and we shall see what came of it. But afterwards he put away Styr's daughter too, and married the King's daughter Ælfgifu.

In the year 1008, however, Æthelred seems to have acted rather more wisely; for he took advantage of the time when the Danes were away to get together a great fleet. The Wise Men ordered that one ship should be built for every 310 hides of land all over England. That is, I suppose, the owners of that quantity of land were to join together to have one ship built. The fleet was made, and it was stationed at Sandwich next year.[1] But in this reign everything went wrong. There was one Wulfnoth, a South-Saxon "child" or thane, who was one of the captains. He was falsely accused to the King by Brihtric[2] the brother of Eadric, who seems to have been as bad as Eadric himself. So Wulfnoth, for fear of being seized, fled away with twenty of the ships, and turned Sea-king

---

[1] Henry of Huntingdon says that Æthelred now sent to his brother-in-law Duke Richard for help and counsel, but he does not say whether he got any of either.

[2] The same name as Beorhtric, only spelled in a way more like the modern way.

on his own account, and began to plunder. Then, as the Chronicle says, " Brihtric took to him eighty ships, and thought that he should work for himself mickle words [gain much fame], for that he should get Wulfnoth quick or dead. But as they thitherward were, there came such a wind against them as no man ere minded, and all the ships it beat and thrashed and on land *warped*[1] ; and came Wulfnoth soon and the ships burned. When this quoth [told] was to the other ships where the King was, how the other ships had fared, it was as if it all redeless[2] were ; and the King got him home and the Aldermen and the high Wise Men, and forlet [forsook] the ships thus lightly. And the folk that on the ships were brought the ships eft to London, and let all the people's trouble thus lightly come to naught ; and was the victory no better that all English kin had hoped for."

Just after this wretched business another great Danish fleet came in August. This time King Swegen did not come himself, but the fleet came in two divisions, the first commanded by Earl Thurcytel or Thurkill, the second by his brothers Heming and Eglaf. From this time till the end of Æthelred's reign we read of nothing but the ravages of the Danes. These lasted till 1013, when Swegen came again himself. It would be almost endless to tell you all their marches to and fro, all the parts of the country that they ravaged and all the towns that they burned ; but you should mark that they now get far away from the sea, burning Oxford and Northampton and other quite inland places. I will only pick out a few of the more re-markable things which happened during these four dreadful years.

As I said before, in this reign everything went wrong. If one man or a few men tried to do their duty, some one else was sure to stand in the way, till at last, as the Chronicle says, when the King and the Wise Men did settle something, " it did not stand for one month ; and next was there no headman[3]

---

[1] " Awearp." *Threw* or *cast.* We now use this verb, which is the same as the High-Dutch *wurfen*, only in a rather different sense. But we talk of " the *warp* and the woof," and in some parts a mole is called a " *mouldwarp*," because he *warps* or throws up the mould.

[2] Without *rede* or counsel, as Æthelred is called the Unready.

[3] *Heafodman*, headman, captain, like the High-Dutch *Hauptmann.*

that troops would gather ; and ilk man fled as he most might ; and the next thing was that no shire another would help." Thus, in 1009, when Æthelred did get together an army and seemed really disposed to fight, Eadric betrayed them. The next year, when the Danes came into East-Anglia, the brave Alderman Ulfcytel met them again, but only the Cambridgeshire men would fight ; the others ran away, one Thurcytel setting the example. Thurcytel was doubtless a Dane by descent ; but so was Ulfcytel, and yet he did his duty. So the Danes were let into the heart of England and burned Northampton. Next year, 1011, the King and his Wise Men asked for peace, and offered money and food, if the Danes would leave off plundering. Now let us hear the Chronicle.

"All this ill luck fell on us through unrede[1] [lack of counsel], that man would not bid [offer] them *gafol* [tribute] in time ; and when they most evil had done, then made man *grith* and *frith* [truce and peace] with them, and nathless for all this grith and frith and gafol, they fared everywhere by flocks, and harried, and our poor folk robbed and slew."

This year, 1011, the Danes took Canterbury, which was betrayed to them by Ælfmar the Archdeacon, whose life had once been saved by Archbishop Ælfheah. The Danes are said to have committed every sort of cruelty ; it is said indeed that they regularly massacred nine people out of ten in the city. The Chronicle, however, does not speak so much of killing people as of taking them away prisoners, no doubt to sell them as slaves. That they plundered the city and burned the Minster I need hardly say. But what has made this taking of Canterbury most famous is the martyrdom of Archbishop Ælfheah, or Saint Alphege. This the Chronicle describes at length. We have also two other accounts which go more into detail. One is a life of Saint Alphege, by one Osbern, who lived about sixty years after, and who also wrote a life of Archbishop Dunstan. Osbern, like most writers of the lives of saints, is fond of marvels and of talking in a grand kind of way, and he says some things which are clearly not true. For instance, he makes Eadric join the Danes and help to take

---

[1] This is no doubt said with a play on Æthelred's name and nickname ; the *noble counsellor* had no counsel.

Canterbury, because one of his brothers had been killed by
the thanes of Kent. But it is worth noticing that a great part
of Osbern's account appears also in Florence ; either Florence
copied so much of Osbern as he thought agreed with the
Chronicle, or else both Florence and Osbern copied from
somebody else. The other account is in the history of Thietmar Bishop of Merseburg, a German historian who lived at the
time, and who says that he heard the story from a man who
had just come from England. This then is better authority
than Osbern, indeed almost as good as the Chronicle itself.
And Thietmar's account, without contradicting the Chronicle,
helps to make the whole story more intelligible.   Thietmar
however makes one very strange mistake, for he calls the Archbishop Dunstan instead of Ælfheah. No doubt the name of
Dunstan was famous all over Christendom, while people in
Germany had probably never heard of Ælfheah till they heard
of his murder. So, if the man who told Thietmar only talked
of the Archbishop of Canterbury without mentioning his name,
Thietmar might write down the name of the only Archbishop
of Canterbury he had ever heard of. Still it is strange that,
if Thietmar knew anything of Dunstan at all, he did not know
that he had been dead more than twenty years. I tell you all
this, because it is well that you should know how much and
how little people in other countries knew of what was going
on in England. But I think I cannot do better than give you
the account as it is in the Chronicle.

"They went to their ships and led the Archbishop with them.

Was there a captive[1]	Where man ere
He that ere was	Saw bliss,
Angle-kin's head	In that wretched borough
And Christendom's.	Whence to us came erst
Then man might there	Christendom and bliss
See wretchedness	Fore God and fore world.

And they had the Archbishop with them so long as to that time
that they him martyred.

"MXII. On this year came Eadric Alderman and all the

[1] *Ræfling*, one robbed or taken away.

oldest[1] Wise Men, ordered and lewd[2] [priests and laymen], of the English kin to London-borough, before Easter. Easter day was that year on the Ides of April [April 13th]; and they there were so long as till all the *gafol* was paid ; that was eight thousand pounds. Then on the Saturday was the host much stirred against the Bishop, for that he would not to them fee [money] promise, and forbad that man nothing [anything] for him should sell [pay]. Were they eke very drunken, for that there was wine brought from south. They took then the Bishop and led him to their husting,[3] on the Sun-eve,[4] the octave of Passover, and him there then pelted with bones and neats' heads, and slew him then one of them with an axe iron on the head, that he with the dint nether [down] sank, and his holy blood on the earth fell, and his holy soul he to God's kingdom sent. And they the dead body[5] in the morn carried to London ; and the Bishops Eadnoth and Ælfhun and the borough-folk him took with all worship, and him buried in Saint Paul's minster, and there God now shows forth the holy martyr's might."

Thus it stands in the Chronicle ; the account there must have been written within eleven years, for in 1023 Ælfheah's body was *translated*, that is solemnly moved, from London to Canterbury. Florence says that on Saturday the 19th the Danes told Ælfheah that he must pay three thousand pounds for his life and freedom ; if not, they should kill him the next Saturday. As he had forbidden that anything should be paid for him, they brought him forth and killed him as is said in the Chronicle. He adds that the Dane who at last killed him was

---

[1] Not necessarily the *oldest* in age, but the highest in rank ; the same sort of use as the word Alderman.

[2] This word is the same as the High-Dutch *leute*, and simply means *people*, especially the laity as opposed to the clergy. Thence it comes to mean ignorant, and so bad in other ways, as we read in the Acts of the Apostles of "certain lewd fellows of the baser sort," as we should say blackguards or ruffians ; but here you see it is still quite an honourable word.

[3] The Danish place of assembly ; we still keep the word to mean the sort of raised platform on which the speakers stand at the election of members of Parliament.

[4] The eve of Sunday, that is Saturday—*Sonnabend* as it is called in German ; before it is called *Sæternesdæg* or *Sæterdæg*.

[5] *Lichamon*, the same word that we have in *lich*gate, the city of *Lich*-field, &c.; the same as the High-Dutch *Leich*.

one Thrum, whom he had converted and baptized in his prison, and had confirmed only the day before. Thrum did it, they say, " moved by an impious piety,"[1] that is, he wished to put an end to Ælfheah's sufferings. Thietmar says that Ælfheah had promised to pay the Danes money to let him go, and had fixed a time, but that when the time came, he said he had none to pay, and told them to do what they pleased with him. He also said that Thurkill the Danish Earl tried to save him,[2] but that the other Danes would not hearken. Now this account perhaps takes away somewhat from the beauty of the story, but for that very reason it is more likely to be true ; it also explains why the Danes kept Ælfheah so long, and why they were so very bitter against him. Again, Thietmar's story about Thurkill agrees with the account in the Chronicle, which seems to speak of a mere tumultuous attack of the soldiers rather than of a fixed meeting, such as it seems to be in Florence. It also agrees with Thurkill's conduct afterwards.

This is said to have happened at Greenwich where the church of Saint Alphege now stands. Of course the English looked on Ælfheah as a martyr. In after-times, after the Norman Conquest, Lanfranc the Italian Archbishop said that he was no martyr, because he had not died for the Christian faith ; but Saint Anselm, who was afterwards Archbishop, said that he was a true martyr, for that he died for righteousness and charity ; that is, that he chose to die rather than let his people be further oppressed to raise money to ransom him.

Just after the death of Ælfheah the money was paid to the Danes, and their fleet dispersed, save forty-five ships, which entered Æthelred's service with Thurkill at their head.[3] The King was to feed and clothe them, and perhaps to give them lands in East-Anglia, as Alfred did to Guthorm. You see how

---

[1] Or *pity.* " Pietas " means either, and *piety* and *pity* are the same word.

[2] Thietmar makes Thurkill talk of "the Lord's anointed" as if he had been a Christian. He certainly was a Christian afterwards, and we shall presently see that he very likely was one now. William of Malmesbury makes him the chief leader in the Archbishop's murder, which he certainly was not.

[3] It is only William of Malmesbury who distinctly mentions Thurkill, but we find him directly afterwards in Æthelred's service ; so it was no doubt now that he entered it.

this conduct of Thurkill quite agrees with what Thietmar says about his trying to save the Archbishop's life. Æthelred seems to have used this moment of rest to punish the Welsh, who, we may suppose, had not been very regular in paying their tribute. For we read in the Welsh Chronicle that in 1012 the Saxons, under " Edris," which must mean Eadric, harried St. David's. This, you will see, is just of a piece with Æthelred's former conduct towards Cumberland and Normandy. He was idle when he should have acted vigorously, and active when he had better have kept quiet.

For it was a very short moment of peace that England now had. In 1013 Swegen came again. One can hardly believe William of Malmesbury, when he says that Thurkill invited him, as Thurkill seems to have been, now at least, quite faithful to Æthelred. One writer at the time[1] indeed says that one object of Swegen in coming was to punish the treason of Thurkill. However this may be, it is plain that Swegen had now fully made up his mind to conquer all England. Instead of merely plundering the South of England, he now set steadily to work, first to secure the part of England which was largely inhabited by Danes, and then to conquer the purely English part by their help. This, you will see, is something quite different from any of the earlier invasions, and it shows a distinct and settled policy unlike anything that we have seen before. So when, in August this year, he came to Sandwich, he stayed there only a few days, and then sailed round the coast of East-Anglia to the mouth of the Humber, and then up the Trent as far as Gainsborough. Here all the people of the North-East of England, all the Danish part, submitted to him ; first the men of Lindesey, and then Uhtred the Earl of the Northumbrians. You will remember Uhtred, who delivered Durham in 1006. Some time before King Æthelred had given him his daughter Ælfgifu in marriage ; he had seemingly got rid of his second wife as easily as he did of his first. Next came the men of the Five Boroughs. You remember them, Leicester, Lincoln, Nottingham, Stamford, and Derby, and how King

[1] The author of the *Encomium Emmæ.* He was a foreigner, and writes wholly in the interest of Cnut and Emma, and there are many strange mistakes in his accounts of English affairs.

Edmund recovered them from the Danes in 941. They are still spoken of as if they formed a sort of Confederacy, and no doubt their people were mainly of Danish blood. In a little time all the people beyond Watling Street submitted, so that Swegen had now won without a blow all the country which had been given up to the Danes in Alfred's time, and all the work of King Edward and the other Kings after him was undone. And now it was just forty years since Edgar, King of the English and Lord of all Britain, had been rowed on the Dee by his vassal Kings. Such a difference there was between the father and the son, and between a counsellor like Dunstan and a counsellor like Eadric. But it was not enough for Swegen to have the Danish country; he would have all England. So he made all the men of the North swear to him and give hostages and also horses and food to his army. Then he gave the hostages and the fleet to his son Cnut[1]—the Great Cnut, of whom we now hear for the first time—and went on himself over Watling Street, right through Mercia, through a country which had seen hardly any fighting for a hundred years and more. There he ravaged and burned and massacred more cruelly than he or any of them had ever done before. He took Oxford again, which had been burned only three years before; then he went to Winchester, where the citizens made peace and gave hostages. Thence he went to London, where King Æthelred was, and, what was better than King Æthelred, the brave Dane Thurkill. So the citizens stood a siege and fought manfully, and drove Swegen away. You see through the whole story that the English wanted nothing but good leaders. But it was only for a little time that the Londoners could hold out. For Swegen went away to Wallingford and

---

[1] *Cnut* or *Knut* is his real name, in Latin *Cnuto.* He is often called *Canutus* or *Canute,* because when a later Danish King of the name was to be made a Saint, Pope Paschal the Second could not say *Cnut,* and so called him "Sanctus *Canutus.*" The change was likened to the change of *Abram* into *Abraham.* It is better to call him by his own name, only sound the *c* as you would in German, and make the *u* long. If you use the other form, at least say *Canúte* and not *Cánute.* But I suspect that very few people know that Cnut's real Christian name was *Lambert.* He was baptized either by Archbishop Unwan of Bremen or by Æthelnoth, who was afterwards Archbishop of Canterbury. But we do not call him Lambert or his father Otto, any more than we call Rolf Robert. See p. 141.

thence to Bath, harrying the land as he went. And at Bath Æthelmær the Alderman of the Defnsætas and all the thanes of the West came to him and submitted and gave hostages. Thus Swegen had got the whole land except London, and men now counted him for full King over all England ; but he could hardly have been hallowed as King by any Bishop. So Florence says that he was not King but only Tyrant, and goes on speaking of him as the Tyrant. So when the men of London saw that Swegen had won all England save their own city, they thought it was no use holding out any longer, and they too submitted and gave hostages. So King Æthelred and Thurkill left London and went to Thurkill's fleet, the forty-five ships which were lying at Greenwich. But Æthelred sent the Lady Emma and their two sons, the Æthelings Edward and Alfred (of both of whom you will hear again), to Duke Richard in Normandy. And presently, after Christmas, he himself went across to Duke Richard. But Thurkill stayed with the fleet, and both he and Swegen laid on taxes to keep their fleets and plundered the people and did much evil.

Thus you see that Swegen was the first Dane who was King, or, as Florence calls him, Tyrant, over all England. But he did not long enjoy the greatness which he had won by so much cruelty. For about Candlemas next year, 1014, he died. Florence here, for once, tells a tale which I will tell you.

The Story of the Death of Swegen the Tyrant.

Now when Swegen had conquered all England and had driven King Æthelred out of the land, he kept his court at Gainsborough. Now in times past, in the days of Alfred the Great King of the West-Saxons, there was an Under-king of the East-Angles, whose name was Edmund. He was a good man and an holy, and the Danes who came into his land slew him, for that he would not forsake the faith of Christ. Wherefore men called him Edmund the saint and martyr, and a goodly minster was builded over his grave, and men called the minster and the town after his name, Saint Edmund's Bury. Now when

Swegen the Tyrant was in this land, he greatly hated Saint Edmund and his minster and his priests and all that belonged to him, for that Saint Edmund had been slain by men of his own people in past time. And he said that Saint Edmund was no saint,[1] and mocked greatly at him. So Swegen the Tyrant sent to the priests of Saint Edmund's Bury, saying : "Give me a great sum of money ; and if ye give it me not, I will come and burn your town and all the folk that are in it ; and I will pull down your minster to the ground, and you that be priests and clerks I will put to death with all manner of tortures." And Swegen the Tyrant gathered together his Wise Men and his captains and all his host, and spake unto them in the like manner. And he sat on a goodly horse at the head of his host. And while he was yet speaking, he saw one coming towards him like an armed man with a spear in his hand ; but no man saw him save only Swegen the Tyrant. And Swegen cried, " Help, help, my soldiers, for lo, the holy King Edmund cometh against me to slay me." So Saint Edmund smote Swegen the Tyrant with his spear, so that he fell from his horse, and died that night in great pain and anguish. Thus did Saint Edmund avenge his minster.

There is most likely so much truth in this story as this, that Swegen had done, or threatened to do, some mischief to the minster at Bury, and that, when he died soon after, men said it was God's judgement for the wrong done to Saint Edmund. Then it would be easy to say, in a kind of figure, that Saint Edmund killed him, and so the story would grow up. It is known to Danish as well as to English writers. But I will come back to our history.

When Swegen was dead, the Danes of his fleet chose his son Cnut to be King. But the Wise Men of England came together and sent over to Æthelred in Normandy, and said that no lord was dearer to them than their lord by birth, if he would only govern them better than he did before. So Æthelred first sent

---

[1] The sort of half belief attributed to Swegen in this story fits in very well with the position of one who had been a Christian, but who had gone back to idol-worship.

over his son Edward with messengers, and greeted all his people, and said that he would be good lord to them, and would make better all the things that they eschewed, and would forgive all things that had been said or done, if they would all receive him with one accord and without treachery. So the Wise Men plighted full friendship to him and declared every Danish King an outlaw in England for ever. So in Lent in the year 1014 King Æthelred came over to England and all men received him gladly. But I do not see that he reigned any better than he did before ; only now his brave son Edmund, whom, because of his strength and daring, men called Ironside, was able to lead the people and fight against the Danes. For remember that Cnut was still in the land of Lindesey, and he agreed with the men of the land that they should give him horses and join him in harrying the rest of England. But King Æthelred got an army together, and came on them before they were ready ; so Cnut was driven out and took to his ships. He then went to Sandwich, and cut off the ears, noses, and hands of the English hostages who had been given to his father. He then went back to Denmark, and the land was free from the Danes for a little time. But King Æthelred caused 21,000 or, as some say, 30,000 pounds to be paid to his own Danish fleet at Greenwich, and this seems to have been thought almost as great a grievance as if Cnut and the other Danes had stayed in England.

The next year, 1015, a great meeting of the Wise Men was held at Oxford. To that meeting came Sigeferth and Morkere, two brothers, who were the chief men among the Five-Burghers, and Eadric persuaded them to come to his own house, and there gave them wine to drink and had them murdered. But their followers took refuge in the tower of Saint Frideswide's minster, which is now Christ Church. So Eadric set fire to the minster and burned them there. It does not seem clear whether King Æthelred actually ordered these murders, but at any rate he did not punish Eadric, and, like Ahab, he took the spoil to himself. For he seized all the goods of the two thanes and sent Sigeferth's widow Ealdgyth a prisoner to Malmesbury. But the Ætheling Edmund had seen her and wished to have her for his wife ; so he went to Malmesbury and married her against his father's will. The Ætheling then went

Q

to the Five-Boroughs and took possession of Sigeferth and Morkere's property, and the people submitted to him. Edmund had thus got a kind of principality of his own in the North, which helped him for some while.

But this year Cnut came again with a great fleet. Some say[1] that Thurkill had gone over to his side, and had sailed to Denmark, and prayed him to come ; but this is not in the Chronicle. Anyhow Cnut came to Sandwich ; perhaps he had a battle there with the English fleet ; he then went and plundered in Wiltshire, Dorsetshire, and Somersetshire, while King Æthelred lay sick at Corsham in Wiltshire. And now Eadric filled up the measure of his wickedness. The Ætheling gathered an army in the north and Eadric gathered one in the south, and when the two came together, Eadric tried to kill the Ætheling by guile, so that nothing was done. Then Eadric went over to Cnut with forty ships, no doubt the Danish ships in Æthelred's service. The West-Saxons then submitted to Cnut and gave him hostages. Things were thus for a little while turned about, Cnut the Dane having got possession of the purely Saxon country, while Edmund was still strong in that part of Mercia where the people were chiefly Danish.

So in the next year, 1016, Cnut set forth out of Wessex, with the Danes and West-Saxons, and crossed the Thames at Cricklade, and harried the land of the Hwiccas. So the Ætheling came against him with an army from the north ; but his men said they would not fight unless King Æthelred and the Londoners were there ; so Edmund sent and prayed his father and the Londoners to join him ; and so they did, but when they came together, the King was told that there were traitors in the camp, so he went away to London, and the army dispersed. But the Ætheling rode to Northumberland to his brother-in-law Earl Uhtred, for Uhtred was strong on his side, and when Cnut sent asking him to join him, he said he would do no such thing, but would ever be faithful to his lord King Æthelred. So Edmund and Uhtred joined their forces, and between them the whole land was harried, Edmund and Uhtred harrying on one side and Cnut and Eadric harrying on the other. But Cnut marched straight through Mercia and came to York while

[1] It is so in the *Encomium Emmæ*.

Uhtred and Edmund were away. So when they heard this, Edmund went to his father in London, and Uhtred went to York and submitted to Cnut. Cnut most likely looked on him as a traitor, because he had submitted to Swegen and had afterwards joined Edmund. So when Uhtred's enemy Thurbrand begged Cnut that he would let him have Uhtred killed, Cnut gave him leave. So Uhtred was summoned to Cnut's court at Wihæl, but when he came, armed men were placed beyond a curtain, who burst out and killed Uhtred and forty of his men. The Chronicle says that Cnut made Eric the Dane Earl of the Northumbrians, but Simeon says that Eadwulf the brother of Uhtred succeeded him in his Earldom.[1] I suppose that Cnut made Eric Earl of the whole Kingdom of Northumberland, and that Eadwulf was Earl of Bernicia under him. Cnut then went to his ships, and after Easter he made ready to sail against London. But before he came King Æthelred died on Saint George's day, and was buried in Saint Paul's minster in London. After all that had happened, he was only forty-eight years old.

§ 2. THE REIGN OF KING EDMUND IRONSIDE.
April 23—November 30, 1016.

When King Æthelred died, there was what might be called a double election of a King. Many of the chief men, Aldermen, Bishops, and others, thought that it was no use trying to resist the Danes any longer, and that the best thing was to choose Cnut King of the English. So they met and chose Cnut King, and they went to Southampton, where he then was, and swore oaths to Cnut, and said that they forsook the whole house of Æthelred for ever. Then Cnut swore oaths back again to them that he would be a faithful lord to them both in the things of God and in the things of the world.[2] Cnut therefore was already a

---

[1] Simeon says Eadwulf was a weak and timid man, and that for fear of the vengeance of the Scots he gave up Lothian to them. If it be true that King Edgar granted Lothian to Kenneth, perhaps Uhtred had got it back again after his defeat of the Scots at Durham.

[2] This account of Cnut's election is not in the Chronicle, but as it is in Florence, I do not doubt about accepting it, the more so as the Chronicle itself mentions only the Wise Men that were in London and the citizens of London as joining in Edmund's election.

Christian. But the citizens of London and such of the Wise Men as were in London had nothing to do with this election of Cnut. They at once chose Edmund in the place of his father, and he was crowned in Saint Paul's minster by Archbishop Lyfing ; so there were two Kings in the land. Edmund was a valiant warrior, and very likely, if he had come sooner, he might have done as much as any of the great Kings, Alfred or Edward or Æthelstan, and might have delivered the land altogether from the Danes. It seems to have been nothing but treason and mismanagement which caused England to be so badly defended, for whenever there was a pitched battle, the English always fought well ; only some traitor almost always either hindered a battle from being fought or else drew off his troops during the fighting. Now that the English had got this brave King Edmund at their head, they did what they could. We hear no more of any shrinking or running away or paying money. For the few months that Edmund was King we hear of nothing but hard fighting, in which the English commonly get the upper hand. Still it perhaps was too late anyhow really to win, and King Edmund did not live long enough to finish his work. In times like those which we are reading about, almost everything depended on the goodness or badness of this or that man. A man like Alfred can save a kingdom, and a man like Æthelred can let a kingdom go to ruin. In settled times like ours, no one man can do either so much good or so much harm.

You will remember that Cnut was now in possession of Wessex, while Edmund held the city of London, whose importance is now always coming out more and more strongly. Cnut's great object was to take London, and Edmund's great object was to get back Wessex, where you may suppose that the people had submitted to Cnut only for fear. In Northumberland and East-Anglia we can well believe that many people, being of Danish descent, really wished to have a Danish King, but we may be sure that none of the Saxons in Wessex, or even of the Angles in Mercia, wished for any such thing. So first of all Edmund got stealthily out of London and went into Wessex to gather troops. Meanwhile Cnut's fleet came against London, and they besieged the town and made a ditch round it, and there was much fighting, till at last the Danes broke up the siege, and went away into Wessex after Edmund, leaving only a part of the army to guard the ships. So Edmund and Cnut met and fought a battle at Pen Selwood on the borders of Somersetshire, Wiltshire, and Dorsetshire, where the English had the victory. Then after midsummer Edmund got a greater army, and fought another battle at Sherstone in Wiltshire, on the borders of the land of the Hwiccas. King Edmund had with him the men of Dorsetshire and Devonshire and part of Wiltshire, besides whatever troops he had brought with him from London. King Cnut had his Danes; and three English Aldermen, Eadric and Ælfgar and Ælfmær called Darling, had brought to him the men of Hampshire and part of Wiltshire. This was a very great battle and lasted two days. On Monday both armies fought all day without either getting the better, and in the evening they parted for sheer weariness. On Tuesday they began again, and the English had the better, and the Danish account says that King Edmund himself got so near to King Cnut that he cut through his shield. The Danes however pressed round their King and saved him, but they were beginning to yield, when Eadric cut off the head of one Osmær, who was very like King Edmund, and held it up saying, " Flee, English; flee, English; dead is Edmund." So the English fell back a little, but when they knew that King Edmund was not dead, they turned again, and the two armies again fought all day without either side gaining the victory. Then King Cnut broke up secretly in the night and marched off to London and began the siege again. Then Alderman Eadric, seeing how strong King Edmund was, changed sides yet again, and went over to King Edmund and swore oaths, and King Edmund was foolish enough to trust him. Then King Edmund marched to London and delivered the city and drove the Danes to their ships. Two days afterwards he crossed the Thames at Brentford, and fought a third battle and defeated the Danes again. But many of the English were too eager after booty and were drowned in the river. Then King Edmund marched again into Wessex to gather more troops, and the Danes again besieged London, but they could not take it. Then the Danish fleet sailed up the Thames and harried Mercia, while the land army went and harried Kent. So King

Edmund marched back from Wessex with his new troops, and came into Kent, and fought a fourth battle with the Danes at Otford, and beat them again so that they fled to the Isle of Sheppey, and all men said that he would have destroyed them utterly, had not Eadric beguiled him to stop the pursuit at Aylesford. So King Edmund went back into Wessex and Mercia, and King Cnut crossed into Essex and thence into Mercia, harrying everywhere that he went. And when the Danes had got much plunder, they began to go back to their ships. But King Edmund followed them with an army gathered from all England, and fought the fifth battle at Assandun[1] in Essex by the river Crouch. This was again a very fierce battle. King Edmund drew up his men in three divisions, and he stood between his great Standard and the other ensign, which was the Dragon of the West-Saxons,[2] and he bade his men fight bravely. And the Danes set up their standard the Raven, and Thurkill, who was now on Cnut's side, said that the Raven moved its wings, and that the Danes would have the victory.[3] So King Edmund and King Cnut both led on their armies, and both fought very valiantly, and the Danes began to give way. Then wrought Eadric a worse treason than he had yet wrought, for he had promised King Cnut that he would betray his lord King Edmund and his army. Now Eadric commanded the Magesætas, the men of Herefordshire ; and when he saw the Danes giving way, he drew off his troops. So had Cnut the victory, though all the folk of England fought against him. There died many and good men, Ælfric the Alderman, and Godwine the Alderman of Lindesey, and Ulfcytel the brave Alderman of the

---

[1] That is *Ass-down, Mons Asini* as Florence has it. *Assan* is the genitive of *assa*, a he-ass, but the name of the place has got corrupted into *Assington*, or Ashington, as if it were the town of the *Assingas* or *Æscingas*. So Huntandun, Abbandun, Ethandun (the place of Alfred's battle), have been corrupted into Huntingdon, Abingdon, Edington.

[2] Henry of Huntingdon gives a full account of this, which must be taken from a ballad.

[3] I get this from the *Encomium Emmæ*, though both this writer and Henry of Huntingdon have confused this battle with the battle of Sherstone. But it is worth noting that the superstition about the Raven, which we saw in the time of Alfred, lasted still.

East-Angles, of whom we have heard before, and Æthelweard the son of Æthelwine Alderman of the East-Angles, whom men called the Friend of God. And there too were slain Eadnoth the Bishop of Dorchester and Wulfsige the Abbot of Ramsey, who had come to pray for King Edmund and his host. Well-nigh all the Aldermen and great men of England were slain ; yet did not King Edmund's heart fail him, but he got together another army, and marched into the land of the Hwiccas, and Cnut marched after him, and they both made ready to fight a sixth battle. But Eadric and certain other of the Wise Men persuaded King Edmund that he should not fight another battle, but that he and Cnut should divide the land. To this King Edmund at last agreed, though it was much against his will. So the two Kings met near Deerhurst, in an island of the Severn called Olney, and there they made a peace and gave hostages, and they swore to be brothers to each other, and they divided the Kingdom. King Edmund was to be the head King, and to have Wessex, Essex, and East-Anglia, with the city of London, and Cnut was to have Northumberland and Mercia. This, you will see, was not the same division which was made between Alfred and Guthorm ; for Edmund gave up to Cnut all the English part of Mercia which Alfred had kept, while he kept East-Anglia and Essex which Alfred had given to Guthorm. So Edmund and Cnut exchanged arms and clothes in token of friendship, and agreed about the money to be paid to the fleet. But the Danes went away with their plunder, and the men of London made peace with them and with Earl Eric who was their chief, and let them winter in the city.

This is the story as I find it in the Chronicle and in Florence ; but there is another story, which there is no good authority for, but which has grown up into a famous legend. The tale runs that, just as the two armies were ready to fight the sixth battle in Gloucestershire, Edmund proposed to Cnut that, instead of their armies fighting a battle, they two should fight in single combat, and so settle who should be King. According to William of Malmesbury, Cnut refused the combat, because he was a small man, while Edmund was very tall and strong. so that it would not be a fair battle ; but he said that, as each of them had a good claim to a Kingdom which had been held by his father, the fairest thing would be to divide it. Others say that the two Kings were just going to fight, or had actually begun fighting, when Cnut proposed to divide the Kingdom instead.

This way of settling differences by single combat was very common in the North, and about this time most nations in Europe began to adopt it as a way of settling difficult causes, for they thought that God would always give the victory to the right side. In deciding quarrels between whole nations, we often hear of it in an early state of things, but not as men get more settled and politic. For the meaning of a war is that that one of the powers at war which is really the stronger will get what it wants from the other. Now the loss of a battle may really compel the weaker people to give in, but the mere loss of one champion in no way compels them to give in, though they may be bound to do so by agreement. So in stories of single combat, as in that of David and Goliath, we often find that the two armies did fight after all. You will see presently that when William Duke of the Normans challenged our King Harold to settle their claims to the crown by single combat, King Harold refused, and very rightly ; for if William had killed Harold in single combat, it would not have given William any better right to the crown of England ; and if Harold had killed William, it was not likely that the Norman army would go home quietly. But as for the division of the Kingdom, it was perhaps as wise a thing as could be done. You will remember that England had been one Kingdom for so short a time that the notion of dividing it did not seem so strange and shocking as it would now.

We will hope that Cnut was really honest in this treaty, and that he did not merely mean it as a trick to deceive Edmund. Anyhow, on Saint Andrew's day in the same year King Edmund Ironside died, and men commonly thought that Eadric had contrived to kill him. He had reigned only seven months, and he had in that time fought five great battles ; he was victorious in three and he was not fairly beaten in any. All this shows how completely it was the fault of Æthelred and Eadric that England was conquered at all. The strange thing is that not only

Æthelred, but Edmund too, should have trusted Eadric after he had committed so many treasons. King Edmund, like so many of his family, must have been quite young when he died. You will remember that the year before he had married Ealdgyth the widow of Sigeferth. He left two little sons, Edmund and Edward, who, one would think, must have been twins. Of his brothers three at least were living, Eadwig son of Æthelred by his first wife, and Alfred and Edward, the sons of Emma of Normandy. Æthelstan, the eldest son of Æthelred, was most likely killed during the war.

King Edmund was buried by his grandfather Edgar in the Minster at Glastonbury.

I have now ended the Danish wars, which I have told at some length. I do not expect you to remember all the names of persons and places; indeed I cannot myself remember all of them without the book; but I am sure that you will better understand what a long and fearful struggle it was, and how great a difference there was between Æthelred and Edmund or between Eadric and Ulfcytel, if you try to follow the campaigns on the map, and try to understand the deeds and characters of some of the chief actors. I dare say you will forget many of the names and dates, but I think you will carry off a fuller and clearer notion of the whole story than if I had told it you in a short and dry way. At any rate I have now done with the Danish wars, and we shall hardly have any fighting in England itself for fifty years, and then will come a still more famous fight than any of those between Cnut and Edmund.

§ 3. THE REIGN OF KING CNUT.

1016—1035.

When Edmund was dead, no one seems to have said anything against Cnut's taking the whole Kingdom. You know by this time that it was not likely that any one should set up either of Edmund's little sons to be King; had things been quiet, the Wise Men would most likely have chosen Eadwig, Edmund's brother, who was much beloved by the people.[1] But I suppose that by this time everybody was quite tired of fighting, and that, as Cnut had already got half the Kingdom, it was thought better to let him have the other half too than to run the chance of any more wars between the two parties. So Cnut the Dane, the son of Swegen, was chosen King over all England and was crowned in Saint Paul's by Archbishop Lyfing. It is said that Cnut called together all the Wise Men at London, and asked those who had been witnesses of the treaty between him and Edmund, whether anything had then been settled about Edmund's sons or brothers, and whether they ought to reign in Wessex if Cnut were alive? Then the Wise Men of the West-Saxons answered that nothing had ever been said about Edmund's brothers, and that Edmund had not left them any part of his Kingdom; and that as for his little sons, he begged that Cnut would be their guardian and take care of them till they were old enough to reign. But we are told that in all this the Wise Men of the West-Saxons lied for fear of Cnut, and it is plain that, if Edmund was murdered by Eadric, he could hardly have had time to make a will or settle anything. So they all swore oaths to Cnut, and the chief men of the Danes swore oaths to them, and they all said that none of Edmund's sons or brothers should be King, and they said that it would be wise to have the Ætheling Eadwig outlawed. But Cnut thought that, if it was wise to have him outlawed, it would be safer to have him killed. So he called Eadric the traitor into a room by himself, and bade him beguile Eadwig that he might die. But Eadric said, "There is one Æthelweard, a chief man among the English, who can beguile Eadwig better than I.[2] Call him to thee, and promise him gifts and honours that he may slay Eadwig." So Cnut called Æthelweard and said, "Thus and thus spake Eadric the Earl to me, saying that thou canst beguile Eadwig the Ætheling that he may die. Now then do as I bid thee, and thou shalt

---

[1] "Edwius, egregius et reverendissimus Regis Eadmundi germanus."— Flor. Wig.

[2] Eadric most likely meant that Eadwig would not trust or listen to him, while he would trust Æthelweard.

enjoy all the honours of thy fathers. Bring me the head of Eadwig, and thou shalt be unto me dearer than a brother." So Æthelweard promised to slay Eadwig; yet he meant not to do the deed, and he did it not. For he promised only from fear of Cnut; for he was of the noblest stock among the English.

I hardly know what to make of this story. It is in Florence, but it is not in the Chronicles, and it is hard to make it agree with what follows. For in the course of the year 1017 it is certain that Eadwig the Ætheling was outlawed, and with him another Eadwig was outlawed, of whom we have no account save that he was called "King of the Churls," so that we may suppose that he too was much beloved by the common people. This we get in the Chronicles, but Florence goes on to say that Eadwig the King of the Churls made his peace with the King, but that Eadwig the Ætheling was soon after murdered by some men who he thought were his best friends. Now the story which I just told you reads very much as if it were the same story over again. Anyhow there is no doubt that Cnut tried to get all the members of the old royal family out of the way. The two young sons of Æthelred and Emma, Edward and Alfred, were safe with their mother in Normandy. But the two little children whom Edmund had left, Edward and Edmund, were sent by Cnut to his half-brother Olaf or James, King of the Swedes, who was the first Christian King who reigned in Sweden. Cnut, it is said, wanted to have them killed in Sweden, as he did not like the shame of having them killed in England. But Olaf would not kill them, though he was too much afraid of Cnut to keep them in Sweden. So he sent them over into Hungary, where they were well taken care of. For the King of the Hungarians then was Stephen, the first Christian King in Hungary, who is called Saint Stephen, and who has been much reverenced ever since. You may perhaps remember that, when the present King of Hungary was crowned, he was crowned with the Crown of Saint Stephen. King Stephen took good care of the little Æthelings. Edmund died young; but Edward lived, and Stephen's Queen Gisela, who was a sister of the Emperor Henry the Second, the last of the Saxon Emperors, gave him her niece Agatha in marriage.   We shall hear of this Edward and his children again.

This same year, 1017, Cnut, now being King over all England, divided the land into four parts.   He kept Wessex himself and set Earls over the three other parts, namely Eadric over Mercia, Thurkill over East-Anglia, and Eric, another Dane, who had married his sister, over Northumberland.   But before the year was out, Eadric, who had betrayed so many people, was put to death,—"very rightly," says one copy of the Chronicles; but as several other people of whom we do not know any harm were put to death too, perhaps it was not very lawfully.   For though Eadric had many times deserved to die at the hands of Æthelred and Edmund, it does not appear that he had at all sinned against Cnut.   There are two stories about his death. The first is that, as soon as Edmund was dead, Eadric came to Cnut saying, "Hail, sole King of the land."   And Cnut answered, "Wherefore callest thou me sole King, while Edmund reigneth in the land of the West-Saxons?"   And Eadric answered and said, "Lo, Edmund thine enemy is dead, for I have caused him to be slain by craft."   Then said King Cnut to him : "Then hast thou served me well, and for this deed will I set thy head above the heads of all the men of all England."   So Cnut called for an executioner, and he caused the head of Eadric to be cut off, and they set it on a pole and put it on the highest gate of London.   Thus was the head of Eadric the traitor set above the heads of all the men of all England.

Now this story cannot be true, because we know that Eadric was not killed till the year after Edmund's death.   The other story *may* be true, because it does not contradict anything in the history.   But it is the sort of story which one doubts about, because it reads, as many other stories do, like a piece of the Old Testament stuck in.   This says that Cnut and Eadric had some quarrel,[1] and that they disputed together.   Then said Eadric, "Lo, I forsook Edmund my King and my brother for thy sake,

---

[1] William of Malmesbury says, honestly enough, that he does not know what the quarrel was about.   But Roger of Wendover, a later writer, first tells us about the appointment of the different Earls and how Eadric was made Earl of the Mercians, and yet directly after he makes Eadric come to Cnut and complain of having the Earldom of the Mercians taken from him.   He then goes on like William of Malmesbury.

and for thy sake I slew him ; and thus it is that thou rewardest me." Then was King Cnut very wroth, and his countenance was changed against Eadric, and he said, "Now shalt thou die, and rightly ; for thou art guilty of treason towards God and towards me, for thou hast slain thine own lord, and my brother who was bound to me by an oath. Thy blood be upon thine own head, for thine own mouth hath witnessed against thee that thou hast stretched forth thine hand against the Lord's anointed." Yet would not King Cnut slay him openly, for fear of the people, lest a tumult should be made. So he made them smother Eadric then and there in the chamber, and they threw his body through the window into the river of Thames.

This last story, you will at once see, is taken from the account in the Old Testament of the conduct of David to the Amalekite who killed Saul and to the men who killed Saul's son Ishbosheth.

Now of all this the Chronicles only say, "And this year was Eadric Ealdorman slain," to which one copy, as I said, adds, "in London, very rightly." Florence says, "And on the Nativity of the Lord, when he was in London, he bade the faithless Earl Eadric be slain in the palace, because he feared that he might some time be entrapped by him with snares, as his former lords Æthelred and Edmund had often been entrapped by him ; and he bade that his body should be thrown over the wall of the city and left unburied." Here we most likely have the true account, and from what Florence says about throwing his body over the wall we can understand how the two other stories arose about throwing his body through the window and setting his head on the gate of London.

This same year, but seemingly before the death of Eadric, namely in July, Cnut sent over to Normandy and brought thence the Lady Emma or Ælfgifu and married her. This is one of the strangest marriages that one ever heard of. Cnut was quite a young man, only about twenty-two, but Emma must have been much older, as it was now fifteen years since her former marriage with Æthelred. It is not certain whether he had ever seen her, and, if he merely wanted to connect himself with the Dukes of the Normans, Duke Richard had several daughters, and it would have been more natural to ask for one of them than for their aunt. And on the other hand, it seems strange that Emma should wish to marry a man who had fought against and dethroned her former husband, and had driven her and her children out of the land. But she may have got used to England, and may have been well pleased to go back there again as Lady on any terms. Anyhow, as she was safe with her brother at Rouen, it is quite certain that she need not have married Cnut or gone back to England. if she had not wished it. It is said however that she made Cnut promise that the Crown of England should go to his children by her, which would cut off both her own children by Æthelred, and two sons of Cnut's, Swegen and Harold, who were born already. But of course no such agreement could be made without the consent of the Wise Men, and we shall find that, when Cnut died, he was not at once succeeded by Emma's son, but by one of those other sons. So Emma came over to England and married Cnut, and they had two children, Harthacnut and Gunhild.

The next year, 1018, Cnut laid a very heavy tax on all England, and especially on London, to pay his Danish fleet, the greater part of which he then sent home. This is the last act of anything like oppression on Cnut's part. And this need not have really been oppression ; I mean that, though it must have been a very heavy burthen and hard for the English to pay, yet it may well have been the best thing to get rid of the Danes in this way, at whatever cost for the time. But from this time onward Cnut seems to have set himself steadily to work to mend his ways, and to rule his Kingdom of England well. If we compare him with the next Conqueror of England, we shall find that Cnut began a great deal worse than William, but ended a great deal better. Indeed no one could well have begun worse than Cnut, but from this time onwards we shall find him, as far as England is concerned, always getting better and better. I say, as far as England is concerned, because he was always waging wars, and some of them unjust wars, in the North, and one or two great crimes are recorded of him, especially the murder of his brother-in-law, the Earl Ulf. It seems that Ulf had rebelled or conspired against Cnut, but it also seems plain that Cnut had Ulf put to death without any form of law, after he had been pardoned. And though, besides England and Denmark, he won before his death all Norway and part of Sweden. Cnut seems to have been fonder of England than of any other part of his dominions, and to have spent most of his time there. He seems to have been loved by the English, and, as he went on, he trusted them more and more, and put Englishmen again in all high offices. Thus it is in his time that we first hear of the great Earls Godwine and Leofric, who were afterwards so famous. He made Leofric Earl of the Mercians, and Godwine, of whom I shall have a great deal more to tell you, was in 1020 made Earl of the West-Saxons, for Cnut found that he was obliged to have an Earl under him even in Wessex itself. But no doubt a good many Danes settled in the land, and Cnut kept a body of soldiers about his person, called his *Thingmen*, or *House-carls*, who were originally Danes, though Englishmen and men of all nations were allowed to enlist in the force. As far as I can see, he wished to mix the two nations together as much as might be. And some say that the Danes complained of his promoting Englishmen in Denmark, which he certainly did in the matter of Bishopricks. In England he lived on the best terms with the clergy, especially with the good Archbishop Æthelnoth. Also he and Earl Thurkill built a minster at Assandun, where they won their great victory over Edmund, and gave it to a priest named Stigand to pray for the souls of the men who were killed there. Of this Stigand you will often hear again. He was very liberal to other churches, especially to Saint Edmund's Bury ; you will easily see why, if you remember the story of the death of his father. Hitherto there had been secular canons in the church of Saint Edmund, but now Cnut put in monks. And he also showed great respect to the church of Glastonbury, partly perhaps because Edmund, whom he called his brother, was buried there. He came to Glastonbury in 1032 with Archbishop Æthelnoth, who had once been a monk there, and he granted a charter to the Abbey, which was signed in the wooden church.[1] This means the old church of all, the Welsh church, which stood where Saint

---

[1] There is some doubt whether this charter is really genuine, but we may trust it for the bit about the wooden church, because that is just the sort of thing about which a forger would take care to be accurate.

Joseph's Chapel stands now. The great church built by Dunstan was to the east of this, where the great Abbey church is still. But in process of time both churches were rebuilt as you see them now, and in the thirteenth century the two churches were enlarged so as to touch. And in 1023 Cnut had the body of Saint Ælfheah moved, or, as it is called, *translated*, from London to his own church at Canterbury. In all these things Cnut was clearly trying to atone for all the mischief that he and his countrymen had done in past times. And there is a famous story told of Cnut, which I dare say you have heard before. It is told by Henry of Huntingdon, which, though not the best authority of all, is a great deal better than such stories generally have. I mean how King Cnut was one day by the sea-shore near Southampton, and when some of the men who were with him spoke of his power and greatness,[1] he bade a chair to be placed close to the water's edge. Then said Cnut, "O sea, I am thy lord ; my ships sail over thee whither I will, and this land against which thou dashest is mine ; stay then thy waves, and dare not to wet the feet of thy lord and master." But the waves came on, for the tide was now coming in, and they came round the chair on which Cnut was sitting and they wetted his feet and his clothes. Then spake King Cnut to the men that were with him : "Ye see now how weak is the power of Kings and of all men, for ye see that the waves will not hearken to my voice. Honour then God only and serve Him, for Him do all things obey." Now from that day would not King Cnut wear his crown, but he put it on the head of the image of our Lord in the Old Minster at Winchester.

King Cnut seems also to have been very fond of the church of Ely, which then was not a Bishoprick but an Abbey. So the Ely monks had two or three stories to tell about him. He used often to come with the Lady Emma and some of his chief men and keep the Feast of the Purification or Candlemas-Day with them. One time he was going by water, and as he saw the minster rising above him on the island, and heard the

---

[1] This is not in Henry's story, but it seems implied to give the tale any meaning.

voices of the monks singing in the choir, he was much pleased,
and at once himself made a song in English, of which the
beginning was :

> Merie sungen ðe muneches binnen Ely,
> Ða Cnut ching reu ðer by ;
> Roweð, cnites, noer the land,
> And here we þes muneches sæng.

I do not know whether you can make that out ; I think you
should be able to do so, all except the word *binnen*, and there
your High-Dutch will help you. But the words, as we have
them, can hardly be so old as Cnut's time ; but I copy them,
as they are, out of the History of Ely, which goes on to say
that the song of which these lines were the beginning was sung
in choirs—can this mean choirs of churches?—and became a
proverb. So King Cnut, as he made his song, went on singing
till he came to land, when the monks met him in procession
and led him to the minster, where he confirmed all their rights
and privileges, and laid the charter on the high altar by the
tomb of their great saint Æthelthryth, called in Latin Etheldreda. And another Candlemas they tell us that there was a
great frost, so that there was no going by water ; the King
therefore got a sledge, but, as they were not sure whether the
ice would bear the sledge, a churl of those parts named
Brihtmær, who, because he was very stout and fat, was called
Budde,[1] offered to go first, because if the ice would bear him it
would bear anything, much more King Cnut, who was a small
man. So Brihtmær went first, and, as the ice bore him very
well, King Cnut followed in his sledge, and he gave to Brihtmær and his lands certain rights, which Brihtmær's descendants
still enjoyed when the account was written.

These are pleasant stories enough, and I know no reason
why they should not be true. But we will go back to greater
matters which are written in the Chronicles. I told you that
in 1018 the great tax was laid on. In the same year there was
a great meeting of the Wise Men, both English and Danish, at
Oxford, and they renewed "Edgar's Law." This is a form
of words which you will often meet with in these times. People

---

[1] So it is in the Ely History ; but I do not know what word is meant.

R

ask for the Law of a particular King, generally the last who was thought to have reigned well, or who was looked back to with any sort of love. It means much more than merely to have the laws enforced as they stood in his reign ; it means that people wished to be governed in the same good way in which they were governed in his time. So now, after all the wretchedness of the reign of Æthelred, men looked back to the great King Edgar's days as the happy time, and they asked for·Edgar's Law. Some time later we shall find the men of Northumberland in the same way asking for Cnut's Law. And after the Norman Conquest everybody asked for King Edward's Law, and the Norman Kings often promised to give it ; but they could not give King Edward's Law in the sense in which the English people meant, unless they and all the Normans who had come into the land had gone away again.

I told you that Cnut was constantly warring in the North, and many Englishmen served in those wars, and Earl Godwine in particular is said to have greatly distinguished himself. But in England itself everything was very quiet, and it must have been felt as a very happy time after all the wretched years of fighting with the Danes. So the Chronicles have really hardly anything to tell us all through Cnut's reign, only such things as the deaths and appointments of Bishops, the translation of Saint Ælfheah, and a little about Cnut's Northern wars.

One of the most remarkable things in Cnut's life is his pilgrimage to Rome. I think I explained to you about pilgrimages when I was talking about King Æthelwulf going thither. Next in merit, men thought, to praying at the tomb of our Lord at Jerusalem was praying at the tombs of the Apostles Peter and Paul at Rome. So a great many people made the pilgrimage to Rome, and, busy as Cnut was with his many Kingdoms, he found time to make it also. This was in the year 1027. It was the year in which the Emperor Conrad was crowned at Rome at Easter, and Cnut and King Rudolf of Burgundy were both at the crowning, and the Emperor walked from Saint Peter's church to his palace between the two Kings. Of course Cnut made great gifts and gave great alms both at Rome and in other places that he went through, and he procured that the English school at Rome should be free from all taxes. But the most notable thing about Cnut's pilgrimage is the letter which he wrote from Rome to the people of England, and sent home by Lyfing, Abbot of Tavistock, who was afterwards a very famous Bishop. It is just like the letter of a father to his children, and it makes us think better of Cnut than anything else that we know of him. It is addressed to the Archbishops Æthelnoth and Ælfric, to the Bishops and great men, and to the whole nation of the English, both nobles and commons. He tells them, just as a father who was away from home might tell his children, all that he had seen, how he had visited the holy places, and how he was there at Easter with Pope John and the Emperor, with King Rudolf and a great number of other princes and people of all sorts, and how much honour everybody paid him, and what rich gifts everybody gave him, especially the Emperor. Then he goes on to say how he had a talk with the Pope and the Emperor and with King Rudolf—because he commanded the passes of the Alps—and other princes, and persuaded them to take away various tolls and other annoyances by which English and Danish travellers, both pilgrims and merchants, had been aggrieved. Then he tells them how he complained to the Pope of the great sums which were wrung from English Archbishops when they went to Rome for the *pallium*, and how the Pope promised that it should not be so any more. And then comes the best part of the letter. For Cnut there says that he has made up his mind to amend his life in every way, and to rule all his Kingdoms and nations justly and piously, and to do right judgement in all things, and that anything that he has done wrong through the violence or carelessness of youth he hopes, by God's help, to set right. Then he bids all his governors and officers everywhere to deal justly with all folk, rich and poor, and to do violence to no man, and not to make the King's needs an excuse for any wrong, "for I have no need of money gathered by unrighteousness." Then he says that he is going into Denmark to settle matters there, and that he shall then come into England. He says he tells them all this, because he is sure they will be glad to hear how well he has fared on his journey, and how they know that he has not spared any trouble, and never will, to do anything that can be for the good of all his

R 2

people. He then winds up by telling them that they must pay all church-dues before he comes back, and that, if he finds anything of the sort unpaid when he does come, he shall exact it all without fail. Now surely one cannot help thinking well of the man who could write such a letter as this ; there is something so honest and earnest about it. Also at some time of his reign after 1028 Cnut put out a Code of Laws by the authority of the Wise Men. Like most of these codes, they are mostly the old laws over again, and a great part consists more of moral and religious advice than of what we should call Laws. And the substance of all is to be found at the beginning, which runs thus :—

" That is, then erst [first] that they, over all other things, one God ever would love and worship, and one Christendom with one mind hold, and Cnut King love with right truth."

Some part however are real laws, and Cnut, like Edgar, orders very cruel punishments against thieves. The West-Saxons, the Mercians, and the Danes are all to keep their own customs. All heathendom is to be forsaken ; no doubt some of the Danes were still heathens, and even some of the English may have gone over to their worship when the heathen Gods seemed to be the stronger. Every man might hunt on his own ground, but there are strict laws against those who poached on the royal forests. But these last are chiefly found in some Latin laws, about which learned men are not so sure as about the others whether they are really of Cnut's making or not.

Another thing that I have to tell you about this great King is that in 1031 he fully brought Scotland to submission. We may be sure that, all through the reign of Æthelred, the submission of the Scots and the other vassal nations had been very doubtful. We have heard of one or two incursions of the Scots in Æthelred's reign ; and just at the beginning of Cnut's reign, before his power was well established, Malcolm King of Scots again invaded Northumberland and defeated the English in a battle at Carham. It is also said that Duncan the Under-king of Cumberland, the nephew of Malcolm, refused to become Cnut's man, saying that Cnut was not the lawful King of the English. But he was made to submit to Cnut all the same.

But it is more certain that Cnut now went into Scotland, and that Malcolm King of Scots "bowed to him ;" and so did two other Kings, Under-kings no doubt of Malcolm, whom our Chronicles call Mælbæthe and Jehmarc. This Mælbæthe must be the same as Macbeth, who was afterwards King of Scots, of whom you will hear again, and whose name, as well as Duncan's, has been made famous by one of Shakespere's plays.

Through all the time of Cnut's reign we hear of no wars at all in England itself. For Cnut's hand was quite strong enough to keep down everybody within the country, and those who used to come and invade England, the Danes and Northmen, were now fellow-subjects of the English. But it seems that once during his time a foreign enemy thought of attacking England. You will remember that the two Æthelings, the sons of Æthelred and Emma, Alfred and Edward, were still in Normandy under the care of their uncle Duke Richard. In 1026 Duke Richard died, and the next Duke, his son Richard the Third, died very soon after him. Then in 1028 Robert, the younger son of Richard the Good, succeeded. He was the father of William the Conqueror and was called Robert the Magnificent, and sometimes, I know not why, as he was not a very bad man, Robert the Devil. The Norman writers tell us that he thought of doing something for his cousins, and sent an embassy to Cnut bidding him "give them their own," which I suppose means the Crown of England. You may be sure that Cnut was not likely to do any such thing ; so, when he refused, Duke Robert fitted out a fleet to conquer England and bring back the Æthelings by force. But the ships were driven back, and many of them were broken by a contrary wind ; so they got no further than the Isle of Jersey. Duke Robert's son fared better when he set sail to get England, not for his cousin, but for himself. But the Normans tell us, though one can hardly believe it, that Cnut was so frightened that he promised to leave half the Kingdom of England to the Æthelings at his death. You must remember that the mother of these young men, Emma, was all this while Cnut's wife ; but she seems to have quite forgotten her former husband and children, and to have thought only about her children by Cnut, Harthacnut and his sister Gunhild. Gunhild was married to King Henry, the son of the Emperor Conrad, who was afterwards the Emperor Henry the Third.[1] But she was not the mother of his son the Emperor Henry the Fourth, who was the son of Henry's second wife, Agnes of Poitiers.

In the year 1035, on November 11, being, it seems, only forty years old, King Cnut died at Shaftesbury, and was buried in the Old Minster at Winchester.

§ 4. The Reign of King Harold the Son of Cnut.

1035—1040.

King Cnut left a son named Harthacnut, who was the child of the Lady Ælfgifu-Emma. There were also two other young men who were said to be the sons of Cnut and of another Ælfgifu, the daughter of Earl Ælfhelm who was murdered by Eadric. Their names were Swegen and Harold. But many people did not believe that they were Cnut's sons at all, so that, when the King died, there was a great question as to who should succeed him. It seems that, of Cnut's three Kingdoms, Swegen got Norway and Harthacnut got Denmark without any trouble. But in England men were much divided. The Wise Men met at Oxford, and Earl Leofric and most of the Thanes north of Thames and the seafaring men of London were all for Harold, but Earl Godwine and the West-Saxons were for Harthacnut. This seems odd, as one would have thought that Harold, who may have been the son of two English parents, would have seemed more of an Englishman than Harthacnut, who was the son of a Danish father and a Norman mother. I can only suppose that Cnut had reigned so well in the latter part of his time that men were anxious to do whatever he wished, and that they liked one who was undoubtedly his son rather than anybody else. Emma too had lived so long in England as

---

[1] The Emperors of the name of Henry are reckoned in two ways. This Henry who married Gunhild is called by the Germans Henry the Third, by the Italians Henry the Second. This is because he was the third German King of the name, but only the second Emperor. For you know that the first King Henry, Henry the Fowler, was never crowned Emperor, nor ever went into Italy at all. The Italian way of reckoning is therefore the more accurate, but the German way is more commonly used in England.

the wife of two Kings that she perhaps seemed to the people by this time to be one of themselves. So, after a good deal of disputing, the Kingdom was divided, as it had been between Cnut and Edmund. Harold reigned to the North of the Thames, and Harthacnut to the South. Or in truth we cannot say that Harthacnut reigned at all, for he stayed in Denmark, and his mother Emma and Earl Godwine governed in his name. This Earl Godwine was now, for a long time onwards, the greatest man in England, and we shall always find him standing up for the rights and freedom of England against strangers. Yet it is very hard to say who he was. He was certainly in favour with Cnut from quite the beginning of his reign, and he distinguished himself, as I have told you, in Cnut's wars in the North. He married a Danish wife, Gytha, the sister of Ulf, a Danish Earl, who was himself married to Estrith, Cnut's sister. Some make out that Godwine married a sister or daughter of Cnut himself, but that cannot well be. Godwine and Gytha had many children, of all of whom you will hear again, of one especially, namely Harold, our last English King. But, though we know a great deal about God-wine's children, it is not so easy to say anything about his parents. His father's name was Wulfnoth. Some make out that he was the son of Wulfnoth who ran away and burned the ships in 1009, and also that he was the great-nephew of Eadric. Now he could not very well have been both these at once, and he could hardly have been the great-nephew of Eadric in any case. For Eadric married Eadgyth or Edith the daughter of King Æthelred, and Godwine's daughter Edith married King Edward the son of King Æthelred. Now Edith the daughter of Æthelred was several years older than her half-brother Edward, and no doubt both Eadric and King Edward were a good deal older than their wives. Still, even allowing for all this, it is not likely that a man should marry the great-granddaughter of the brother-in-law of his half-sister.[1] Another story is that,

---

[1] Edward was born between 1002 and 1005. He must therefore have been forty or more when he married Edith in 1045. We do not know when Edith the daughter of Æthelred was born; it must have been before 1002, when her father married again; it is not likely to have been much before 990, as Æthelred was born in 969, and we do not know that she was his eldest child.

after the battle of Sherstone between Edmund and Cnut, the Danish Earl Ulf lost his way, and fell in with a young man named Godwine, who led him to the house of his father Wulfnoth, seemingly a well-to-do yeoman in those parts. Ulf was so pleased with young Godwine that he took him with him, introduced him to Cnut, did all he could for his advancement, and gave him his sister in marriage. Such, according to this story, was the beginning of the fortunes of the great Godwine, Earl of the West-Saxons, and father of Harold, King of the English. Now I do not at all tell you that this story is true ; but I think that all these contradictions help to show that very little was known about Godwine's real birth, and that therefore he was most likely not of any illustrious family. Anyhow he made his way by his own valour and ability, which seem to have won him the favour first of the Ætheling Æthelstan the brother of King Edmund, and afterwards of Cnut himself. Very early in Cnut's reign he was made an Earl, and a few years afterwards Cnut made him Earl over all Wessex, to rule in his name when he was out of England. So when Cnut died, he remained Earl of the West-Saxons under Harthacnut, Harold, and Edward.

In the next year, 1036, a great crime was done, which has brought Earl Godwine's name into great disgrace, but I cannot see any proof that he had anything to do with it. The story is told in a great many ways ; so I must tell it you in the way which seems to me most likely to be true. Though Harthacnut had been made King over part of England, that is, over Wessex,[1] he still stayed in Denmark, and people in England began to be displeased with him for not coming over. It was most likely this which made Alfred, the son of Æthelred and Emma, think that he might have some chance of getting for himself the crown of England, or, at any rate, the crown of Wessex. I do not know whether Emma or Godwine or any one else invited him, but it is quite certain that he came over from Normandy, where he had been staying, as you know, all the time of Cnut's reign, and that he brought a good many Norman followers with him. It is not clear whether he ever

---

[1] Wessex, you will remember, now takes in Kent and Sussex ; all England, in short, south of the Thames.

saw his mother or not; indeed some say that Emma was so much fonder of her children by Cnut than of her children by Æthelred that she herself had a hand in the bloody work that followed. It seems that Earl Godwine met the Ætheling at Guildford, with what object it is not easy to say. Soon after this the Ætheling was seized by Harold's servants, his companions were killed, tortured, or mutilated, and he himself was taken to Ely, where his eyes were put out, and he soon afterwards died. Now it is clear that some people at the time attributed all this cruelty to Godwine, and many later writers have charged him with it. But the evidence does not seem at all strong enough to convict him,[1] and it is most unlikely that he should have had any hand in any such business. For Godwine was not the minister of Harold, but of Harthacnut; he had opposed Harold's election, and he had no motive to betray the Ætheling to him. It is far more likely that Harold's people were looking out, and that they seized Alfred without Godwine's having anything to do with the matter.

The next year, 1037, men got quite tired of waiting for Harthacnut, so Harold was chosen full King over all England by the whole people. Emma was now driven out of the land. She was afraid to go back to Normandy, where things were just now in great confusion, as I shall tell you presently. So she went to live at Bruges in Flanders, where the Marquess Baldwin received her very kindly.

During the two next years nothing is mentioned except the succession of Bishops, and some fighting, as usual, with the Welsh.

In 1040 Harold died at Oxford, and was buried at Westminster; he was the first King who was buried there.

---

[1] Godwine is charged with this crime in one version, but one only, of the Chronicles, and the story can hardly be reconciled with the history as given in the other versions. The *Encomium Emmæ* tells the tale much as I do.

§ 5. The Reign of King Harthacnut.

1040—1042.

When King Harold died, Harthacnut was at Bruges with his mother, having joined her there the year before. He was now chosen King, and messengers were sent to bring him over. So he came and became King over all England, but he reigned only two years, and did no good while he reigned. He brought with him sixty ships with Danish crews, and the first thing he did was to lay a heavy tax on the whole land to pay these Danes, much as we read of in times past. He then caused the body of the late King Harold to be dug up and thrown into a fen, and he sent Ælfric Archbishop of York, and Earl Godwine, and several other great men, to see this pleasant piece of work done. Ælfric then accused Godwine and Lyfing Bishop of Worcester of having had a hand in the murder of Alfred the King's half-brother. Harthacnut was very wroth and took away Lyfing's Bishoprick, which he gave to Ælfric to hold with his own Archbishoprick. Perhaps you will think that this does not say much for the worth of Ælfric's witness against Lyfing. As for Godwine, he made oath after the usual fashion that he had not done the crime with which he was charged, most of the Earls and Thanes of the land swearing with him. This is what is called *compurgation*. He had however to purchase the King's favour by giving him a splendid ship, manned by eighty picked men, all magnificently armed.

The tax had now to be levied, and the next thing was that Harthacnut in 1041 sent his housecarls through the land to gather it. I told you a little about the housecarls when I was speaking of the reign of Cnut. I will now tell you a little more, as you will often hear of them again. They were the first soldiers that were regularly kept and paid in England. In old times, Kings and Aldermen had their own followers, and every man was bound to serve when he was wanted, but there was no *standing army* as there is now, no men who were soldiers as their regular calling, and who were always under arms and always paid. Cnut was the first King to keep a force of this kind, which he made of picked men, Danes, Englishmen, and others. These housecarls were very good soldiers, and we shall afterwards see the use of having such a force, but they were not at all the right people to be tax-gatherers. So at Worcester the people revolted and killed two of the housecarls who had taken refuge in the tower of the minster. Harthacnut was very wroth at this, and he sent all the great Earls, including the three famous ones, Godwine Earl of the West-Saxons, Leofric Earl of the Mercians, and Siward Earl of the Northumbrians, and bade them kill all the people of Worcester, burn the city, and ravage the country. I suspect that the Earls did not much like their errand, and that they let the people know what was coming; for hardly anybody was killed, the people all getting away into an island in the Severn, called Beverege, that is Beaverey or Beaver-Island.[1] But the town was burned and so was the minster, and the country round about was harried. I do not know whether the King thought that Archbishop Ælfric, who was then Bishop of Worcester, had anything to do with the murder of his housecarls. At any rate he took away the Bishoprick from him, and gave it back again to the former Bishop Lyfing. Lyfing had also the Bishopricks of Devonshire and Cornwall, which in the time of the next King, Edward, were joined into the one Bishoprick of Exeter.

I suppose that the Lady Emma had come back again with her son Harthacnut in 1040. The King now sent over to Normandy for his half-brother Edward, who came and lived at his court.

The next year, 1042, King Harthacnut died on the 8th of June. He was at Lambeth, at the wedding-feast of Gytha the daughter of Osgod Clapa, a man of great power. She was married to Tofig the Proud, a Dane and the King's standard-bearer. This Tofig was the first founder of the church at Waltham, of which you

---

[1] You see that there used to be beavers in England, though there are none now. Giraldus Cambrensis, who wrote in the time of Henry the Second and his sons, says that there were none left in his time in any part of Britain, save only in the river Teifi in Cardiganshire.

will hear more. The King stood drinking, I suppose to the health of the new-married pair, when he suddenly fell down, and died. He was carried to Winchester and buried by the side of his father Cnut.

We have now done with the Danish Kings. If Cnut's sons had been like himself, his descendants might very likely have gone on reigning in England. But people were tired of Kings like Harold and Harthacnut, and they were determined to have again a King of their own people. So you will see that two more English Kings reigned before the coming of William the Conqueror and his Normans.

CHAPTER XI.

§ 1. FROM THE ELECTION OF KING EDWARD TO THE BANISH-
MENT OF EARL GODWINE.

1042—1051.

ALL folk, we now read, chose Edward to be King. This was
Edward the son of Æthelred and Emma. He was in truth the
only man of either the English or the Danish royal family who
was at hand. We hear nothing of any children of either
Harold or Harthacnut, and, if there were any, they must have
been quite little ones. And the other Edward, the son of
Edmund Ironside, was away in Hungary. There seems to
have been a Danish party in favour of Cnut's nephew Swegen
Estrithson, the son of his sister Estrith and the Earl Ulf, but
the English were determined to have a King of the old house,
so they chose Edward at once at London, even before Harthacnut was buried. I am inclined to think, for one or two reasons,
that Edward, though he was now living with his brother Harthacnut, was just at this moment in Normandy, on a visit to
some of his friends there or on a pilgrimage to some Norman
church. It is certain that his coronation happened at Easter
the next year, when he was crowned at Winchester; and that,
before that, there was another meeting at Gillingham in Dorsetshire, at which Edward was finally chosen. The chief leaders
in this business were Earl Godwine and Bishop Lyfing.
Godwine was a very eloquent speaker, and could win over
everybody to his side. Still there were some people who
opposed Edward's election and who were afterwards banished
and otherwise punished. It was for this, I suppose, that Osgod

Clapa was banished, and that Æthelstan, the son of Tofig the Proud,[1] lost his estate at Waltham, of which I shall speak again.   Earl Godwine now became the King's chief adviser, and nearly two years after his coronation, in January 1045, Edward married Godwine's daughter Edith, but they had no children.

The English no doubt thought that, in choosing Edward, they were choosing an English King once more.   But in truth, except so far as Earl Godwine did what he could to keep matters straight, they were really better off under such a Dane as Cnut than under such an Englishman as Edward.   They hardly remembered that, though Edward was born in England, he had been taken to Normandy when he was a boy, and had lived there all the time of Cnut and Harold.   He had in fact been brought up as a Frenchman ; all his feelings and notions were French and not English ; he was very fond of his young cousin Duke William ; and his chief thought was to get his other French[2] friends over to England, and to give them as many estates and offices as he could.   You may suppose that the English people, with Earl Godwine at their head, did not at all like this, and it soon, as you will see, led to great disputes.

There was however one person of Norman birth in the land for whom King Edward had not much love.   This was his own mother Emma, the Queen Dowager, as we should now call her, or, as the Chroniclers call her, the Old Lady.   I told you that she cared much more for Cnut and her children by him than for her sons by Æthelred, and she is said to have treated Edward harshly.   It is hard to see when this could have been, as, since he was a child, she had hardly seen him till the time when he came back to England under Harthacnut.   But at any rate mother and son were not fond of one another.   So in the November of the year in which he was crowned, King Edward, with the three great Earls, Godwine, Leofric, and Siward, rode straight from Gloucester, where they had been holding a meeting

---

[1] He could not have been the son of Gytha whom Tofig had just married ; so she must have been his second wife.

[2] As the Normans now spoke French, our Chroniclers always call them Frenchmen.   So when men are called Frenchmen in the Chronicles, they may either be Normans or men from other parts of Gaul.   Edward had plenty of both sorts about him.

of the Wise Men, to Winchester, where the Old Lady was living. They took away all her treasures of gold, silver, and precious stones, but they left her enough to live on, and bade her stay quietly at Winchester.

For two or three years we do not hear much except about the appointments and deaths of Bishops and Abbots. But of these Prelates I must mention one in particular, namely Stigand the King's chaplain, who had been priest of Cnut's minster at Assandun, and who in 1044 became Bishop of Elmham or of the East-Angles. We shall often hear of him again. Also in the same year we hear of the banishment of Gunhild, the niece of King Cnut. She was the daughter of his sister and of Wyrtgeorn King of the Wends. The Wends are the Slavonic people in Mecklenburg and all that part of Germany, with whom the Danish Kings often had wars. She was first married to Hakon, who was called the doughty Earl, and who was banished by Cnut and afterwards died at sea. She then married another Earl, Harold, who was also dead, and now she and her two sons, Thurkill and Heming, were banished. I suppose they had had some hand in the opposition to King Edward's election. So she went away, as everybody seems to have gone about this time, to Marquess Baldwin at Bruges, and thence into Denmark.

King Edward, however, was on good terms with Swegen of Denmark. This King Swegen was a nephew of the great Cnut, being a son of his sister Estrith by the Earl Ulf, the same whom Cnut had killed, and who is said to have brought Earl Godwine forward in his youth. You will remember that Gytha, Godwine's wife, was Ulf's sister, so that she was aunt to King Swegen. At this time, in 1045, Magnus, King of the Norwegians or Northmen, thought of invading England. He said that he and Harthacnut had settled that, whichever of them died first, the other should succeed him, so he thought that he ought to have both England and Denmark, and not either Edward or Swegen. But Edward is said to have answered—perhaps Godwine put the words in his mouth—that he was King by the choice of the whole people of England, and that he would not give up his crown to any man while he lived. So King Edward got ready a fleet at Sandwich to fight against Magnus if he came. But there was no need for any fighting, because King Swegen of Denmark met the Northmen on the way and hindered them from coming. Two years after this, in 1047, Swegen was fiercely attacked by Magnus ; so he very naturally asked for help from England in return for the great service which he had done. So the Wise Men met to settle what should be done. And Earl Godwine proposed to send fifty ships to Swegen's help. But Earl Leofric spoke against this, and the more part voted with him ; so no help was sent to Swegen, and he was driven out of his kingdom, only presently Magnus died, and then Swegen got his kingdom again. Magnus was succeeded in Norway by Harold, surnamed Hardrada,[1] of whom we shall hear again.

Though the English would not help Swegen, yet they soon were engaged in a war with which it would seem that England had less to do than with the war in the North. In 1049 the Emperor Henry, King Edward's brother-in-law, was at war with Baldwin of Flanders, because he had burned his palace at Nimwegen. So he called on King Swegen, who was his vassal, to help him with his fleet, which he did, and he begged[2] King Edward, not as a vassal, but as a friend and brother, to watch with his fleet lest Baldwin should escape by sea. So King Edward watched with his fleet at Sandwich till the Marquess had submitted to the Emperor.

These were all the foreign wars of this reign, if we can call them wars, when there seems to have been no fighting after all. At home there was always some fighting with the Welsh, and a good deal more was going on which I will now tell you in order. First, in 1046, Ealdred Abbot of Tavistock became Bishop of Worcester ; we shall often hear of him. And it was in this same year that Osgod Clapa was banished. And now we begin to hear of the sons of Godwine. Perhaps the great Earl was, like many other fathers, too anxious about advancing his children. I have told you that his daughter was married to the King, and two at least of his sons were already Earls. The eldest, Swegen, was Earl of a very odd government, partly in

---

[1] In English, *Hard-rede* = stern in counsel.
[2] Florence uses the word *mandare* when he speaks of the Emperor's message to Swegen, *rogare* when he speaks of his message to Edward. Swegen he had a right to command, but not Edward.

Wessex, partly in Mercia, and taking in both Somersetshire and Herefordshire. The second son, Harold, was Earl of the East-Angles, taking in not only Norfolk and Suffolk, but Cambridgeshire, Huntingdon, and Essex. Gytha's nephew Beorn, brother of King Swegen of Denmark, was also an Earl, most likely of the Middle-Angles. Swegen was a brave young man, and he afterwards showed that he had some good in him ; but he was revengeful and violent in all his passions, and therefore he fell into some great crimes. As Earl over Herefordshire, you may be sure he had some fighting to do with the Welsh, and in 1046 he had to go against the South-Welsh King Gruffydd,[1] and he overcame him. On his way back, he sent for Eadgifu (in Latin Edgiva), the Abbess of Leominster, a great monastery in Herefordshire, and kept her with him for some time, and wanted to marry her. But this could not be, because she was a nun. So he threw up his Earldom, and left England, and went away, like everybody else, first to Bruges and then to Denmark. The King seems to have divided his lordships and property between his brother Harold and his cousin Beorn. But when King Edward lay with the fleet at Sandwich, Swegen came with eight ships and prayed the King to take him back, and to restore his lands to him. But Harold and Beorn both said that they would not give up what the King had given them. And I suppose that Earl Godwine himself approved of their refusal, for King Edward would not let Swegen come in. Just now news came that Osgod Clapa had come back with some ships from Denmark, and was lying off the coast of Flanders. So they stayed to watch him. Osgod himself soon went back to Denmark, but some of his ships harried the coast of Essex. So there was much sailing backwards and forwards of Earl Godwine and Earl Harold and all the people ; and at last Swegen persuaded Beorn, who was at Pevensey in Sussex, to get into his ship and go with him to Sandwich to the King, and try to get him into the King's favour again. But, instead of sailing to Sandwich, Swegen put Beorn in bonds, and sailed west to Exmouth, and there slew him and

---

[1] There were two Gruffydds at this time, one in North, the other in South Wales ; you must be careful to distinguish the two. Gruffydd of North Wales was just now for a time in alliance with Swegen against his namesake.

S

buried him, and got back again to Flanders. Everybody was very much enraged at this. Most likely, if Swegen and Beorn had quarrelled and fought, and if one of them had killed the other in fair fight, few people in those fierce times would have seen much harm in it. But for a man to kill another, especially his near kinsman, by guile was thought base and cowardly. So the King and all the army declared Swegen an outlaw and a " nithing," the most disgraceful name in the language, meaning an utterly worthless fellow. Of his eight ships, all but two forsook him. Then Earl Harold and all Beorn's friends and the sailors from London went to Exmouth and took up the body of Beorn and carried it to Winchester, and buried it in the Old Minster by his uncle King Cnut. But it is strange to read that in the next year Bishop Ealdred persuaded the King to " inlaw "[1] Swegen and to give him his Earldom again. Ealdred is said to have been a great peacemaker, and to have been able to reconcile the bitterest enemies. But one is surprised to find him exerting himself on behalf of one stained with such crimes as those of Swegen. But perhaps Swegen already showed signs of repentance and amendment. We hear nothing more of him but what is good.

But before Swegen came back, indeed before the year 1049 was out, Bishop Ealdred had less luck in another business, which you will perhaps say was not so much in his own line. In August thirty-six Danish ships from Ireland sailed up the Bristol Channel to the mouth of the Usk. There Gruffydd the South-Welsh King met them, and joined his forces with theirs, and they crossed the Wye and did much damage. Then Ealdred got together some troops from Gloucestershire and Hereford- shire. Gloucestershire, you will remember, was in his Diocese as Bishop of Winchester. But of his troops some were Welshmen: part of Herefordshire certainly, and perhaps Gloucestershire west of the Severn, was still largely Welsh, just like Cornwall and Devonshire. So the Welshmen in the Bishop's army sent to King Gruffydd, and begged him to make a sudden attack on the English. This they did, both Danes and Welsh ; and most of Ealdred's men were killed, and the rest took to flight.

---

[1] The opposite to " outlaw ; " to restore a man to his country and to the rights and property which he has forfeited.

All this time King Edward was promoting Frenchmen and other foreigners more and more, especially to Bishopricks. He had already given the Bishoprick of London to a Norman monk named Robert, who had been Abbot of Jumièges by the Seine. I know no good of him, except that he built the great minster at Jumièges, which is now in ruins. And now this year the Bishoprick of Dorchester[1] was vacant, and the King gave it to another Norman named Ulf, making a very bad choice, for, as the Chronicles say, he "did nought bishop-like." He went to Rome, and Pope Leo, who was a very good Pope, was very near depriving him of the Bishoprick ; he "almost broke his staff," as the Chronicle says, because Ulf was so unlearned that he could hardly read the Church service. But Ulf bribed, not the Pope himself, I am quite sure, but people about him, and so kept the Bishoprick. And the next year, 1050, when Eadsige, the Archbishop of Canterbury, died, King Edward gave the Archbishoprick to Bishop Robert, even though the monks of Christ Church and Earl Godwine wished him to give it to one Ælfric an Englishman. All this must have seemed very strange and irksome to the English people. There had not been a foreigner Archbishop of Canterbury, perhaps not Bishop of any see at all, since the days just after the conversion of the English, when of course they were obliged to have Romans and other foreigners for a little while. And now, as if there was nobody in England good enough for any high place, these Frenchmen were given Bishopricks and other high offices, and were generally set to suck up the fat of the land. Even those who did not stay in England to hold estates and offices came over to see their good friend the King and to get what they could out of him. Archbishop Robert especially was always foremost in mischief ; he tried to set the King against Earl Godwine and to make him believe that Godwine had had a hand in the death of his brother Alfred. Then again the King's sister Godgifu had married a Frenchman, Drogo Count of Mantes, and her son Ralph had an Earldom, and other Normans and Frenchmen had offices and estates, and they began to build castles, after

---

[1] That is Dorchester in Oxfordshire, which I spoke of in p. 61 ; the Bishoprick was afterwards moved to Lincoln. It was the largest Diocese in England, stretching from the Thames to the Humber.

the fashion of their own country, which was not yet in use in England. The towns in England were fortified, as you have often heard from the time of the great fortress-builders, Edward the Elder and his sister the Lady of the Mercians. But men had not begun to build themselves castles, as they did in Normandy, on their own estates. These castles were great, strong, square towers. The White Tower, the oldest part of the Tower of London, built by William the Conqueror, is perhaps the grandest in England. Of course those belonging to private lords were not so large and grand as the Tower of London, which was the King's palace. But men greatly disliked these foreign lords and their castles, which gave them the means of oppressing the people in many ways which the natural English Earls and Thanes never thought of. You may be sure that people would not bear all this very long; and you will soon hear how the crash came at last. But there is one thing more to tell before I come to this part of my story. Early in 1051 King Edward dismissed a great many of his ships, and let off the English from the payment of the tax called *Heregeld*, which was levied for the crews, and which had been paid for thirty-eight years, ever since his father Æthelred had taken Thurkill the Dane into his service.

And now things came to such a pitch with the King's French favourites that men could bear it no longer. Drogo of Mantes, the husband of the King's sister Godgifu, was dead, and she married another Frenchman, Eustace Count of Boulogne. So, not long after his marriage, Count Eustace came over like other people to see his brother-in-law, and got from him all that he asked for. Then he turned about to go home. So he and his people came to Dover, and, thinking they might do just what they pleased, Count Eustace and some of his followers wanted to lodge in the house of one of the townsmen against his will. When the master of the house would not let them in, they killed him; meanwhile his fellow-townsmen had come to help him, and there was a general battle, in which about twenty people were killed on each side. But at last Count Eustace and his men were driven out of the town : so they rode back to the King, who was at Gloucester, and told the story their own way, making out that it was not they who were to blame, but the men of Dover. So King Edward was very wroth, and bade Earl Godwine, as Dover was in his Earldom, go and chastise the people of the town for the wrong done to his brother-in-law. You may remember that Godwine, and others with him, had been sent on the like errand to Worcester in the time of Harthacnut. They had then done their countrymen as little harm as they could; but now Earl Godwine was much more powerful, and could speak out more boldly. So he answered the King plainly that he would do nothing of the kind; no man in his Earldom should be put to death without trial; if the Dover men had done anything wrong, let their magistrates be brought before the Meeting of the Wise Men, and there be tried fairly. Meanwhile some Frenchmen [1] from Herefordshire came about the King and set him still more against Godwine and his people. So Earl Godwine and his sons, Earl Swegen and Earl Harold, got together all the men of their Earldoms, and assembled at Beverstone in Gloucestershire, on the top of the Cotswolds near Tetbury. Meanwhile the King sent to Siward, the great Danish Earl of the Northumbrians, and to Leofric Earl of the Mercians, and to his nephew the French Earl Ralph, and they came with what forces they could muster, but they could not get together such an arm as Godwine's, for, besides the men of his own and his sons' Earldoms, many of the best men of all England came to him. Then, as the King had done no justice, Earl Godwine and his men demanded that Count Eustace and the other Frenchmen who had done such wrong in their Earldoms should be given up to them. The King refused, and his army was very anxious to fight with Godwine's army. No doubt in the King's army were many Frenchmen, and Earl Siward and his Danes had very likely

---

[1] The Chronicles call them *Welshmen*; but it is plain what sort of Welshmen they were. You will remember that *Wealh* or *Welsh* originally meant foreigners of any sort, and that the Britons were called *Welsh* because they were foreigners. Our forefathers, and the Teutonic people generally, called all who spoke the Romance languages Welsh. So the French are the *Gal-Wealas*—the Welsh of Gaul, and the Italians the *Rum-Wealas*—the Welsh of Rome. These Welshmen at Herefordshire were *Gal-*Welshmen and not *Bret-*Welshmen. This should be noted, because William of Malmesbury has made a mistake, and thought they were *Bret-Welsh*.

no great love for Godwine and his Saxons. But Godwine and his men did not want to fight against the King, if they could help it; so they gladly listened to Earl Leofric, who proposed that hostages should be given on both sides, and that the Wise Men should meet at London and settle everything. Perhaps Godwine would have done better to have pressed his advantage at once, for he did not fare nearly so well at London as he had done at Gloucester. The Wise Men met, and the King gathered a great army from all parts. Godwine also came with many men, but they gradually dropped away from him. The Wise Men then declared Swegen an outlaw and summoned Godwine and Harold to appear before them. This was treating them as criminals; so they refused to come, unless they had a safe-conduct and hostages. That is, they required that the King should pledge his word that they should come and go safely, and also that he should put some of his friends into their hands as sureties for his keeping his word. This was often done, and in such a case as this it was quite reasonable. But the King refused to give the hostages; so Godwine and his sons refused to come. The Wise Men then declared them all outlaws, only they gave them five days to get them out of the land. So Earl Godwine and his wife Gytha, and their sons Swegen, Tostig, and Gyrth, took refuge with Baldwin at Bruges. Tostig had just before married Baldwin's sister Judith; indeed Godwine and his sons were called away from the wedding feast—the *bride-ale*[1] as our fathers called it— to go and settle all these matters. They went first to the Earl's house at Bosham in Sussex, and thence set sail for Flanders in a ship filled full of treasure. So they stayed the winter in Flanders, but, as you will see, they did not, like so many other people, go on into Denmark. But Godwine's other sons, Harold and Leofwine, went westwards to Bristol. Bishop Ealdred was bidden to go after them and catch them, but he and his men loitered on purpose; so they got off safe in a ship which Swegen had got ready, and sailed to Ireland, where they were well received by Dermot King of Leinster, and passed the winter in Dublin.

[1] The *bridal*, which people sometimes use wrongly as if it were an adjective.

So you see the patriotic leaders were driven out of the land, and the Frenchmen had it all their own way for a while. First of all, the Lady Edith, Earl Godwine's daughter, was robbed of all her treasures, and was sent away from court and shut up in the monastery at Wherwell, which you will remember was founded by Ælfthryth the King's grandmother. Then more Frenchmen got honours. When Robert was made Archbishop, the King gave the Bishoprick of London to Spearhafoc (that is *Sparrowhawk*) Abbot of Abingdon. But Robert said that Pope Leo had forbidden him to consecrate Spearhafoc as a Bishop; so, when Godwine was gone, the King gave the see to a Norman chaplain of his named William. William however was different from some of his countrymen, and made a really good Bishop. One Odda was made Earl over all the west part of Godwine's Earldom and part of Swegen's, namely over Somerset, Devon, Dorset, and "the Wealas," that is, no doubt, over Cornwall. Some make out Odda to have been a Frenchman also, partly because he is called the King's kinsman. But he might easily be the King's kinsman in other ways. And as he had a brother named Ælfric and a sister named Edith, two purely English names, I think he must have been an Englishman. But it must have been much the same as if he had been a Frenchman, as he throughout took the side of the strangers against Earl Godwine and the patriots. In other respects however Odda is very well spoken of; he was at any rate very fond of the monks, and himself turned monk before he died. He built the church of Deerhurst in Gloucestershire, which is now standing. Harold's Earldom was given to Ælfgar, the son of Leofric Earl of the Mercians.

Now that Godwine was gone, King Edward had a visitor come to see him, who perhaps would not have come, or have been allowed to come, while Godwine was at home. This was no other than his cousin William Duke of the Normans, who lived, as you know, to conquer and reign in England. This Duke William was now about twenty-three years old, and he had been Duke ever since he was seven years old. For his father Duke Robert went on a pilgrimage to Jerusalem, from which he never came back; but before he went he made the Normans swear oaths to his little son. William's mother was

named Herleva or Arlette ; she was the daughter of a tanner at
Falaise, where Robert had a castle in which he lived before he was
Duke. Herleva had never been married to Robert, and many of
the Normans did not think it right that her son should be Duke;
so there were many disputes and conspiracies against him. But
William, while he was a boy, had a wise and good guardian called
Count Gilbert, and at this time his lord the King of the French,
Henry the First, did his duty very faithfully by his young vassal.
So young William kept his Duchy through all these difficulties,
and, as he grew up, he showed himself to be very brave and
wise, and in 1047 he gained a great victory over the rebels
at a place called Val-ès-Dunes, where King Henry came to
help him. Duke William governed his Duchy very well and
wisely, and under him Normandy became one of the most
flourishing parts of Europe. He also encouraged learning and
the arts, and built several grand churches, and for the most
part put very wise and good men in his Bishopricks and
Abbeys. In short William was a very great prince, and, had
he stayed in his own country, we might have called him a
very good prince also. But he was very ambitious, and
always bent on having his own way. and though I do not
think he was one of those who took any pleasure in cruelty, he
did not scruple to do the most cruel things if they at all
served his purpose. Well, this Duke William came over to
see his cousin Edward, and, with so many Frenchmen in the
land, he must have felt himself quite at home. Most likely
it was now that he began to think that it might not be a hard
matter to succeed his cousin in a Kingdom which already
seemed half Norman. And as William always said that Edward had left him the English crown, it is most likely that
Edward did make him some kind of promise at this time.
But you know that a King of the English could not leave
his crown to whom he pleased ; he could at most recommend
the Wise Men to choose this or that man, and it rested with
them whether they would do so or not. And when the time
came, King Edward did not recommend Duke William to
the Wise Men. Still I think he must have made him some
kind of promise, or William could hardly have said so much
about it as he did. At any rate Duke William and many

of his companions were received with great honour by the King and went away loaded with precious gifts.

Lastly, during the time that Earl Godwine was away, namely in March 1052, the Old Lady Emma or Ælfgifu, the widow of two Kings and the mother of two others, died at Winchester, and was buried there in the Old Minster by her husband King Cnut. You see that she had been a long time in England, and had done very little good all the time she was here. You now pretty well understand what mischief had been brought about by Æthelred's fancy for marrying a foreign woman. Ever since her marriage the land had been gradually filled with Normans and Frenchmen, who did nothing but mischief, and who made ready the way for William to come over and conquer the land altogether. It is odd however that Emma and her son Edward agreed so badly. There is a story told, though it is not in any writer who lived at the time, that she was once brought to trial on various charges of public and private misconduct, but that she cleared herself by the ordeal of walking blindfold over red-hot ploughshares without being hurt. This sort of trial and others of the same kind were anciently allowed when the evidence was not clear either way; for men thought that God would not allow an innocent person to be hurt. But there are several reasons why this is not at all likely to have happened in the case of Emma, and no good writer speaks of it.

Thus we leave England almost wholly in the hands of the King's Frenchmen. But this state of things did not last very long. You will be glad to hear, in my next section, how Earl Godwine and his son Harold came back the next year, and made England England again for fourteen years, till William and his Normans came in altogether, and could not be got rid of any more.

§ 2. From the Return of Earl Godwine to the Death of King Edward.

1052—1066.

Things did not go on well in any way while Earl Godwine was in banishment. Gruffydd, the North-Welsh King, thought it was a good time for an inroad; so he entered Herefordshire,

and harried as far as Leominster.   Then many Englishmen
went out against him, and the Frenchmen too from the castles
which they had built.   But Gruffydd fought against them and
beat them and slew many men, both French and English.
Meanwhile Earl Godwine and his sons thought of coming home
again.   They tried what they could to be reconciled with the
King, and they had got both the Marquess Baldwin and Henry
the King of the French to plead for them.   But the Normans
would not let the King hearken.   So they now thought it was
high time to try what they could do for themselves, especially
as they knew quite well that most people in England would be
very glad to have them back.   So they set out, no doubt by
agreement, from Flanders and Ireland, where they had passed
the winter.   King Edward knew that they were likely to come,
and sent a fleet to Sandwich to watch, under the two Earls
Ralph and Odda, of whom you will remember that Ralph was
a Frenchman.   Meanwhile Harold and Leofwine sailed over
from Ireland with nine ships, and landed at Porlock in Somersetshire.   The people here did not wish them to come in, and
fought against them.   Perhaps they were obliged to do so by
their Earl Odda, or perhaps, as Swegen had been their ruler,
they did not love Godwine and his house so much as men did
in other parts.   Or it may have been only because Harold was
obliged to plunder to get food for his men.   At any rate there
was a battle, and thirty thanes and other men besides were killed,
and Harold and Leofwine took cattle and other things on board
their ships, and sailed round the Land's End to meet their
father.   Meanwhile Earl Godwine sailed forth from Bruges,
and when the King's two Earls heard of it, they sent for more
ships and more men, but Godwine escaped from them.   Then
there came on a great storm, and Godwine went back to
Bruges.   Then the King's fleet, which had done nothing at
all, sailed back to London, very much like Æthelred's fleet in
1009.   Then King Edward said that he would send the fleet
again with other Earls to command it—most likely the English
sailors did not obey the French Earl Ralph at all willingly, nor
Earl Odda either when he was taking part with the Frenchmen.
But he was so long about it that all the sailors dispersed
and went home.   So Godwine could do just what he pleased :

he therefore set out again from Bruges, and sailed to the coast
of Kent, and all along the coast of Sussex and Wight to Port-
land, where he met Harold and Leofwine. In most places,
especially along the coast of Sussex, where Godwine had large
estates, people were very glad to see them, and came flocking
to the coasts, saying that they would live and die with Earl
Godwine. But in some places, chiefly in Wight, either people
did not love the Earl so well, or else they were afraid of the
King and his Frenchmen ; so Godwine had to plunder to get
provisions. By thus sailing about, Godwine gradually got him
a great fleet, till he thought he was strong enough to sail up to
London. So he did on the 14th of September, the day of the
Exaltation of the Holy Cross, and he found the King and the
other Earls ready to meet him with fifty ships. Then Godwine
sent to the King and asked that the Earldoms and everything
that had been wrongfully taken from him and his sons should be
given back to them. But the King refused, and tried to get an
army together. But he could not get anybody to fight against
Earl Godwine, for the men who came to him said, "Shall we
Englishmen slay one another, only that these outlandish folk
may the more reign over us ?" But Godwine's men were very
wroth because the King refused to do justice, and they were
very eager to fight against the King's men, but the Earl hindered them, though he had much trouble to do it. At last
there came Bishop Stigand and others who wished to make
peace, and they settled that hostages should be given on both
sides, and that all things should be judged in a Meeting of the
Wise Men. When the Frenchmen heard that, they saw that
there was no more hope for them ; so they got them on their
horses and rode off hither and thither to their castles that they
had built. Earl Leofric let some of them pass through his
land into Scotland to Macbeth the King of Scots, who received
them gladly. And the two bad Bishops, Robert of Canterbury
and Ulf of Dorchester, rode out of the East-gate of London,
cutting about and killing as they went, till they got to the
coast, and there they got into a crazy ship and sailed away, and
never came back. Bishop William of London went away too,
but I do not think that he killed anybody on the road. The next
morning the Wise Men met, and Earl Godwine arose and made

a speech—you know how well he could speak—and said that he
and his sons were guiltless of all that had been laid to their
charge. And all the Wise Men hearkened to him, and they
decreed that Godwine and his sons should have all their estates
and honours back again. And they outlawed all the Frenchmen, because it was they who had stirred up strife between the
King and the Earls. Only they let a few stay, of whom the
King was very fond, and who had done no mischief. And they
let Bishop William of London come back to his Bishoprick,
because he had been a good Bishop and not like Robert and
Ulf. So Earl Godwine and Gytha his wife and his sons Harold
and Tostig and Gyrth and Leofwine, and all the men that were
with Godwine, were taken back into the King's full friendship,
and had again whatever they had had aforetime. So Godwine
was again Earl of the West-Saxons, and Harold again Earl of
the East-Angles. And Edith the Lady came back from her
monastery, and had all her goods and honours again. And to
Stigand the Bishop, who had been the first to make peace, was
given the Archbishoprick of Canterbury, from which Robert
the Frenchman had run away. But Swegen the Earl came not
back ; for he had gone away out of Flanders already, because
his heart smote him for that he had slain Beorn his cousin by
craft, and he went to Jerusalem to pray at the tomb of our
Lord, and he died on his way homeward and saw his native
land no more.

The next year, 1053, when the King was keeping the Epiphany at Gloucester, men brought him the head of Rhys, the
brother of Gruffydd the South-Welsh King. This Rhys had
plundered and done much mischief; so the King and his Wise
Men, at their Christmas meeting, ordered him to be put to
death. It is strange that they found means to do it, and that
so soon. But a much greater man died before the year was
out, no other than the great Earl Godwine himself. At the
Easter-feast he was dining with the King at Winchester, when
he suddenly dropped down in a fit. His sons carried him out,
and four days afterwards he died, and was buried in the Old
Minster.

Now you may suppose that the Normans and all the Frenchmen and foreigners of all sorts hated Earl Godwine while he

was alive, and loved to tell tales against him when he was dead. Besides that most unlikely story that he had a hand in the blinding and death of Alfred, they had all kinds of lies to tell of him and his sons. Now I have told you the real story of his death, as it is in the Chronicles, I will tell you the Norman story, and I think you will be able to see how such stories were made up by putting together pieces of different tales.

The Story of the Death of Earl Godwine.

When Edward the Saint was King of the English, he kept one year his Paschal feast in the royal city of Winchester, and Godwine the traitor, who was the Earl of the West-Saxons, was at meat with him. This is that Godwine who betrayed Alfred the Ætheling to Harold the son of Cnut, and they slew his comrades, and put out his eyes that he died. Wherefore King Edward ever hated Godwine, because that he had slain his brother. Yet was Godwine so mighty that the King was constrained to let him dwell in the land, and be the chief of the people. And Godwine made the King marry Edith his daughter; yet the King loved neither her nor her father. Now as Godwine and the King sat at meat, the King's cup-bearer came near to pour out wine for the King. And the cup-bearer's foot slipped so that he was nigh unto falling, yet he saved himself with the other foot. Then said Godwine, "So brother helpeth brother." Then said King Edward, "And I had a brother once who might have helped me; but he is dead through the treason of Earl Godwine." Then spake Godwine to the King, "Many a time, O King, hast thou said that I betrayed and slew Alfred thy brother; now I call God to witness that I betrayed him not neither slew him, neither had I any hand in the doings of them that slew him." Then took Godwine a morsel of bread from the table, and said, "May this morsel of bread choke me if I had any hand in the blinding or death of Alfred thy brother." Then Godwine swallowed the morsel of bread, but it stuck in his throat and choked him, so that he fell down and died. Then said King Edward, " Drag out this dog, and bury him in the highway, for he is not worthy to have the burial of a Christian man." Howbeit Harold and Tostig and his sons took his body and buried it in the Old Minster, the King not knowing thereof. Thus God avenged the blood of Alfred upon Godwine the traitor.

I think that by this time you know better than to believe stories of this kind. No doubt Earl Godwine had his faults like other men, and very likely he was ambitious and grasping and too fond of advancing his own family. But that he was a true lover of his country, and ruled his Earldom well, and defended England against strangers, no man can doubt. The English people wept for him as for their friend and father ; only they rejoiced that he had left a son to walk in his ways. For, when Godwine died, Harold his son was made Earl of the West-Saxons, and his Earldom of the East-Angles was again given to Ælfgar the son of Leofric, who had held it while Harold was in banishment. Thus the four great Earls were Harold in Wessex, Leofric in Mercia, Siward in Northumberland, and Ælfgar in East-Anglia. Thus the house of Leofric gained by the death of Godwine, as now they had two Earldoms, while the house of Godwine had only one. Before Godwine's death it had been just the other way.

From this time Earl Harold was the greatest man in the Kingdom, and he became so still more when the old Earls Leofric and Siward died. He and King Edward were very good friends, and Harold in fact governed the Kingdom. One can well believe that Godwine, a man who had made his own fortune, was rougher with the King, and did not know how to manage him so well as Harold did. Anyhow it is certain that, great as Godwine was, he never had things so completely in his own hands as Harold had. King Edward after all was really a good man. only his fondness for Frenchmen made him quite unfit to govern the Kingdom. So it was well that he had a man like Harold to rule in his name. The King was very fond of hunting, which one would hardly have expected ; otherwise his time was chiefly spent at his prayers, and in building churches and collecting relics. His great object was to build a great monastery in honour of Saint Peter at Westminster, which he did, but it was not finished till just before his death. This is the famous Abbey of Westminster, where our Kings are crowned and where so many of them are buried. The church has been rebuilt, so that there is nothing of Edward's work left except the bases of a few pillars. But in the other buildings of the monastery, outside the church, there is a great deal of Edward's work still to be seen. Earl Harold too built a great church ; but I want you particularly to notice that, while the King and almost everybody else was gone nearly mad after monks, Earl Harold did not favour them, but when he built his church he put secular priests into it. This was the minster of Waltham in Essex. The first man who built a church at Waltham was Tofig the Proud, at whose bride-ale Harthacnut died. Tofig had lands in Somersetshire as well as in Essex, and the story is that in Cnut's time, at the place which was then called Lutegarsbury and is now called Montacute, a cross was found at the top of the pointed hill from which the place is called Montacute, that is *Mons acutus*, the sharp hill. This cross was thought to be miraculous and to be able to work wonders. So they were minded to set it up in some great minster, and they put it in a cart drawn by oxen to take it away. So they named Canterbury and Glastonbury and other great churches, but the oxen would not stir. At last, in despair, Tofig named Waltham, and then the oxen at once set out to go. Now at Waltham there was no town or village or church, but only a hunting-seat which Tofig had built in the wood. So Tofig built a church at Waltham, and put the cross in it, and set two priests to minister there, and certain men who had been healed by the power of the cross came and lived round about the church. And as they lived there and as pilgrims came to worship, so gradually there grew up the town which is now called Waltham Abbey or Waltham Holy Cross. I do not expect you to believe all this story, but there is no doubt that Tofig built the first church at Waltham, and that there was a cross in it which was thought to work miracles. Afterwards Tofig's son Æthelstan lost his estates, most likely for opposing King

Edward's election. His lands were given to Earl Harold, and Harold pulled down Tofig's small church and built a much larger and grander one, and instead of Tofig's two priests he founded a Dean and twelve Canons. Now I want you to take notice that Earl Harold, in founding this church, took great care that there should be some one in his College able to teach ; so he made the "Childmaster" be one of the chief among the Canons, and he sent to Germany for one Adelhard of Lüttich, which in French is called Liège, who, under the great Emperor Henry the Third, had reformed many churches in Germany. This Adelhard he made Childmaster at Waltham. For though Harold took care that the Frenchmen should never again have power in England, he had no dislike to foreigners as such. But the men whom he brought from foreign parts were all from Lorraine or the Netherlands, where people spoke the Low-Dutch tongue, which was then not very different from English. I do not think you will find any Frenchmen promoted after Godwine's return, while, besides Adelhard, several men from Lorraine got Bishopricks, which they could hardly have done against Harold's will. Harold himself visited foreign countries more than once. He made the pilgrimage to Rome, like Cnut and many other great men, and on his way he travelled in France, on purpose to see what was going on and to know the state of Europe thoroughly. Harold's church at Waltham was not finished and hallowed till 1060, and the foundation was not fully completed till 1062. But I mention it here, because no doubt he began it long before, and also because all these things help to show how great a man our last true English King really was, at once how wise and how bountiful, and how anxious for everything which could be for the good of his country. I do not mean to say a word against King Edward and his Abbey of Westminster, but after all it was only a pious fancy. But Earl Harold's College at Waltham, his choice of secular priests, his care to make his foundation really useful, to get fit men even from foreign countries, show that he was not only lavish of gifts to the Church, like so many others, but that he was really wise and thoughtful and anxious to improve himself and his countrymen in every way. Of course the Normans tell every sort of lie of him as well as of his father, but if you go to the accounts of those who really knew him, you will see that Earl Harold was really one of the greatest and best rulers that England ever had.

I mentioned a little time back that the King of Scots now was Macbeth, whose name is very famous, because Shakespere made a play about him. In 1031 we find that Macbeth was an under-King in Scotland, and that he did homage to Cnut along with the head King Malcolm. I suspect that Macbeth was not so black as he is painted. There are no Scottish writers or documents of the time, so we really know next to nothing of Scottish affairs. But Scottish tradition says that Macbeth ruled very well and that Scotland was better off under him than under any other King for a long time before or afterwards. It is also certain that he had a claim to the Scottish crown, and it is all a false tale that he invited Duncan to his castle, and killed him there treacherously by the counsel of his wife. The truth seems to be that there was a battle between Macbeth's party and Duncan's party, and that Duncan was beaten and ran away, and was pursued and killed. Also Duncan, the grandson of Malcolm, instead of being an old man, was quite young; and as for Macbeth's wife, Gruach, we really know nothing about her except her gifts to certain churches. Thus you see how history gets perverted. So Macbeth became King of Scots, and most likely he had as good a right to the crown as anybody else, except that he may have taken it without the leave of his Lord the King of the English. I suppose this was so, or I do not see why King Edward should have been anxious to turn him out, or why Harold should have approved of the expedition against him, as I suppose he did. In the year 1050 Macbeth is said to have spent a great deal of money at Rome, scattering it about among different people. This looks very much as if he knew that some mischief was brewing, and so wanted to get the Pope on his side. But at any rate, in 1054, the year after Godwine's death, now that things were quiet in England, men began to think of what was going on in Scotland. Earl Siward, the great Earl of the Northumbrians, was very anxious to drive Macbeth out, perhaps all the more because

T

Duncan had married a kinswoman of his. So he got leave of the King, and went with a great host by land and sea to invade Scotland. Macbeth met them in battle, and he had on his side the Normans who had taken refuge with him. It was a very hard fight; many thousands of the Scots were killed, and, we are told, all the Normans. But many of Siward's Danes and Englishmen were killed too, especially of his own house-carls, and among them his own son Osbeorn and his sister's son Siward.[1] However Siward got the victory and carried off such plunder as no man had ever seen before. Malcolm the son of Duncan was then proclaimed King of Scots. According to Shakespere Macbeth was killed in this battle, but this was not so. There was war for some years between Malcolm and Macbeth, and, after Macbeth's death, between Malcolm and one Lulach, who succeeded Macbeth. But in the end Malcolm got all the Kingdom of Scotland. You will often hear of this King Malcolm again. The next year, 1055, Earl Siward died. A story is told that, when he knew that he was dying, he felt ashamed that he was dying quietly in his bed, "like a cow," as he said, instead of dying in battle. So he sent for his armour and put it on, so that, as he could not die in battle, he might at least die as if he were ready for battle. You see how fierce and fond of fighting men were in those days, and how much more so among the Danes in Northumberland than they were in the southern parts of England. We do not hear any such stories of Godwine or Leofric, though Godwine at least could fight well enough when fighting was wanted. Siward himself had got his Earldom by killing the former Earl Eadwulf, so that he was himself no better than Macbeth. Well, he now died and was buried in the minster at Galmanho in the suburbs of York, which he had himself built and hallowed to God and Saint Olaf. This is Olaf King of the Northmen, who had much fighting with our King Cnut. He had also much trouble with his own people; for many men in Norway were still heathens, and Olaf was a zealous Christian, just like the other Olaf Tryggvesson, and, just like Olaf Tryggvesson too, he tried to make all his people Chris-

---

[1] Shakespere is wrong when he makes young Siward the son of the old Earl.

tians like himself, not quietly, as our Kings had done, but by force. So many of the Northmen would not submit, and they slew King Olaf in battle. But for his zeal he was called a saint and a martyr, and he became a favourite saint among the Danes in England. So Earl Siward dedicated his church to him. Out of that church grew the famous Abbey of Saint Mary at York, of which some very beautiful ruins are still to be seen, and there is also a parish church called Saint Olave's. When Siward was dead, his Earldom was given to Tostig the son of Godwine and brother of Harold. Earldoms, you know, were not hereditary; the King and the Wise Men could give them to whom they pleased. But, just as with the Kingdom, the son of the last Earl was more likely to be appointed than any one else, if he was at all fit for the place. But Siward's eldest son Osbeorn had, as you have heard, just been killed, and his other son Waltheof, of whom you will often hear again, was still quite young. Tostig therefore got the Earldom ; so there were now again two Earldoms in the house of Godwine. There were two also in the house of Leofric. Harold and his brother Tostig, Leofric and his son Ælfgar, had all England among them.

The same year that Siward went into Scotland, Osgod Clapa died suddenly in his bed. And the same year too Bishop Ealdred was sent on an embassy into Germany to the Emperor Henry the Third. One object of the embassy was to get the Emperor to send into Hungary for the Ætheling Edward the son of Edmund Ironside. You will remember how he was sent into Hungary when he was a babe, with his brother Edmund. Edmund was dead, but Edward was still living in Hungary. He had married Agatha, a niece of the Emperor Henry the Second, the last of the Saxon Emperors, and he had three children, Edgar, Margaret, and Christina. You will hear of them again ; but I want you to mark now that the boy had an English name, and the girls Greek names. As his uncle King Edward had no children, this Ætheling Edward and his children were the only people left in the royal family ; so it was natural to send for them, so that the Ætheling or his son might succeed to the crown whenever King Edward died. The King was now about fifty-two years old and the Ætheling about thirty-nine.

Bishop Ealdred was a whole year away on his embassy. He spent the time at Köln, which in French is called Cologne, where he was received with great honours both by the Emperor and by Hermann the Archbishop of Köln. The English and the Germans were at this time very good friends, as they always ought to be, and the men of Köln had much trade with London. The old Low-Dutch or Saxon tongue was still spoken in that part of Germany, so that Ealdred no doubt felt himself almost at home.

I have told you of the death of Earl Siward in 1055. The same year, the King and his Wise Men, in a meeting at London, outlawed Earl Ælfgar. He was charged with treason; but some say that he was not guilty. However he soon made himself guilty, if he was not so before. For he went over to Ireland and got him eighteen pirate-ships, no doubt from among the Danes on the east coast of Ireland. So he sailed back and made a league with King Gruffydd in Wales, and they agreed to make war upon King Edward. So Ælfgar and Gruffydd and their host marched into Herefordshire and began to harry the land. Now you may remember that Ralph the Frenchman, the King's sister's son, was Earl of that shire. So he got together the men of his shire, and also some Normans and other Frenchmen whom he had with him. Now you know that in those days Englishmen never fought on horseback. The great men and the housecarls rode to the field of battle, but when the fighting was to begin, they got down and fought on foot like the others with their great axes. But in Normandy, and in France generally, all who were gentlemen fought on horseback, with swords and long spears. Ralph thought that the way of his own country was the best, and he insisted on his Englishmen fighting in the French way on horseback. This was not the way to make them fight well, but at any rate he might have set them a good example himself and have shown them how to fight after his own fashion. But instead of this, when they came near to the army of Gruffydd, about two miles from Hereford, Earl Ralph was the first to turn his bridle and ride off, and his Frenchmen seem to have followed him. So when the English were forsaken in this way, they very naturally rode away too, and the enemy had the victory and killed about five hundred men. Then Gruffydd and Ælfgar marched to the city of Hereford, and they came to Saint Æthelberht's minster—you remember Saint Æthelberht who was killed by Offa—and killed seven of the Canons who tried to keep the great door against them. They killed several other men, and burned the church and the town, and went off with much spoil and many captives. When this kind of work was going on, it was plain that quite another sort of captain from Ralph the Frenchman was needed. So the King ordered an army to be gathered from all England at Gloucester, and he gave the command of it to Earl Harold. Neither Gloucester nor Hereford was in Harold's own Earldom, but Earl Leofric was getting old, and perhaps it would hardly have done to send him to fight against his own son. So Earl Harold set to work like a man, and followed after Gruffydd and Ælfgar and drove them out of Herefordshire and pitched his camp in Gruffydd's own country. Now Gruffydd and Ælfgar knew very well with what kind of man they had now to deal, so they were afraid to fight against Earl Harold, and fled into South-Wales. Harold then divided his army into two parts. One part he sent into South-Wales to watch Gruffydd and Ælfgar, and, if need be, to fight against them. With the rest he himself went to Hereford, and dug a ditch and built a wall round the city, that it might not be taken again so easily. Meanwhile messages were going to and fro, and at last peace was made at Billingsley in Shropshire. You will find that Earl Harold, though so valiant in war, was always ready, sometimes too ready, to make peace. One is surprised to hear that Ælfgar, after all that he had done, was allowed to go to the King and get back his Earldom. But no doubt his father Leofric pleaded hard for him, and Harold may well have remembered that he had himself been in banishment, and that he had himself used more violence than was needed when he landed at Porlock. In any case he had not done anything like what Ælfgar had done; but we can well believe that he might not think it right to press very hardly upon him.

Early in the next year, 1056, died Æthelstan Bishop of Hereford. He it was who had built the minster which Ælfgar and Gruffydd had burned. He had been blind for thirteen

years before he died, and one Tremerin, a Welsh Bishop, had
acted for him all that time. In his stead Leofgar, a chaplain of
Earl Harold's, was made Bishop, but he held the see not quite
twelve weeks. For there was a Welsh war again, and the
new Bishop went out to fight, but King Gruffydd met them
at Cleobury and there slew the Bishop and some of his clerks,
and Ælfnoth the Sheriff. The English fared very badly along
the border all the days of Earl Ralph. So Earl Harold and
Earl Leofric and Bishop Ealdred came, and they again made
peace with Gruffydd and he swore to be a faithful under-King
to King Edward. The same year Earl Odda or Æthelwine,
who had become a monk, died in his own monastery which he
had built at Deerhurst, and was buried at Pershore.

The next year, 1057, the Ætheling Edward and his children
came to England. You will remember that Bishop Ealdred
had gone to the Emperor three years before to see about this
matter, and now the Ætheling actually came home. But he
never saw his uncle the King; for, soon after he came to
England, he died in London and was buried in Saint Paul's
minster. Through his death the royal family was almost ex-
tinct; there was no male descendant left except young Edgar
the Ætheling's son. There were also Edgar's sisters, and there
must have been people both at home and abroad who were
descended from various Kings' daughters. But it had never
been the custom in England to elect a Queen—Sexburh in
Wessex, long before, is the only case at all like it—nor were
those who were connected with the royal house only in the
female line held to have any claim on the crown. And you
will remember that even a King's son or brother had no
absolute right to succeed; he was simply to be preferred to
anybody else, if he was at all fit. And again, do not forget
that young Edgar was not, according to our modern notions,
the heir of his great-uncle King Edward. Edgar was the
grandson of the King's elder brother Edmund Ironside, so
that, as the law now stands, Edward would have been the heir
of Edgar, not Edgar the heir of Edward. As the law and
custom of England then stood, if, when King Edward died,
young Edgar had been a grown man and at all fit to reign,
it would have been the regular thing to choose him rather

than any one else.   But he had no right to the crown beyond
this.

This same year Earl Leofric died, and was buried at Coventry.   He was a great builder of churches and monasteries,
both he and his wife Godgifu, and the minster of Coventry was
one of their building.   Of course most of their buildings have
been rebuilt, but in the church of Stow in Lincolnshire there
is still some work of Earl Leofric's time.   Coventry Cathedral
is quite gone, having been pulled down in Henry the Eighth's
time.   Godgifu, Leofric's wife, is the Lady Godiva of whom a
silly story is told how she begged her husband to let off the
people of Coventry from a certain tax, which he said he would
do only if she would ride naked through the city.   So the
Lady gave orders that all people should shut up their windows
and doors, and she rode naked through the town and delivered
them from the tax.   Now all people did as the Lady bade them,
and shut up their windows, save one Tom, called Peeping
Tom, who looked out and was struck blind.   This is not
one of the real old legends, which, though not true, are
still for many reasons worth telling.   It is a mere silly tale,
which was not heard of till long after Leofric's time.   And it
really makes one almost angry to think how many people know
such a foolish tale as this who never heard anything besides
about the great Earl Leofric and his wife.   And it is some comfort to think that, if there was a Peeping Tom of Coventry at
this time, he must have been one of King Edward's Frenchmen,
for Englishmen, as you know by this time, did not use Scrip-
ture names.   Leofric was succeeded in his Earldom by his son
Ælfgar.   Godgifu outlived her husband and her son and some
of her grandchildren, and died some years after the coming in
of William the Norman.   In this same year also died Ralph
the French Earl and was buried at Peterborough.   Herefordshire was so important a part of the country, as being so close
on the Welsh border, and the city of Hereford, now Harold
had strengthened it, was so important a frontier post, that it was
thought that no one but the first man in England could be trusted
with it.   So Hereford and all Herefordshire became part of the
Earldom of Harold.   Ralph left a little son named Harold,
perhaps a godson of the great Earl, but he did not do anything

famous, though the castle and parish of Ewias Harold in Herefordshire were called after him. And great changes were made
in the East of England. Ælfgar's Earldom of the East-Angles,
or at any rate Norfolk and Suffolk, and most likely Bedford and
Cambridgeshire, was given to Harold's brother Gyrth, who afterwards had Oxfordshire also. And Essex, Kent, and the other
shires about London were made into an Earldom for the other
brother Leofric. Thus the sons of Godwine had now all England
in their hands, except the part of Mercia which belonged to
Ælfgar. And by these new divisions Harold and his brothers
had not only all Wessex, but all the country which had been
West-Saxon in quite early times before the Mercian Kings
began to conquer. And I have little doubt that from about
this time, now that the Ætheling was dead, men began to think
that, when King Edward should die, it would be the right thing
to choose Earl Harold as King in his stead.

The next year, 1058, the new Earl of the Mercians was outlawed again, but he came back to his Earldom by force, by the
help of his old friend King Gruffydd and of some Norwegian
ships, seemingly Wikings who were cruising about and who
now entered his service. I suppose it was about this time that
Ælfgar gave Gruffydd his daughter Ealdgyth in marriage. We
shall hear of her again. There is something very strange in
all these doings of Ælfgar and Gruffydd, and it shows how
strong the power of the house of Leofric must have been in
Mercia, for Ælfgar to be able thus to get his Earldom back
again twice. This last time we hear nothing of Harold; it has
sometimes come into my head that it must have been this year
that he went on his pilgrimage to Rome, so that Ælfgar and
Gruffydd were better able to do as they pleased while he was
away. And, however this may be, it was not Harold's wish
or policy for many reasons to press hard at any time on the
great rival house.

For several years there is very little to tell. Things seem
to have been more quiet than usual, and we hear of hardly
anything besides appointments to Bishopricks and matters of
that kind. In 1058, the year of Ælfgar's second outlawry and
return, Bishop Ealdred hallowed the minster at Gloucester and
made one Wulfstan Abbot of it. This is not Saint Wulfstan

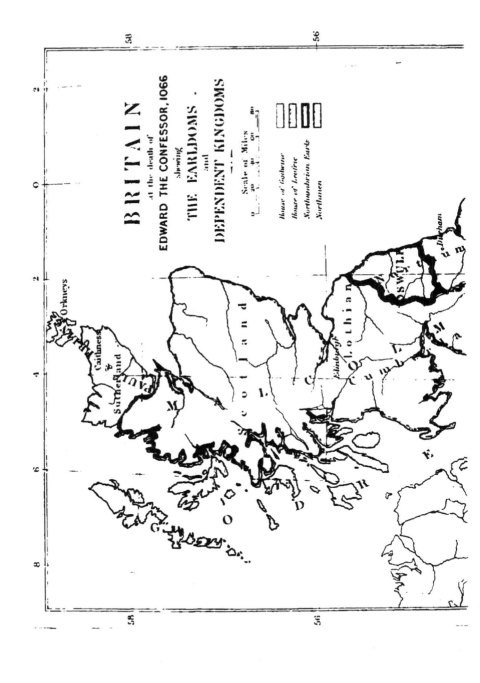

BRITAIN
at the death of
EDWARD THE CONFESSOR, 1066
shewing
THE EARLDOMS
and
DEPENDENT KINGDOMS

Scale of Miles

House of Gothwine
House of Leofric
Northumbrian Earls
Northmen

Orkneys

Caithness

Sutherland

M

S c o t l a n d

O

G

D

R

O

Edinburgh

L o t h i a n

OSWULF

Durham

Cumberland

E

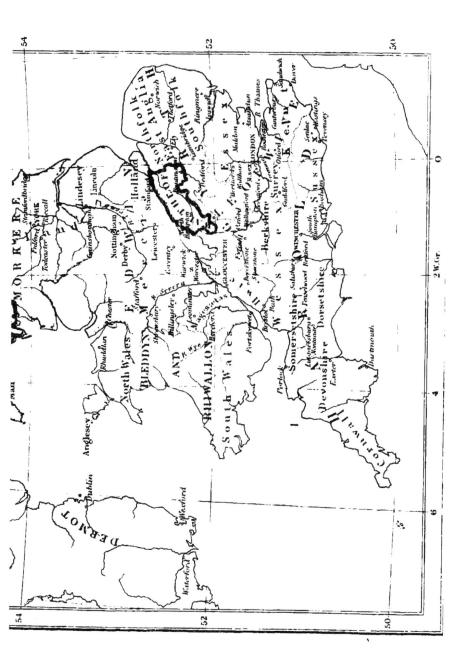

who was afterwards so famous and of whom you will hear something very soon. When Ealdred had done this, he went on a pilgrimage to Jerusalem, a thing which no English Bishop had ever done before. It must have been soon after he came back, in 1060, that Cynesige Archbishop of York died and Ealdred succeeded him. The consecration of Earl Harold's minster at Waltham, which, I told you, happened in 1060, must have been one of Cynesige's last public acts. Ealdred at first kept his Bishoprick of Worcester with the Archbishoprick, which was not a right thing, but which several Archbishops of York had done before him. In 1061 he went to Rome to get his pallium from Pope Nicolas, and with him went Earl Tostig and his wife Judith and several other people as pilgrims. With them also went two men who had been appointed to Bishopricks the year before, namely Walter of Hereford and Gisa of Wells.. They went to be consecrated by the Pope, because there was some doubt whether Stigand was a lawful Archbishop according to the canons of the Church. He had been appointed during the lifetime of Robert the Norman Archbishop, who ran away as you will remember. You will also remember that Robert had been deposed by the King and people of England in the great meeting which restored Earl Godwine in 1052. And this Englishmen thought quite enough to deprive him of his See, but as Robert had never been deposed by the Pope or by any ecclesiastical Council, Stigand was a long time without his pallium, till at last he got it, most likely by Earl Harold's influence on his pilgrimage, from Pope Benedict. But Benedict was not looked upon as a lawful Pope ; so this only made matters worse. People thought less of questions of this sort in England than perhaps anywhere else in the West ; so that it is not wonderful to find that not only the King's Frenchmen, but other foreigners, made difficulties about things which very few Englishmen would have thought of at all. Walter and Gisa were not Frenchmen ; they came from that part of Lotharingia which is now in the Kingdom of Belgium, and they no doubt spoke Low-Dutch. Godwine and Harold had promoted several men from those parts. But they, as well as the French-men, seemed afraid to acknowledge Stigand as Archbishop.

And when the thing was once talked of, Englishmen began to be afraid also. Saint Wulfstan chose to be consecrated by his old friend Ealdred, and not by his proper metropolitan Stigand, and we have seen that Earl Harold himself had had his minster at Waltham hallowed by Cynesige and not by Stigand. Bishop Gisa, of whom I just now spoke, is a memorable man in the history of our church of Wells. He had a quarrel with Earl Harold about the lordships of Banwell and Congresbury and about some other property belonging to the late Bishop Duduc, which Gisa said belonged to the see, but which it seems most likely was Duduc's private property which had come to Harold as Earl.[1] There seems to have been a good deal of trouble about the matter, but in the end Gisa and Harold were made friends. I tell you this, because this matter about Gisa has grown into a story of Harold robbing the church of Wells of all its estates and driving out the Canons to beg their bread, for all which there is no authority at all. This Bishop Gisa did another thing at Wells, which you should know of, but which I think must have happened a good while after this time. The Canons had before this lived each man in his own house, as they do now, and it is even possible that some of them were married. Of this Gisa did not approve ; so he made his Canons live together after the custom of Lotharingia, which had been drawn up in a set of rules long before by Chrodegang Bishop of Metz. He built them a cloister and a *dorter* or common sleeping-room, and other common buildings. It does not seem that he actually made them take vows as monks ; but this was making them live somewhat more in the way of monks, and we can fancy that his object was in the end to have monks instead of Canons at Wells, as had been done in so many other churches. But this never happened ; because after the Conquest the next Bishop altered matters in quite another way.

I have been led astray to talk about Bishop Gisa and our own church of Wells till I have almost forgotten about Arch-

---

[1] Duduc, like Gisa, was a foreigner, a Saxon, who had been made Bishop in Cnut's time. He would therefore most likely have no heirs in England, so that any private property of his would on his death *escheat*, as it is called, to the King or perhaps to the Earl.

bishop Ealdred going to Rome for his pallium. You will remember that Earl Tostig and several other people had gone with him. When they got to Rome, Pope Nicolas was quite ready to consecrate Walter and Gisa, but he did not think it right that Ealdred should keep the Bishoprick of Worcester as well as his Archbishoprick. So, instead of Ealdred's getting the pallium, the Pope and his council professed to deprive him of his Bishoprick of Worcester also and to send him home altogether empty. So he and Earl Tostig and the two newly-made Bishops turned about to go home again. But when they had got a little way from Rome, they were set upon by robbers who stripped them of all that they had, leaving them only their clothes. So they went again to the Pope and Earl Tostig spoke out like a stout Englishman. It was all very well for the Pope to be so fierce to people who came from a long way off, when nobody minded at all about him close under the walls of Rome. Here they all were, robbed of everything they had, and he was not at all sure that the Pope might not have had something to do with the robbery. If strangers and pilgrims were treated in this way when they came to Rome, the Pope could not expect that they would care much about his excommunications when they got to their own countries. At any rate he knew what he would do himself. If the Pope did not cause everything that had been taken away to be made good to them, as soon as he got back to England, he, Earl Tostig, would tell the King and the whole English people how they had been treated, and he would take care that not a penny of English money was paid to the Pope any more. When Pope Nicolas heard this, he began to be afraid, and he not only made good all that Tostig and Ealdred and the other Englishmen had lost, but he gave Ealdred the pallium and said that he might keep the Archbishoprick, only he must give up the Bishoprick of Worcester. So in the next year, after Pope Nicolas was dead, the next Pope, Alexander the Second, sent two Legates into England, who had to settle some matters about the King's new Abbey of Westminster and also about appointing a successor to Ealdred in the see of Worcester. · Ealdred himself seems to have had a good deal to do with choosing his successor, and he certainly made a very good choice. For he chose Wulfstan who was afterwards called Saint Wulfstan, who was at this time Prior of his cathedral church at Worcester. You will often hear of him again. He was a very holy man and a great preacher, and it is said that he used to go about the country round Worcester and baptize the children whom the parish priests would not baptize unless their parents paid them a fee. But perhaps this is only one of the stories which the monks so often got up against the secular clergy. At any rate there is no doubt as to Wulfstan's goodness and as to the great honour in which he was held by everybody at the time. He was much reverenced by Earl Leofric and his wife Godgifu, and he was a special friend of Earl Harold's, who would go many miles out of his way to talk to him and ask for his prayers. So when the King and his Wise Men met at Gloucester, and were told that the clergy and people of Worcester all wished to have Prior Wulfstan for their Bishop, everybody spoke in his favour. The Pope's Legates and the two Archbishops and Earl Harold and Earl Ælfgar all spoke for him. Nobody in short said anything against it except Wulfstan himself, who, when he was sent for and was brought before the Wise Men, said that he would rather have his head cut off than be made a Bishop. And indeed he held out for some months before he would take the Bishoprick, and at last he was only persuaded by a holy hermit, who had lived by himself for forty years, who told him that it was his duty to do what everybody wished him to do. So at last Wulfstan became Bishop of Worcester, but he would not be consecrated by Stigand because, as I said, he was held not to be Archbishop according to the law of the Church. But as he was Archbishop by law, Wulfstan made profession of obedience to him, but he went to York to be consecrated by Archbishop Ealdred, and Archbishop Ealdred had to declare that he claimed no sort of authority over Wulfstan or over the church of Worcester.

I have now not much to tell you for some time except that in 1061, while Tostig and Ealdred were away, Malcolm King of Scots, though he had become Tostig's sworn brother, invaded and harried Northumberland and gave special offence by not sparing Saint Cuthbert's Holy Isle of Lindesfarne.

Now I said before that it was most likely while Earl Harold was away on his pilgrimage that Ælfgar came back by force; so it seems to have been dangerous for an English Earl to go away so far from his Earldom, especially under a King like Edward, when the Earls were the real rulers of the country. The next thing that I have to tell you is that in 1062, the year in which Wulfstan became Bishop, Earl Harold quite finished his College at Waltham. The church, you will remember, was hallowed in 1060. He now got the King's charter, which confirmed all his gifts, and he settled all the details about the incomes, rights, and duties of the different people belonging to the College. He had time to settle such things in 1062; in 1063 he had quite other matters to look to. For by this time Gruffydd's disturbances had got beyond all bearing, and it was now determined really to put a stop to everything of the kind. This must have been settled at the Christmas meeting of the Wise Men, which was held as usual at Gloucester. So Earl Harold marched straight to Rhuddlan, where Gruffydd had a palace; but Gruffydd had just time to get away in a ship. Of course what was meant by this sudden march in the winter was to seize Gruffydd himself, for winter was not a time to make war in such a country as Wales. So when Gruffydd had thus got away, Earl Harold burned his palace at Rhuddlan and his ships, and went back again to Gloucester. It was no doubt settled to carry on the war decisively when the summer came. So when all things were ready and it was now May, Earl Harold set out from Bristol with a fleet, and his brother Earl Tostig set forth with a land-force, and Harold sailed round Wales till he met his brother, and then the two set to work manfully and harried the whole land. Earl Harold had learned something in his former war with the Welsh, and he saw that the English way of fighting did not always do in a Welsh war. The English housecarls with their heavy coats of mail and their great axes were as good soldiers as could be in a pitched battle; but the Welsh took care there never should be any pitched battles, and the housecarls were not at all suited to chase the nimble and light-armed Welsh among the hills and dales of Wales. So Earl Harold made his men lay aside their heavy harness and weapons and learn to fight in the Welshmen's own way. So he was able to go through the whole land, beating them everywhere, till at last the Welsh gave in, and deposed their King Gruffydd and gave hostages and swore oaths and promised to pay tribute. And in the month of August Gruffydd was killed by his own people, because, we are told, of the war which he had waged with Earl Harold. I dare say that at first all the Welsh people were quite as anxious for war with the English as Gruffydd himself, but no doubt they were by this time quite tired of Earl Harold's way of making war, which you see was rather different from Ralph's. Gruffydd was the last Welsh King of any great power or who reigned over all Wales. Those who killed him brought his head and the beak of his ship to Earl Harold, who sent them on to King Edward. The King then gave the Welsh land to the brothers of Gruffydd, whom the Chronicles call Blethgent and Rigwatla, but whose real names seem to have been Bleddyn and Rhiwallon. The new princes gave hostages and swore oaths both to the King and to Earl Harold, that they would be faithful by land and sea and do and pay all that the Welsh land had ever done and paid to any English King.

This complete conquest of Wales, by which the country was brought more thoroughly into subjection than it had ever been since Edgar's time, was one of Earl Harold's great exploits. People remembered them long after, even when they had been long taught to look upon Harold as an usurper and a wicked king altogether. There is a great deal about Harold's war with Gruffydd in two writers who lived in the time of Henry the Second, John of Salisbury and Giraldus Cambrensis. They both tell us how thoroughly Harold did his work, and John of Salisbury picks out this story to show the difference between a good general and a bad one, and he wishes that there were men in his own time to guard the marches as Harold did. Giraldus, who was born in Wales and who knew the country well, says that at every place where Harold had fought with the Welsh he set up a stone with the writing on it, "Here Harold conquered." You may be sure that these great successes endeared him still more both to the King and to the people. No doubt by this time he was thinking that he might very likely be chosen King whenever Edward died. Indeed one or two things look as if he had been made something more than a common Earl, even while King Edward was alive. For Florence in one place calls him *Subregulus* or *under-King*, a name which is often given to the Princes of Wales, but which I do not remember to have seen given to any other Earl since Alderman Æthelred of Mercia in the days of Edward the Elder. And it is worth notice that the Welsh Princes swore oaths to Earl Harold as well as to King Edward, which looks very much as if people expected that Harold would be King after Edward.

Under the year 1064 the Chronicles tell us nothing, but Florence puts the death of Gruffydd and the final submission of Wales in that year instead of in 1063.[1] It was perhaps about this time that a thing happened which is told with such great differences that it is very hard to get at the exact truth, though it seems most likely that something of the kind really did happen. I mean the oath which Earl Harold is said to have taken to Duke William to be his man and to receive him as King whenever King Edward should die. The Norman writers all assert this very strongly, and it was, according to them, the chief ground on which William justified his attack on England. But our English writers say nothing whatever about it. But I cannot help thinking that their saying nothing about it rather proves that something of the kind did happen. For most of the Norman lies about Godwine and Harold we can easily answer. The English writers either contradict them in so many words or else give an account which shows that they cannot be true. But of this matter of Harold's oath they say nothing at all; whereas, if the Norman story had been a mere lie from beginning to end, we may be sure that they would have been glad to have been able to say so. We know also that Harold did visit France and Rome and other parts of Europe, so that it is very likely that he visited Normandy also. So on the whole I think it is most likely that Harold did at some time make some kind of oath to William, as I think it is most likely

[1] The two Welsh Chronicles put the death of Gruffydd, one in 1063, the other in 1064.

that Edward did at some time make some kind of promise to William. If both stories had been mere inventions of William's, we should surely find Harold's contradiction in some shape or other. But, if you ask me for time, place, and circumstance, I can only say once more that the English writers say nothing about it, and that the Norman writers contradict one another in such a way that I can tell you hardly anything for certain. But I think it is most likely that Harold was sailing in the Channel, either merely for pleasure or on a voyage somewhere, and that he was driven by bad weather on the coast in the dominions of Guy Count of Ponthieu. Now it is worth notice that in many places there has been a very strange and wicked feeling about shipwrecks and persons cast on shore by shipwreck, some traces of which exist even now. In Cornwall, not so very long ago, people used to live by wrecking, that is by plundering shipwrecked vessels, and sometimes, I am afraid, even murdering any people who might be on board. Others would put out false lights so as to cause ships to be wrecked, and some would even pray to God for good shipwrecks. I fancy that sometimes people committed crimes of this sort who would not have robbed or murdered in any other case ; they had a kind of notion that neither the laws of the land nor the common laws of right and wrong had anything to do with things at sea. They seem to have fancied that shipwrecked things and people were forsaken of God, and given over into their hands, so that they might do what they pleased with them. Our law is that anything that is thrown ashore by the sea, and of which the owner cannot be found, belongs to the King, or, by his grant, to the lord of the manor. And in early times it would even seem that the King or other lord had a right to all wrecks, even though the owner was known : still, though this was very harsh and unjust, it gave no power to hurt any human being who might be cast on shore. But in the times of which I am writing the lords of some coasts pretended a right of wreck over persons as well as over things, so that, if any man was shipwrecked, instead of being helped in any way, he was clapped in prison till he paid a ransom. Count Guy claimed this as the law of his county of Ponthieu ; so when the great Earl of the West-Saxons, the brother-in-law of the King of the English, was wrecked on his shore, Guy clapped him in prison, and demanded a ransom. But Guy could not have everything his own way; for he was a vassal of William Duke of the Normans. So Earl Harold contrived to send a message to Duke William, telling him of the wrong that his vassal had done to him. We have no reason to doubt that William would be really anxious to redress a wrong of this sort done by any one who was at all under his control. At the same time, as he had doubtless, long before this, begun to aim at the English crown, we may be quite sure that he would be very glad of the opportunity of laying Earl Harold under an obligation to him, perhaps of getting him personally into his power. So Duke William sent to Count Guy, and by threats and promises made him give up his prisoner. He then received Earl Harold at his court with all honour, his Duchess Matilda and every one joining to pay all respect to so illustrious a guest. It is even said that he persuaded Harold to accompany him in a campaign against Conan Count of the Bretons, in which Harold greatly distinguished himself, especially by pulling out and saving many of the Normans when they were likely to be swept away by the river Coesnon which divides Normandy and Britanny, close by Saint Michael's Mount. You may see this in the Bayeux Tapestry, where Harold is shown lifting up two Normans at once. The English generally were taller and stronger men than the Normans, and Earl Harold is spoken of as being the tallest and strongest, as well as the wisest and bravest, man among them. As a general rule, in those times, a man's body was of almost as much account as his mind. It was not indeed always so, for you will remember that both Edgar and Cnut were small men; but a man who, like Harold or Edmund Ironside, was vigorous in body as well as in spirit, was thought much more of on account of it. Earl Harold then helped Duke William in his war against the Bretons; perhaps he liked the notion of fighting the Welsh on both sides of the Channel.

After this Breton war, William "gave arms" to Harold, making him a knight after the fashion of the Normans. And now it was, we are told, that Harold swore to be Duke William's man, and to receive him as King when King Edward died, and

U

meanwhile to give him up the castle of Dover, and to marry one of Duke William's daughters, and to give a sister of his own to marry one of Duke William's lords. Earl Harold, we are told, swore to all this, and left his young brother Wulfnoth as a hostage, and then went home. But the whole thing is told with such contradictions that one hardly knows what to believe. On the whole, putting everything together, I am inclined to think that what Harold really swore was simply to marry William's daughter, and that he did homage to William as his future father-in-law. I think you will see that, though this would not be an oath to do all that is said in the other story, yet the other story could easily grow out of it. I need hardly tell you that Harold did not keep his oath even to marry William's daughter, still less to do all the other things which he is said to have sworn. Of these things you will easily see that some were things which he could not do and which it was not right that he should do. Harold of course had no right to promise the Crown of England to any man, as, whenever King Edward should die, it would belong to the Wise Men to choose whom they would. So too he had no right to give up a castle in England to a foreign prince. Indeed for a man in Harold's place, so likely to be the next King, even to marry the daughter of a foreign prince, though not absolutely unlawful, was a thing likely to be dangerous, and of which the English people were not at all likely to approve. In truth whatever sin there was in Harold's conduct was not in *breaking* his oath, but in *taking* it. It was something like when Herod in the Gospel swore to cut off the head of Saint John Baptist ; his sin would have been much less if he had broken his oath. And of course in strictness Harold ought to have suffered anything rather than take an oath to do things which he could not do and which it would have been wrong for him to do. The truth is that oaths of this kind were in those days—as perhaps some kinds of oaths have been in our time—lightly taken and lightly broken. Men did homage and became one another's men on all sorts of occasions and on account of almost any kind of favour that they received. A man sometimes had several lords, and it was not easy to be faithful to all at once. Duke William himself was the man of the King of the French, but there is some reason to believe that he had become the man of King Edward when he promised him the crown. It is certain that William in several charters and letters calls Edward his Lord. So it was not at all wonderful if Harold became William's man, when William had done him so great a service as to set him free from Guy's prison, to say nothing of his promising to marry William's daughter and serving under him in the Breton war. Now in all these cases, when one man became the man of another, he was bound to his Lord by oaths, and those oaths were so easily and so constantly broken that men came to think but little of it. Every time that any Earl or under-King, like Ælfgar or Gruffydd, rebelled, he was breaking his oaths; so was every prince in Germany or France who fought against the Emperor or the King of the French. But this kind of oath-breaking, even when it was done quite wrongly and without any provocation, seems to have been easily passed by and forgiven. Harold most likely felt that he was in William's power, and that he could not get away against William's will, and he may have felt less scruple about taking an oath which it must have been plain that he could not keep if he wished to do so. William had anyhow taken an unfair advantage of him, and he may have thought to repay him in his own coin. I do not say that, in strict morals, Harold was right in doing this; but I say that, with the feelings of those times, he might easily think that the fault was a slight one, and I do very distinctly say again that, whatever blame he deserves, he deserves wholly for taking the oath, not at all for breaking it. If he really swore all that is said, something quite beyond the common oath of homage, it is plain that he was unfairly entrapped into taking the oath. He ought then in strictness to have refused at all risks to take it; but no one can say that, because he had taken it, it was his duty to betray his country to the Norman Duke, which was, in plain words, what he is said to have sworn to do.

I cannot tell whether anybody in England knew anything about the oath which Harold had taken to William. If men did know of it, most likely they looked on it as quite a light matter. But this oath of Harold's gave William the greatest possible advantage when he came to put forward his own claim to the crown. In truth Harold's oath could not give William

any more right to the crown than he had before ; but it gave
him the opportunity of calling Harold usurper and perjurer
and so of setting men's minds in other lands against him.   And
William is said to have further entrapped Harold in another way
about this oath.   We are told that he took care that it should
be something more solemn than the common oath of homage
for which men had come to care so little.   He caused Harold,
when he swore, to put his hand on a chest, and, when he had
sworn, he showed him that this chest was full of the most
venerated relics of the saints gathered from all the churches
of Normandy.   Now in those times nothing was set more
store by than the relics of saints, and it was thought that
he who in any way insulted them—and of course to swear
falsely by them was the greatest of insults—would at once
bring their vengeance upon his head.   Now the story says
that Harold did not at all know that he was swearing on the
relics ; so one would have thought that, if departed saints
really could feel human passions and could have anything
to do with the affairs of this world, Harold was not the
person with whom they had the greater reason to be angry.
Surely the worse sinner was William in profaning such holy
things to obtain such a mean advantage.   But men, at least in
other lands, seem not to have thought so.   Men who would
perhaps have thought very little of the breach of a common
oath of homage were shocked at the notion of an insult to the
holy relics, and they looked on Harold's perjury as something
frightful beyond measure.   Of course this was a very low form
of superstition.   An oath must be just as binding in whatever
form it is taken, and with a really good man a promise is just
as binding as an oath.   The truth is that the fewer oaths and
promises men load themselves with the better, as they cannot
always tell whether they shall be able to keep them.   But
men thought otherwise at the time, and their thinking so
did great harm to Harold and to England.   But I think you
will agree with me in holding that—supposing of course the
story to be true at all—though Harold, in order to act quite
rightly, ought never to have taken the oath, yet he would
have done much worse to have kept it, and also that William,
by taking such a shabby advantage of Harold, and especially

by playing him that disgraceful trick about the relics of the saints, was really a much greater sinner in the matter than Harold was.

We are now getting near the end of the days of our true native Kings, for we have reached the year 1065. It was a very troubled year. In July Earl Harold, as the Welsh were now so utterly conquered, ordered a house to be built at Port-skewet or Porth-iscoed in the land of Gwent, at one of the points where the mouth of the Severn is crossed. This house was to be a hunting-seat for King Edward, who, as I told you, was fond of hunting. So Earl Harold bade many workmen to be gathered together, and much food and drink and other good things. Now I think I told you that there were two Gruffydds about this time. The one of whom we have heard so much was Gruffydd the son of Llywelyn of North Wales. He had killed Gruffydd of South Wales and had taken his Kingdom. But Gruffydd of South Wales had left a son called Caradoc, which, as you will remember, is the same name as Caractacus. On Saint Bartholomew's day this Caradoc came with so many men as he could get together, and killed all Earl Harold's workmen and carried off all the meat and drink and other things. No doubt Caradoc did not like to see an English King's house set up on Welsh ground, and he may also have been angry that, when Gruffydd the son of Llywelyn was conquered, he did not get his father's dominions back again. No doubt Earl Harold would have chastised this insult, but just now there were much more important matters to be looked to in the North of England. The Northumbrians did not at all agree with their Earl Tostig, Harold's brother. By great good luck we get the story from both sides. There is no sort of doubt that the people of Northumberland were at this time far more barbarous than the people of the rest of England, that murders and robberies were very common, and that it needed a very strong hand to keep them in anything like order. It is said that robbers were so numerous and so bold that it was hardly safe to travel, even in parties of twenty or thirty. Earl Siward, though he had come to his Earldom by a great crime, had yet done some good by keeping a tight hand on these wild people. Earl Tostig, we are told, worked hard to keep them in order, and to establish at least as peaceful a state of things as he was used to in the South of England. In doing this, he used great severity against all offenders, and even chastised some of the chief men for their misdeeds. On the other hand, the Northumbrians complained of Tostig's unbearable tyranny, of the heavy taxes which he laid upon them, and how some of their chief Thanes had been treacherously murdered. One of them, named Gospatric, they said, had been, through Tostig's devices, murdered by order of the Lady Edith, when he came to the King's Court the Christmas before. Two others, they said, Gamel the son of Orm, and Ulf the son of Dolfin, had been murdered by Earl Tostig's own orders in his own chamber at York, when he had just pretended to make peace with them. You will remember several stories of murders of this sort, and they are nowhere so common as in the history of the Northumbrian Earls. Probably there was truth on both sides. The biographer of King Edward, who lived at the time, and who gives us Tostig's version of the matter, lets it out as it were that though Tostig's object was a good one, to keep order in his Earldom, yet he set about in too harsh and violent a way, and that he did not behave in the mild and winning way in which his brother Harold always did. Now, if this be so, it is even possible that, if there were any powerful men, whose crimes deserved death, but who were too strong to be got at in the way of regular justice, he might think himself justified in entrapping them to death in the way of which the Northumbrians complained. I cannot tell this for certain, but it seems a likely way of explaining the two accounts. Anyhow the Northumbrians now rebelled against Tostig. On the 3d of October the Thanes of all Northumberland held at York what was clearly meant to be a meeting of the Wise Men of the Earldom, though it must have been a rather disorderly meeting. Earl Tostig was now with the King, with whom he was a great favourite, at Bretford in Wiltshire. The Northumbrians then in their meeting declared Tostig deposed from his Earldom and outlawed from Northumberland, and they chose Morkere the son of Ælfgar to be their Earl. This was acting as if Northumberland had been a dependent Kingdom like Wales or Scotland, and not a part of the Kingdom of England.

Ever since there had been one King over all England, it had belonged to him and the Wise Men of the whole land to name Earls over the different parts of the Kingdom. Then they not only did this, but killed as many of Tostig's housecarls and friends as they could find, to the number of two hundred and broke open the Earl's treasury and carried off all that was in it, gold, silver, weapons, everything. Then Morkere, whom they had chosen for their Earl, came to them and marched southward at their head. The men of Lincolnshire, Nottinghamshire, and Derbyshire, where many of the people, especially the chief men and the men of the Five Boroughs, were of Danish blood, joined them, and they marched on to Northampton. There came Morkere's brother Edwin to meet him. He was now Earl of the Mercians; it is not certain when he succeeded his father Ælfgar, the date of whose death is not mentioned, but it must have been at some time between 1062 and 1065. Edwin now brought a large body of his Mercians and also many Welshmen; you see the friendship between his family and the Welsh still goes on. At Northampton Earl Harold met them and held a great meeting. The King sent, charging the Northumbrians to leave off their rebellion, and to have everything that they complained of tried quietly. They in return demanded that Earl Harold himself should go to the King and lay their complaints personally before him, and should demand that Tostig should be banished from the King's presence and from the whole Kingdom; otherwise they would deal with the King as an enemy. So Harold went to the King with their message; on which Tostig charged Harold most unjustly with having set on the Northumbrians to make these charges against him. Nothing could be more unlikely, as Harold had no kind of motive for doing so. Harold at once denied the charge on oath.[1] But though Harold had no motive to stir up the Northumbrians to rebellion, he had an obvious motive not to push them to extremities now they had rebelled. His disposition and policy was always to be as

---

[1] The biographer here makes a very curious remark. He laments that Harold was rather too hasty in taking oaths. This can only be an allusion to Harold's oath to William, though he never directly mentions that oath in his story.

conciliatory as possible, and just now, when he was hoping to be chosen King at the next vacancy, he clearly could not afford to make enemies of a large part of the Kingdom. However he did what he could for his brother. While he was with the King, the Northumbrians had been dealing with Northamptonshire as with an enemy's country. They not only seized many thousand cattle, which perhaps they could not help if they were to be fed, but they burned houses and corn and slew some men and carried off sóme hundreds as captives to the North. You see the sort of people whom Tostig had to deal with. The King was very anxious to send an army against the rebels and to restore his favourite Tostig by force. But Harold and others shrank from a civil war, and besides winter was drawing on, so that it was not a good time for warfare. So they persuaded the King to give up the thought of war. Then Harold went and held another meeting at Oxford, the Northumbrians having marched so far southward. He and others tried to persuade the Northumbrians to take Tostig back again, but they would not hearken. So Morkere the son of Ælfgar was confirmed in the Earldom of the Northumbrians, and Tostig the son of Godwine was outlawed and banished. And whatever we say of the conduct of the Northumbrians, and however good Tostig's intentions may have been in his general government, still, if he really had put men to death by guile, we cannot but say that he was rightly outlawed and banished. In this same meeting they renewed Cnut's Law. You know now what that means, and you will remember how in Cnut's time they renewed Edgar's Law. So Tostig went away with his wife and children to the Marquess Baldwin at Bruges. We have seen that everybody who was banished from England used to go to Baldwin; but of course Tostig had a special reason for going to him, as Baldwin was his wife's brother. King Edward was very angry at having to part with his favourite, and at not being allowed to punish his enemies. But Earl Harold knew that it must be so, and the King had nothing left to do but to pray that God might punish them. The Northumbrians certainly suffered evil enough in the next year and for many years to come. But I do not think we have any right to say that it was because they had driven out Earl Tostig.

King Edward now fell sick, and saw that his end was nigh. So his great object was to finish his great church at Westminster and to have it hallowed before he died. He lived just long enough to have this done. He kept Christmas and had the Christmas meeting of the Wise Men in London instead of at Gloucester as usual. And on Innocents' day the new minster was hallowed, but the King was too sick to be there; so the Lady Edith stood in his stead. And on January 5th, 1066, King Edward the son of Æthelred died. He counselled the Wise Men to choose Earl Harold as King in his stead, and he commended to his care his sister Edith, and those who had left their own country for his sake, that is to say, the Frenchmen whom he had brought over to England. The next day, being the feast of the Epiphany, he was buried in his own new church at Westminster. Miracles were soon said to be wrought at his grave, and about a hundred years after his death he was canonized as a saint. He was the last male descendant of Cerdic who reigned over England.

CHAPTER XII.

WE have now come to the great and terrible year 1066. In the course of that year England had three Kings, I might almost say four ; and in the course of that year it was that the line of our native Kings came to an end, and that England had to receive a foreign King. And the King, before long, divided all the great honours and offices, and the greater part of the lands of England, among his foreign followers. No year, before or after, since the English came into Britain, was so full of great events as this. The year 597, when Christianity was first preached to our forefathers, was doubtless still more important in its results, but it could not have struck men's minds at the time in the same way.

King Edward then was dead, and the Wise Men had to choose a King to reign in his stead. It was Christmas-tide, when, as you know, a meeting was commonly held, and this time King Edward had gathered together all the great men of the land for the hallowing of his new minster of Saint Peter. So no doubt there was a great meeting from all parts. Now you know very well by this time the old law about choosing Kings. If Edward had left a son or a brother who was a grown man and in the least fit to reign, he would have been chosen before anybody else. But there was no such person. There was no one left in the royal family but young Edgar and his sisters. Now Margaret afterwards showed herself so wise and good a woman that, if it had been the custom of our forefathers to set women to reign over them, perhaps they could not have done better than to choose her. But it was not usual to choose Queens, and most likely no one thought of such a thing at all. And moreover she must then have been quite young. As for Edgar, he too was quite young, he was hardly an Englishman, having been born in a foreign country, and he was not, which was then so much thought of, the son of a crowned King. He therefore hardly seemed to men to have that sort of right which an Ætheling commonly had. It was clear too that his election would have been most unwise, as he was in no way fit to reign. The Wise Men therefore were obliged to look for a King who was not of the royal family. This was the first time they had done so, unless you reckon the elections of Swegen and Cnut, who, after all, were a King and a King's son, though not of the line of English Kings. This was the first and only time that they ever chose an Englishman who was not of royal blood. They were obliged to look beyond the royal family; but when they had once done that, they had not to look very far. There was one man ready, and only one. As there was no Ætheling fit to reign, whom could they choose but the great Earl Harold? He had been the chief ruler of the realm for many years ; he had shown himself wise and valiant in war and peace, and he had been recommended to their choice by the late King. So the Wise Men of all England met and chose Harold the son of Godwine to be King. And on the same day on which King Edward was buried, most likely as soon as the funeral service was over, Earl Harold was hallowed as King in the West Minster by Archbishop Ealdred. Stigand had always been a firm friend of him and his house ; but as Stigand was said not to be lawful Archbishop, the new King thought it safer to be crowned by Ealdred, against whom there was nothing to be said.

I cannot fancy there being, in any land which is ruled by Kings at all, a greater or more glorious day than this, the feast of the Epiphany, 1066. Then our forefathers chose to themselves a man to reign over them, not because he was the son or grandson of this or that man who had been King before him, not because he was a foreigner who had conquered them and whom they could not help choosing, but simply because he was the bravest and wisest and best man in the land.   If there ever was a lawful King in this world, King Harold was one ; for he reigned by the best of all titles, the choice of the people.

So Harold the son of Godwine was King of the English and Lord of the Isle of Britain.   But there were some people in Northumberland who did not at once acknowledge him. But King Harold behaved in the wise and mild way in which he always did.   He did not fight against them or use any harshness, but he went to York, and took with him his friend Wulfstan, the holy Bishop of Worcester.   Wulfstan, besides his holiness, was a great speaker, as to be sure Harold was himself.   So Wulfstan and Harold talked to the Northum-brians, most likely in a meeting of their own Wise Men, and they came round and acknowledged the new King.   So Harold was King over all the land without any shedding of blood.   And it was, I think, most likely at this time that King Harold married Ealdgyth the daughter of Earl Ælfgar and widow of King Gruffydd of North Wales.   It is certain that he did marry her some time, and I think that this is altogether the most likely time.   For the King to marry the sister of Edwin and Morkere was a good way to seal, as it were, his new friendship with the men of Northumberland.

King Harold then came from York to Westminster to keep Easter.   The Chronicles say that he had little stillness while he reigned, and so it was.   Soon after Easter a comet was seen, which shone with great brightness for seven days.   In those days men thought that appearances of that sort foretold some-thing wonderful which was going to happen, especially that some great King or Kingdom was about to be overthrown. And indeed they might well think so just then.   For King Harold had two enemies to strive against at once.   Though he had been chosen King by the whole people of England, there were two men in the world who fancied they knew better who ought to be King in England than the English did them-selves.   These were the King's brother Tostig and William Duke of the Normans.   Tostig before his banishment had most likely hoped to be chosen King himself on Edward's death, and of course the Wise Men might, if they pleased, have chosen him instead of Harold; but he had quite lost any chance that he had by his doings in Northumberland. He seems now to have got quite reckless, and to have settled in his own mind to make his way into England again on any terms and at any risk, never minding how much mischief he did to any one. And Duke William, it is said, sent an embassy over to Harold almost as soon as Edward was dead to demand that he should resign the crown to him according to his oath, or at all events that he should hold it of him and marry his daughter. But King Harold, we are told, answered that his oath was void in itself, because he had sworn to do what none but the whole people of England could do, and now the whole people of England had chosen him for their King, and he could not give away the crown which they had given him. And he added, we are told, that an English King could not marry a foreign wife without the consent of the Wise Men. You must remember that all this is not in the Chronicles, but it is most likely that William did send an embassy to Harold, very likely more than one. But I do not suppose that William really thought that King Harold would really give up the crown at his asking. But he could now say that he had tried to get what he called his rights peaceably. So now he began to think of coming over to conquer England, and he set about trying to get friends everywhere. How far Duke William really persuaded himself that he had any right, of course we cannot tell; but he showed great skill in the way in which he mixed up different pretences together to deceive other people. First, he said that the English crown was his by right, as he was next of kin to Edward. Now he was not so near of kin to Edward as young Edgar was, and his being of kin to Edward was nothing to the purpose, if he had been never so near. For his kindred was only through Edward's mother Emma; William was not of the royal house of England, he was not a descendant of Cerdic, Ecgberht, and Alfred.[1] And, as you know, if he had been, it would have given him no actual right, but only a preference. Secondly, he said that Edward had left him the crown. Now I have told you that most likely Edward had once made him some promise of this kind; but

---

[1] William's wife Matilda was descended from Alfred in the female line, but he does not seem to have put this forward at all.

you know that the King could not leave his crown to whom
he pleased; he could only recommend to the Wise Men; and
whatever promise Edward had made to William he had re-
voked by recommending Harold.   Lastly, he said how Harold
had sworn to him and had broken his oath, how he had profaned
the relics of the saints, and so forth.   Now, as I have told you, it
is by no means clear what Harold really did swear, but supposing
he swore all that any one pretends that he swore, still, though this
might be a crime and a wrong in Harold, it could give William
no more right to the English crown than he had before.   Then
with all this he artfully mingled up stories about the massacre
of the Danes and the death of Alfred, and how the English,
especially Godwine and his sons, had unjustly driven out Archbishop Robert and the other Normans, and a great deal more
which might stir up men's minds, but which could not really
have anything to do with the matter.   You will see how very
artfully all this was put together.   No one thing by itself proved
anything, but altogether it sounded as if William had had
some great wrong done to him.   I see no reason to believe
that William had a single Englishman on his side, except it
was one Ralph of Norfolk, whose father had been *Staller* or
Master of the Horse to King Edward, and who now seems to
have been banished.   His mother was a Breton and he had
lands in Britanny; so he went over there and joined himself to
the Bretons who served under William.   And it is very likely,
though we do not know for certain, that some of the Frenchmen whom Godwine and Harold had allowed to stay in England may have done what they could for William.   But William,
by his clever way of putting things, made people on the Continent believe that he was all in the right.   And he sent to Rome,
and set forth how Harold had profaned the relics of the saints,
and he asked the Pope to bless his undertaking, and promised
that, if he succeeded, he would make England more obedient
to the Roman See and would take care that Peter's pence should
be paid more regularly.   This was a sum of a penny yearly for
each house, which used to be paid to the Pope.   The Pope at
this time was Alexander the Second, but the man who really
managed everything at Rome was the Archdeacon Hildebrand,
who was afterwards the great Pope Gregory the Seventh.

Some of you know his name as the Pope who made King Henry of Germany, who was afterwards Emperor, stand three days in the snow. I cannot say whether Hildebrand really thought William right or not, and it is certain that many of the Cardinals greatly withstood him, and said that the Church ought to have nothing to do with a matter which would bring about so much bloodshed. So there must have been some good and wise men in the Pope's Council. But Hildebrand insisted on helping William, because, whether William was right or wrong, his scheme at any rate opened a great opportunity for increasing the power of the Pope in England. So he made Pope Alexander approve of William's undertaking, and, when William was going to set out, he sent him a hair of Saint Peter in a ring, and a consecrated banner. So Duke William spent all the former part of the year in getting over people to his side, and in gathering together his army, and having his ships built. You may see the whole story in the Tapestry, from the very beginning. Duke William orders a fleet to be built, and you see men cutting down the trees.

Duke William however did not at first find his own Normans very willing to undertake such a great and perilous enterprise as the conquest of England. They said it was their duty to fight for their Duke in any common war at home, but that they were not bound to follow him to get crowns beyond the sea. So he held an Assembly at Lillebonne near the Seine, in a grand old hall—it was a new one then—which was pulled down some years back, and tried to persuade them. At first he met with great opposition, but the Barons were gradually won over, chiefly by William's great friend William Fitz-Osbern, though in the end they were rather tricked than persuaded. But when they were once in for it, however unwillingly, they did not draw back, but helped the Duke manfully. So Duke William began to get ready his fleet and army, and many men came to him not only from his own Duchy but from other countries. When King Harold heard of Duke William's preparations, he began to get ready the greatest host by land and by sea that had ever been known in England, and he set troops at different parts of the coast wherever the Normans were likely to land. You see this was very different from the way in which things were done in Æthelred's time. And most likely King Harold would have been able to keep the Normans out altogether, if he had had only the Normans to fight against; but it was as the Greek proverb says, Even Hêraklês cannot fight against two. For early in the year Tostig had gone into Normandy to try to get Duke William to help him. But William was much wiser than Tostig, and he was not in so great a hurry. So Tostig had pretty much to shift for himself. But soon after Easter he had got together some ships somehow; so he came from Flanders to the Isle of Wight, and began to plunder and make people pay tribute to him, and then he plundered all the coast as far as Sandwich. Meanwhile King Harold was in London, getting together his great army, and as soon as he was ready, he marched towards Sandwich, and then Tostig sailed away. So King Harold spent the whole of the summer in the south, arranging his fleet and army as I told you for the defence of the coast. But they waited, and Duke William did not come. It was the hardest thing in the world to keep an army together in those days, and the wonder is that Harold was able to keep his great army together so long as he did. But at last, on September 8th, after waiting so many months. there was nothing more for them to eat; so he was obliged to let his people go home again. That is, I mean, the great mass of the people of the southern shires, who were thus gathered together and taken away from their homes. Of course he kept his own housecarls, and no doubt his kinsfolk and friends and his own Thanes would mostly stay with him. If he could only have guarded the coast a few weeks longer, and if he had not been wanted elsewhere, things would have turned out very differently from what they did.

For when Tostig sailed away from Sandwich, he sailed to Lindesey and there plundered and slew men. But the two Earls, Edwin and Morkere, the sons of Ælfgar, came against him and drove him out, so he went away to Scotland to King Malcolm, and stayed there all the summer. According to the Norwegian account, he went to his cousin King Swegen in Denmark, and asked him to help him, saying how Cnut his uncle had conquered England, and how he, Swegen, could conquer it too. But Swegen answered: "Cnut was a great man, and I am a small man. Cnut won Norway without slash or blow, while it is as much as I can do to keep Denmark." So Tostig went on into Norway to King Harold Hardrada, the brother of Saint Olaf, of whom you have heard before. This Harold Hardrada was thought to be the greatest warrior of the North, and he had done all kinds of exploits in all parts of the world. He had served in the armies of the Eastern Emperors at Constantinople, who always kept a body of Scandinavian soldiers in their pay, and he had fought in Africa and Sicily, and had made the pilgrimage to Jerusalem, and after he came back to Norway he had carried on a long war with Swegen of Denmark. Tostig had told him that so great a warrior as he was would soon conquer England, and that moreover many of the people would join him, Tostig. But some of the Northmen thought it would not be so easy to conquer England; they said that our King Harold had with him his housecarls or *Thingmen*, any one of whom was a match for two men anywhere else. But at last Tostig persuaded Harold of Norway to set out. So say the Norwegians; but our English Chronicles say nothing about Tostig going to Denmark or Norway; they seem rather to imply that Tostig found Harold Hardrada sailing about somewhere near Scotland or the north of England, and their account reads almost as if his coming into Britain was quite unexpected, which it could hardly have been if Tostig had been going about to Denmark and Norway. Harold Hardrada had with him his son Olaf, and Paul and Erling the Earls of Orkney, who had joined him when he was sailing about Scotland. The Norwegians say that he also took his wife Elizabeth and his two daughters with him, but that he left them in Shetland. Anyhow Tostig and Harold Hardrada met at the mouth of the Tyne, and Tostig submitted to him and became his man, and they sailed together to the mouth of the Humber, plundering as they went. They then sailed up the Ouse to a place called Riccall, and there left Earl Paul with the ships and marched inland.

The Norwegian story has many wonders to tell us about this expedition, and how King Harold Hardrada and others in his fleet saw many strange omens and visions, most of which

x

boded ill to them. For instance, one Thored dreamed a dream how they landed in England and saw the English host coming with banners displayed, and before the host rode a huge witch-wife on a wolf, and as she rode she fed the wolf with the carcases of men, and as soon as he had eaten up one carcase, she gave him another, and she sang this song ; ·

> "The armed host lifts the bright red shield,
> As men are marching to the field ;
> The woman sprung of giants old
> Doth the King's sad fate behold ;
> Into the jaws of the swart-haired beast
> She sweeps men's corpses for his feast ;
> The wolf's fierce jaws with blood are red,
> By that woman ever fed."

Now they had got near to York as far as Fulford by the Ouse, and there the Earls Edwin and Morkere met them on the eve of Saint Matthew and fought against them, and both sides fought very valiantly, and the English made part of the Northmen to flee and followed after them : but then came up King Harold of Norway with his banner called the Landwaster, and he pressed mightily against the English that they fled, and more of them were drowned in the river than they whom the Northmen slew with the sword. So the Northmen had possession of the place of slaughter, and the city of York made peace with them and gave them one hundred and fifty hostages, and the Northmen gave to the men of York one hundred and fifty hostages. And the men of York received King Harold of Norway for King, and they swore to join him in making war on King Harold of England. And they said that other hostages should be given for the whole shire of York,[1] and King Harold of Norway and the Northmen went away to Stamfordbridge by the river of Derwent, and to Aldby the house of the old Kings, to wait for the hostages. But meanwhile the news was brought to King Harold of England that Earl Tostig and King Harold of Norway had landed in Northumberland. So King Harold got together his host, his Thanes and his housecarls and such men

---

[1] Deira is now beginning to be called Yorkshire, and Bernicia to be distinguished as Northumberland.

as he could get together speedily, to fight against King Harold of Norway and his host. And men told a tale how King Harold fell sick and was made whole again, which tale I will tell you in the way in which I tell you other such tales.

The Story of King Harold's Sickness and Recovery.

Now when Harold the son of Sigurd, King of the Northmen, and Earl Tostig the son of Godwine came into this land to subdue it, the news was brought to Harold the son of Godwine, King of the English. And King Harold sent forth to gather together his Thanes and his housecarls and all his men of war to go and fight against Earl Tostig his brother and against Harold King of the Northmen. But while he was gathering together his host, he was smitten with a great sickness. But he strove to hide his sickness from all men, and day by day he worked manfully to gather together his host, and in the night, when he could not sleep, he prayed to God and sought for the help of the Holy Rood in whose honour he had builded his minster at Waltham. Then Æthelsige the Abbot of the minster at Ramsey saw a vision by night, for the holy King Edward appeared to him and said, " I am Edward, who was but a little time ago King of the English. Go now to Harold who reigneth in my stead, and say unto him, ' Hearken, O King, to my words. Edward, who was King before thee, hath sent me to thee to speak a word in thine ears. Know then that thy prayer is heard, and be thou strong and of a good courage, and gather together thine host, and go forth to fight against the men who have come into thy land. Fear not, neither be dismayed ; for King Edward will pray for thee and for thine host, and thou shalt fight against thine enemies and overcome them and slay them with a great slaughter. And if thou doubtest whether King Edward hath sent me, or whether King Edward hath power to help thee, lo, this shall be a sign unto thee. Thou art sick with a great sickness, and no man knoweth thereof, for that thou hast hidden thy sickness from all men and hast striven manfully to gather together thine host. But Edward the King knoweth it well, and he knoweth

X 2

well how thou hast prayed to God and to the Holy Rood, and God hath heard thy prayer, and thou shalt recover of thy sickness, and go forth and deliver thy land out of the hand of Harold King of the Northmen.'" Then Æthelsige the Abbot arose from his sleep, and he did as the holy King Edward had bidden him, and he went to King Harold and spake unto him the words which the holy King Edward had put in his mouth. And when King Harold heard that saying, he was greatly comforted, and he arose up quickly, and straightway he was healed of his sickness and his strength came again unto him, and he gave great thanks to God, and he gathered together his host and went forth to fight against Harold King of the Northmen.

Now I do not ask you to believe this tale as it stands, and yet it is one which is well worth reading and thinking about. It may or it may not be true that, when King Harold was setting forth to march to the North, he fell sick and recovered. If it were so, we can quite understand how such a story might grow up. And there is another thing that you may remark in it. Edward appears to Æthelsige and bids him take his message to Harold, when one would have thought that he might just as well have appeared to Harold himself. But you will generally find in what are called ghost stories that the ghost does not go to the person with whom his business really is, but goes to some one else and sends him on his errand. And some of you may perhaps remember a story in the early Roman History how Jupiter has a message for one of the Consuls, and how, instead of going to the Consul himself, he goes to a poor man in the country and bids him go to the Consul, and how the poor man is afraid to go, and how his son dies and how he himself loses the use of his limbs, till at last he is carried to the Consul with the message, and then Jupiter gives him the use of his limbs again, but I do not remember that his son came to life again. You will see that all these are stories of the same kind. But the reason why I wish you specially to remark this story is this. It is plain the men who put this story together looked on Edward as a saint who was able to work wonders. But it is also plain that they did not look on Harold as a bad King or an usurper, or one with whom Edward was likely to be angry; but they looked on Edward and Harold as being good friends, and they thought that Edward would be likely to use his power as a glorified saint to help the King whom he had himself chosen to reign in his stead. Now you see that this quite falls in with the true history, and this no doubt long remained the English way of looking at things, in opposition to all the Norman lies and slanders which I have so often told you of. I must now go back to my History.

When King Harold had got together his army, he marched along the old Roman road from London to York, and he pressed on as fast as he could, stopping, so the Chronicles say, neither day nor night. Of course we must not take this quite literally; it only means that they marched on as fast as men and horses could go. It must have been while they were on their march that the battle of Fulford was fought, and no doubt the news would make them go on even quicker than before. You will remember that the battle of Fulford was fought on Wednesday, and that York surrendered to Harold of Norway on the next Sunday. On that Sunday evening, September 24, King Harold of England reached Tadcaster on the Wharf, which was the last stage of the Roman road from London to York, and near which the famous battle of Towton was fought about four hundred years afterwards. Here King Harold found the English fleet, which had sailed up the Wharf to get out of the way of the fleet of the Northmen when they sailed up the Ouse. So King Harold reviewed the fleet, and the next morning, Monday September 25, he set out again and marched through York, where the people received him gladly, but where he could not now stay long. So he pressed on to Stamfordbridge and came upon the Northmen unawares. They seem to have been spread abroad on both sides of the Derwent, and those who were on the right bank, the side nearest to York, seem to have been in bad order and not to have had on their full harness. Still they fought very bravely against the English, but they were most of them killed or driven into the river. Then one of our Chronicles tells us how one valiant man of the Northmen guarded the bridge against the host of the English, so that men could not pass the bridge. And he slew as many as forty men with his axe. And one man shot at him with an arrow, but it slew him not. Then went another Englishman in a boat below the bridge and smote him under the corslet that he died. Then King Harold and all his host crossed the bridge and fought against the Northmen who were on the other side. And now came the hardest part of the fighting. For the Northmen on the left bank of the river had now had time to put themselves in battle array. And with them were King Harold of Norway and Earl Tostig and all the most valiant men of the host. So there was hard fighting for a long while, and many men on both sides were killed, but in the end the English had the victory, and King Harold of Norway and Earl Tostig were killed, and King Harold of England and his host overcame the Northmen and smote them and slew them with a great slaughter. And the English had possession of the place of slaughter. And King Harold took oaths and hostages of Olaf son of King Harold of Norway and of Paul Earl of the Orkneys, who had stayed by the ships, and he let them go in peace. So King Harold the son of Godwine won the great fight of Stamfordbridge, and saved England out of the hand of Tostig his brother and out of the hand of King Harold the son of Sigurd.

This is the true story as far as I can make it out from our own books. The Chronicles tell us something, and still more may be made out from Henry of Huntingdon, who gives a very full and spirited account. There can be no doubt that he put it together out of a ballad which was made at the time, such an one, we may be sure, as the Song of Maldon. This is the real account, as far as we can see, but the Norwegian story has a great deal more to tell, much of which cannot be true, but as it is a famous and beautiful tale, I will tell it you as a tale.

The Story of the Fight of Stamfordbridge.

Now Harold the son of Sigurd King of the Northmen had come into England with a great host, and with him came Earl Tostig the son of Godwine, who had fled out of the land from the face of his brother Harold King of the English. So they sailed up the river of Ouse, and they landed near the city of York, and there fought against them Morkere and Waltheof the Earls, and King Harold the son of Sigurd and Earl Tostig smote them, and slew Earl Morkere, and Earl Waltheof fled into the castle of York and saved himself there. And then many of the men of the land submitted to King Harold the son of Sigurd and to Earl Tostig. So King Harold marched towards York to Stamfordbridge to take the castle, and the men of the castle and of the city held a meeting, and they submitted to King Harold and gave him hostages. This was on a Sunday, and on the Monday there was to be another meeting, when King Harold was to settle everything for the government of the city and of the land. So King Harold went back to his ships for the night. But that same evening came Harold the son of Godwine, King of the English, to the city with a great host of horsemen and footmen, and he came into the city and the men of the city received him gladly. But King Harold the son of Sigurd and all the host of the Northmen knew not that he was there.

So in the morning King Harold the son of Sigurd blew a trumpet and bade his men go on shore. For now would he go and take full possession of the city of York. So of every three men two went with the King and one stayed with the ships. And with the King went Earl Tostig the son of Godwine, but with the ships stayed Olaf the King's son, and Paul Earl of the Orkneys, and Eystein Orre, a brave man whom the King loved and to whom he had said that he would give Mary his daughter to be his wife. Now the day was hot, so they laid aside their harness and marched along merrily. But as they drew near to the city, they saw a great dust as of men and horses marching. And presently they saw the flash of arms and of burnished shields. And King Harold of Norway halted his men, and said to Earl Tostig, "Knowest thou what is this host that cometh towards us?" And Earl Tostig answered, "I know not as yet of a surety what it is; perchance it is the host of the English coming against us; perchance it is only some of my kinsfolk and friends coming to welcome us and to bow to thee and be thy men." Then said King Harold of Norway, "Then will we halt awhile, till the host draws nearer." So they halted, and the host drew nearer, and they saw that it was a very great host, and the arms of the men of the host shone like glancing ice. Then said King Harold of Norway, "Lo, verily this is the host of the English, and King Harold the son of Godwine cometh against us; let us now devise good rede for ourselves." Then spake Earl Tostig, "Let us go back to our ships, and get us our harness and the rest of our men, and then let us fight; or rather let us go on board of our ships and fight from thence, for then the horsemen of the English cannot harm us." Then spake King Harold of Norway, "Nay, let us rather abide here and send three men on swift horses to the ships, and bid the rest of our men come to help us. Verily the English shall see some hard hand-play before I yield unto them." Then spake Earl Tostig, "Be it, O King, as it seemeth good unto thee; of a truth I have no mind to flee before my brother and his host." Then King Harold the son of Sigurd spake unto Frirek his banner-bearer, and bade him set up his banner which men called the Landwaster. And he marshalled his host around the banner, and set them in a circle with their shields set firmly together, which men call the shield-wall, and he bade them hold their spears well against the horses of the English. Then King Harold the son of Sigurd rode round his host to see that all was as he had bidden. Now King Harold rode on a black horse, and his horse stumbled, and the King fell to the ground. And he arose speedily and said "Truly, a fall is lucky for a traveller." Now by this time the host of the English had come near, and King Harold of England saw King Harold of Norway fall. And with King Harold of England were certain Northmen who knew King Harold of Norway.

Then spake Harold the son of Godwine, King of the English, " Know ye who is that goodly man who hath fallen from his horse, he with the blue kirtle and the goodly helm?"

Then the Northmen who were with him answered the King, " Of a truth that goodly man who hath fallen from his horse is Harold the son of Sigurd, King of the Northmen."

Then spake Harold the son of Godwine, King of the English, " Truly he is a tall man and of a goodly presence, but I ween that his luck hath left him."

Then there rode forth from the host of the English twenty men of the Thingmen or Housecarls, any one man of whom, men said, could fight against any other two men in the whole world. And they and their horses were clothed with armour all over. And they drew nearer to the host of the Northmen, and one of the horsemen of the English spake and said, " Is Earl Tostig the son of Godwine in this host?"

And Earl Tostig answered, " It cannot be said that he is not here."

Then the horseman answered, and said, "King Harold of England greeteth well Earl Tostig his brother, and saith that he shall again have all Northumberland; nay rather than that his brother should be his enemy, he will give him a third of his kingdom to reign over with him."

Then Earl Tostig answered and said, " Truly last winter my brother had nought for me but words of scorn and hatred, but now he speaketh me fair. Had he spoken me thus fair last winter, truly many men who are now dead would be still alive. But tell me this also, If I hearken to the words of my brother and make peace with him, what will my brother King Harold of England give to King Harold of Norway for his toil in coming hither?"

And the horseman answered and said, " Seven feet of the ground of England, or more perchance, seeing he is taller than other men."

Then Earl Tostig answered and said, " Go thy way then, and tell King Harold of England to gird up his loins for the battle ; for never shall men say in Norway that Earl Tostig left King Harold the son of Sigurd and went over to his foes. Know this, that we will either die here like men or we will win England for our own with our own arms."

And when the horsemen of the English heard that saying, they spake not again, but rode away to the host of the English. Then spake Harold the son of Sigurd, King of the Northmen, "Who is that man who spake so well unto thee?" And Earl Tostig answered and said, "That man who spake so well unto me is my brother Harold the son of Godwine, King of the English." Then spake Harold the son of Sigurd, King of the Northmen, "Then didst thou wrong to hide this thing so long from me; for truly he had come so near to our host that he should never have gone back to tell of the slaughter of our men." Then spake Earl Tostig the son of Godwine, "True, O King; and verily it was not wise in so great a King thus to risk himself. Yet knew I that my brother would offer me great gifts and rich lordships, and, had I betrayed him, I should have been the murderer of my brother. Now if one of us twain must fall, rather would I that he should be my murderer than that I should be his." Then Harold the son of Sigurd, King of the Northmen, turned away from Earl Tostig, and spake unto his own men, and said, "Lo, yonder man is little of stature, yet sat he well in his stirrups."

And now King Harold of Norway began to make him ready for the battle. And he put on his coat of mail which was called Emma,[1] and which was so strong that no man could pierce it. And he made a song and sang it, and the song pleased him not, and he made another song which pleased him better, and he sang that instead. And now the battle began, for the horsemen of the English came riding up against the Northmen, and the Northmen kept them off with their spears. And this happened divers times, and at last the English began to fail and rode not up so fiercely as they had ridden at first. Now as long as the Northmen kept the shield-wall which they had made, no man could come near them to hurt them. But when the English began to give way, the Northmen broke the shield-wall and followed them. And when the shield-wall was broken, the English turned, and rode up from all sides, and hurled darts at the Northmen and shot at them with arrows. Now King Harold the son of Sigurd stood by

---

[1] I suppose this is Emma, a woman's name. The Northmen often gave names to their swords, so perhaps they did to their coats of mail also.

his banner the Landwaster in the midst of the host. But when he saw that the shield-wall was broken, he gat him to the front of his host and laid about him with his two-handed sword, so that the English were wellnigh put to flight. But one of the English shot him with an arrow in the throat that he died. Then Earl Tostig took the King's place by the King's banner the Landwaster, and the fight stopped for a while, now that King Harold the son of Sigurd was dead. Then King Harold the son of Godwine spake yet again to Tostig his brother, and offered him peace, and offered quarter to all the Northmen who still lived. But all the Northmen answered with one voice and said, "We will take no quarter from the English ; we will rather die, one man's body over the other." So the battle began again. And then came up Eystein Orre with the rest of the host, all in full harness. And now was the fiercest fighting of all, and Eystein's men slew many of the English, and wellnigh put them to flight. And at last Eystein's men waxed as it were mad, and that they might fight the more easily, they threw away their shields and their coats of mail. But thereby did the English smite them the more easily that they died. So the more part of the chief men of the host were slain, and at eventide the remnant turned and fled, and King Harold of England had the victory, and the English had possession of the place of slaughter. So died Harold the son of Sigurd, King of the Northmen, and with him died Tostig the Earl, the son of Earl Godwine of England.

This is a very fine story, and well told, and the characters are well preserved, for the speeches put into the mouths of the two Harolds and of Tostig are just such as they would be likely to make. But we cannot trust the story ; it is so full of mistakes. For instance the Norwegian, or rather Icelandic, writer, whose name is Snorro, says that Morkere and Waltheof were brothers of King Harold, as if Godwine must have been everybody's father, whereas we know that Morkere was a son of Ælfgar and Waltheof was a son of Siward. Whether Waltheof was at Stamfordbridge we cannot say, but Snorro directly after gives quite a wrong account of his death, and we know that Morkere was not killed at Fulford, for he lived long after. Then the account of the battle is very strange and cannot be right. For you all know well that it was not the manner of the English to fight on horseback or to trust much to arrows; and there are many things in the story of the battle which really sound as if they were copied from the account of the Battle of Senlac (of which we shall hear presently) only putting the English instead of the Normans. Snorro wrote in the thirteenth century, and I can only suppose that he described our King Harold's army after the pattern of an English army of that time, when the English horsemen, and the English archers still more, were getting famous; that is to say, by Snorro's time the English had learned the Norman way of fighting. But in the time of the two Harolds, the English had very few archers, and no horsemen. I mean that they had no men who fought on horseback, for you know that the great men, and seemingly the housecarls too, rode to the fight, but they got off their horses when the fighting began. If our Harold had had such horsemen as Snorro says at Stamfordbridge, he would not have been without any at Senlac. And the account of Harold Hardrada being shot by the arrow almost seems as if it were taken from the death of our Harold. The description of the Northmen fixing their spears and the English riding against them is just like what we read of King Edward the First's battles with the Scots. In truth at the time of the battle of Stamfordbridge the English and the Northmen fought in nearly the same way, only the Northmen seem still to fight with swords, while the English had taken to use axes. Then, if the story in Snorro had really been written at the time, surely that account of the one Northman keeping the bridge, which one English Chronicler has preserved, would not have been left out. And Snorro shows that he knew nothing at all of the geography, for he fancies that Riccall and Stamfordbridge were close together and that both were close under the walls of York. And he seems to have had no notion at all of the river Derwent and the bridge. So we cannot believe his story, but we must be satisfied with what we can find in our books. And from them we may be sure that our men did not win the battle by the help of horsemen or archers, but that they fought and won in the old way, fighting on foot, and cleaving down the shield-wall hand to hand with their axes.

Tostig had two sons, Ketil and Skule. They both settled in Norway and left many descendants. So if we wish to see descendants of Earl Godwine in the male line, Norway is the place where we are most likely to find them.

The battle of Stamfordbridge was fought on the 25th of September, and four days later Duke William landed in Sussex. Had there been no war in the North, he hardly could have landed. But you see that the force of the country had just been disbanded because they had no more to eat, and Harold's own followers, his housecarls and the men who were his own thanes and friends and kinsfolk were with him at Stamfordbridge. So the Normans were able to land without any man withstanding them. They sailed across from Saint Valery at the mouth of the Somme, in the land of Count Guy of Ponthieu, and landed at Pevensey. There are the walls of the Roman city of Anderida still standing, the city which the Welsh had, almost six hundred years before, defended against the South-Saxons, and which Ælle and Cissa had stormed, and left not a Welshman alive. One story, a story told also of Cæsar when he landed in Africa, says that, as Duke William landed, he stumbled, and, as he got up with his hands full of earth, one of his men said, "This is a good omen, my Lord Duke, thou hast already taken *seisin* of the land of England." For, when a lord granted lands to a vassal, he often gave him *seisin* or personal possession of the lands by giving him a clod of earth from those lands as a sign. So Duke William was said to have taken seisin of England, because his hands were full of English earth. Some say that he burned his ships that his men might have no retreat if they were beaten, and might therefore fight the more valiantly. But this is not true. William found no one to withstand him at Pevensey, so he occupied the town, and made a fort, seemingly in a corner of the old Roman walls. He then marched on to Hastings, and abode there, making himself a castle of wood on the hill where the ruins of the later stone castle now stand, and from Hastings he harried the country all round for fifteen days, up to the day of the great battle.

Now there was a Norman favourite of Edward's, named Robert the son of Wymarc,[1] who was his Staller and who had watched by his death-bed, and to whom he had given lands in divers places. This Robert now sent to Duke William, saying "My Lord Duke, I come of thy land, and I wish thee well, and I should be grieved if any evil were to betide thee. Know then that King Harold the son of Godwine is gone to the North with all his mighty men, and he hath smitten Tostig the Earl his brother and King Harold the son of Sigurd the mightiest of all warriors, and if thou abidest here he will come hither and smite thee also and thine host, for no man may stand before him. Get thee back then into thine own land before he cometh; for I would not that thou and thine host should be smitten." But Duke William answered and said, "I will not get me back into mine own land; for this land is mine also, and I come but to win the Crown which is mine of right. And now have I with me sixty thousand men; but if I had but ten thousand, I would not turn back till I had smitten Earl Harold and chastised him for the false oath which he sware unto me." But before this time, while the Normans were yet at Pevensey, an English Thane had seen them land, and he went and mounted his horse, and rode northwards, and rested not day or night till he came to York, where King Harold and his host were resting after their great fight at Stamfordbridge. So the Thane came to King Harold, and said "My Lord O King, Duke William and his Normans have landed in Sussex, and they have built them a fort at Pevensey, and they are harrying the land, and they will of a truth win thy Kingdom from thee, unless thou goest speedily and guardest thy land well against them." And presently there came a churl also who had come from Hastings, and he told King Harold how that the Normans had marched from Pevensey to Hastings, and how they had built

[1] You might not have guessed that Wymarc was a woman's name, but so it seems to be, and Robert seems to be called from his mother. I cannot tell who he was, save that he is called a kinsman of King Edward's. But so are a great many people so called both in England and in Normandy of which it is hard to trace the pedigree.

them a castle at Hastings and how they were harrying the land far and wide. Then King Harold answered and said, " This is evil news indeed; would that I had been there to guard the coast, and Duke William never should have landed ; but I could not be here and there at the same time." Then King Harold got together his own following, his housecarls and his own Thanes and kinsfolk and friends, the men who had fought with him at Stamfordbridge, and he marched with all speed to London. And he sent through all the land, bidding all men everywhere to come to his standard and fight against Duke William and the Normans. And the men of Wessex and East-Anglia came gladly, and many of the men of Mercia also, from all those shires through which the King marched on his way to London, and from the shires which were under the King's brothers, and under Waltheof the son of Siward. But from the other shires of Mercia men came not, nor did they come from any part of Northumberland, save only such as followed the King straight from York. For Edwin and Morkere the Earls remembered not how King Harold had saved them and their land out of the hand of Earl Tostig and out of the hand of King Harold of Norway. And they thought not how he had married Eald-gyth their sister, and how he had kept back King Edward from making war on them. For they said in their hearts, " What care we if Harold falls and if Duke William reigns over Wessex? We shall be the better able to keep Mercia and Northumberland, and to be Kings instead of Earls." So Edwin and Morkere and all the men of the North came not to King Harold's muster.

As we are now coming so near to the great battle, I think it right to tell you whence it is that we get our knowledge of the battle and the whole campaign. The English writers, both the Chronicles and Florence, give us very few details. It is plain that they did not like to talk about it, and that they cut the story as short as they could. From them we should hardly learn more than that a battle was fought at such a time and place, in which the Normans had the victory, and in which King Harold and his brothers and many other good men were killed. It is therefore from the Norman writers, who naturally write much longer accounts, that we have to learn all our details ;

but of course we must use a certain caution in following them. There are three chief Norman accounts. The first is the Life of William by William of Poitiers, who was Archdeacon of Lisieux and the Duke's chaplain. His book stops suddenly short long before the end of William's reign, for it was written during his lifetime more as a panegyric or book written in William's praise than as anything else. William of Poitiers is very partial to his own master, and he reviles Godwine and Harold in the most savage way; still his book is very valuable as being a book written at the time, and it gives a full account of the battle and of the whole campaign. The second is a poem in Latin elegiacs, expressly about the battle, called "Carmen de Bello Hastingensi." This was written by Guy Bishop of Amiens, who was of the house of the Counts of Ponthieu. He also lived at the time, and part of the poem is addressed to William in the second person. Guy gives a full account of William's voyage and landing, of the battle itself and of the whole story down to William's coronation. He tells us a great many things which are not to be found in any other account, and he gives a very clear picture of the ground and of the array of the two armies. The third account and, I am inclined to say, the best of all the three, was not written with a pen but was wrought in stitch-work. This is the famous Tapestry of Bayeux, where the whole story from Harold's setting out to go to Normandy till the end of the battle is all worked in pictures, with Latin legends over each scene. There is no doubt that it was wrought very soon after the battle, but there is no reason at all to think that it was wrought by William's Queen Matilda. It is plain that it was wrought by order of Bishop Odo and was given by him to his cathedral church at Bayeux, where it used to be kept, though it is now in the Library there. That it was made for Odo and for Bayeux is plain, because several people are made very prominent in it, whom we hear nothing of anywhere else, but whom we know from Domesday to have been followers of Odo's, and who were therefore no doubt well known at Bayeux. This Tapestry gives the best and fairest account of all the Norman authorities; you will easily see, if you think a moment, that though the Tapestry might show any part of the story in quite a wrong way, yet it could not colour and insinuate in the way that a story told or written can do. And it is a great thing to see the men as well as to hear about them, and to know what sort of clothes and armour and weapons they had, all which the Tapestry tells us better than anything else. Besides these three accounts, there is the account given by Master Wace, who was a Canon of Bayeux and born in Jersey, and who wrote a book in Old-French verse called the *Roman de Rou*. This is a history of the Dukes of Normandy, and it is very valuable both in itself and as an example of the Old-French tongue. Master Wace did not finish his book till the reign of Henry the Second, but I think that he must have been an old man then, and that he must have been getting together materials for many years, as in one place he seems to imply that his father crossed over with William and that he heard part of his tale from him. Anyhow, though he did not live at the time, he was a very honest and careful writer, and he takes great pains to compare one story with another, and, when he does not know a thing, he fairly tells you that he does not know it. So I set great store by him. Besides these chief accounts, several things may be picked up from William of Malmesbury and Henry of Huntingdon, and also some things special about the place are found in the Chronicle of Battle Abbey and in a little book called " Brevis Relatio," a short and generally very bitter account of the Conquest, written in Henry the First's time. From all these accounts it is, I think, not very hard to get a good and full account of the battle. But I doubt whether anybody will quite fully understand it, if he does not go over the ground as I have done, with the original books in his hand or at any rate fresh in his head. I will now go back to my story.

While the English host was gathering in London, King Harold and Duke William seem to have sent messengers to one another, as if it had been possible for them to come to any agreement without fighting. Of course William was most anxious to make his cause look as fair as possible, and he would not lose any chance that could help him. But our own writers, as I said, seem not to have liked to write about so sad a story more than they could help ; so they cut everything very

Y

short, and tell us nothing about these messages; and the Norman writers tell the story with such contradictions that it is impossible to make out what really happened. It was a case where messages were of no use, because it was quite impossible that any real agreement could be come to. Thus we are told that Harold offered William money to go away quietly, as if he had been a Danish pirate. We are told too that William offered to Harold at different times that, if he would give up the crown, he should have all Northumberland, and that Gyrth should have his father Godwine's Earldom of Wessex. Then William offered that the Pope should judge between them, which must have been a mere cheat, as the Pope had already judged in William's favour. Then we are told that William said that it would be a great pity to kill so many men in both armies to decide a quarrel between their two selves. He and Harold would do better to fight, man against man, and let the one that killed or beat the other be king. You see the cunning of this; it was at once an appeal to Harold's personal bravery and to his humanity. It was easy to say, if Harold declined the challenge, either that he was afraid or that he did not care how many men were killed in his own quarrel. Of course William wanted people to believe that it was merely a personal quarrel between himself and Harold. But our great King was much too wise to be caught in any of Duke William's traps. He answered that it was not his quarrel, but the quarrel of the people of England. I told you once before, when I was talking about Cnut and Edmund, that, if Harold and William had fought and if Harold had killed William, it was not the least likely that the Norman army would have gone quietly home again. And if William had killed Harold, it would have given him no more right to the crown of England than he had before, and it is not the least likely that the English people would have submitted to him without fighting. In either case there would have been a battle all the same; only one or the other army would have had to fight without its great leader. It is hard to tell how much of all these stories of messages is true, and, if any be true, how much happened while Harold was still in London and how much after he came into Sussex, the whole is told with such utter confusion. Then there are

other stories ; how Harold sent spies to Duke William's camp,
and how Duke William let the spies be taken through the
camp and shown everything, and then let them go in peace.
Those of you who have read any Grecian history will remember
exactly the same story of Xerxes. Then we are told how Duke
William himself met Harold's messenger, and told him that he
was only the Duke's seneschal, and got out of him all that he
could, and then brought him before all his chief men, and then
said, " I am William Duke of the Normans." Then we read
a more foolish story than all, how Harold's mother Gytha
wanted him to stay in London and not go out to fight with the
Normans, and how he spurned her away with his foot. Against
this we may set a story equally silly, which is told by Snorro
the Icelander. This is that, when Duke William was setting
out, his wife Matilda wanted him to stay behind, so he kicked
her in the breast, and his spur ran into her breast that she died.
Now Matilda did not die till many years after this time ; but
even if it were not so, I think you know by this time what to
say to stories like these. Indeed it is plain enough that the
story about Harold's mother and the story about William's wife
are really only one story, fitted with different names in the way
that I have so often told you of.

But meanwhile I will tell you an English story, which is at
least better worth hearing.

The Story of the Holy Rood of Waltham.

You have heard long ago how the Holy Rood was found at
Lutgaresbury in the land of the Sumorsætas, which men now
call Montacute or the Peaked Hill ; and how the Rood was
brought of oxen to Waltham of the East-Saxons ; and how
Tofig the Proud built there a church and set two priests to
serve God therein ; and how Earl Harold the son of Godwine
built there a greater and a fairer church, even the great minster
of the Holy Rood at Waltham, and how he enriched it with
many goodly gifts and set thirteen priests to serve God in the
same. And when Earl Harold was chosen King over the whole
people of the English, still he loved the church of Waltham,

which he had built, and he sought to enrich it with yet goodlier gifts and more holy relics than he had given aforetime when he was but an Earl. And when King Harold had gone to the North, and had fought the great fight which men call the fight of Stamfordbridge, and had smitten Tostig the Earl his brother and Harold the son of Sigurd, King of the Northmen, then came he back to his own house at Waltham, and dwelt there awhile in peace.[1] And while the King dwelt at Waltham, there came a messenger to him saying, " Lo, William Duke of the Normans hath landed at Pevensey of the South-Saxons, and hath built him a fort at Hastings and is harrying the whole land." Then King Harold answered and said, " Then will I go forth and fight against him, and by God's help I will smite him and his host, even as I have smitten Harold the son of Sigurd, King of the Northmen."   But the King's friends said to him, " Tarry awhile, O King, till thou canst gather a greater host than thou hast ; for the men who fought with thee at Stamfordbridge are scattered every man to his own home."   But the King would not hearken, and he said, " Nay, but I will go forth with such men as I have, that I may come upon the Normans unawares and smite them suddenly, before other men come across the sea to help them."   But before the King went forth, he arose early in the morning to pray in the minster of the Holy Rood. And he took with him certain relics from his own chapel, and he put them upon the altar, and he vowed a vow to God that, if God would give him victory over the Normans, he would give to the church of Waltham yet greater gifts and would set yet more priests to serve God therein, and that he would give himself to serve God as it were a slave redeemed from bondage. Then the canons and all the priests and the singers and all the men of the church of Waltham formed in a procession and led the King to the door of the church where the Holy Rood was.   And King Harold fell down before the Holy Rood with his face to the ground and his arms spread out like the arms

---

[1] You see this cannot be true, as we know that Harold heard the news of William's landing while he was still at York, and that he then marched straight from York to London. But that, while he was waiting in London, he went to Waltham to pray in his own church, before he went forth to the war in Sussex, is very likely indeed.

of one nailed to the cross. And he prayed. Now before this the face of our Lord on the Holy Rood looked upwards. But as King Harold lay on the ground and prayed, lo, the image bowed its head towards the King as he lay. And ever since that day the head of the image on the Holy Rood hath been bowed to the ground. And I who tell this tale[1] have spoken with many men who saw the Holy Rood while the face of our Lord thereon looked upwards. But one man only saw the image bow its head while King Harold lay praying. This was Thurkill the sacrist, who stood by the King, and from him I heard it; for I saw him two years before he died and I helped to bury him. So Thurkill the sacrist saw this great wonder, that the image bowed and looked sad. And he feared greatly, for he thought that it was an evil sign, and he feared that some great harm would come upon King Harold and upon all England. So he told his brethren the canons, and when King Harold went forth to fight in Sussex, they sent two of the chief of them, Osgod and Æthelric the Childmaster, that they might see how it fared with King Harold and with all their friends that were with him, and that if he or they should die in the fight, they might bring their bodies home to bury them in the minster of the Holy Rood.

King Harold stayed about six days in London, gathering men together from all parts, and he made ready to go forth to the war against Duke William. And a story is told how Earl Gyrth his brother counselled him to abide in London and gather more men, and to let him, Gyrth, go forth with the host to the war. "Thou hast sworn," he said, "to the Duke, and perchance thou mayest meet him in battle face to face, and it were not well to meet one to whom thou hast sworn. But I have sworn to no man save to thee, and I can meet any man in the world with a safe conscience. Let me then go forth and fight, and do thou abide here, and gather fresh troops, and

---

[1] The story is told by one who had been canon of Waltham and who wrote the book "De Inventione Sanctæ Crucis Walthamensis." According to his account, Thurkill died in 1126, while the writer was a boy attached to the College.

then go forth and lay waste all the land as thou goest, that the Frenchmen may not be able to find food." And King Harold answered, " Thy counsel is wise, my brother ; yet may not a King of the English fall back before the foe. And God forbid that I should ever lay waste mine own land and harm mine own folk ! Hath not this people chosen me to be their King? I must therefore guard them and fight for them while I live, and I will never lay waste their land." You may believe this story or not as you please; it is only Norman writers who tell it ; but anyhow it sets before us how even his enemies knew Harold for a King who loved his people and would not harm his own land.

So King Harold set forth from London, with Earl Gyrth his brother and Earl Leofwine his brother, and all his house-carls, and the men of London and of Kent and very many of the men of all the southern and eastern shires of England, Now King Harold had an uncle whose name was Ælfwig ; he was the brother of Earl Godwine, and he was a monk, and he was Abbot of the New Minster at Winchester. But when Duke William landed and harried the land, and when King Harold his nephew called all men to join his standard, then Ælfwig thought that those were times when even priests and monks ought to fight. So he and twelve of his monks put harness over their monks' garb and went forth and joined King Harold on his march. And Leofric the Abbot of Peterborough, who was the nephew of the great Leofric the Earl, came also from his monastery of Peter-borough, which men call the Golden Borough, and he too joined the King's standard. And the King marched on through the land of the South-Saxons, and he came to the hill which men then called Senlac, whereon now is the town of Battle, and there he pitched his camp by the hoar apple-tree.[1]

The place was then all wild, seemingly without any house or church or anything ; but it was a very strong post, being the last spur of the hill country in the north of Sussex, standing out like a sort of peninsula, as it were to meet the hills that are nearer to the sea. A little way off to the south is a

[1] So says one of the Chronicles. You must fancy some very aged and famous tree, perhaps a sacred tree in the days of heathendom.

small detached hill, which I fancy was made use of as an outpost. On the main hill King Harold took up his post and fenced it in with a palisade. I wish you to mark how wise a captain our great King was, and how well he suited his way of fighting to the enemies whom he had to fight against. The Norwegians and the English fought very much in the same way, forming with the shield-wall, hurling their javelins, and then fighting hand to hand with their great swords and axes. But now Harold had to deal with an enemy who fought in quite another way. I told you before, when I was telling you about Earl Ralph and his bad luck in the Welsh war, how the English, even their greatest men, fought on foot, while among the Normans and other French all at least who were gentlemen fought on horseback. Also the Normans had many very skilful archers, while the English had scarcely any. Now you will at once see that it would never have done for our men to charge, axe in hand, on the Norman horsemen, as they had done on Harold Hardrada's shield-wall. The best thing for them was to encamp on a place where the Normans would have to attack them, where they could make their own shield-wall as strong as possible, and where the Norman horses would be of the least possible use. So King Harold pitched his camp on the hill, so that it would be the hardest thing in the world for the Norman horsemen to ride up the sides. For as they were coming up, the English would hurl their javelins at them, and when they came close they could not well ride up through the barricades, with our men behind the barricades with their axes ready to cut down any one who came near. I am no soldier myself, but, as far as I can understand such matters, King Harold seems to me to have been one of the greatest generals that ever lived, and if all his troops had only done as he bade them, it is quite certain that the Normans never could have won the battle.

The English seem to have stayed only one night on the hill. The stories of the messages which passed between Harold and William are, as I told you, so confused that it is hard to tell whether they all took place while Harold was still in London or whether any of them happened after he had reached Senlac. But there is one story how King Harold sent a spy to the Norman camp, and how the spy came back and said that among the Frenchmen there were many times more priests than there were soldiers. He called them priests because they had their upper lips shaven. But King Harold told him that he would find these French priests right valiant soldiers indeed. And another story is that King Harold and his brother Earl Gyrth rode out themselves to spy the Norman camp, and how they quarrelled and nearly fought, but that when they got back to the camp they let no one know that they had quarrelled. Now could any Norman know about this? That some messages passed between the armies, and that Harold refused either to give up his crown or to stake it on a single combat, is likely enough, but I can tell you nothing for certain.

It was now Friday evening, the 13th of October, 1066, and all men in both armies knew that the fight would be on the morrow. The English ate and drank and were merry, and they sang the old songs of their fathers. Cannot you fancy them sitting by their fires and singing the songs about Brunanburh and Maldon? I do not think they would fight any the worse for doing so. And they had priests and monks in their army too to pray with them and bless them, and no doubt they did so. But we have no account of these things from any English writer, and the Normans wish to make out how much more pious they were than the English. They tell us how, while the English did nothing but drink and sing, the Duke's army spent the night in prayers, and processions, and how Bishop Odo of Bayeux went through the camp exhorting and blessing and hearing confessions. Most likely Abbot Ælfwig and Abbot Leofric did the same. But however either army spent the night, it is quite certain that both sides were equally ready for very sharp work in the morning.

So on Saturday morning, being the feast of Saint Calixtus the Pope, Duke William arose early in the morning, and heard mass and received the holy communion, and then marshalled his army and made a speech to them. He told them that he had come into England to assert his just right to the crown which King Edward had left him, and to punish Earl Harold, who had become his man and had broken his oath to him. He reminded them of the fame of the Normans in war, how they had won their land in Gaul with their own swords, and how they had given law to the Kings of the Franks, and how they had conquered all their enemies everywhere. But the English, he told them, had never been famed in war ; the Danes had conquered them and taken their land whenever they pleased. Then he went on to tell of all the wrongs which he said the felon English had done : how they had slain the Danes, the kinsmen of the Normans, on the day of Saint Brice ; how they had betrayed and slain their own Ætheling Ælfred, the Duke's cousin, and the Normans who came with him ; how they had driven out Archbishop Robert and so many other Normans at the time when Godwine came back from banishment. All these wrongs he said he had come to avenge ; and God, he knew, would maintain their righteous cause. The army then marched from Hastings to the hill which is called Telham, whence they could see the English camp on Senlac. There the knights put on their coats of mail and changed the light horses on which they rode from Hastings for the war-horses which they were to use in battle. Then Duke William called for his coat of mail, and went about to put it on, but the fore part of the coat was turned backwards. Then said Duke William, " Now is this a good sign and a lucky ; the Duke shall this day be turned into a King." Then the Duke looked out on the English camp on Senlac and he saw King Harold's Standard, and he vowed that where that Standard stood he would build a great minster in honour of Saint Martin the Apostle of the Gauls. And so in after time he did. And now all was ready and the host marched forward in battle array. Now the host was marshalled in three parts. On the left were the Bretons and Poitevins and men of Maine. Their captain was Alan of Britanny. On the right were all the hired men and adventurers of all kinds from France and Picardy and other places. They were led by Roger of Montgomery, a mighty man among the Normans. And in the midst of the host were the Normans themselves, under the command of the Duke himself. In each division were archers, and heavy armed foot and horse. And in the centre of all rode Duke William. He rode on a noble horse given him by Alfonso King of

Galicia in Spain. Round his neck he wore the choicest of the relics on which he said that Harold had sworn, and in his hand he carried, not a sword or a spear, but a mace of iron. Close by him rode his brother Bishop Odo; he was the son of the Duke's mother Herleva, who after Duke Robert's death had married a knight named Herlwin. This Odo had the Bishoprick of Bayeux given him when he was only about twelve years old, and he was now quite a young man, and as fond of fighting as if he had not been a priest. He too, like the Duke,. had a mace of iron; for the laws of the Church said that a priest might not shed blood; so Odo would not fight with sword or spear, but he said that it was not shedding blood to smite men with his mace of iron. Hard by these two great ones rode William's other half-brother, Robert, another son of Herlwin and Herleva, to whom William had given the county of Mortain and who had afterwards great estates in England and was Earl of Cornwall. So the three brothers were near together, and close by them rode a knight called Toustain the White, who carried the banner which Pope Alexander had sent to the Duke. So they rode across the ground between Telham and Senlac till they came to the foot of the hill.

King Harold had also risen early and had put his men in order. On the slope of the hill, just in the face of the army as it came from Hastings, he planted the two ensigns which were always set up in an English royal army, and between which the King had his royal post. The one was the golden Dragon, the old ensign of Wessex, of which we have heard so long ago as when Æthelhun carried it so bravely at the battle of Burford. The other was the Standard, which seems to have been the King's own device. King Harold's Standard was a great flag, richly adorned with precious stones and with the figure of a fighting-man wrought upon it in gold. As the English thus had two ensigns, they had also two war-cries. They shouted "God Almighty," which I take to have been the national war-cry, and they also shouted "Holy Cross," that is no doubt the Holy Cross of Waltham which King Harold held in such reverence. Perhaps this last was the cry of the King's own men. For you must remember that there were in the English army two very different sorts of men. There were King Harold's own followers, his own kinsmen and friends and Thanes and house-carls, the men of whom the Northmen said that any one could fight any other two men. These were in short the men who had won the fight of Stamfordbridge. These wore coats of mail, and they had javelins to hurl at the beginning of the fight, and their great two-handed axes to use when the foe came to close quarters. And with these picked troops I suspect were reckoned the men of Kent and London, who are spoken of in a special way. But besides these tried soldiers there were the men who came together from the whole south and east of England, who were armed as they could arm them-selves, many of them very badly. Most of them had no coats of mail or other armour, and many had neither swords nor axes. Most of them had pikes, forks, anything they could bring; a very few seem to have had bows and arrows. Now in a battle on the open ground these men would have been of no use at all; the Norman horsemen would have trampled them down in a moment. But even these badly armed troops, when placed on the hill side, behind the barri-cades, could do a good deal in driving the Normans back as they rode up. But as far as I can see, King Harold put these bad troops in the back, towards what we may call the isthmus of the peninsula, where the worse troops on the other side were likely to make the attack. But his picked men he put in front, where the best troops of the enemy were likely to come. So when they were all in order, King Harold rode round the hill to see that they were all ready, and he, like Duke William, made a speech to his men. He told them plainly that Duke William had come across the sea to conquer them if he could; they had nothing to do but to stand firm and defend themselves against him. He told them that the Norman horsemen were most brave and terrible soldiers; if they once got on the hill, there would be very little hope; but, if the English only kept firm in their ranks, they never could get on the hill. Let the English only stand still and cut down every one who came near the barricades, and the day was sure to be theirs. When the King had gone all round, he rode to the Standard, alighted from his horse, prayed to God for help, and stood ready with his axe till the enemy drew near. An English King, as you know, always fought on foot, that he might share all the dangers of his people, and that, where the King fought, no man might think of flight. By the King stood his brothers Gyrth and Leofwine and his kinsfolk and chief friends. If we were on the hill of Senlac, I could show you within a few feet where the Standard was pitched and where King Harold stood. For in after times, when King William the Conqueror built his great minster there, called the Abbey of the Battle, the high altar of the minster was placed where King Harold's Standard had stood. So it is easy to find the place.[1]

Thus the English stood on the hill ready for the French host, horse and foot, who were coming across from Telham to attack them. About nine o'clock on Saturday morning they came near to the foot of the hill, and now began the great Battle of Senlac or Hastings. The Duke's army I told you was in three parts. Alan and the Bretons had to attack on the left, to the west of the abbey buildings. Roger of Montgomery with the French and Picards were on the right, near where the railway station is now. Duke William himself and the native Normans were in the midst, and they came right against the point of the hill which was crowned by the Standard, where King Harold himself stood ready for them.

And now began the great battle. First of all, the Norman archers let fly their arrows against the English; then the heavy-armed foot were to come up; and lastly the horsemen. They hoped of course ,hat the shower of arrows would kill many of the English and put the rest into confusion, and that the heavy-armed foot would then be able to break down the barricades, so that the horsemen might ride up the hill. But first of all a man named, or rather nicknamed, *Taillefer* or *Cut-iron*,[2] rode out alone from the Norman ranks. He was a juggler or minstrel, who could sing songs and play tricks, but he was a brave man all the same, and he asked Duke William's leave that he might strike the first blow, hand to hand. So Taillefer

---

[1] The place actually shown is a wrong one, as the altar of the Lady Chapel has been mistaken for the high altar, but it is easy to tell within a few feet where the high altar must have stood.

[2] In Latin he is called *Incisor Ferri.*

the minstrel rode forth, singing as he went, like Harold Hardrada at Stamfordbridge, and, as some say, throwing his sword up in the air and catching it again. Now perhaps you will wonder when I tell you what his song was about, for he sang of the Emperor Charles the Great and of Roland his captain, how he died in the fight of Roncesvalles in the Pyrenees. For French people had even then begun to fancy that the great German King was a Frenchman, and they had begun to tell stories and to sing songs about him by his French name of Charlemagne.[1] So Taillefer now sang about Charlemagne, as about a hero of his own land, just as our men no doubt sang about Alfred and Æthelstan. As he came near to the English line, he managed to kill one man with his lance and another with his sword, but then he was cut down himself. Then the French army pressed on at all points, shouting " God help us," while our men shouted " God Almighty" and " Holy Cross." They tried very hard, first the foot and then the horse, to break down the barricade. But it was all in vain. The English hurled their javelins at them as they were drawing near, and when they came near enough, they cut them down with their axes. The Norman writers themselves tell us how dreadful the fight was, and how the English axe, in the hand of King Harold or of any other strong man, cut down the horse and his rider with a single blow. Duke William and his army tried and tried again to get up the hill, but it was all in vain ; our men did not swerve an inch, and they cut down every Frenchman who came near, King Harold himself and his brothers fighting among the foremost. Soon the French lines began to waver ; the Bretons on the right turned and fled, and soon the Normans themselves followed. The English were now of course sorely tempted to break their lines and pursue, just what King Harold had told them not to do. Some of them, seemingly the troops in the rear, where the Bretons had first given way, were foolish enough to disobey the King's orders, and to follow their flying enemies

---

[1] That is *Carolus Magnus* = Charles the Great. So Hugh the Great is called Hugues *le Magne*. But it is possible that there is also some confusion between *Karl* and his brother *Karlmann*. The best way is to use the form Charlemagne only when one is speaking of him distinctly as a subject of French tales.

down into the plain. It seemed as if the French were utterly beaten, and a cry was raised that Duke William himself was dead. So, just as our King Edmund had done at Shenstone, he tore off his helmet that men might see that he was alive and cried out, " I live, and by God's help I will conquer." Then he and his brother the Bishop contrived to bring their men together again. They turned again to the fight; those who were pursued by the English cut their pursuers in pieces, and another assault on the hill began. Duke William this time had somewhat better luck. He again tried to get straight to the Standard and meet King Harold face to face. This however he never actually did at any time of the battle. We hear much of the exploits of both Harold and William, but they never met face to face. But just at this stage of the battle they were nearer meeting than at any other. William got so near to the barricade just before the Standard that Earl Gyrth, who we know fought near his brother the King, was able to hurl a spear directly at him. It missed the Duke, but his horse was killed and fell under him, as two others did before the day was out. Duke William then pressed on on foot, and met Gyrth face to face, and slew him with his own hand.[1] Earl Leofwine too was killed about the same time, and Roger of Montgomery and his Frenchmen to the right contrived to break down part of the barricade on that side. So this second attack was by no means so unsuccessful as the first. The two Earls were killed, and the barricade was beginning to give way. Still Duke William saw that he could never win the battle by making his horsemen charge up the hill in the teeth of the English axes. He saw that his only chance was to tempt the English to break their shield-wall, and come down into the plain. So he tried a very daring and dangerous trick. He had seen the advantage which by his good generalship he had contrived to gain out of the real flight of his men a little time before ; so he ordered his troops to pretend flight, and, if the English followed, to turn upon them. And so it

---

[1] There are several accounts of the death of Gyrth. One makes him die the last man at the Standard after Harold was killed. But, on the whole, the evidence seems to be in favour of his being killed at this stage of the battle, and by William's own hand.

was; the whole French army seemed to be fleeing a second time; so a great many of the English ran down the hill to chase them. As far as I can make out, it was only the light-armed, the troops on the right, who did this; I do not think that any of King Harold's own housecarls left their ranks. So the Normans seemed to fly, and the English followed after them. But presently the Normans turned, and now the English had to fly. It was most foolish of them to disobey the King's orders, and this disobedience lost the battle, and lost everything; still we must say that those who had made this great mistake did their best to make up for it. Some managed to seize the little hill which I before spoke of, and thence they hurled down javelins and stones on those who attacked them, and thus they completely cut off a party who were sent against them. Others, who knew the ground well, led the French-men who chased them to a place near the isthmus—I wish we were there that I might show it you—where the ground is very rough, and where there is a little narrow cleft with steep sides, all covered with bushes and low trees. So the Nor-mans came riding on, and their horses came tumbling head over heels into the trap which was thus ready for them, and the English who were flying now turned round and killed the riders.

All this was bravely and cleverly done; but it could not recover the battle, now that King Harold's wise orders had once been disobeyed. The English line was now broken; the hill was defenceless at many points; so the Normans could now ride up, and the battle was now fought on the hill. The fight was by no means over yet; the English had lost their great advantage of the ground; but King Harold and all his mighty men were still there; so they still formed their shield-wall and fought with their great axes. Now if you think a moment, you will easily see that the English must have got tired much sooner than the Normans. It is a very wearying thing to stand still for a long time together, watching for the moment when one has to strike or to do anything. It is far more wearying to do this than to ride or walk or run backwards and forwards, which is what the Normans had to do. I suppose it was through sheer weariness that the English seem to have gradually lost their close array, so that the battle changed into a series of single combats; here one or two Frenchmen cutting down an Englishman, here one or two Englishmen cutting down a Frenchman. Very valiant deeds of this sort were done by many men in both armies. They had now been fighting ever since nine in the morning, and twilight was now coming on. Luck had no doubt now turned against the English; still they were by no means beaten yet, and it is by no means clear that they would have been beaten after all, if King Harold had only lived till night-fall. Here, as always in these times, everything depended on one man. Harold still lived and fought by his Standard, and it was against that point that all the efforts and all the devices of the Normans were now aimed. The Norman archers had begun the fight and the Norman archers were now to end it. Duke William now bade them shoot up in the air that the arrows might fall like bolts from heaven. This device proved the most successful of all; some men were pierced right through their helmets; others had their eyes put out; others lifted up their shields to guard their heads, and so could not wield their axes so well as before. King Harold still stood—you may see him in the Tapestry—standing close by the golden Dragon, with his axe in his hand, and his shield pierced with several arrows. But now the hour of our great King was come. Every foe who had come near him had felt the might of that terrible axe, but his axe could not guard him against this awful shower of arrows. One shaft, falling, as I said, from heaven, pierced his right eye; he clutched at it and broke off the shaft; his axe dropped from his hand, and he fell, all disabled by pain, in his own place as King between the two royal ensigns. Twenty Norman knights now swore to take the Standard, now that the King no longer defended it; they rushed on; most of them were killed by the English who still fought around their wounded King; but those who escaped succeeded in beating down the Standard of the Fighting Man and in bearing off the Golden Dragon. That ancient ensign, which had shone over so many battlefields, was never again carried before a true English King. Then four knights, one of whom was Count Eustace, rushed upon King Harold as he lay dying; they killed him with several wounds, and mangled his body. Such was the end of the last native King of the English, Harold the son of Godwine. He fell by the most glorious of deaths, fighting for the land and the people which he had loved so well.

But still the fight was not over. Such of the housecarls and other picked men as still lived still fought on, and, as far as I can see, they were all killed at their posts. Abbot Ælfwig and his twelve monks were all killed, and Abbot Leofric was sore wounded, but he got home to Peterborough and died soon after. I fancy that he must have been one of those who were carried off the next day among the dead bodies. One story says that King Harold himself was carried off in this way, and lived for some time after, but we know that this is not true. I fancy that all those of the picked men who escaped at all escaped in this way. We hear nothing of any prisoners being taken, nothing of any of the axemen taking to flight. But as it grew dark, those of the light-armed men who were left fled, some of them on the horses on which the leaders, though they fought on foot, had ridden to the battle. Duke William and the Normans followed them, but the English, who knew the ground, were able even now to do the Normans a great damage. On the north side, near where the parish church now stands, the side of the hill is very steep and the ground at the bottom is swampy. The English had the art to entice the pursuers to follow them to this point, where, now in the dark, they had even worse luck than they had had on the other side of the hill earlier in the day. Again the Norman horses and horsemen came tumbling down the steep place, where some were choked in the swamp, and others were killed by the English, who turned and took no small vengeance for their own defeat and the death of their King. Thus the Normans suffered a very heavy loss even after they had gained the day, besides all the men who had been killed earlier in the battle. I do not suppose there ever was a more hard-fought battle, or one in which more courage and skill was shown on both sides. The English lost the day, but, as far as good fighting was concerned, they certainly lost no honour. Even the great fault of those who broke their line, and so lost the day, was not a fault

z

of cowardice but of over-eagerness. This great battle, like everything else in these times, shows how great was the difference
between one King or leader and another. Under Æthelred and
his favourites Englishmen could do nothing ; under Edmund or
Harold they could do everything. And Harold was better off
than Edmund in having no traitor in his camp. Edwin and
Morkere were indeed almost as bad as Eadric ; but then they
kept away from the battle altogether.

The great battle being over, Duke William came back to the
hill, and stayed there all night. He had the dead bodies swept
away around where the Standard had stood, and there he
pitched his tent and did eat and drink. The next day he had
the dead among his own men buried, and he gave leave that the
women and people of the country might take away and bury
the bodies of the slain English. So many women came and
took away the bodies of their husbands and sons and brothers.
Then the two canons of Waltham, who had followed the army,
Osgod and Æthelric the Childmaster, came to the Duke and
craved that they might take the body of their founder King
Harold, and bury it in his own minster at Waltham. And
Gytha the mother of the King also craved the body of her son.
I cannot say for certain whether she too had followed the army,
or whether she only sent word by the canons, but she offered
the Duke King Harold's weight in gold if she might have his
body to bury at Waltham. But the Duke said Nay ; for that
Harold was perjured and excommunicated, and might not be
buried in holy ground. Now there was in the Norman army one
William Malet, a brave knight, who was in some way or other
a friend or kinsman of King Harold's ; so Duke William bade
William Malet to take the body of his friend and bury it on
the sea-coast, under a heap of stones, which men call a cairn.
For Duke William said : "He guarded the shore when living,
let him guard it now that he is dead." But no man could find
the body ; even Osgod and Æthelric, who knew him well, could
not find it, for it was all defaced and mangled, and it had been
thrown aside when the bodies were cleared away for William's
tent to be pitched. But there was a lady called Edith,
whom for her beauty men called *Swanneshals*[1] or the Swan's

---

[1] You know the word *hals* in German, and it is also still used in Scotland.

Neck, whom King Harold had loved in old times when he was Earl of the East Angles. Either she had followed the canons from Waltham, or they went and fetched her. So Edith went and looked for the body of King Harold among the heaps of the slain English. And she knew him not by his face, which was all mangled so that no man could know him, but by a mark on his body. So William Malet and the canons took up the body of King Harold and buried it under a cairn on the rocks by Hastings. But after a while, when Duke William was crowned King of the English, he relented, and men took up the body of King Harold from under the heap of stones, and buried it in his own minster at Waltham. And there might men see the tomb of the great King Harold, until such time as Waltham and so many other churches were spoiled and the tombs of our Kings and great men broken down. The choir of Waltham Minster has long been pulled down, and I cannot show you the tomb of King Harold any more than the tomb of King Alfred. But I can tell you this. When the great King Edward, called the First, because he was the first of the name who reigned after the Norman Conquest, died in the North of England, they took his body to bury it in the Abbey of Saint Peter at Westminster, a great part of which he himself had rebuilt. And on the way they rested at Waltham, and the body of the great King Edward was laid for a while in the Minster of the Holy Cross. So the bodies of the two greatest Kings that ever reigned over the whole Kingdom of England lay for a short space side by side.

CHAPTER XIII.

You will understand quite well that, though Duke William had won the great battle, and though King Harold was dead, that did not at once make the Duke King of the English. You know by this time that in those days a man who was chosen King, where the Kingdom was elective, or who succeeded by right of birth, where the Kingdom was hereditary, still was not fully King till he was crowned, generally by the chief Bishop of the country. Such a man's birth or election gave him a right to claim to be crowned King, but he was not King till he was crowned. So Duke William, though he gave out that he alone had a right to be King of the English, still did not call himself King after he had won the battle any more than he did before. And it was not yet at all clear that he ever would be King. He had, after all, only won one battle, and got possession of part of one shire. You know that both Swegen and Cnut had to do a great deal more than this before they were Kings over the whole land. And no doubt, had there been one man in the land like Harold or Edmund or Alfred, Duke William would have had to fight many another battle, and perhaps he never would have been King at all. You remember all the battles which Edmund fought, even when England was quite worn out with all the wretchedness of the reign of Æthelred. And England was far better able to resist now than she was then. But she had now no leader, any more than in Æthelred's time. There was nobody now left like Harold or Edmund. Gyrth and Leofwine were dead as well as their brother, and Waltheof and Hereward, who afterwards did such great things, had not yet been heard of as great captains. So, after the battle of Senlac, William never again met Englishmen in a pitched battle. But he was very far from getting possession of the land all at once. It took him about five years really to conquer the whole Kingdom, even after he had been crowned King. Still he had never again to meet the whole nation, or any large part of it, in battle. Men resisted and revolted here and there, this shire or that town, and they often fought very bravely and gave William a good deal of trouble to overcome them. But there was no general resistance of the whole nation, because there was no one man worthy to lead the nation. So of course the land was conquered bit by bit. I want you particularly to bear in mind that England was conquered only in this gradual way, even after William was crowned King, and that, till he was crowned, he did not profess to be King at all.

I told you that Edwin and Morkere, the two Earls, the King's brothers-in-law, betrayed King Harold and kept away from the battle. As soon as they heard the news of his death, they came to London, and took their sister the Lady Ealdgyth, the King's widow, and sent her away to Chester. Then the Archbishops Ealdred and Stigand, and the Earls Edwin and Morkere, and the citizens and the sailors of London, and such of the other Wise Men as could be got together, met to choose a King. If they had known what traitors the two Earls were, the wisest thing they could have done, as one of the Chroniclers says, would have been to choose William at once. But they naturally thought that, with all the force of Northumberland and most part of that of Mercia, they could still resist. So they chose young Edgar the Ætheling. Of course Edgar was quite unfit to be the leader of the nation at such a time ; but there was nobody else to choose, unless they had chosen Edwin, as he seems to have hoped. There was nobody else in the old royal family; Harold's brothers were dead, and though he had left three sons, they seem to have been mere youths, and so were no better than Edgar. So young Edgar was chosen King, but it does not seem that he was ever crowned. And Edwin and Morkere promised to be faithful to him and to go and fight for him against Duke William. So the citizens of

London and all the men who were at all brave and true of heart made ready to go out and fight. But the Earls forsook them and went away with their men to their Earldoms. I suppose that they did not care to fight for a West-Saxon King, whether he were Harold or Edgar, and perhaps they fancied that they might be able to divide the Kingdom with William, as had been done in the time of Edmund and Cnut. They perhaps thought that William would think it enough to be King in Wessex, and would leave them to be Kings north of the Thames, instead of being merely Earls under Harold or Edgar. Anyhow they were thorough traitors, first to Edward, then to Harold, then to Edgar, and afterwards to William also. They kept faith with nobody, and in the end they were punished as they deserved.

Meanwhile Duke William first went back to Hastings, and left a garrison in the fort which he had built there. He waited there some days thinking that people would come in and submit to him, but nobody came. So he set out to conquer the country, bit by bit. First he went to Romney. It seems that some of his people had been there already; perhaps one or more of the ships had gone astray and got on shore there. At all events there had been a fight between some of his men and the men of Romney, in which many were killed on both sides, but in the end the English had driven the Frenchmen away. So Duke William now, we are told, took from the men of Romney what penalty or satisfaction he chose for the men whom they had killed, as if he had been making them pay a wergild. I suppose this means that he put them all to death. Then he went on, still along the coast, as far as Dover. Here was one of the very few castles which were then in England; it had most likely been built by Harold himself. So Dover was thought to be stronger than any other place, and many people from all parts round about had come into the town for safety. The castle was strong and stood on the cliff; but the commanders of the garrison were cowardly, and surrendered at once. So some of the Normans, who had hoped to have the plundering of the town, got angry, and set fire to some of the houses, and a good deal was burned. But the Duke paid the owners of the houses for what they had lost. You may here see his crafty policy. As he gave himself out to be the lawful heir to the Crown, his plan was to treat everybody who opposed him as a traitor, and everybody who submitted to him as a loyal subject fulfilling his duty. So you see he was harsh at Romney and gentle at Dover. He then caused the castle to be further strengthened. He stayed some time at Dover, because many of his army fell ill—from eating fresh meat, it is said. Meanwhile the fear of him went abroad. "The powerful metropolis," we read in William of Poitiers, "trembled." Now what place do you think is meant by "the powerful metropolis"? Perhaps some of you will at once say, London, because I dare say you have often heard people who like to use long words call London "the metropolis." But the place here meant is Canterbury. Some of you have learned Greek enough to know that Metropolis (μητρόπολις) means the *mother-city*. When a Greek city sent out a colony, the city whence the colonists went was called the *metropolis*, as we now talk about the *mother-country*. And in ecclesiastical language Metropolis means an Archbishop's see, and in England at least very rightly. For Canterbury and York were the first churches planted in the south and north of England respectively, and all the other churches of England are in a manner colonies of one or other of those two, so that the churches of Canterbury and York are rightly called Metropolitan churches and their Bishops Archbishops and Metropolitans. But no place in England[1] is in any sense, ecclesiastical or civil, a colony of London. London is the *capital*, the head-town, the largest town and the seat of government, but not, in any strictness of speech, the Metropolis. Yet I have known people who ought to know better call Saint Paul's church in London "the metropolitan cathedral," instead of Christ Church at Canterbury or Saint Peter's at York. So Canterbury was the metropolis which trembled; we shall hear about London presently. So Duke William set out, and received the submission of the citizens of Canterbury and the rest of the men of Kent at a place called the Broken Tower,

---

[1] But London is, in the strict Greek sense, the metropolis of Derry in Ireland, to which London sent a colony in the time of King James the First, whence it is called Londonderry.

which seems to have been not far from Canterbury. There is a story told how the Kentishmen came to meet William in arms, and how they hid themselves and their arms with branches of trees, so that they looked like a walking wood. Then suddenly they threw aside the branches, and stood before him as an army ready for battle. Then the Duke was afraid, and he and the Kentishmen came to an agreement, that they would submit to him, but only on condition of having all their ancient laws and customs confirmed to them. And this is the reason why so many old laws and customs still remain in Kent, which have gone out of use in the rest of England. I think you will see how unlikely a story this is in itself, and there are other reasons why it cannot be true. It is one of those stories which, as I have so often told you, go the round of the world. It is the same story which you will find in Shakespere's play of Macbeth, about Birnam wood going to Dunsinane. There is no authority for it at all, and in truth Kent submitted much more easily than many other parts of the Kingdom. It is no wonder that it did so; the Kentishmen had been among the foremost at Senlac, and no doubt all the bravest men of the shire had been killed, and had left hardly any strength to withstand William. It is indeed quite true that William did not abolish the old laws in Kent, but that is because he did not do so anywhere, nor is there anything to show that he treated Kent either better or worse than the rest of the Kingdom.

While Duke William was at or near Canterbury, he fell sick, which hindered him from marching on for a whole month. But he was not idle even during his sickness. About this time he heard that Edgar the Ætheling had been chosen King in London. Now the Duke's great object was of course to get London into his hands, and also Winchester. Now Winchester had been given as her dower to the Lady Edith, the widow of King Edward and sister of King Harold. Now as William professed to have come into the land as the heir and kinsman of Edward, it was of course his policy to show all respect to his widow. It is indeed not quite certain that Edith was not on William's side; it is quite possible that she, like her husband, had been bewitched by the Frenchmen. And it is quite certain that, in the quarrel between her brothers, she had taken the part of Tostig against Harold. So all that William asked from Winchester was tribute, no doubt whatever the city had been used to pay to the old Kings. And this the Lady and the chief men of the city easily agreed to give.

But the chief thing was to take London; so as soon as William was well enough, he set forth again on his march. He first sent out five hundred horsemen, who must have gone more to *reconnoître*, as it is called, that is to look about and to see how the land lies, than with any hope that such a force could take the city. But they had a skirmish with some of the citizens and drove them within the walls, and they burned the suburb or work on the south of the Thames, called Southwark. Now you may mark here the difference between William's campaign and those of Swegen and Cnut. The Danes had commonly attacked London with their ships; but William, though he had not destroyed his ships, had left them behind. He seems to have meant to use them only as transports and not at all as war-ships. So you see that he could not get at the city, because he could not cross the river. He had therefore to march a long way up the stream, till he could come to a bridge which was not guarded or to a place where the river could be forded. The Norman writers say that he went on like a King on his progress, doing no harm on his march, while the English talk much of the ravages of his army. I dare say there is some truth in both accounts. It was William's policy to strike hard whenever he was resisted, but not to do any needless mischief to the country which he claimed as his own. He would not, like Swegen, give his men orders to do all the harm possible, but most likely quite the contrary. But in such cases it always happens that an army does a great deal more harm than its general means it to do. And if the people anywhere at all withstood him, William would himself harry and slay without mercy. So I think we can understand both accounts. So William marched up along the right bank of the Thames—I hope you know which is the right bank of a river—as far as Wallingford in Berkshire, where his army crossed the river, partly by a ford and partly by a bridge.

Now the commander of the forces in London at this time was named Esegar. He was the son of Æthelstan, the son of Tofig the Proud, and he had been Staller both to King Edward and to King Harold. His father had, as you will remember, lost his estate at Waltham, but Esegar had large estates in different parts of the country, and he was one of the chief men in England. He was now Sheriff of the Middle-Saxons, which most likely accounts for his commanding in London. He had fought at Senlac, and he had been so badly wounded there that he could not walk, but was carried about in a litter. So you see that he could not have been one of those who fled just at the end of the battle. I should think that he must have been one of those who were left for dead, and carried off among the dead bodies. Esegar kept up the spirits of the citizens as long as he could ; but at last, we are told, though it seems a very strange story,[1] that he told them that, as William's power was increasing every day, their only hope was to send and make a feigned submission, that so, I suppose, they might gain time. But William took the messenger in by his show of power and by his gifts and his kind way of talking. So when the messenger came back, he gave the citizens such an account that they agreed to surrender in spite of Esegar. However this may be, about this time they did agree to submit, and Edgar the King-elect, and Archbishop Ealdred, and some other Bishops, and the best men of London, and many Thanes from other parts, met the Duke at Berkhampstead, and swore oaths to him and gave hostages ; and the Duke promised to be good lord to them, and yet the Chronicles say that he let his army harry the land as before. So he came on to London, and on Midwinter-Day, that is Christmas Day, he was crowned in King Edward's new church, the West Minster. Some say that he refused to be crowned by Stigand because he was not a lawful Archbishop ; others say that Stigand refused to crown him because he was not a lawful King. I should like to believe this last story if I could, but it is only found in later writers, and it seems from Bishop Guy of Amiens that Stigand was actually one of the Bishops who took a part in the coro-

---

[1] This story comes from the Latin poem of Bishop Guy of Amiens. There can be no doubt that by " Ansgardus " he means Esegar.

nation. But the actual *celebrant*, as it is called, the Bishop who anointed the King and put the Crown on his head, was Archbishop Ealdred of York, who thus crowned two Kings, and two such different Kings, in one year. The church was full of people, Normans and English, and some Norman soldiers were set to keep guard outside. Then Geoffrey Bishop of Coutances got up and said to the Normans in French, " Will ye that William your Duke be crowned King of the English ?" Then Archbishop Ealdred spoke to the English in English, saying, "Will ye that William Duke of the Normans be crowned King of the English ?" So all the people, both Normans and English, clapped their hands and shouted " Yea, yea." So there was a great noise in the church. And the Normans who were set outside fancied, or pretended to fancy, that somebody was hurting the Duke. If so, one would have thought the right thing would have been to run into the church and help him, but instead of that they began to set fire to the houses round about. So the people began to run out of the church, some trying to put out the fire and some trying to plunder in the confusion. So Duke William was left with hardly any body in the church except the Bishops. Then he swore the oath of the old Kings, to do justice and mercy and to rule his people as well as any King had ever ruled them. Then Archbishop Ealdred anointed him and put the crown on his head, and he became King of the English.

Thus it was that Duke William came into England and overthrew King Harold at Senlac and became King in his stead. And now I will bring my History to an end for the present. I have now gone through all that we can strictly call Old-English History, the History of the times when everything in England was purely English, before the Normans came and gradually brought in so many new words into our language and so many new ideas into our laws. These early times are times which I wish you specially to attend to and to remember about, because they are times which are so often neglected and so often misunderstood. And yet the right understanding of them is most needful, if only for the right understanding of the times that come after. And I think you will see by this time that they are times whose history is most important in itself, and that, if we only take care rightly to distinguish between true history and legend, it can be made both as useful and as pleasant to read as the history of any other time. Surely there is no time which we ought to care to know more about than about the beginnings of our own nation and of all that belongs to us, and the deeds of those of our Kings who were most truly Englishmen. So now that I have brought this time to an end, it seems a good point to stop at, at any rate for a while. For I do not say that I may not some day begin again and tell you, if not the whole History of England, which would be rather too long a business, yet at any rate something about William himself and the times soon after him, down to the time when the changes which were caused by the Norman Conquest were fully brought about. But there are two things which I wish you specially to remark and to remember now. The first is that William was not called the Conqueror because he overcome King Harold in battle and got the crown by force. To *conquer* means to *purchase*, and to *purchase* in law means to get property by any means other than regular descent, whether it is by bequest or by paying money or in any other way. William, you know, said that Edward had left him the crown ; so he took it by *conquest* or *purchase*. Still, though this is the first meaning of the word *Conqueror*, and the meaning in which the word was first applied to William. still it is quite true to call him William the Conqueror in the other sense also, for he did con-quer the land with the sword, and got it in no other way. And besides *Willelmus Conquæstor*, we also in some old books find him called *Willelmus Triumphator*, and there can be no doubt at all what that means. So you may very well call him William the Conqueror in either sense. The other is that at the time when he was crowned, he had not as yet conquered all the land by a great deal. But now he is crowned we must call him King William instead of Duke William, though you see that he had as yet possession only of the south-eastern part of the country, and it was a long time yet before he became really King over the whole land. Still he was the King, chosen, crowned and anointed, if not by the real will of the people like Harold, at any rate with their outward

consent. And no one ever was able to drive him out of the
land, and the Crown of England has ever since been held by
his descendants, though in the direct male line it did not go
beyond his own sons. And though William professed to hold
the Crown, not by force of arms, but by right, and though it is
quite a mistake to think that he tried to root out the old laws
and language of England, yet very great changes in laws and
language and everything else followed step by step after his
coming in. It was not merely because the King himself was
a stranger, but because he found means step by step to give
all the greatest offices in the country to Normans and other
strangers, and even to take away the lands of all the chief
men of England and to give them to these strangers. And as
the followers of William were not men of kindred speech like
the followers of Cnut, but men whose speech and habits and
feelings about everything were quite different from those of
Englishmen, it is no wonder that quite a new state of things
began with his coming. In short, with the crowning of our
first King who was altogether a stranger I say that our true
Old-English History ends, and I will therefore end my story,
at least for a while.

I N D E X.

INDEX.

AACHEN, capital of Charles the Great, 85.

Abel, Patriarch of Jerusalem, Alfred sends an embassy to, 132.

Adelhard of Lüttich, Childmaster at Waltham, 272.

Ælfgar, Ælfric's son, his eyes put out by Æthelred, 205.

—— Alderman, at the battle of Sherstone, 229.

—— son of Leofric, Earl of the East-Angles, 263, 270, 275 ; makes war upon Edward, 276 ; outlawed, *ib.* ; restored to his earldom, 277 ; succeeds his father in his earldom, 279 ; again outlawed, 280 ; returns, *ib.* ; gives his daughter to Gruffydd in marriage, *ib.* ; date of his death, 295.

Ælfgifu, Æthelstan's sister, 146.

—— mother of Swegen and Harold, 246.

—— wife of King Eadwig, 169.

Ælfheah, Bishop of Winchester, persuades Dunstan to become a monk, 164.

—— or Saint Alphege, 206 ; confirms Olaf, *ib.* ; made Archbishop of Canterbury, 214 ; his martyrdom, 217 ; Saint Anselm's opinion of him, 220 ; his body translated to Canterbury, 240.

Ælfhelm, Earl of Deira, murdered by Eadric, 214, 246 ; his son's eyes put out, 214.

Ælfhere, Alderman of the Mercians, 183, 184, 186.

Ælfhun, Bishop of London, 219.

Ælfmær, Archdeacon, betrays Canterbury to the Danes, 217.

—— called Darling, 229.

Ælfnoth, Sheriff of Herefordshire, slain by the Welsh, 278.

Ælfric, Alderman of the Mercians, 190, 205 ; his treason, 213.

—— Alderman, killed at Assandun, 230.

—— Archbishop, 243, 250, 251.

—— kinsman of Godwine, see of Canterbury refused to him, 259.

Ælfsine made Archbishop of Canterbury, 176 ; his death, *ib.*

Ælfthryth, daughter of Alfred the Great, 137.

Ælfthryth, wife of Edgar, story of, 178 ; different versions of the story, 182.

Ælfwig, Abbot, King Harold's uncle, 326, 328 ; killed, 337.

Ælfwyn, daughter of Æthelflæd, 143.

Ælla, King of the Northumbrians, story of him and Ragnar Lodbrog, 108, 162.

Ællandun, battle of, 97.

Ælle, first King of the South-Saxons, 34, 317.

Æscesdun Ashdown, battle at, 111, 128.

Æthelbald, King of the Mercians, 75, 77 ; his death, 76.

—— son of Æthelwulf, conspires against his father, 105 ; his reign, 106 ; married his father's widow, Judith, *ib.* ; his death, *ib.*

Æthelberht, King of Kent and third Bretwalda, 45 ; he marries a daughter of Chariberht, *ib.* ; his conversion, 47.

—— King of the East-Angles, murdered by Offa, 86 ; churches called after him, 87.

—— son of Æthelwulf, King of Kent, 106 ; his reign over Wessex and death, 107.

Æthelburh, daughter of Æthelberht, marries Edwin, 55 ; driven out of Northumberland, 59.

—— wife of Ine of Wessex, 69 ; persuades her husband to forsake the world, 71.

Æthelflæd, daughter of Alfred, Lady of the Mercians, given in marriage to Alderman Æthelred, 125, 137 ; her fortifications, 140, 143 ; her death and character, 143.

—— wife of Edgar, 178.

—— wife of Brihtnoth, 191.

Æthelfrith, King of the Northumbrians, defeats the Welsh at Chester, 50.

Æthelgifu, Alfred's daughter, Abbess of Shaftesbury, 131, 137.

Æthelheard, King of the West-Saxons, 72, 74, 75.

Æthelhelm, Alderman of the Wilsætas, 136 ; dies, 137.

Æthelhun, "the proud Alderman," his bravery at the battle of Burford, 75.

Æthelmær, Alderman, submits to Swegen, 223.

Æthelnoth, Alderman, 136.
—— Archbishop, 222, 239.
Æthelred the First, 107 ; his battles, 111 ; his death, 112.
—— the Second, 178, 182 ; proposed for the kingdom at his father's death, 183 ; chosen King, 189 ; his character, 190 ; called the *Unready, ib.* ; puts out the eyes of Ælfric's son, 205 ; equips a fleet to repel the Danes, 207 ; harries Cumberland and sends his fleet against Normandy, 208 ; marries Emma, 210 ; flees to Normandy, 223 ; restored to the crown, 225 ; his death, 227.
—— the Mickle or Big, father of Alfred's wife Ealhswyth, 116.
—— Alderman of the Mercians, 125 ; London handed over by Alfred to, 133 ; defeats the Danes at Buttington, 136.
Æthelric the Childmaster craves the body of Harold, 338.
Æthelsige, Abbot of Ramsay, story of his vision, 307.
Æthelstan, son of King Ecgberht, succeeds Æthelwulf as King of Kent, 99.
—— son of Edward, 145 ; his reign, 148 ; all the Princes of Britain submit to him, *ib.* ; his wars with the Welsh, 152 ; he fortifies Exeter, 153 ; his victory at Brunanburh, 153–158 ; his death, 158 ; his character, 159.
—— son of Æthelred, 211, 233, 248.
—— son of Tofig the Proud, 254.
—— Bishop of Hereford, Saint Æthelberht's minster built by, 277 ; his death, *ib.*
Æthelswyth, sister of Alfred, 103.
Æthelthryth, Saint, patron of Ely, 241.
Æthelwald, son of Æthelred, 138 ; rebels against Edward the Elder, 139 ; slain, *ib.*
—— Alderman, 178 ; his legendary history, 179–183 ; his battles, 183.
—— Bishop of Winchester, favours the monks, 168, 177.
Æthelwealh, first Christian King of the South-Saxons, 61.
Æthelweard, son of Edward, 147.
—— Alderman, his History, 167 ; advises giving money to the Danes, 190, 205 ; his mission to King Olaf, 206.
—— son of Æthelwine, his death at Assandun, 231.
Æthelwine, surnamed the Friend of God, Alderman of the East-Angles, favours the monks, 183.
Æthelwulf, son of Ecgberht, made King of Kent, 97 ; succeeds Ecgberht as King of the West-Saxons, 99 ; gives his kingdom of Kent to his son Æthelstan, *ib.* ; his reign, 102 ; goes on a pilgrimage to Rome, 104 ; marries Judith, daughter of Charles the Bald, *ib.* ; gives up to Æthelbald the kingdom of the West-Saxons, 105 ; his death, 106.

Æthelwulf, Alderman, fights the Danes at Englefield, 111 ; killed at Reading, *ib.*
Agatha, niece of the Emperor Henry the Second, wife of the Ætheling Edward, 275.
Agricola, Julius, his final conquest of Britain, 17 ; the Orkneys found out by, *ib.*
Aix-la-chapelle, French name for Aachen, 85.
Alan of Britanny at the battle of Senlac, 329, 332.
Alban, Saint, abbey and town of, 21, 81 ; founded by Offa, 78.
Alban's, Saint, Head, 69.
Alcuin or Ealhwine, his favour with Charles the Great, 84, 86.
Alderman (*Ealdorman*), the title of, 35, 194.
Alexander the Second, Pope, sends legates to England, 283 ; gives William a banner, 303.
Alfonso, King of Galicia, 329.
Alfred the Great, his life by Asser, 103 ; adopted and hallowed by Pope Leo, 104 ; his battles in the time of Æthelred, 111, 112 ; his reign, 113 ; compared with Saint Lewis. *ib.* ; his character, 114 ; story of him and his mother, 115 ; marries Ealhswyth, 116 ; gains the first English victory at sea, 118 ; he retreats to Athelney before the Danes, 120 ; story of the cakes, 121 ; his victory at Ethandun and peace at Wedmore, 123 ; story of his going into the Danish camp in disguise, 126 ; story of Saint Cuthberht and, 127 ; his literary works, 130 ; his collection of laws, 131 ; his attention to religious matters, *ib.* ; founds a monastery at Athelney, 132 ; equips a fleet, *ib.* ; it is defeated, *ib.* ; repairs London, 133 ; his later wars, 135 ; improves his ships, 136 ; dies, 137.
—— the town-reeve of Bath, his death, 140.
—— Ætheling, conspires against Æthelstan, 150.
—— son of Æthelred and Emma, put to death by Harold Harefoot, 248 ; Earl Godwine charged with his murder, 248, 269.
Alphege, Saint. *See* Ælfheah.
Anderida, taken by Ælle and Cissa, 34.
Andover, Olaf received at, by Æthelred, 206.
Angeln, 1.
Angles, begin to settle in Britain, 30 ; give their name to the land, 32 ; their kingdoms in Britain, 37, 39.
Anglesey, why so called, 55.
Anglo-Saxon, meaning of the name, 31, 138.
Anlaf, Danish Kings of the name in Northumberland, 151, 153, 162, 163.
Anselm, Saint, his opinion of Saint Ælfheah, 220.

Antoninus Pius, Emperor, wall of, 20.
Appledore, Alfred takes a fort at, 135.
Archers, Norman, 327, 332, 336.
Arminius, or Irmin, the deliverer of Germany, 22.
Arnulf, Emperor, 134; his victory over the Northmen at Löwen, 135.
Arthur, the Briton, resists the English, his victory at Badbury, 35.
Arwald, King of the Jutes in Wight, 67; his sons murdered by Ceadwalla, 68.
Aryan languages, why so called, 6.
Ashdown (Æscesdun), Alfred's battle at, 111, 128.
Assandun, battle of, 230; meaning of the name, ib.; Cnut and Thurkill build a minster at, 239.
Asser's Life of King Alfred, 93, 103, 131.
Athelney, Alfred builds a fort at, 123; abbey founded by Alfred, 132.
Augustine, Saint, his mission to Britain, 42; he preaches to Æthelbert, 45; his conference with the Welsh Bishops, 48; his Abbey, ib.
Augustine's Oak, 48.

Bæda, his Life and History, 42, 50, 74; his History translated by Alfred, 130.
Baldred, King of Kent, driven out by Ecgberht, 97.
Baldwin, first Count of Flanders, marries Judith, 107.
—— the Second, Count of Flanders, marries Alfred's daughter Ælfthryth, 137.
—— the Fifth, receives Emma, 249; also Gunhild, 255; the Emperor Henry wages war with, 256; Earl Godwine and Gytha take refuge with, 262; pleads for Earl Godwine, 266; Earl Tostig takes refuge with, 296.
Baldwinsland, Flanders so called, 107.
Bamborough, lords of, 165.
Bangor Iscoed, slaughter of the monks of, 50.
Barbarians, meaning of the word, 23.
Bartholomew, Saint, Alfred's embassy to the Christians of, 132.
Basing, Alfred's battle at, 112.
Basques, the, 6.
Bath, taken by Ceawlin, 36; Edgar crowned at, 175; Swegen acknowledged King at, 223.
Battle. *See* Senlac.
—— Abbey, the Chronicle of, 321; founded by William, 332; position of the high altar at, ib.
Bayeux, Bishoprick of, 142; Danish language survives at, 142, 210; tapestry of, 289, 320, 336.
Beavers in Britain, 251.
Benedict Biscop, Abbot of Wearmouth, 74.
—— the Tenth, Pope, gives the pallium to Stigand, 281.

Beorhtric, King of the West-Saxons, 90; poisoned by his Queen, 93.
Beorhtwald, first English Archbishop of Canterbury, 73.
Beorhtwulf, King of the Mercians, defeated by the Danes, 102.
Beorn, King Edmund's huntsman, legend of, 108.
—— Gytha's nephew, slain by Swegen, 257.
Beornicia, division of Northumberland, 38; made a separate Earldom by Edgar, 174; gets the name of Northumberland, ib.
Beornred, King of the Mercians, 80, 82.
Beornwulf, King of the Mercians, drives out Ceolwulf, 88, 96; killed by the East-Angles, 98.
Berengar, King of Italy, 134.
Berkhampstead, Edgar and others submit to William at, 346.
Beverege, island in the Severn, 251.
Billingsley, peace made between Gruffydd and Harold at, 277.
Birinus, Bishop, Wessex converted by, 61.
Bleddyn, brother of Gruffydd, King of Wales, 286.
Boadicea, revolt of, 16.
Boethius's Consolation of Philosophy translated by Alfred, 130.
Boniface, Saint, Apostle of Germany, 62, 73.
Bosham, Godwine sails from, 262.
Boso, King of Burgundy, 133.
Boulogne, Danes sail from, to England, 135.
Bradford-on-Avon, battle of, 65.
Bramsbury, fortified by Æthelflæd, 140.
Brecknock, taken by Æthelflæd, 143.
Brentford, Edmund's victory at, 229.
Bretwalda, meaning of the word, 40; analogy of with the Emperors, 96.
Brevis Relatio, the, an account of the Norman Conquest, 321.
Brice, Saint, massacre of, 211.
Bride-ale, meaning of the word, 262.
Brihthelm, Bishop of Somersetshire, refused the see of Canterbury, 176.
Brihtmær, surnamed Budde, 241.
Brihtnoth, Alderman of the East-Saxons, 183; his death at Maldon, 191; his character, ib.; Ely Abbey partly founded by, ib.
Brihtric, brother of Eadric, accuses Wulfnoth, 215.
Bristol, Harold sets sail from, 262, 285.
Britain, the name the same as Brittany, 1; force of the name *Great* Britain, ib.; why called England, 2; character of its early inhabitants, 7, 8; how conquered by the Romans, 9–15; a Roman province, 16–21; Roman remains in, 17; how it became England, 21–31; foundation of the English kingdoms in, 32–41; English conquest of, 32.

Brittany, language of, 5; Harold's campaign in, 289.
Broken Tower, submission of Kent to Duke William at, 343.
Bromton's Chronicle, 178.
Bruges, Emma takes refuge at, 249: also Gunhild, 255; Swegen, 257; Godwine, 262; Tostig, 296.
Brunanburh, battle of, 154; song of, 155.
Buonaparte, Napoleon, 209.
Burford, battle of, 75, 330.
Burgundy, kingdom of, 24; many meanings of the name, 134.
Burhred, King of the Mercians, 103, 109; runs away from his kingdom, 117.
Bury Saint Edmund's, monastery of, 223, 224.

Cadiz, or Gades, when founded, 11.
Caedmon, the first Christian poet in England, 74.
Cadwalla, King of the Strathclyde Welsh, defeats and kills Edwin, 59.
Caerleon, places so called, 50, 120; British Archbishoprick. 21.
Caesar, Caius Julius, invades Britain. 13.
—— Caius Julius Octavianus, first Augustus, 14.
—— Caius, called Caligula, threatens to invade Britain, 14.
Calixtus, Saint, battle of Senlac fought on his day, 328.
Calne, meeting of the Wise Men at, 134.
Canons, Chrodegang's rule for, 282.
Canterbury, meaning of the name. 34; Augustine preaches at, 47; taken by the Danes, 217; submits to William, 343.
Caradoc, or Caractacus, resists the Romans, 15.
—— son of Gruffydd of South Wales, kills Harold's workmen at Portskewet, 293.
Carham, battle of, 244.
Carthage, a Phoenician colony, 11; capital of the Vandals, 24.
Castles, the building of, introduced into England, 259.
Ceadda or Chad, Saint, Bishop of Lichfield, 61.
Ceadwalla, King of the West-Saxons, his character, 67; murders Arwald's sons, 68; baptized by Pope Sergius, ib.; his death, 69.
Ceawlin, King of the West-Saxons and Bretwalda, his victories over the Welsh, 36.
Celtic languages, their extent, 5.
Cenhelm. See Kenelm.
Cenwealh, King of the West-Saxons, his victories, 61, 65.
Cenwulf, King of the Mercians, his victories, 98.
Ceolred, King of the Mercians, defeated by Ine at Wanborough, 70.

Ceolwulf, King of the Mercians, driven out by Beornwulf, 87, 88. 96.
—— made King of the Mercians by the Danes, 118, 120.
Cerdic, founds the kingdom of the West-Saxons, 35; nearly all the Kings of England descended from, ib.; Edward the Confessor the last King in the male line, 297.
Charlemagne, French name of Charles the Great, 333.
Charles the Bald, King of the West-Franks and Emperor, 104.
—— the Fat, Emperor, 133; deposed, 134.
—— the Great, King of the Franks and Emperor, his greatness, 81, 83; Queen Eadburh repairs to, 94; succeeded by Lewis the Pious, 104; division of his dominions, 104, 133.
—— the Simple, King of the West-Franks, brother-in-law of Edward the Elder, 141; deposed, 146.
Chester, force of the name, 50; Æthelfrith defeats the Welsh near, ib.; Edgar's triumph at, 175; Ealdgyth, widow of Harold, sent thither, 341.
Chichester, see of Selsey moved to, 62.
Christina, daughter of Edward and Agatha, 275, 278.
Chrodegang, Bishop of Metz, his rule for Canons, 282.
Chronicles, English, 32.
Churl, meaning of the word, 41.
Cirencester, taken by Ceawlin, 36; stay of the Danes at, 125.
Cissa, invasion of, 34, 317.
Civil war, meaning of, 14.
Claudius, Emperor, visits Britain, 15.
Cleobury, defeat of Bishop Leofgar at, 278.
Cnut, son of Swegen, 222; true form of the name. ib.; chosen King by the Danish fleet, 224; driven out of England, 225; returns and wars with Edmund, 226; chosen King by the English at Southampton, 227; his wars with Edmund, 229-231; makes peace with Edmund at Olney, 231; tale of their single combat, ib.; finally chosen and crowned, 234; sends Edmund's sons to Sweden, 235; stories about Eadric and, 236; his marriage with Emma, 237; murders Earl Ulf, 238; he and Thurkill build a minster at Assandun, 239; grants a charter to Glastonbury Abbey, ib.; translates the body of Saint Ælfheah to Canterbury, 240; story about his rebuking the sea, ib.; his visits to Ely Abbey, 240, 241; his pilgrimage to Rome, 242; his letter from thence to the people of England, 243; his Code of Laws, 244; brings Scotland to submission, ib.; his death, 246; his campaign

against London contrasted with William's, 340, 345.

Cnut's Law renewed by Harold, 296.

Coifi, high priest of Woden, his argument against his idols, 57 : he destroys the temple at Godmundingham, 58.

Cologne, French name of Köln, 276.

Colonies planted by the Phœnicians, 10.

Comet, appearance of, in 1066, 300.

Compurgation, meaning of, 230.

Conan, Count of the Bretons, expedition of William and Harold against, 289.

Conqueror, sense in which William was first so called, 348.

Conrad the Second, Emperor, Cnut present at his coronation, 242.

Constantine, the first Christian Emperor, first proclaimed in Britain, 21.

—— the Sixth, Emperor, deposed, 84.

—— King of Scots, does homage to Æthelstan, 148 ; shelters Guthfrith, 151, 152 ; defeated at Brunanburh, 153.

Corfes Gate, 184 ; Edward the Martyr murdered at, 185.

Cornwall, boundary and language of, 153, 263 ; practice of wrecking in, 288 ; Robert of Mortain, Earl of, 330.

Coutances, peninsula of, 210.

Coventry minster built by Earl Leofric, 279.

Cromlechs, 7.

Crowland Abbey founded by Æthelbald of Mercia, 78 ; its destruction by the Danes, 110.

Cumberland, ravaged by Æthelred, 207.

Cumbra, Alderman, murdered by Sigeberht, 76.

Cuthberht, Saint, and King Alfred, story of, 127.

Cuthred, King of the West-Saxons, defeats the Mercians at Burford, 75 ; his death, 76.

Cwenthryth, daughter of Cenwulf, charged with the murder of her brother Cenhelm, 87.

Cwichelm seeks to slay Edwin, 56 ; first Christian King of the West-Saxons, 61.

Cyneberht, Abbot, baptizes the sons of Arwald, 68.

Cynegils, first Christian King of the West-Saxons, 61.

Cyneheard, Cynewulf killed by, 89.

—— Bishop of the Sumorsætas, 177.

Cynesige, Bishop of Lichfield, brings back Eadwig to the banquet, 170.

—— Archbishop of York, hallows the minster at Waltham, 281.

Cynethryth, mother of Archbishop Dunstan, 164.

—— wife of Offa, murders Æthelberht of East-Anglia, 86.

Cynewulf, King of the West-Saxons, his victories over the Welsh, 76 ; defeated

by Offa at Bensington, 82 ; killed by Cyneheard, 89.

Cynric, son of Cerdic, 35.

Danegeld, meaning of, 207 ; laid on, 250.

Danes, their language, 6 ; beginning of their invasions, 91 ; three periods of their invasions, 92 ; wars with Charles Great, 96 ; wars with Ecgberht, winter in Sheppey, 102 ; their ravages in Æthelberht's reign, 107 ; great invasion in Æthelred's reign, 108 ; their settlements in Northumberland, Mercia, and East-Anglia, 109; divide Northumberland among them, 118 ; divide the kingdom with Alfred, 125 ; submit to Edward, 144 ; their invasions begin again, 187, 191 ; their relations with the Empire, 189 ; their settlement in Cumberland, 207 ; massacred by Æthelred, 211 ; take Canterbury, 217 ; settle in England under Cnut, 239.

Dannewerk, made by Gorm and Thyra, 188.

David's, Saint, ravaged by Eadric, 221.

Deerhurst, church of, built by Odda, 263 Odda dies there, 278.

Deira, Division of Northumberland, 38 . Pope Gregory's pun on the name, 44 ; made an Earldom by Edgar, 174.

Denewulf, Bishop, legend of, 121.

Deorham, battle of, 36.

Dermot, King of Leinster, receives Harold and Leofwine, 262.

Devonshire, conquered by Ecgberht, 96 ; traces of the Welsh in, 152.

Diuma, the Scot, first Bishop of the Mercians, 61.

Dorchester, Oxfordshire, foundation of the Bishoprick of, 61 ; extent of, 259.

Dover, outrages of Eustace at, 260 : castle of, built by Harold, 342 ; surrenders to William, *ib.*

Dragon, golden, the ensign of Wessex, 75, 230, 330.

Drogo, Count of Mantes, 259, 260.

Dublin, Harold takes refuge at, 262.

Duduc, Saxon Bishop of Somersetshire, 282.

Dufnal, Prince, 175.

Duncan, Under-king of Cumberland, 244 : killed by Macbeth, 273.

Dunstan, Archbishop, sketch of his life, 164, 168, 177 ; King Eadred's chief minister, 165 ; driven out of the Kingdom by Eadwig, 167, 170 ; recalled by Edgar, 170 ; his influence in Edward the Martyr's reign, 184 ; in that of Æthelred the Second, 190 ; his death, *ib.*

Durham, the Bishoprick of, 174 ; the city besieged by Malcolm, 214.

Eaba, first Christian Queen of the South-Saxons, 61.

Eadbald, King of the Kentishmen, forsakes and returns to Christianity, 61.

Eadberht, King of the Northumbrians, takes Alcluyd, 77; his friendship with Pippin, *ib.*

—— Pren, King of the Kentishmen, taken prisoner by Cenwulf, 87.

Eadburh, wife of Beorhtric of Wessex, 90; story of, 93.

—— daughter of Edward the Elder, story of, 146.

Eadgifu, daughter of Edward the Elder, marries Charles the Simple, 141, 146.

—— her sister, married to Lewis, King of Provence, 146.

—— Abbess of Leominster, her misconduct, 257.

Eadgyth. *See* Edith.

Eadhild, King Æthelstan's sister, married to Hugh the Great, 146, 159.

Eadmund. *See* Edmund.

Eadnoth, Bishop of Dorchester, translates Ælfheah, 219; slain at Assandun, 231.

Eadnoth, Bishop of London, dies, 137.

Eadred, King, 145; his reign, 165; his death, 166.

Eadric Streona, favourite of Æthelred, 212; marries his daughter Edith, *ib.*; murders Ælfhelm, 214; made Alderman of the Mercians, *ib.*; betrays Æthelred's army, 217; harries Saint David's, 221; murders Sigeferth and Morkere, 225; joins Cnut, 226; his treason at Sherstone, 229; joins Edmund, *ib.*; flees at Assandun, 230; different accounts of his death, 236.

Eadsige, Archbishop of Canterbury, 259.

Eadwig, son of Edmund, 165; his reign, 166; drives Dunstan out of the kingdom, 167; marries Ælfgifu, 169; revolt against, 170; separated from Ælfgifu, *ib.*; his death, 171.

—— brother of Edmund Ironside, 233, 234.

—— King of the Churls, 235.

Eadwine. *See* Edwin.

Eadwulf of Bamborough, 148.

—— Uhtred's brother, Earl of Bernicia, 227; killed by Siward, 274.

Ealdgyth, Sigeferth's widow, married to Edmund Ironside, 225, 233.

—— daughter of Ælfgar, given in marriage to Gruffydd, 280; marries King Harold, 300, 319; sent by Edwin and Morkere to Chester, 341.

Ealdhelm, first Bishop of Sherborne, 69, 74.

—— first Bishop of Wells, 147.

Ealdhun, first Bishop of Durham, 215.

Ealdorman (Alderman), the title of, 35, 165, 194.

Ealdred, son of Eadwulf of Bamborough, 148.

Ealdred, Abbot of Tavistock, becomes Bishop of Worcester, 256; persuades the King to "in-law" Swegen, 258; sent after Earl Godwine's two sons, 262; his embassy to Germany, 275, 276, 278; makes peace with Gruffydd, 278; hallows Gloucester minster, 280; goes on a pilgrimage to Jerusalem, 281; succeeds Cynesige as Archbishop of York, *ib.*; goes to Rome for his pallium, 283; consecrates Wulfstan, 284; crowns Harold, 299; helps to choose Edgar, 341; submits to William, 346; crowns him, 347.

Ealdwulf, the only Archbishop of Lichfield, 83.

Ealhmund, father of Ecgberht, 94.

Ealhstan, Bishop of Sherborne, his warlike exploits, 97, 102, 103; conspires against Æthelwulf, 105; his death, 108.

Ealhswith marries Alfred the Great, 116; dies, 139.

Eanwulf, Alderman of the Sumorsætas, 102; conspires against Æthelwulf, 105; his death, 108.

Earl, first meaning of the word, 41, 155; Danish use the same as Alderman, 157, 165, 236.

East-Angles, foundation of the kingdom of, 38; invite Ecgberht's help against the Mercians, 97, 98; make peace with the Danes, 109; conquered by the Danes, *ib.*; nature of the conquest, 110; the land divided, 125; East-Anglian Danes help Hasting against Alfred. 135, 136; their wars with Edward the Elder, 139; their treaty with him, 139, 140; submit to Edward the Elder, 144; inclined to Danes in Æthelred's time, 213; retain their own meeting of Wise Men, *ib.*; extent of their Earldom, 280; join Harold at Senlac, 318.

East-Saxons, foundation of the kingdom of, 38; submit to Ecgberht, 97.

Ecgberht, King of the West-Saxons, banished, 92; elected King, 93; his conquests, 95; comparison with Charles the Great, *ib.*; wars with the Welsh, 96; with Mercia, 97, 98; Northumberland submits to him, 98; becomes lord of all the English and Southern Welsh, 99; his wars with the Danes, *ib.*

—— King in Northumberland under the Danes, 109.

Ecgfrith, King of the Northumbrians, drives out Wilfrith, 62.

—— King of the Mercians, 87.

Ecgwyn, mother of Æthelstan, 150.

Edgar, son of Edmund, 165, 166; chosen King, 170; his prosperous reign, 171; charge against him of encouraging foreigners, 173; his friendship with the Emperor Otto, *ib.*; surnamed the

Peaceful, 173; his doings in the north of England, *ib.*; hallowed as King, 175; his titles, *ib.*; story about him and Kenneth King of Scots, 176; favours the monks, 177; his death, 178; story of Ælfthryth and, *ib.*; different versions of the story, *ib.*

Edgar, son of Edward and Agatha, 275, 278, 298, 299; chosen King, 341, 344; submits to William, 346.

"Edgar's law," renewal of, 241, 296.

Edinburgh founded by Edwin, 38, 174.

Edith, daughter of Edward the Elder, marries Otto the Great, 146, 173.

—— Saint, daughter of Edgar, 178.

—— daughter of Æthelred, marries Eadric, 247.

—— daughter of Earl Godwine, 247; marries Edward the Confessor, 254; sent to Wherwell monastery, 263; returns, 268; murders Gospatric, 294; favours Tostig against Harold, 344; pays tribute to William for Winchester, 345.

—— *Swanneshals*, finds the body of Harold, 339.

Edmund, King of the East-Angles, martyred by the Danes, 110; legend of his vengeance on Swegen, 223.

—— the Magnificent, his exploits at Brunanburh, 155; succeeds Æthelstan as King, 162; his wars with the Danes, 163; his conquest of Cumberland, *ib.*; murdered, *ib.*

—— son of Edgar, 179, 182.

—— Ironside, son of Æthelred, 211; marries Ealdgyth, 225; his wars with Cnut, 226; chosen King, 227; his battles with Cnut, 229, 230; divides the kingdom with Cnut, 231; his death, 232.

—— son of Edmund Ironside, 235, 275.

Edward the Elder, chosen King, 138; first lord of all Britain, *ib.*; his wars with the Danes, 139, 144; his fortresses, 140; all the princes of Britain submit to him, 145; his death, *ib.*; his children, *ib.*

—— the martyr, son of Edgar and Æthelflæd, 178; chosen King, 183; story of his death, 185.

—— son of Edmund Ironside, 235, 275; comes to England, 278; his death, 279.

—— the Confessor, son of Æthelred and Emma, 223; recalled by Harthacnut, 251; chosen King, 253; his fondness for Normans, 254; his dealings with his mother, 254, 265; his monastery at Westminster, 271; his fondness for Tostig, 296; leaves the crown to Harold, 297; his death, *ib.*

—— the First (after the Conquest), his dealings with the Scots and Welsh, 145; his body rests awhile in Waltham Abbey, 339.

Edwin, Bretwalda and first Christian King of the Northumbrians, 50; story of his conversion, 52-59; killed by Cædwalla and Penda at Heathfield, 59.

Edwin, son of Edward the Elder, 147; story of, 160.

—— Earl, son of Ælfgar, Earl of the Mercians, 295; joins the Northumbrian revolt, *ib.*; drives Tostig from Lindesey, 304; defeated at Fulford, 306; fails to support Harold, 319; betrays Edgar, 341, 342.

Eglaf, brother of Thurkill, invades England, 216.

Eiréné, deposes her son Constantine the Sixth, 84.

Elbe, lands near, first seats of the English, 1, 8.

Elizabeth, wife of Harold Hardrada, left in Shetland, 305.

Ely Abbey, foundation of, 191; Brihtnoth buried at, *ib.*; Cnut's visit to, 240; the Ætheling Alfred murdered at, 249.

Emma, daughter of Richard the Fearless, marries Æthelred, 210; sent into Normandy, 223; marries Cnut, 238; regent for Harthacnut, 247; driven out by Harold, 249; recalled by Harthacnut, 251; spoiled by Edward, 254; her death and legend, 265.

"Emma," Harold of Norway's coat of mail so called, 314.

Emperor, origin of the title, 14; break in their succession, 134; English Kings why so called, 139.

Emperors, Eastern, 24, 83; supplanted by the French, 85; keep Scandinavian mercenaries in pay, 335.

Empire, Roman, continued in the East, 24, 83; transferred to the Franks, 85; united with the crowns of Germany and Italy, 134.

England, why so called, 1, 31; nomenclature of, 26.

Englefield, Danes defeated at, 111.

English, their conquest of Britain, 14; their character, and difference from other Teutonic conquests, 27; their true name, 31; remain heathens in Britain, 42; their conversion to Christianity, 42-50.

English language, its relations to other tongues, 2-5; a Teutonic language, 25; its relations to German and French, *ib.*

Ereri, Welsh name of Snowdon, 98.

Eric (Eoric, Danish King of East-Anglia, death of, 139.

—— son of Harold Blaatand, his short reign in Northumberland, 165.

—— King of Swedes, drives out Swegen, 206.

—— Earl of Northumberland under Cnut, 227, 236.

Erling, Earl of Orkney, joins Harold Hardrada, 305.

Escheat, law of, 282.

Esegar the Staller, grandson of Tofig the Proud, commands the Londoners at Senlac, 346; his wounds there, *ib.*; his dealings with William, *ib.*

Estrith, daughter of Swegen, marries Ulf, 247.

Ethandun, Alfred's victory at, 122–124.

Eustace, Count of Boulogne, marries Godgifu, 260; his outrages at Dover, *ib.*; helps to kill Harold when wounded, 336.

Exeter, taken and retaken in Alfred's wars, 119, 120; meaning of the name, 119; greatness of, 120; Welsh expelled from, by Æthelstan, 152; fortified by Æthelstan, *ib.*; his laws published at, 143, 159; the Danes beaten off by the citizens, 211; marriage-gift of Emma, 212; betrayed to Swegen, *ib.*; Bishoprick of, founded, 251.

Exmouth, Beorn murdered at, 257.

Eyder, boundary of Germany and Denmark, 96, 188.

Eystein Orre, legend of his exploits at Stamfordbridge, 311, 315.

Fins, their language, 6.

Five Boroughs, recovered by Edmund, 162; submit to Swegen, 221; their Thanes murdered by Eadric, 225; occupied by Edmund Ironside, 226.

Florence of Worcester, his chronicle, 218.

Fortification, advance in, under Æthelstan, 152.

Fræna, Danish Earl, killed at Ashdown, 111, 112.

—— Thane of Lindesey, his cowardice, 205.

France, called from the Franks, 24; beginning of the modern kingdom of, 105; descent of the later Kings of, 134; old boundaries of, 209; conquests of, from Germany and Burgundy, *ib.*

Francia, meaning of name, 210; mercenaries from, at Senlac, 329.

Franks, their territories in Germany and Gaul, 24; countries called from them, *ib.*; Æthelberht marries a Frankish princess, 45; their language, 46; their Kings and Dukes help the English missionaries in Germany, 73; their power in Italy, 84; their Kings become Kings of all Germany, 85; kingdoms of the East and West, 105; united under Charles the Fat, 133; finally divided, 134.

French language, origin of, 25; not known in the time of Charles the Great, 85; beginnings of, 105; supplants German in Gaul, 141; adopted by the Normans, 142, 209.

Frirck, banner-bearer of Harold Hardrada, 312.

Frisians, in Alfred's service, 136; their connexion with the English, 137.

Fulford, battle of, Harold Hardrada defeats Edwin and Morkere at the, 306.

Gainsborough, Swegen receives submission at, 221; dies at, 224.

Gallia, meaning of name, 210.

Gamel murdered by Tostig, 294.

Gaul, conquest of, by Cæsar, 13.

Geoffrey, Bishop of Coutances, his share in William's coronation, 347.

Gerent, Welsh King, his wars with Ine, 70.

German language, its relations to English, 3, 25; spoken by Charles the Great, 85; spoken by the West-Frankish Kings, 105; dies out in Gaul, 141, 209.

Germany not conquered by the Romans, 22; English missionaries in, 62; first united by Charles the Great, 83; end of the kingdom, 85; separation from France and Lorraine, 105; Italy united to, 134.

Gilbert, Count, guardian of William the Conqueror, 264.

Gillingham, Edward the Confessor chosen King at, 253.

Giraldus Cambrensis, his account of Harold's campaign, 286.

Gisa, Bishop of Somersetshire, consecrated at Rome, 281; his quarrel with Earl Harold, 282; his changes at Wells, *ib.*

Gisela, Queen of the Hungarians, 235.

Glass, in windows, introduced into England by Benedict Biscop, 74.

Glastonbury, Arthur buried at, 35; becomes English, 66; legend of Alfred at, 127; Dunstan, Abbot of, 164; Edmund the Magnificent buried at, *ib.*; Edgar buried at, 178; Edmund Ironside buried at, 233; Cnut's visit and charter to, 239; two churches at, 240.

Gloucester taken by Ceawlin, 36; meetings held at, 255, 260, 268, 284, 285; armies gathered at, 277–285; minster hallowed by Ealdred, 280.

Gloucestershire, speech of, 37; traces of the Welsh in, 258.

Goda, Devonshire Thane, killed at Watchet, 190.

Godgifu, daughter of Æthelred and Emma, marries Drogo, 259; her son Ralph, *ib.*; marries Eustace, 260.

—— wife of Leofric, legend of, 279; her building of churches, *ib.*; her great age, *ib.*; her reverence for St. Wulfstan, 284.

Godwine, Thane of Lindesey, his cowardice, 205.

—— Alderman of Lindesey, killed at Assandun, 230.

—— Earl of the West-Saxons, 239; his exploits in the North, 242, 247; supports Harthacnut against Harold, 246; governs in Wessex for Harthacnut, 247;

marries Gytha, 247 ; question as to his father, 247, 248 ; his favour with the Ætheling Æthelstan, 248 ; with Cnut, *ib.*; charged with the murder of the Ætheling Alfred, 249 ; unlikelihood of the story, *ib.* ; sent to dig up the body of Harold, 250 ; makes compurgation for the murder of Alfred, *ib.* ; sent against Worcester, 251 ; promotes the election of Edward, 253 ; becomes his chief adviser, 254 ; opposes the Normans, *ib.* ; helps to despoil Emma, *ib.* ; proposes to help Swegen, 256 ; refuses to punish the men of Dover, 261 ; gathers a force at Beverstone, *ib.* ; demands justice against Eustace, *ib.* ; outlawed by the Wise Men at London, 262 ; takes refuge at Bruges, *ib.* ; sets sail from Bruges, 266 ; reaches London, 267 ; demands restoration, *ib.* ; is restored by the Wise Men, 268 ; dies at Winchester, *ib.* ; legend of his death, 269 ; his character, 270 ; the power of his house, 280.

Gorm the Old unites Denmark in one kingdom, 188 ; his wars with Henry the Fowler, *ib.*

Gospatric murdered by Tostig and Edith, 294.

Goths, East, Theodoric King of, reigns in Italy, 24 ; West, under Alaric, take Rome, *ib.*; their kingdom in Spain and Aquitaine, *ib.*

Greeks, 9 ; their colonies, 11 ; later, called themselves Romans, 24 ; Greek language, its connexion with English, 9 ; spoken in the Eastern Empire, 85 ; ignorance of, in the West, 130.

Greenland discovered by the Northmen, 91.

Greenwich, Saint Ælfheah martyred at, 220 ; Thurkill's fleet lies at, 223.

Gregory the Great, Pope, 43 ; story of, and the English boys, 45 ; sends Augustine to Britain, *ib.*; his works translated by Alfred, 130.

—— supposed son of Edward the Elder, 147.

—— the Seventh, Pope. *See* Hildebrand.

Grimbald, of Flanders, encouraged by Alfred, 131.

Gruach, wife of Macbeth, 273.

Gruffydd ap Llywelyn, King of North-Wales, in alliance with Swegen against Gruffydd of South-Wales, 257 ; invades Herefordshire and defeats the French, 265 ; joins Ælfgar and defeats Ralph, 276 ; burns Hereford, 277 ; flies before Harold, *ib.* ; peace made with, *ib.*; rebels again, and defeats Leofgar, 278 ; submits again, *ib.* ; helps Ælfgar, 280 ; marries his daughter Ealdgyth, *ib.* ; Harold's great campaign against, 285 ; deposed and killed by his own people, 286 ; his

head sent to Edward, 286 ; date of his death, 287.

Gruffyd ap Rhydderch, King of South-Wales, defeated by Swegen, 257 ; joins the Danes, invades Gloucestershire, and defeats Bishop Ealdred, 258 ; killed by Gruffydd of North-Wales, 293.

Guildford, the Ætheling Alfred seized at, 249.

Gunhild, daughter of Harold Blaatand, killed in the massacre of St. Brice, 211.

—— daughter of Cnut and Emma, 238 ; marries Henry the Third, 245.

—— niece of Cnut, banished, 255 ; her husbands and children, *ib.*

Guthfrith or Godfrey, Danish King of Northumberland, driven out by Æthelstan, 148 ; his wars with Æthelstan, 151, 152.

Guthmund, Norwegian chief, at the battle of Maldon, 191 ; money paid to, 205.

Guthorm, Danish King of East-Anglia, invades Wessex, 119 ; baptized, and makes peace with Alfred, 123-125 ; his second war with Alfred, 132 ; confounded with Æthelstan, 159.

Guy, Count of Ponthieu, imprisons Harold, 288 ; gives him up to William, 289.

—— Bishop of Amiens, his "Carmen de Bello Hastingensi," 320 ; his account of William's coronation, 346.

Gyrth, fourth son of Godwine, takes refuge at Bruges, 262 ; William's offer to, 322 ; his advice to Harold, 325 ; marches to Senlac, 326 ; Norman stories of, 328 ; killed by William's own hand, 334.

Gytha, sister of Ulf, marries Godwine, 247 ; takes refuge at Bruges, 262 ; legend of her and Harold, 323 ; asks for Harold's body, 338.

—— daughter of Osgod Clapa, marries Tofig, 251.

Hadrian, Emperor, visits Britain, 20 ; his wall, 20, 83.

—— Pope, his dealings with Offa, 83.

Hakon, King of Norway, called Æthelstan's Foster, 159.

—— the Doughty Earl, marries Gunhild, 255 ; banished and drowned, *ib.*

Halfdene, Danish King at Ashdown, 111 ; divides the lands of Northumberland, 118.

Hampshire, origin of the name, 107.

Harold Hardrada, King of the Northmen, 256 ; meaning of his surname, *ib.* ; his exploits in the East, 305 ; his war with Swegen, *ib.* ; his invasion of England, *ib.* ; lands at Riccall, *ib.* ; prodigies attending his voyage, 306 ? defeats Edwin and Morkere at Fulford, *ib.* ; receives hostages from York and Yorkshire, *ib.*; encamps at Stamfordbridge, *ib.* ; defeated and slain by Harold of England,

310 ; legend of his interview with Harold of England, 313 ; of his death, 315.

Harold, Danish Earl, killed at Ashdown, 111, 112.

—— Blaatand, King of the Danes, 165 ; his dealings with Normandy, 189, 210 ; with Northumberland, *ib.*; does homage to Otto the Second, and is baptized, *ib.* ; deposed by his son Swegen, 189.

—— son of Cnut, 238 ; reigns north of the Thames, 247 ; chosen King over all England, 249 ; dies at Oxford, *ib.*; buried at Westminster, *ib.*

—— Earl, husband of Gunhild, 255.

—— son of Ralph, Ewias Harold called from, 279.

—— second son of Godwine, 247, 248 ; Earl of the East-Angles, 257 ; refuses to restore Swegen's lordships, *ib.* ; buries Beorn, 258 ; joins his father at Beverstone, 261 ; outlawed, 262 ; pursued by Ealdred, *ib.*; takes refuge at Dublin, *ib.*; sets sail from Ireland, 266 ; plunders at Porlock, *ib.* ; joins his father, 267 ; restored to his Earldom, 268 ; succeeds his father as Earl of the West-Saxons, 270 ; chief ruler under Edward, *ib.*; he favours the secular clergy, 271 ; founds the College of Waltham, 272 ; his character, 272, 273 ; favours Germans, 272 ; his travels and pilgrimage, 280 ; his prospect of the crown, 280, 287 ; his friendship for St. Wulfstan, 284 ; marches from Gloucester to Rhuddlan and burns Gruffydd's palace, 285 ; sails from Bristol, and subdues all Wales, 285, 286 ; makes the English adopt the Welsh tactics, 285 ; receives the oaths of the Welsh, 286 ; traditions of his Welsh campaign, *ib.*; stories of his oath to William, 287, 288 ; shipwrecked on the coast of Ponthieu, 288 ; imprisoned by Guy, *ib.*; set free by William, 289 ; stays at William's court, *ib.*; helps William in his Breton campaign, *ib.*; his oath, *ib.*; different accounts of it, 290 ; its probable nature, *ib.*; where his real fault lay, 291 ; builds a hunting seat at Portskewet, 293 ; receives demands of the Northumbrians at Northampton, 295 ; his policy, *ib.*; meets the Northumbrians at Oxford and confirms their demands, 296 ; recommended by Edward to the Wise Men, 297 ; chosen King, 299 ; crowned by Ealdred, *ib.*; lawfulness of his title, 300 ; the Northumbrians refuse to acknowledge him, *ib.*; he wins them over without bloodshed, *ib.* ; marries Ealdgyth, *ib.*; his answer at William's embassy, 301 ; his defence of the coast, 303 ; he is forced to disband his fleet and army, 304 ; marches against Harold Hardrada, 306 ; legend of his sickness and recovery, 307 ; value of the story, 308 ; reviews his fleet at

Tadcaster, 309 ; passes through York, *ib.*; his victory at Stamfordbridge, 310 ; makes peace with Olaf and Paul, *ib.*; legend of his answer to Tostig, 313 ; hears of William's landing, 318 ; marches to London 319 ; refuses William's offer of single combat, 323 ; legend of his visit to Waltham, 324 ; sets forth from London, 325 ; refuses to ravage the land, 326 ; pitches on Senlac, *ib.*; his generalship, 327 ; stories of his spies, 328 ; marshals his men for the battle, 330, 331 ; his speech, 331 ; his personal exploits, 334 ; his death, 336 ; legend of his escape, 337 ; his body found and buried on the seashore, 338 ; translated to Waltham, 339 ; destruction of his tomb, *ib.*; his sons, 341 ; Dover Castle built by him, 342.

Harthacnut, son of Cnut and Emma, 238 ; succeeds his father in Denmark, 246 ; reigns south of the Thames, 247 ; stays in Denmark, *ib.*; deposed, 249 ; chosen King over all England, 250 ; lays on a Danegeld, *ib.* ; digs up the body of Harold, *ib.* ; causes Worcester to be burned, 251 ; recalls his brother Edward, *ib.* ; dies at Lambeth, *ib.*

Hasting leads the Danes into Gaul, 125 ; his invasion of England, 135.

Hastings, William encamps at, 317, 318.

Helen, mother of Constantine, 21.

Heming, brother of Thurkill, invades England, 216.

—— son of Gunhild, banished, 255.

Hengest settles in Kent, 33.

Hengestesdun, Ecgberht defeats the Danes and Welsh at, 96.

Henry, King and Emperors or the name of, how reckoned, 246.

—— King of the East-Franks, an ally of Edward the Elder, 146 ; his wars with the Danes, 188 ; founds the mark of Sleswick, *ib.*

—— the Second, Emperor, the Ætheling Edward marries his niece, 235.

—— the Third, Emperor, marries Gunhild, daughter of Cnut, 245 ; his war with Baldwin, 256 ; his alliance with England, *ib.*; embassy of Ealdred, 275.

—— the Fourth, Emperor, his treatment by Hildebrand, 303.

—— the First, King of the French, helps William of Val-ès-Dunes, 264 ; pleads for Godwine, 266.

—— of Huntingdon, his account of the battle of Stamfordbridge, 310.

Heptarchy, meaning of the word, 40.

Herakles, Greek proverb of, 304.

Hereford, Church of, founded by Offa, 87 ; Welsh do homage to Æthelstan at, 152 ; Gruffydd defeats Ralph near, 276 ; church and city burned, 277 ; restored by Harold, 277–279.

Herefordshire, traces of the Welsh in, 258 ; Frenchmen in, set Edward against Godwine, 261 ; ravaged by Gruffydd, 265, 276 ; added to Harold's Earldom, 279.

Heretoga, meaning of the word, 205.

Hereward, his exploits, 341.

Herleva, mother of William the Conqueror, 264 ; marries Herlwin, 330.

Herlwin, husband of Herleva, 330.

Hermann, Archbishop of Köln, receives Ealdred, 276.

Herodotus, stories found in, recurring in Teutonic legends, 78.

Hildebrand, Archdeacon of Rome, wins over Pope Alexander to support William, 303.

Holland, why so called, 78.

Holms, Steep and Flat, sufferings of the Danes on, 143.

Holy Rood, legend of, 271, 323–325; English war-cry, 330.

Honorius, Emperor, recalls the Roman Legions from Britain, 30.

Horsa settles in Kent, 33.

Horses not used in battle by the English, 276, 327.

Housecarls, force founded by Cnut, 239; nature of the force, 250; their arms, Harthacnut's Danegeld, *ib.*; their arms, 285, 331; their fame in Norway, 305; they fight to the last at Senlac, 337.

Howel the Good, King of the Welsh, his laws, 148.

Hroald, Danish Earl, ravages Wales, 142.

Hubba. *See* Ingwar.

Hugh the Great, Duke of the French, marries Eadhild, daughter of Edward the Elder, 146; helps to restore Lewis, 159.

—— Capet, chosen King of the French, 209; the crown remains in his family, *ib.*

—— the French Churl, betrays Exeter to Swegen, 212.

Hun, Alderman, killed at Ellandun, 97.

Hungary, language of, 6 ; Kings of, Emperors and Kings of Germany, 85 ; Stephen first Christian King of, 235 ; Kings of, crowned with Saint Stephen's crown, 235 ; embassy, 275.

Hwiccas, in Gloucestershire, &c., 39, 61, 82 ; fight between them and the Wilsætas, 93 ; their land harried by Cnut, 226.

Iceland, discovered by the Northmen, 91.

Iceni revolt under Boadicea, 16.

Idwal, Prince of South-Wales, subdued by Edgar, 173.

Image worship, disputes about, 84.

India, language of, 6 ; Alfred's embassy to, 132.

Ine, King of the West-Saxons, his wars and laws, 69, 70; founds the Church of Wells, 69 ; founds Taunton, 70 ; his battle with Ceolred of Mercia at Wanborough, *ib.*; goes to Rome and dies, 71 ; legend of, *ib.*

Ingulf, Abbot of Crowland, 110.

Ingwar puts Saint Edmund to death, 110.

Interregnum in 1066, 340.

Ipswich plundered by the Norwegians, 191.

Ireland, language of, 4 ; people of, called Scots, 48 ; Danes in, 143, 151, 162 ; Danes from, ravage England, 258 ; Harold and Leofwine take refuge in, 262 ; return from, 266 ; Ælfgar raises a fleet in, 276.

Italy, kingdom of, 134 ; united to Germany, *ib.*

Ithamar of Rochester, first English Bishop, 61.

James, first Christian King of the Swedes, protects the children of Edmund, 235.

Jedburgh, Archbishop Wulfstan imprisoned at, 165.

Jehmarc, Under-king in Scotland, does homage to Cnut, 245.

Jersey, Duke Robert's fleet driven back from, 245.

Jerusalem, Alfred's embassy to, 132 ; pilgrimage to, of Robert, 263; of Swegen, 268 ; of Ealdred, 281 ; of Harold Hardrada, 305.

John, the Old-Saxon, encouraged by Alfred, 131.

—— the Tenth, Pope, perjury of the Ætheling Alfred before, 150.

—— the Twelfth, Pope, gives the pallium to Dunstan, 177 ; crowns Otto the Great, *ib.*

—— the Fifteenth, Pope, makes peace between Æthelred and Richard, 210.

—— the Nineteenth, Pope, receives Cnut at the coronation of the Emperor Conrad, 242, 243.

—— of Salisbury, his account of Harold's Welsh campaigns, 286.

Judith, daughter of Charles the Bald, marries Æthelwulf, 104 ; marries Æthelbald, 106, 107; mistakes about, 116.

—— sister of Baldwin, marries Tostig, 252 ; goes with him to Rome, 281.

Julian, Emperor, called the Apostate, 21.

Jumièges, Church of, 259.

Jupiter, story of, 308.

Justin, Norwegian chief at the battle of Maldon, 191 ; money paid to, *ib.*

Jutes, first Teutonic settlers in Britain, 30, 32 ; their kingdoms in Kent and Wight, 33; of Wight conquered by Ceadwalla, 67 ; Alfred's mother sprung from, 115.

Jütland, peninsula of, 210.

Kenelm, Saint, legend of, 87.

Kenneth, King of Scots, his dealings with Edgar, 174, 175 ; legend of, 176.

Kent, first Teutonic kingdom in Britain, 32 ; keeps its Welsh name, 33 ; two kingdoms in, 34 ; decline of, 95 ; becomes an appanage of Wessex, 95, 97 ; its two bishopricks, 139 ; men of, distinguished at Senlac, 326, 331 ; legend of their submission to William, 344.

Kings, English, their powers limited by law, 41 ; commonly married English-women, 45 ; seldom chosen in their father's lifetime, 106 ; called Emperors of Britain, 139 ; force of the title, *ib.* ; lords of all Britain, 145 ; right of the Wise Men to choose, 299 .

Kingston, kings crowned at, 148.

Köln, Ealdred stays at, 276 ; trade of, with London, *ib.*

Lady, title of King's wife in Wessex, 94, 212 ; Old, or Queen Dowager, 254.

Lambert, Cnut's real Christian name, 222.

Landwaster, Harold Hardrada's banner, 306, 312.

Laon, royal city of the West-Franks, 134, 141, 209.

Latin language, when spoken in Britain, 19 ; languages derived from it, 25 ; names preserved in Southern Europe, 26.

Leicester taken by Æthelflæd, 143 ; by Edmund, 163.

Leo the Third, Pope, 83 ; suppresses the Archbishoprick of Lichfield, *ib.* ; crowns Charles the Great, 85.

—— the Fourth, Pope, hallows Alfred as King, 104.

—— the Ninth, Pope ; his dealings with Ulf of Dorchester, 259 ; forbids Robert to consecrate Spearhafoc, 263.

Leofgar, Bishop of Hereford, killed by Gruffydd, 278.

Leofric, Earl of the Mercians, 239 ; supports Harold and Cnut, 246 ; sent against Worcester, 251 ; helps to despoil Emma, 254 ; refuses help to Swegen, 256 ; joins Edward at Gloucester, 261 ; makes a compromise between Edward and God-wine, 262 ; lets the Normans pass through his Earldom, 267 ; greatness of his family, 270, 280 ; dies, 279 ; his reverence for St. Wulfstan, 284.

—— Abbot of Peterborough, joins Harold at Senlac, 326 ; escapes and dies, 337.

Leofwine, fifth son of Godwine, takes refuge at Dublin, 262 ; returns with Harold, 266 ; marches to Senlac, 326 ; his death, 334.

Leominster, Monastery of, 257.

Lewis the Pious, Emperor, division of his dominions, 104.

—— King of the East-Franks, oath taken by his soldiers, 105.

Lewis, son of Arnulf, last Carlovingian King in Germany, 134.

—— King of Provence, marries Eadgifu, daughter of Edward the Elder, 146.

—— son of Charles the Simple, seeks shelter in England, 146, 159 ; restored by Æthelstan, 159.

—— Saint, compared with Alfred, 113.

Lichfield, single Archbishop of, 83.

Lillebonne, William assembles the Norman barons at, 303.

Lindesey conquered by the Danes, 117 ; meaning of name, 205 ; submits to Swe-gen, 221 ; to Cnut, 225 ; plundered by Tostig, 304.

Lindisfarne ravaged by Malcolm, 284.

Liofa murders Edmund, 163.

Lithuania, language of, 6.

Liudhard, Frankish Bishop in Kent, 46.

Lombards settle in Italy, 83 ; conquered by Charles the Great, 84.

London, first mention of, 16 ; Boadicea defeated near, *ib.* ; said to have been a Welsh Archbishoprick, 21 ; keeps its Welsh name, 26 ; taken by the Danes, 102 ; repaired by Alfred, 133 ; occupied by Edward the Elder, 140 ; burnt, 191 ; Swegen and Olaf beaten off by its citizens, 205 ; Swegen beaten off again, 222 ; submits to Swegen, 223 ; the citizens choose Edmund King, 228 ; besieged by Cnut, 228 ; assigned to Edmund, 231 ; Eric and the Danes winter in, *ib.* ; seafaring men of, support Harold the son of Cnut, 246 ; Edward the Confessor chosen King at, 253 ; Godwine and his sons restored at, 267, 268 ; trade of, with Germany, 276 ; men of, distinguished at Senlac, 326, 331 ; joins in the election of Edgar, 341 ; citizens eager to fight with William, 342 ; their skirmish with his horsemen, 345 ; forces of, commanded by Esegar, 346 ; submit to William, *ib.*

Londonderry, why so called, 343.

Lothar, Emperor, son of Lewis the Pious, 104, 105.

Lotharingia or Lorraine, origin of the name, 105 ; men of, favoured by Harold, 272, 281.

Lothian, part of Northumberland, 3 ; said to be granted by Edgar to Kenneth, 174; language of, 175 ; said to be ceded by Eadwulf, 227.

Löwen Louvain), Arnulf defeats the Danes at, 135.

Ludeca, King of the Mercians, killed by the East-Angles, 98.

Lulach succeeds Macbeth, 274.

Lutgaresbury, old name of Montacute, 271, 323.

Lyfing, Archbishop, crowns Edmund, 228; crowns Cnut, 234.

—— Abbot of Tavistock, brings home

Cnut's letter from Rome, 243; Bishop of Worcester, Devonshire, and Cornwall, 250, 251; charged with the murder of Alfred, 250; promotes the election of Edward, 253.

Macbeth does homage to Cnut, 245; receives the Norman exiles, 267; legends of, 273; how he became King of Scots, *ib.*; spends money at Rome, *ib.*; defeated by Siward, 274: his death, *ib.*

Magesaetas settled in Herefordshire, 75; flee at Assandun, 230.

Magnus, King of the Northmen, threatens England, 255; his war with Swegen Estrithson, 256; his death, *ib.*

Maine, men of, at Senlac, 329.

Mainz, see of, founded, 63.

Malcolm, King of Scots, receives Cumberland from Edmund, 163.

—— Under-king of Cumberland, refuses to pay Danegeld, 208; King of Scots, 214; besieges Durham, 215: defeated by Uhtred, *ib.*; defeats the English at Carham, 244; dwes homage to Cnut, 245.

—— Canmore, son of Duncan, proclaimed King of Scots by Siward, 274; his wars with Macbeth and Lulach, *ib.*; becomes Tostig's sworn brother, 284; harries Northumberland, *ib.*; receives Tostig, 304.

Maldon, battle of, 191; song of, 192.

Malmesbury, Abbey of, Æthelstan buried at, 158.

Man, ravaged by Æthelred, 208.

Manchester, taken by Edward the Elder, 144.

Margaret, daughter of Edward the Ætheling, 275; her character, 298.

Marinus, Pope, his dealings with Alfred, 132.

Mark, meaning of, 188.

Martin, Saint, William vows a church to, 329.

Mary, daughter of Harold Hardrada, betrothed to Eystein Orre, 311.

Matilda, wife of William the Conqueror, her descent, 137; her courtesy to Harold, 289; Bayeux tapestry not made by, 320; Snorro's legend of her death, 323.

Mercia, origin of the kingdom, 39; mixture of races in, *ib.*; becomes Christian, 61; growth of, 65; its greatness under Æthelbald, 75; under Offa, 82; submits to Ecgberht, 98; asks help of Ethelwulf against the Welsh, 103; end of the kingdom of, 118; divided by the Danes, 120; divided between Alfred and Guthorm, 125; English portion of, governed by an Alderman, 125, 126; governed by Æthelflæd, 140; united to Wessex by Edward the Elder, 143, 144; Danish portion of submits to Edward the Elder,

144; chooses Æthelstan King, 148; Edgar made Under-king of, 166; revolts against Eadwig and chooses Edgar, 170; ravaged by Swegen, 222; holds out for Edmund Ironside, 226; which shires of join Harold's muster, 319.

Merton, Cynewulf killed at, 89; Ethelred and Alfred, defeated by the Danes, 112.

Metropolis, meaning of, 343.

Michael, Saint, Mount, monastery on, 210; William and Harold pass by, 289.

Middle-Saxons, London in their land, 38.

Middleton, Church of, founded by Æthelstan, 158.

Milan, Kings of Italy crowned at, 134.

Mona, both isles so called conquered by Edwin, 55.

Montacute, story of the Cross of, 271.

Morkere, Thane of the Five Boroughs, murdered by Eadric, 225.

—— son of Ælfgar, chosen Earl by the Northumbrians, 294; marches to Northampton, 295; confirmed in the Earldom by Edward, 296; drives Tostig away from Lindesey, 304; defeated by Harold Hardrada at Fulford, 306; keeps back the Northumbrians from Harold's muster, 319; joins in the election of Edgar, 341; forsakes him, 342.

Mul, brother of Ceadwalla, killed by the Kentishmen, 67.

Naval affairs under Alfred, 118, 132, 136; under Edgar, 172; under Æthelred, 215.

Neal, Viscount of St. Saviour's, withstands English invasion, 210.

Neot, Saint, legend of, 121.

Nicholas, Pope, 281; refuses pallium to Ealdred, 283; yields to threats of Tostig, *ib.*

Nimwegen, palace at, burnt by Baldwin, 256.

Nithing, meaning of the word, 258.

Normandy, foundation of the Duchy, 142; origin of the name, *ib.*; invaded by Æthelred, 208; beginning of connexion between England and, *ib.*; practically independent of France, 269.

Normans, called French in the English Chronicles, 254; promoted to English Bishopricks, 259; fly from London, 267; outlawed by the Wise Men, 268; take refuge in Scotland and fight for Macbeth, 274; their use of horses in battle, 276, 327; formed the centre at Senlac, 329.

Northampton, submits to Edward the Elder, 144; burned by the Danes, 216, 217; Northumbrians march to, 295; meeting at, *ib.*; ravages of Northumbrians near, *ib.*

Northmen, beginning of their inroads, 99;

their manners and religion, 91 ; kingdoms founded by them, *ib.* ; three periods of their inroads, 92 ; connexion of their inroads in England and on the Continent, 135 ; in Gaul become Normans, 142 ; adopt the French language, *ib.*

Northumberland, kingdom of, founded by Ida, 37 ; extent of, 38 ; becomes Christian, 60 ; greatness and decline of, 77 ; submits to Ecgberht, 98 ; conquered and divided by the Danes, 109, 118 ; submits to Edward the Elder, 145 ; incorporated with the kingdom by Æthelstan, 148 ; revolts against Edmund, 162 ; recovered by him, 163 ; revolts against Eadred and is finally recovered, 165 ; divided by Edgar into two Earldoms, 174 ; united under Uhtred, 215 ; submits to Cnut, 227 ; fierceness of the people of, 274, 293 ; ravaged by Malcolm, 284 ; Siward and Tostig's government in, 293, 294 ; revolts against Tostig, 294 ; Morkere chosen Earl of, *ib.* ; acts as a separate kingdom, *ib.* ; refuses to acknowledge Harold, 300 ; won over by Harold and Wulfstan, *ib.* ; later use of the name, 306 ; men of, kept back by Morkere from Harold's muster, 319.

Norway, kingdom of, founded, 188 ; conquered by Cnut, 239 ; ships from, help Ælfgar, 280.

Norwich burned by Swegen, 213.

Nottingham fortified by Edward the Elder, 144.

Oaths, feeling with regard to, 290, 291 ; nature of Harold's oath to William, 292.

Ockley, Æthelwulf defeats the Danes at, 102.

Oda, Archbishop of Canterbury, makes peace between Edmund and Anlaf, 163 ; crowns Eadred, 165 ; divorces Eadwig and Eadgifu, 170.

Odda, appointed Earl of the Western shires, 263 ; sent with the fleet against Godwine, 266 ; becomes a monk and dies, 278.

Odo, Count of Paris, chosen King of the West-Franks, 134, 159.

—— Bishop of Bayeux, tapestry made for him, 320 ; his behaviour on the night before the battle of Senlac, 328 ; his behaviour in the battle, 330 ; his parents, *ib.*

Odoacer, King of the Heruli, reigns in Italy, 24.

Offa, King of the Mercians, legend of, 78 ; his wars with the West-Saxons, 82 ; with the Welsh, *ib.* ; his dyke, *ib.* ; his friendship with Charles the Great, 83 ; charged with the murder of Æthelberht of East-Anglia, 86 ; dies, 87.

Olaf Tryggvesson, King of the Norwegians, at the battle of Maldon, 191 ;

money paid to, 205 ; joins Swegen in his invasion of England, *ib.* ; makes peace with Æthelred, 206 ; persecutes his heathen subjects in Norway, *ib.*

Olaf, Saint, his wars with Cnut, 274 ; persecutes the heathens, *ib.* ; killed by his own people, 275 ; favourite saint among the Danes, *ib.*

—— son of Harold Hardrada, accompanies his father to England, 305 ; gives hostages to Harold of England, 310.

Old Testament, stories from, 236, 237.

Ordgar, Alderman of Devonshire, legend of, 179.

Orkneys discovered, 17 ; Olaf Tryggvesson visits, 206 ; Earls of, join Harold Hardrada, 305.

Orosius, his works translated by Alfred, 130, 131.

Osbeorn, son of Siward, killed in the war with Macbeth, 274.

Osbern, biographer of Dunstan and Ælfheah, 217.

Osburh, mother of Alfred, 114 ; legend of, 115.

Osgod Clapa, 251 ; banished, 254, 256 ; dies in his bed, 275.

—— Canon of Waltham, sent to Senlac, 325 ; fails to find Harold's body, 338.

Oslac, Earl of Deira under Edgar, 174 ; banished, 184.

—— maternal grandfather of Alfred, 114.

Oswald, Saint, King of the Northumbrians and Bretwalda, finishes the church at York, defeats Cædwalla at Heavenfield, 60 ; defeated and slain by Penda, *ib.*

—— Bishop of Worcester and Archbishop of York, favours the monks, 177 ; favours the election of Edward the Martyr, 184.

Oswine, King of Deira, slain by Oswiu, 60.

Oswiu, King of the Northumbrians and Bretwalda, defeats and slays Penda, 60 ; advance of Christianity under him, *ib.*

Oswulf, Earl of the Northumbrians, the Earldom remains in his family, 165 ; he retains Deira, 174.

Otford, Edmund's victory at, 230.

Othhere, sent by Alfred on voyages of discovery, 131.

Otto the Great, restores the Empire, 134 ; marries Edith, daughter of Edward the Elder, 146 ; his friendship for Edgar, 173.

—— the Second, Emperor, overcomes Harold Blaatand, 189.

Owen, King of Cumberland, joins the Danes at Brunanburh, 153.

—— King of Gwent, submits to Æthelstan, 148.

Oxford, occupied by Edward the Elder, 140 ; burned by the Danes, 216 ; taken by Swegen, 222 ; great meeting at, 225 ;

INDEX. 367

Sigeferth and Morkere murdered at, *ib.* ;
Edgar's law renewed at, by Cnut, 241 ;
kingdom divided at, 246 ; Harold the
son of Cnut dies at, 249 ; Northumbrians march to, 296 ; meeting at, *ib.* ;
Northumberland pacified and Cnut's law
renewed, *ib.*

Pallig, husband of Gunhild, his treason,
211 ; put to death, *ib.*

Pallium, badge of Archbishops, 176, 177,
243, 281.

Panta, river, battle of Maldon fought on
its banks, 191-194.

Paris, importance of the city, 134 ; its
Counts become Kings of France, 134,
141, 159, 209 ; permanence of their dy-
nasty, 209 ; small extent of their power,
ib.

Parret, the Danes defeated near, by Eanwulf and Ealhstan, 102.

Party-spirit, influence of, 166, 167.

Paschal the Second, Pope, could not pronounce the name Cnut, 222.

Paul, Earl of Orkney, joins Harold Hardrada, 305 ; left with the ships at Riccall,
ib. ; gives hostages to Harold of England, 310.

Paullinus, first Bishop of York, converts
the Northumbrians, 55-59 ; takes refuge in Kent, 59.

Peada, son of Penda, King of the Mercians, converted to Christianity, 61.

Pen, meaning of the name, 65.

Pen Selwood, Edmund's victory at, 229.

Penda, King of the Mercians, defeats and
slays Edwin at Heathfield, 59 ; defeats
and slays Oswald at Maserfield, 60 ; defeated and slain, *ib.* ; drives Cenwealh
out of Wessex, 65.

Penhow, men of Devon and Somerset
defeated by Danes at, 211.

Persia, language of. 6.

Peterborough, monastery burnt by the
Danes, 110 ; called the Golden Borough,
326.

Pevensey, Roman work at, 18 ; taken by
the South-Saxons, 34 ; Swegen and Beorn
at, 257 ; William lands at and builds a
fort, 317.

Phœnicians, their language, 10 ; their
colonies, 11 ; their supposed dealings
with Britain, 12.

Picardy, mercenaries from, at Senlac, 329.

Picts, ravage Roman Britain, 29 ; join with
the Northumbrians against the Strathclyde Welsh, 77.

Pippin, King of the Franks, his friendship
with Eadberht of Northumberland, 77.

Poitou, men of, at Senlac, 329.

Ponthieu, Harold wrecked on coast of, 288.

Popes, origin of their power, 43 ; their power
in Italy, 83, 84.

Porlock, Danes driven off from, 143 ; Harold
and Leofwine plunder at, 266.

Portskewet, Harold's hunting seat at, destroyed by Caradoc ap Gruffydd, 293.

Provence, language of, 25.

Provinces, Roman, 13.

Prussia, language of, 6.

Pucklechurch, Edmund murdered at, 163.

Rædwald, King of the East-Angles, shelters Edwin, 51 ; defeats and slays Æthelfrith by the Idle, 54.

Rægnald Reginald takes York, 144 ; submits to Edward the Elder, *ib.*

—— son of Guthfrith, his wars with Edmund, 163.

Ragnar Lodbrog, legend of, 108 ; the
Raven worked by his daughters, 123.

Ralph, nephew of Edward, receives an
Earldom, 259 ; joins Edward at Gloucester, 261 ; sent with the fleet against Godwine, 266 ; makes the English fight on
horseback, 276 ; flies before Gruffydd,
ib. ; his death, 279.

—— of Norfolk, William's only English
partisan, 302.

Raven, the Danish standard, 123, 230.

Reading, Alfred defeated by the Danes
at, 111 ; burnt by Danes, 214.

Reeve, meaning of the word, 92.

Regular and Secular clergy, difference
between, 168, 169 ; disputes between,
177, 183.

Repton, taken by the Danes, 117 ; ancient
remains at, *ib.*

Rhiwallon, brother of Gruffydd, appointed
Prince of Wales, 287.

Rhodri Mawr, union of Wales under, 133.

Rhone, river, old boundary of France, 209.

Rhuddlan, Gruffydd's palace at, burned,
285.

Rhys, brother of Gruffydd of South-Wales,
beheaded, 268.

Ricardesrice, Normandy so called, 208.

Riccall, Harold Hardrada lands at, 305.

Richard the Fearless, Duke of the Normans, his long reign, 209 ; his quarrel
with Æthelred, 210.

—— the Good, Duke of the Normans, 209 ;
Æthelred's quarrel with, 210 ; peace
between them, *ib.* ; receives Æthelred,
223 ; dies, 245.

—— the Third, his short reign, 245.

Robert, Count of Paris and Duke of the
French, 141 ; King of the French, 146–
159.

—— Count of Mortain, half-brother of
William, fights at Senlac, 330.

—— Duke of the Normans, called the
Devil and the Magnificent, 245 ; father
of William the Conqueror, *ib.* ; attempts
to restore Edward and Alfred, *ib.* ; goes
on a pilgrimage to Jerusalem, 263 ; suc-

ceeded by his son William the Conqueror, 263.

Robert, Abbot of Jumièges, becomes Bishop of London, 259 ; Archbishop of Canterbury, *ib.* ; sets the King against Godwine, *ib.* ; flies from London, 267 ; deprived, 268, 281.

—— the son of Wymarc, his message to William, 318.

Rochester, Danes driven away from, by Alfred, 132 ; lands of the Bishoprick ravaged by Æthelred, 191 ; besieged by Danes, 207.

Roderick. *See* Rhodri.

Roger of Montgomery, commands the Norman right at Senlac, 329, 332 ; he breaks down the barricade, 334.

Roland, song of, 333.

Rolf, Rou, or Rollo, helps Guthorm against Harold, 132 ; does homage to Charles the Simple, 141 ; founds the Duchy of Normandy, 142.

Romans, their character and conquests, 12 ; first entered Britain, 13 ; their conquest of Britain, 15–17 ; their works, *ib.* ; their occupation of Britain, 18 ; their wars with the barbarians, 23 ; their name still preserved in the East, 24, 84 ; their legions recalled from Britain, 30 ; their towns withstand the English, 39 ; choose Charles the Great as Emperor, 84.

Rome, Cnut's pilgrimage to, 242 ; Harold's pilgrimage to, 272, 285.

Romney, men of, beat off the Normans, 342 ; William's harshness to, *ib.*

Rouen, capital and archbishoprick of Normandy, 142.

Rowena, legend of, 33.

Rudolf, King of Burgundy, 242 ; grants privileges to English travellers, 243.

Salisbury, Old and New, 116, 117 ; burned by Swegen, 213.

Sandwich, Swegen sails to, 221 ; Cnut mutilates his hostages at, 225 ; Cnut lands at, 226 ; Edward keeps watch at, against Baldwin, 256 ; against Godwine, 266 ; Tostig driven away from, by Harold, 304.

Saxons, begin to ravage Britain, 29 ; begin to settle in Britain, 30 ; all Englishmen so called by the Celts, *ib.*

—— of Germany, or Old Saxons, conquered by Charles the Great, 83 ; encouraged in England by Edgar, 173 ; their language, 276.

Scilly Isles, Olaf Tryggvesson visits, 206.

Scotland, languages of, 4, 5 , northern parts not conquered by the Romans, 17 ; Swegen takes refuge in, 206 ; Cnut goes to, 245.

Scots, ravage Roman Britain, 29 ; Lowland Scots called Saxons by the High-

landers, 38 ; the Irish called Scots, 48 ; defeated by Æthelfrith, 52 ; their share in the conversion of England, 60 ; submit to Edward the Elder, 144 ; to Æthelstan, 148 ; their Kings learn to speak English, 175 ; submit to Cnut, 244.

Seax, the Saxon weapon, 149.

Seisin, meaning of the word, 317.

Selsey, Bishoprick of, founded, 62.

Selwood forest, between the Somersætas and Wilsætas, 105.

Senlac, battle of, different accounts of, 319–321 ; description of the site, 326 ; the night before the battle, 328 ; tactics of the English, 331 ; beginning of the battle, 332 ; the Normans driven back, 333 ; feigned flight of the Normans, 334 ; fight on the hill, 335 ; end of the battle, 337.

Sergius, Pope, baptizes Ceadwalla, 69.

Severn, boundary of England and Wales, ; 82.

Severus, Emperor, his wall, 20 ; dies at York, *ib.*

Sexburh, Queen of the West-Saxons, 66, 278.

Shaftesbury Monastery founded by Alfred, 131 ; Edward the Martyr translated to, 185 ; Cnut dies at, 246.

Sheppey, ravaged by the Danes, 99 ; Danes winter in, 102 ; Cnut retreats to, 230.

Sherborne, Kings buried at, 106, 107 ; bishoprick of, divided, 147.

Sherstone, drawn battle between Cnut and Edmund, 229.

Shield-wall, array of, 112, 327.

Shipwrecked men, treatment of, 288.

Shrewsbury (Pen-y-wern, taken by Offa, 82.

Sidroc, two Danish Earls so called in Alfred's wars, 111 ; both killed at Ashdown, 112.

Sigeberht, King of the West-Saxons, deposed, 76.

Sigeferth, murdered by Eadric, 225.

Sigeric, Archbishop of Canterbury, advises payment to the Danes, 190, 205.

Sigurd, Earl of Orkney, converts Olaf Tryggves o 1, 206.

Sihtric, Danish King of Northumberland, marries a sister of Æthelstan, 145, 148.

Single combat, practice of, 232, 322.

Siward, Earl of the Northumbrians, sent against Worcester, 251 ; helps to despoil Lunna, 254 ; joins Edward at Gloucester, 261 ; invades Scotland and defeats Macbeth, 274 ; story of his death, *ib.* ; his character, 274 ; his church at Galmanho, 274, 275.

—— nephew of Earl Siward, killed in the war with Macbeth, 274.

Slavery in England, 41.

Snorro, mistakes in his account of Stamfordbridge, 315, 316 ; his legend of William and Matilda, 323.

Somersetshire gradually becomes English, 36 ; traces of the Welsh in, 36, 66, 152 ; state of, in Alfred's time, 123.

Somerton taken by Æthelbald of Mercia, 75.

Southampton, Cnut chosen King at, 227 ; story of his rebuking the sea at, 240.

South-Saxons, kingdom of, founded by Ælle and Cissa, 34 ; converted to Christianity, 62 ; submit to Ecgberht, 97 ; their zeal for Earl Godwine, 267 ; Harold marches through their land, 326.

Southwark burnt by William, 345.

Spearhafoc, Bishop elect of London, consecration refused to, 263.

Staffordshire, victories of Edward the Elder in, 140.

Staller, meaning of the title, 302.

Stamfordbridge, Harold Hardrada encamps at, 306 ; battle of, 309 ; the bridge defended by a single Northman, 310 ; victory of Harold of England, *ib.* ; Norwegian legend of, 311, 315 ; mistakes in the story, 316.

Standard, the English, its device of a fighting man, 330 ; the royal post by, 331, 334–336; its site marked by the altar of Battle Abbey, 332 ; beaten down, *ib.*; William pitches his tent by, 338.

Stephen, Saint, King of the Hungarians, protects the children of Edmund, 235.

Stigand, priest of Assundun, 239 ; Bishop of the East-Angles, 255; makes peace between Edward and Godwine, 267 ; made Archbishop of Canterbury, 268 ; doubts as to his right, 281; gets the pallium from Pope Benedict, *ib.*; why not chosen to crown Harold, 299; joins in the election of Edgar, 341 ; his share in William's coronation, 346.

Stow-in-Lindesey, ancient church at, 279.

Strathclyde or Cumberland, kingdom of, 39; subject to Northumberland, 77 ; submits to Edward the Elder, 145; Owen, King of. joins the Scots and Welsh against Æthelstan, 153; granted to Malcolm by Edmund, 165.

Strength of body, importance of 289.

Succession to the Crown, law of, 278, 298.

Suetonius, defeats Boadicea, 16.

Sweden, kingdom of, founded, 188 ; partly conquered by Cnut, 239.

Swegen, called Fork-beard, King of the Danes, rebels against his father and restores idolatry, 189; joins Olaf Tryggvesson in his invasion of England, 205 ; legendary cause of his invasion, 206; invades England again, 212 ; takes Exeter, *ib.*; his campaign in East-Anglia, 213 ; his final invasion, 221; repulsed from London, 222; acknowledged as King, 223 ; story of his death, 223, 224.

Swegen, son of Cnut, 238; succeeds his father in Norway, 246.

—— son of Ulf and Estrithson, a party in his favour at the death of Harthacnut, 253; his friendship for Edward, 255; keeps Magnus from attacking England, 256; asks help from England, but is refused, *ib.*; helps the Emperor Henry against Baldwin of Flanders, *ib.*; refuses help to Tostig, 305.

—— eldest son of Godwine, his earldom, 256 ; overcomes Gruffydd of South-Wales, 257; carries off Eadgifu, *ib.*; throws up his earldom, *ib.*; returns, but is refused his restoration *ib.*; murders Beorn, *ib.*; declared *nithing* by the army, 258 ; restored through Bishop Ealdred, *ib.*; joins his father at Beverstone, 261 ; outlawed, 262; takes refuge at Bruges, *ib.* ; his pilgrimage to Jerusalem and death, 268.

Swithhun, Saint, Bishop of Winchester, 103.

Tadcaster, Harold reviews his fleet at, 309.

Taillefer, his exploits at Senlac, 332.

Tamar, river, boundary of England and Cornwall, 152.

Tavistock burnt by the Danes, 207.

Telham, hill opposite Senlac, 329.

Teutonic nations, their languages, 5 ; they overrun the Empire, 23 ; their settlements in Southern Europe, 24 ; they become Christians and adopt the Latin language, *ib.*; possible early Teutonic settlement in Britain, 29; various Teutonic tribes in Britain, 30.

Thane, meaning of the word, 41 ; fidelity of the Thanes of Brihtnoth, 191–203.

Thanet, ravaged by Edgar, 173.

Theodore of Tarsus, Archbishop of Canterbury, 73.

Theodoric, King of East-Goths, reigns in Italy, 24; puts Boethius to death, 130.

Theodosius, recovers Valentia, 20, 30.

—— Emperor, 30.

Thetford burned by Swegen, 213 ; drawn battle at, between Swegen and Ulfcytel, *ib.*

Thietmar, Bishop of Merseburg, his account of the death of Ælfheah, 218.

Thingferth, father of Offa, 80, 82.

Thingmen. *See* Housecarls.

Thored, his dream, 306.

Thrum kills Saint Ælfheah, 220.

Thunder, Old-English god, 40.

Thurbrand, Uhtred fails to kill him, 215 ; murders Uhtred, 227.

Thurcytel, Danish Earl. *See* Thurkill.

—— East-Anglian Thane, his cowardice, 217.

Thurfrith, besieges York, 151 ; drowned *ib.*

Thurkill, Danish chief, submits to Ed ard
the Elder, 144.
—— Danish Earl, invades England, 216;
burns Northampton, 217; tries to save
Saint Ælfheah, 220; takes service under
Æthelred, 220, 221; defends London
against Swegen, 222; plunders near
Greenwich, 223; joins Cnut, 226; fights
at Assandun, 230: Earl of the East-
Angles, 236; helps to found the minster
at Assandun, 239.
—— son of Gunhild, banished, 255.
—— Sacrist of Waltham, legend of, 325.
Thyra, wife of Gorm, makes the Dane-
werk, 188.
Tin, Phœnician trade in, 11.
Tofig the Proud, marries Gytha, 251; founds
the church of Waltham, 251, 271, 325.
Tostig, third son of Godwine, takes refuge
at Bruges, 262; made Earl of the
Northumbrians, 275; goes on pilgrimage
to Rome, 281; robbed on his way back,
283; threatens Pope Nicholas, ib.; becomes Malcolm's sworn brother, 284;
joins Harold in his Welsh campaign,
285; discontent against him in Northumberland, 294; his alleged crimes,
ib.; deposed by Northumbrians, ib.;
charges Harold with abbetting the rebellion, 295; Edward and Harold try to
restore him, 296; he is outlawed and
banished, ib.; takes refuge at Bruges,
ib.; his disappointment at Harold's election, 300; seeks help from William, 304;
plunders in Wight, Sandwich, and Lindesey, ib.; driven away by Edwin and
Morkere, ib.; stays with Malcolm, ib.;
seeks help of Swegen, ib.; persuades
Harold Hardrada to invade England,
305; doubts as to the story, ib.; he
joins Harold's expedition, 305; killed
at Stamfordbridge, 310; legendary account of, 310-315; his descendants, 317.
Toustain, carries the Pope's banner at
Senlac, 330.
Tower of London, built by William the
Conqueror, 260.
Tremerin, Welsh Bishop, acts for Æthelstan of Hereford, 278.
Turks, their language, 6; take Constanti-
nople, 24.
Tyrant, meaning of the word, 23; tyrants
in Britain, 19; Swegen so called, 223.

Uhtred, son of Waltheof, delivers Durham,
215; his marriages, ib.; submits to Swegen, 221; joins Edmund against Cnut,
226; submits to Cnut, 227; murdered
by Thurbrand, ib.
Ulf, brother-in-law of Cnut, put to death
by him, 238.
—— Bishop of Dorchester, his lack of
learning, 259; flies from London, 267.

Ulf, son of Dolfin, murdered by Tostig,
294.
Ulfcytel, Earl of East-Angles, his brave
resistance to the Danes, 213; forsaken by
his men at Ringmere, 217; killed at As-
sandun, 230.
Unust, King of the Picts, joins Eadberht of
Northumberland against the Welsh, 77.
Unwan, Archbishop of Bremen, baptizes
Cnut, 222.
Utrecht, foundation of the Bishoprick, 73.

Valery, Saint, William sails from, 317.
Val-ès-Dunes, William defeats the Norman
rebels at, 264.
Vandals, their kingdoms in Spain and Italy,
24.
Verulam, 16; St. Alban martyred at, 21;
forsaken, 21, 81.
Vortigern said to have invited the English,
33.

Wace, Master, his Roman de Rou, 321.
Wall, meaning of the word, 20; walls built
by the Romans in Britain, ib.
Wallingford burnt by the Danes, 214; William crosses the Thames at, 345.
Walter, Bishop of Hereford, consecrated a
Rome, 281.
Waltham, Church of, founded by Tofig,
251, 271, 323; rebuilt by Harold, 271;
growth of the town, ib.; foundation of the
College, 272; consecration of the church,
281; charter granted to, 285; legend of
the Holy Rood of, 323-325; Harold's
body translated to, 339; body of Edward
the First rests there awhile, ib.; the choir
destroyed, ib.
Waltheof, Earl of Beornicia, his remissness,
215.
—— son of Siward, 275; his presence at
Stamfordbridge uncertain, 315; men of
his earldom join Harold, 319.
Wantage, Alfred born at, 114.
War-cries, Norman and English, at Senlac,
330, 333.
Wareham, taken by Guthorm, 119; Edward the Martyr buried at, 185.
Watchet, Danes driven off from, 143;
Danes ravage, 190, 207.
Watling-street, boundary between English
and Danes, 125, 163, 222.
Wedmore, peace of, 123, 125.
Wells, Church of, founded by Ine, 69;
bishoprick founded by Edward the Elder,
147; changes made by Gisa at, 282.
Welsh, meaning of the word, 2, 261, 263;
language, where spoken, 19; Welsh names
in England, 26; Welsh words in English,
28; treatment of the Welsh in the English Conquest, ib.; extent of the Welsh
territory in the sixth century, 30, 39;
their long resistance, 39; their differ-

ences from the Roman and English Churches, 49 ; their power in the North broken by Saint Oswald, 60 ; again by Eadberht, 77 ; growth of in Central Wales under Rhodri Mawr, 133 ; their divisions after his death, and submission to Alfred, *ib.* ; to Edward the Elder, 144 ; to Æthelstan, 148 ; paid tribute to Æthelstan, 152 ; their Princes do homage to Edgar, 175 ; their tactics, 285 ; submit to Harold, 286 ; assist revolt of the Northumbrians, 293.

Wends, Slavonic people of North Germany, 255.

Wergild, meaning of, 70, 342.

Westminster, first King buried at, 249 ; rebuilt by Edward, 271 ; consecrated. 297 ; Edward buried at, 299 ; Harold crowned at, *ib.* ; keeps Easter at, 300 ; Edward the First buried at, 339 ; William crowned at, 346, 347.

West-Saxons, kingdom of, founded by Cerdic and Cynric, 34, 35 ; growth of their kingdom, 34 ; converted to Christianity, 61 ; their losses at the hands of Penda, 65 ; their advances against the Welsh, 65, 66 ; subject to Mercia, 73 ; set free by the battle of Burford, 76 ; supremacy of, under Ecgberht, 100 ; results of their supremacy, 101 ; effects of the Danish inroads on, 101, 102 ; Danish invasion of Wessex, 111 ; Wessex overrun by the Danes, 120 ; Kings of, become Lords of all Britain, 145 ; submit to Swegen, 223 ; submit to Cnut, 226 ; join Edmund, 228, 229 ; double-dealing of their Wise Men, 234 ; kept in Cnut's own hands, 236 ; Godwine, Earl of, 239 ; support Harthacnut against Harold, 246 ; extent of the earldom under Harold, 280 ; join Harold's muster, 319.

West-Welsh, meaning of the name, 148 ; subdued by Æthelstan, 152.

Wherwell, monastery founded, 182, 186 ; Edith the daughter of Godwine sent to, 263.

White Horse, said to commemorate Alfred's victory, 124.

Wight, Jutish kingdom of, conquered by Ceadwalla, 67 ; Godwine plunders in, 267.

Wiglaf, King of the Mercians, becomes Ecgberht's man, 98.

Wihæl, Cnut's court at, 227.

Wilfrith, Bishop, driven from York, converts the South-Saxons, 61 ; preaches to the Frisians, 62 ; rescues part of the people in Wight, 68 ; favours the Papal authority, 73.

William, chaplain of Edward, appointed Bishop of London, 263; flies from London, 267 ; restored to his Bishoprick, 268.

—— Fitz-Osborne, wins over the Norman Barons at Lillebonne, 303.

William of Poitiers, his life of William the Conqueror, 320.

—— Malet, buries Harold, 338.

—— Longsword, Duke of the Normans, learns Danish at Bayeux, 142 ; helps to restore Lewis, 159.

—— the Conqueror, compared with Cnut, 238 ; Edward's friendship for, 254 ; his birth, 263 ; his early history and reign in Normandy, 264 ; his character, *ib.* ; his visit to Edward, *ib.* ; the crown promised to him by Edward, *ib.* ; delivers Harold from Guy, 289 ; receives him at his court, *ib.* ; gives him arms, *ib.* ; his homage to Edward, 291 ; entraps Harold with regard to the oath, 292 ; sends an embassy to Harold, 301 ; his claims on the crown, 301, 302 ; William applies to Pope Alexander, 302 ; his enterprise approved by him, 303 ; he makes ready his fleet, *ib.* ; sails from Saint Valery, 317 ; lands at Pevensey, *ib.* ; encamps at Hastings, *ib.* ; his messages to Harold in London, 322 ; he offers single combat, *ib.* ; his treatment of Harold's spies, 323 ; Snorro's legend of him and his wife, *ib.* ; his last messages to Harold, 328 ; his speech to his army, *ib.* ; he marshals his men on Telham, *ib.* ; story of his coat of mail, *ib.* ; vows an abbey to St. Martin, 329 ; arrangements of his army, *ib.* ; his weapon, 330 ; kills Gyrth with his own hand, 334 ; orders the feigned flight, *ib.* ; pursues the light-armed English, 337 ; pitches his tent on the hill, 338 ; refuses burial to Harold, *ib.* ; afterwards relents, 339 ; not King by virtue of the battle, 340 ; his conquest of England gradual, 341, 348 ; waits at Hastings after the battle, 342 ; takes Pevensey, *ib.* ; Dover submits to him, *ib.* ; Canterbury submits to him, 343 ; his illness, 344 ; marches to Wallingford, 345 ; beguiles Esegar's messenger, 346 ; receives the submission of the English at Berkhampstead, 346 ; crowned at Westminster, 346, 347 ; in what sense called the Conqueror, 348 ; the crown ever since held by his descendants, 349 ; effects of his reign in England, *ib.*

Willibrord, founds the see of Utrecht, 73.

Wilton, Alfred's battle at, 116 ; chief town of the Wilsætas, 117 ; burned by Swegen, 213.

Wimborne, Æthelred the First buried at, 113 ; seized by Æthelwald, 138 ; King Sigeferth buried at, 172.

Winchester, Bishoprick of, founded 61 ; divided, 69 ; two minsters at, 137 ; submits to Swegen, 222 ; Edward the Confessor crowned at, 253 ; Emma lives at, 255 ; Edith lives at, 344 ; pays tribute to William, 345.

Winfrith, or Saint Boniface, Apostle of Germany, 62.
—— legendary name of Offa, 80.
Witan or Wise Men, Assembly of, 41; their power, 41, 76; of Wessex deposes Sigeberht, 76.
Woden, Old-English god, 40, 57, 58; supposed ancestor of the English kings, 40.
Worcester, Harthacnut's housecarls killed at, 251; the city burned and the country ravaged, *ib.*; see of, held with York, 251, 281.
Worr, Alderman, poisoned by Eadburh, 93.
Wreck, right of, 288.
Wulfgeat, favourite of Æthelred, disgrace of, 214.
Wulthere, Christian King of the Mercians, 61.
Wulfnoth, South-Saxon Child, slandered by Brihtric, 215; takes to piracy, 216; whether the father of Earl Godwine, 247.
—— sixth son of Godwine, left as a hostage with William, 290.
Wulfstan, Archbishop of York, supports Anlaf against Edmund, 163; deposed and imprisoned, 165; made Bishop of Dorchester, 166.
—— son of Ceola, defends the bridge of Maldon, 195.

Wulfstan, Abbot of Gloucester, 280.
—— Saint, Prior of Worcester, his goodness, 284; his friendship for Harold, *ib.*; appointed Bishop of Worcester, consecrated by Ealdred, *ib.*; helps Harold to win over the Northumbrians, 300.
Wulfthryth, mother of Saint Edith, 178.
Wye, river, boundary of England and Wales, 152.
Wyrtgeorn, King of the Wends, husband of Gunhild, 255.

Xerxes, his treatment of the Greek spies, 323.

York (Eboracum), Severus dies at, 20; said to have been a Welsh Archbishoprick, 21; capital of Northumberland, 38; title of its mayor, *ib.*; foundation of the church of, 59; taken by the Danes, 109, 144; occupied by Æthelstan, 151; Edgar at, 174; submits to Cnut, 227; origin of Saint Mary's Abbey at, 274, 275; revolt of Northumbrians at, 294; massacre of Tostig's housecarls at, 295; Harold acknowledged at, 300; gives hostages to Harold Hardrada, 306; receives Harold of England, 309; news of William's landing brought to, 318.
Yorkshire, beginning of the name, 306.

THE END.

LONDON: R. CLAY, SONS, AND TAYLOR, PRINTERS.